LEASING PUBLIC LAND

POLICY DEBATES AND INTERNATIONAL EXPERIENCES

LEASING PUBLIC LAND

POLICY DEBATES AND INTERNATIONAL EXPERIENCES

Edited by

Steven C. Bourassa and Yu-Hung Hong

Lincoln Institute of Land Policy
Cambridge, Massachusetts

Library of Congress Cataloging-in-Publication Data

Leasing public land: policy debates and international experiences / edited by
Steven C. Bourassa and Yu-Hung Hong.
    p. cm.
    Papers from a conference sponsored by the Lincoln Institute of Land Policy
and held in June 2000 at the Lincoln House.
    Includes bibliographical references.
    ISBN 1-55844-155-7 (pbk.)
       1. Land tenure—Congresses. 2. Public lands—Management—
Congresses. 3. Leases—Congresses. 4. Land use—Government policy—
Congresses. I. Bourassa, Steven C., 1957– II. Hong, Yu-hung.
III. Lincoln Institute of Land Policy.

    HD1245.L43 2003
    333.1'6—dc21

                                      2003007656

Project management: Ann LeRoyer, Lincoln Institute of Land Policy
Design, copyediting and production: Snow Creative Services
Printing: Webcom Ltd., Toronto, Ontario, Canada

The mere pledge of an Irish landlord that for twenty years he would not claim in rent any share in their cultivation induced Irish peasants to turn a barren mountain into gardens; on the mere security of a fixed ground rent for a term of years the most costly buildings of such cities as London and New York are erected on leased ground.

—Henry George, *Progress and Poverty*

Contents

FOREWORD

I want to begin by congratulating editors Steven Bourassa and Yu-Hung Hong and the authors of the ten case studies on their exemplary achievement. I would also like to take this opportunity to place *Leasing Public Land* in the context of the Lincoln Institute's programmatic interests. This book clearly reflects the scope of our international commitment. It deals, if not with *every* country in which public leasehold systems exist, at least with most of the prominent examples. Merely to recite the list of case studies selected is to be reminded of the tremendous diversity in history and political economy represented by the countries that have been engaged in the leasing of public land.

As with another internationally oriented book published by the Institute, *European Spatial Planning*, edited by Andreas Faludi, this volume presents both lessons that can be found in the experiences of different countries and a policy discourse that will be instructive to those who are embarking on the design of new systems, in this case, of land disposition and land tenure. As the editors make clear, public leasehold is of particular interest in "transforming" economies, where issues of land as private property, emerging land markets, and concern for the social recapture of incremental land value come to the fore. These are places and issues central to our program interests at the Lincoln Institute.

In particular, I would call attention to the concept of value capture, inspired by the writings of Henry George, wherein the location value of land (Ricardian rent), as apart from the value attributable to direct private investment and improvements, is reserved for further public benefit. The leasing of public lands can provide a mechanism for value capture through the collection of land rents, the efficacy of which will vary with the design of the leasing system, as the editors point out in their thoughtful concluding chapter.

I am very pleased that the Lincoln Institute has been able to support the editors and authors of this important work.

Armando Carbonell
Co-Chairman
Department of Planning and Development
Lincoln Institute of Land Policy

PREFACE

The idea of undertaking a project to examine international experiences in leasing public land emerged quite accidentally. In 1999, Yu-Hung Hong, who was a visiting fellow at the Lincoln Institute of Land Policy, wrote a short article for *Land Lines*—the newsletter published quarterly by the Institute—about the public land leasing experiences in Canberra and Hong Kong. Responses to the articles were overwhelming. Some questioned whether Hong's observations, derived from two case studies, could be applied generally to other public leasehold systems. Others wanted to translate the article into different languages to make the information accessible to a wider audience. In view of these reactions, we decided to ask the Institute to sponsor a conference to assemble and analyze information about the current state of public land leasing around the world. The proposal was accepted, and thus began our journey to a two-day conference, which was held in June 2000, and the publication of this volume.

The conference was a tremendous success. In addition to the chapter authors who commented on each others' papers, other invited colleagues reviewed and commented on selected papers. For their valuable contributions, we wish to thank Thomas Atmer, William A. Doebele, Moshe Lipka, Michelle McDonough, Karen R. Polenske and Sidney Wong. The discussion was extraordinarily engaging, and email exchanges among our participants continued for weeks afterwards. To capitalize on their enthusiasms we moved forward quickly to compile the conference papers into an edited book. Our editing work encountered unexpected obstacles, however, among them the untimely death of Max Neutze, who was one of the original editors of the book. Thankfully, the authors and other participating parties did not relinquish their support for the project, showing patience and determination to disseminate our collective knowledge to policy makers and analysts. Without their pledge of confidence, the completion of this book would have been impossible.

At the Institute, we thank H. James Brown, president and chief executive officer, for encouraging us to embark on this intellectual expedition. His unswerving trust in our ability to finish the book made a significant difference to the outcome of our endeavors. We are also grateful for the guidance and help provided by Armando Carbonell, senior fellow and co-chairman of the Department of Planning and Development, at each stage of the planning and execution of the project. There are no words to describe his amazing patience and flexibility in overseeing our progress (or lack thereof). Our thanks also go to Lisa J. Silva, meeting planner, and Laurie Dougherty, contract specialist, who offered their professional assistance in managing the logistics of the conference. Last but not least, Ann LeRoyer, senior editor, and Anna Snow, copy editor, improved the manuscript with remarkable competence, and directed the publication of the book with speed and good spirits. These many contributions, we believe, made this book better and our work more enjoyable.

Finally, we wish to pay a special tribute to Max Neutze, friend and mentor, who had for many years helped to keep research interest in public leasehold alive within the academic community. We dedicate this book to him.

Yu-Hung Hong
Steven C. Bourassa

CONTRIBUTORS

CONFERENCE COORDINATORS AND EDITORS

Steven C. Bourassa
Professor and Director
School of Urban and Public Affairs
University of Louisville
Louisville, Kentucky

Yu-Hung Hong
Visiting Assistant Professor
Department of Public Administration
  and Urban Studies
University of Akron
Akron, Ohio

AUTHORS

Rachelle Alterman
Professor, Holder of David Azrieli
  Chair in Architecture and Town
  Planning
Associate Dean for Research
  and Graduate Studies
Technion: Israel Institute of
  Technology
Haifa, Israel

Christie Baxter
Principle Research Scientist
Department of Urban Studies
  and Planning
Massachusetts Institute of
  Technology
Cambridge, Massachusetts

W. Jan Brzeski
Senior Urban Specialist
The World Bank
Washington, DC

David Dale-Johnson
Associate Professor of Finance and
  Business Economics
Marshall School of Business
University of Southern California
Los Angeles, California

F. Frederic Deng
Visiting Assistant Professor
Department of Geography
  and Planning
State University of New York
Albany, New York

Hans Mattsson
Professor of Real Estate Planning
Royal Institute of Technology
Stockholm, Sweden

Barrie Needham
Professor of Spatial Planning
Faculty of Management Sciences
University of Nijmegen
Nijmegen, Netherlands

Max Neutze (deceased)
Visiting Fellow
Urban and Environment Program
Research School of Social Sciences
Australia National University
Canberra, Australia

Ann Louise Strong
Emeritus Professor of City
    and Regional Planning
University of Pennsylvania
Philadelphia, Pennsylvania

Pekka V. Virtanen
Emeritus Professor of Urban
    Planning, Land Valuation
    and Management
Helsinki University of Technology
Espoo, Finland

A TRIBUTE TO
MAX NEUTZE

8 APRIL 1934 – 19 OCTOBER 2000

I do not want to write about the great achievements of Max Neutze that were linked so strongly to his personal integrity and motivated by his faith and strong concern for the common good. Suffice it to say here that the Australian National University and Australian society had the undivided attention and unambiguous commitment of a truly remarkable man for more than forty years of his life. I simply want to take this opportunity to say something about the man who had a great capacity for friendship and loyalty, combined with a firm critical sense.

Graeme Max Neutze was born in Geraldine, New Zealand. He was the eldest son of four children, born into a hard-working farming family who had struggled to survive the Depression. The family experience taught him essential ethical values about concern for the less fortunate, a commitment to procedural justice, an aversion to waste and display, and a stoicism and determination he retained all his life.

Max excelled in the small country school at Geraldine. Encouraged by the example of his elder sister who became a teacher and his father who reminded him constantly that "farming was a mug's game," he embarked on an agricultural science degree at Lincoln College, in Christ Church, New Zealand. He did so with the expectation that he would return to Geraldine to be a better farmer.

During his studies for the degree he found that agricultural economics interested him more than agricultural science. Max's intellectual curiosity was stimulated by his teachers at Lincoln College, who encouraged him to see a wider world and to apply for a Rhodes scholarship. Max's deeply held conservatism was reflected in the fact that when offered the scholarship in 1957, he declined it, explaining to the registrar of the University of New Zealand that, although he appreciated the offer, he preferred to get married. The registrar pointed out that further studies and marriage were not mutually exclusive.

His sense of frugality and his predilection for understatement were reflected in the telegram he sent his parents, which said, "Awarded Rhodes scholarship. Engaged." He had met Margaret (Peggy) Murray, a farmer's daughter, while working on a farm in Waikato, New Zealand. Peggy traveled to England and married Max in 1959.

Max's studies at Oxford were rewarded by a Nuffield scholarship, which enabled him to continue working for his doctorate. The community of scholars

Max encountered at Oxford, especially at Nuffield, introduced him to a new and exciting world. He originally had sought to deepen his understanding of agricultural economics, but with the support of one of his supervisors, Colin Clark, he began to refocus on the economics of location.

In response to the challenges of leading scholars of the day, Max also explored the problems surrounding the effects of institutions on economic processes. This new way of thinking not only led him to find economics a stimulating discipline, it also contained the seeds of his later disappointments and frustration with the aridity, intolerance and myopia of much of contemporary economics and many of its practitioners.

Following the completion of his doctorate in 1960, he took a position as lecturer in agricultural economics in the Canberra University College, which later became the School of General Studies. His departmental head was Heinz Arndt, who encouraged him to explore the economics of decentralization, which continued his interest in location and institutional structures.

Noel Butlin, of the Research School of Social Sciences at Australia National University, took an interest in Max's work. Butlin's own work on the economic history of Australia revealed the significance of urban investment, and he felt that urban and environmental issues were of increasing importance. Butlin's encouragement led Max to apply for the position of head of the newly created Urban Research Unit—to which he was appointed in October 1965. Before taking the position in January 1967, Max spent a year at Resources for the Future, in Washington, DC, where he conducted the first major study of the suburban apartment boom.

From its inception the Urban Research Unit focused on the process of urban development in Australia with special concern for equity aspects of the operation of its cities. The fact that we now have a recognizably Australian literature on urban issues is a testament to Max, his leadership, scholarship and commitment.

Max led this work, and in 1977 published *Urban Development in Australia*, the first major book devoted to Australia's urban growth. It also was the first book published in Australia by George Allen and Unwin. Reprinted and revised many times, it is regarded as the standard work referred to by students in all social science disciplines. Max regarded his subsequent companion book, *Australian Urban Policy*, published in 1978 by George Allen and Unwin, as the more important work.

The significance of Max's leadership and contribution was recognized by his appointment to the chair in Urban Research. He also was elected as fellow in the Academy of Social Sciences in Australia in this period. Later he was to be elected honorary fellow in the Royal Australian Planning Institute and made an officer in the Order of Australia, in recognition of his contribution to research into our cities.

Max Neutze was a very principled man. He was open and honest to the point of naiveté. He never sought preferential treatment or high office, but was twice pressured to accept senior leadership responsibilities at the university at critical times.

He was always modest in his claims for the research in which he was engaged. He expected colleagues to try to see the role of the school in national terms and to respond with a sense of balance. He did not act politically in the university and to some extent was taken advantage of by those who did.

Max had been a strong Methodist and continued his involvement with the church and the Student Christian Movement while at Oxford. The conservatism of his Methodism gradually evolved, especially as he began to realize that it provided a framework for his increasing radicalism. His engagement and concern with environmental issues, while radical, must be seen as originating in the conservative desire to protect and preserve nature from the mindless outcomes of the market. It was one of the ways he could give effect to his belief that his God loved all creatures great and small.

He increasingly found himself focusing on the social ends of equity and environmental issues, seeing economics or efficiency as a debate about the means to achieve those ends, which was simply an extension of his logic of the right way to do things. His commitment to social justice flowed from his commitment to Christian principles. He felt the gains made by human progress in the rights and humanity of people should be protected. There should be no backsliding.

This basic Christian commitment led him to make a personal, direct sponsorship of and financial support for individual disadvantaged children internationally, and for groups and organizations that worked for underprivileged people.

Through his committment to the indigenous people of Australia, Max viewed reconciliation of this population with the existing government as the logical first step in recognizing their rights, culture and spiritual needs. One of the ways he sought, very practically, to support the cause of justice for indigenous Australians was to devote much of the last five years of his life to assembling and regularizing the information base relating to education, health and welfare services.

His strong defense of the leasehold system in the Australian Capital Territory (ACT) came in part from a concern that its administration produced irregularities, contradictions and possible corruption, which he felt would lead to its destruction. When the ACT Government established an inquiry into the administration of the leasehold system, he was distressed to learn that he had been ruled out from membership of the inquiry committee, on the grounds that he was too radical.

One of the things that struck me over the last twelve months of Max's life, as it became obvious that he was slowly losing his battle with cancer, was the number of people who commented on how modest a gentleman he was. Many noted his thoughtfulness and support for their own research and development. Two of his earliest students, Meredith Edwards and Judith Yates, have both observed how often he went out of his way to help them, and that his role as mentor was important in their subsequent, very successful careers.

I knew Max for thirty-five years. We laughed together—he had a wicked, dry sense of humor. We fought and argued, agreed and disagreed on a range of issues, but we were on the same side on most issues that mattered. We stood together in the rain and cold when it was not fashionable to protest the war in Vietnam, and turned out together to express our support for reconciliation. We argued and protested against the insidious destruction of the leasehold system, and jointly prosecuted the case for public housing and better urban planning. We shared our research interests and worked together on them, endlessly discussing our concerns over the direction the university, to which we have both devoted our lives, is taking. We shared our delights in walking in the Australian bush, and swapped stories about the trials and tribulations of our respective children. He supported me in all my personal travails. In all of his I never heard him complain. He truly did turn the other cheek. He was a great mate and I miss him.

I take solace, as we all must, in the knowledge that his influence will continue through his writing, in the statistics he helped to construct, in his students, and in the influence he had on his colleagues, both in Australia and overseas.

Patrick Troy
Centre for Resource and Environmental Studies
Australian National University

PART I

INTRODUCTION

Why Public Leasehold?

Issues and Concepts

Yu-Hung Hong and Steven C. Bourassa

Land reforms in many former socialist countries and transitional economies seem to have no clear direction. Despite promises from reformists that the restitution of private property in land will bring forth the efficiency of a private land market, mechanisms for allocating land still rely predominantly on officially determined criteria and prices. The absence of market mechanisms, although a so-called land market exists, plagues the restoration of private land ownership with corruption and bitter conflict. These perverse effects could generate disputes over the course of reforms that in turn lead to disillusionment and then to retrenchment. Although all these countries recognize that changes are inevitable, no bet is safe as to where or how fast their reforms will go.

With support provided by the Lincoln Institute of Land Policy, we organized a two-day conference on international experiences in leasing public land—a land disposal method and tenure arrangement considered a viable option for transforming economies. In June 2000 seventeen scholars from nine different countries gathered at Lincoln House. Some presented their research papers, others provided critical comments and insights on the practice of land leasing in selected countries. To make the results of our discussion available to policy makers and analysts, we decided to compile the conference papers into a publication. This edited book is the outcome of that meeting. It contains nine chapters that were presented at the conference. We later added another chapter on the public land leasing system in Beijing, the People's Republic of China (PRC). We are by no means claiming that this volume encompasses all public leasehold systems in the world. Had time been more plentiful, we would have included leasehold systems in Singapore, Vietnam, Russia and many others. Yet, we believe we have covered some major leasing experiences around the world from which we could draw meaningful lessons.

Like many edited books, this is the product of the collective efforts and shared knowledge of all conference participants and authors of individual chapters. Indeed, arguments presented by our authors are, in most cases, so coherent that they echo one another almost to the word. However, the richness and validity of the ideas discussed in the individual chapters of this book cannot be made fully apparent unless they are tied together. Therefore, it is useful to review in this introductory chapter: (1) key issues related to public land leasing and principal questions explored in this book; (2) problems associated with defining public leasehold systems; (3) important institutions and organizations for supporting this land tenure form; and (4) the logic of how we proceed to present our ideas and arguments by introducing the basic structure of the book and individual chapters.

ISSUES

For many years controversies involved in land ownership have remained among the most contentious social, political and economic issues in developed, developing and transitional economies. In the United States, for example, the recent "wise use–property rights" movement exemplifies the persistent tension between the public's right to regulate land uses and private property in land (Jacobs 1998; Last 1998). In Poland, Russia, Ukraine and other transforming countries, debates concerning the method and extent of privatizing land ownership are still lingering 10 years after the collapse of the Soviet Union. These debates are so fundamental that they strike at the core of the economic and ideological aspirations of every citizen in these countries.

There are at least two reasons land ownership is such an intractable issue.[1] First, from an economic point of view, there have been prolonged disputes over the distribution of wealth generated from increases in land values. In most situations a land value increment is a product of both public and private investments. For instance, the value of a privately owned house does not depend solely on its owner's investments in land and building, but also on the overall amenities in the neighborhood. The quality of these amenities is determined by government investments in public infrastructure and social services, as well as property maintenance and improvements undertaken by all property owners in the area. As all experienced developers acknowledge, the three key factors that influence the value of a piece of real estate are: location, location and location. Moreover, general population and economic growth that has little to do with private property investments could increase real estate prices. In principle, because the intrinsic value of a location depends on collective investments and other external factors, rises in the land value of an individual property unrelated to its owner's investments should be recaptured by the government on behalf of the community at large.

Government inability to retain land value increments is an enduring policy issue in some developing countries where land is privately owned. When city

---

[1] There are other sources of contention related to the delineation of land ownership. For example, in some former socialist countries the restoration of private land ownership for individuals whose land was taken away during the communist regime has created conflicting claims to property in land. Because the authors did not cover the relationship between this issue and public leasehold in their case studies, we do not discuss this controversy here.

officials fail to recover even the costs of servicing urban land, their financial ability to increase developable land by extending public infrastructure is impeded. With a limited supply of serviced land to accommodate an expanding urban population, land prices in developed neighborhoods escalate rapidly. On one hand, existing private landowners enjoy substantial increases in personal wealth due to appreciation of property values. City governments and the urban poor, on the other hand, are impoverished because of the rising land cost for building public infrastructure and affordable housing. An uneven distribution of the newly created wealth generated by rapid urbanization may become a major cause of inequity in society. Attempts to redistribute a portion of the wealth accumulated in real property from the hands of private landowners to the community have always been conflict-ridden.

Second, not only is land ownership a set of rules for allocating and accumulating wealth, but it also possesses important ideological and political meanings. For example, one can hardly talk about land ownership in the U.S. without mentioning Thomas Jefferson. For Jefferson, as Jacobs (1998, 249) describes, private property in land "would serve as both the basis for informed democratic decision-making and a linkage for residents to take seriously their role as citizens and members of a community." In other words, private land ownership is the cornerstone of the political and social institutions that ensure liberty and democracy in the U.S. Indeed, many private property rights advocates even argue to the extreme that challenging private property in land is to defy America's way of life and political philosophy.

At the other end of the ideological spectrum, many people in some former socialist countries still believe that governments should not sell or lease public interest in land to private entities for profitable undertakings. This action, they believe, would deprive citizens of their equal entitlement to land. Private ownership also deviates from the dogma (or the legacy) of socialism: the root cause of the exploitation of workers is when they combine their labor with private capital and land in production, but are unable to enjoy their fair share of the wealth (Marx 1978). According to this view, private property will threaten the programs of the socialist state to build an equal society. This ideology is so incompatible with the beliefs of private property rights that when the two collide in former socialist countries, the resulting antagonism adds an emotional dimension that blocks any rational discourse to the already very complex land tenure debates.

This book contributes to these debates by focusing on a commonly recognized, but not well understood, land tenure arrangement—public leasehold. In many transitional economies, such as those discussed in this volume, public officials have been experimenting with public leasehold systems to minimize the economic and political conflicts that arise from land reforms. They hope that leasing public land may lessen the tension between the communists' desire to uphold public land ownership and the reformists' demand for increasing private property rights.

In theory, public leasehold does appear to be a compromise, because the system allows the state to remain as the landowner and lease the development and use rights of land to private individuals. In practice, whether the government or private landholders have real control over land will depend on how lease conditions are constructed. These conditions, in most cases, are the outcomes of political processes—an issue discussed thoroughly in this volume. More important, many scholars and analysts have suggested that public leasehold will enable governments to recapture land value increments by collecting annual land rents and other lease payments from lessees (Bourassa, Neutze and Strong 1997; Farvacque and McAuslan 1992; Hong 1998; Tideman et al. 1991). Some, including several authors in this volume, have even postulated that other policy objectives, such as stabilizing land prices, controlling land uses, and facilitating land redevelopment, could also be achieved through public land leasing (Bourassa, Neutze and Strong 1996).

Despite these suggested benefits, public leasehold remains understudied. Although scholars such as Bourassa, Neutze and Strong (1996; 1997), Hong (1995; 1998), Lai (1998), Neutze (1988), Stein, Troy and Yeomans (1995), and Yeh (1994), have published their research on public leasehold, these publications are scattered across academic journals of various disciplines, as well as relatively inaccessible government documents. Besides, these studies used very different research and assessment methods that make any comparison of their results difficult. Without a set of coherent arguments about land leasing experiences in different countries, scholars and analysts have been unable to agree among themselves on what public leasehold systems can or cannot do for the public or for private lessees.

The lack of comprehensive studies on public leasehold systems has two important implications for the current land tenure debates occurring in transitional economies. First, discussions of the adaptability of public leasehold remain at an abstract level. In some instances, arguments suggested by proponents of public leasehold are based simply on some idealized advantages of leasing public land. As several chapters in this book show, although the public leasehold systems examined here were able to achieve one or two of the desired policy goals established by governments, none of them could accomplish all. Our concern is that overstating the usefulness of a public leasehold system may raise public expectations to an unrealistic level. When the system fails to deliver the promises, it will only lead to major disappointments and open the door for challenges.

Second, there is confusion concerning the framing of the key questions for land tenure debates in general, and for research on public leasehold in particular. The prevailing question in most cases is: should governments in transitional economies adopt a public leasehold or freehold system? Yet, when policy makers and analysts make the comparison, they seldom define explicitly what types of public leasehold and freehold systems they are referring to. In assembling the information presented by our authors in individual chapters, we found that leasing structures of public leasehold systems are diverse. They range from property rights arrangements that resemble fee simple to systems with a high degree of government control over land. These varying structures in different times and spaces make it difficult to pin down a set of coherent characteristics of public leasehold systems. The diversity, we argue, is a logical outcome of the fact that land ownership is a complex and changing legal category. Its meanings are social and political constructs that are subjected to interpretation and reinterpretation according to varying circumstances (Hallowell 1955). Any conceptualization of public leasehold, like the conceptualization of freehold, is bound to be an abstraction that depends on the particularities of institutions that are not universal. We define institutions as formal and informal rules that, through their interactions, generate an incentive system for guiding public and private investments in land and real estate. Formal rules include provisions contained in constitutions and related legislation that govern land uses and property rights in land. Informal rules are social norms, ideology and culture that shape people's expectations and perceptions of property ownership in society.

Without settling problems associated with the elusive definition of public leasehold systems, it is unclear how the debates about public leasehold versus freehold could proceed fruitfully. In some instances, instead of asking how different institutional settings in a specific social and political context shape property relations under a public leasehold (or freehold) system, policy makers and analysts have been arguing endlessly about whether a freehold system is preferable to a public leasehold system based on a set of idealized conditions. As the case studies in this volume indicate, property relations in a specific public leasehold system are the results of a series of political struggles instigated by involved parties with strategies defined and constrained by particular historical and institutional contexts. There is no evidence of an all-inclusive model of public land leasing (or, for that matter, freehold) that, if governments followed diligently, would lead their economies into an inevitable path of prosperity.

Based on this view, this book takes a different tack to examine land tenure debates. We do not intend to argue that governments in transitional countries should establish a public leasehold or freehold system. As a matter of general public policy toward land tenure we believe the two systems are not mutually exclusive (Stein, Troy and Yeomans 1995; Hong 1999). The case studies clearly illustrate that public leasehold and freehold have coexisted in many countries for years. At a site-specific level, one may argue that when a land parcel is assigned to a private entity in fee simple, it is almost always politically, and sometimes financially, impossible to convert the freehold land into public leasehold. Although there is some truth to this argument, the convertibility is still fairly dependent upon prevailing institutions. If the general sentiment of the population, local tradition or market conditions favor public leasehold, the government may be able to buy privately owned land, put in public infrastructure and lease the development rights of serviced sites to private individuals. The "active land policy" in the Netherlands before the 1990s described by Needham (Chapter 3) and the attitude of what Virtanen (Chapter 5) calls "socially bounded land ownership" are good examples. The same argument can be applied to the possible conversion of public leasehold into freehold. For instance, if the majority of citizens in a democratic country prefer fee simple ownership, political forces can shape the property relations of a leasehold system into ones that resemble freehold. Popular demand may even pressure the government to sell public leaseholds to existing lessees as freeholds. The Canberra and Israeli public leasehold systems (Chapters 2 and 6) and the Swedish system (Chapter 4) exemplify these two tendencies, respectively. Certainly, the flexibility of public leasehold, that is, its inherent malleability to rearrange property relations either closer to fee simple or state ownership, may make its transformation to another tenure form less controversial. This is an important distinction between public leasehold and freehold identified by the authors of Chapters 6, 8, 9 and 10, and covered in detail in the concluding chapter.

All in all, our fundamental purpose is to gain a deeper understanding of how institutions shape and are shaped by property relations under public leasehold systems. The debate concerning the choice between public leasehold and freehold is secondary, for we may not have to choose at all: public leasehold and freehold may, in some situations, prove not to be contradictory. Thus, we believe the important questions for studying public leasehold are:

» To what extent can governments accomplish their designed policy goals by leasing public land?

» How do different institutions and organizations affect governments' ability to achieve land leasing objectives?

» If there is a set of enabling institutions and supporting organizations for public leasehold systems, what are the critical issues involved in building these institutions and organizations in countries where governments are experimenting with public land leasing?

Answers to these questions will help policy makers better anticipate the opportunities and risks of adopting public leasehold systems.

DEFINING PUBLIC LEASEHOLD

Although policy makers and analysts have been practicing public land leasing for many years, some are rather casual in defining public leasehold. Some misinterpret public leasehold as government ownership of all interest in land, and overlook the role of the market in facilitating the allocation and exchanges of leasehold rights among private entities. This misconception can be reflected by comments given to us during a meeting with a group of analysts from Poland in 1998: "Leasing is not going to work for us. We need private land ownership and do not want our government to have any control over land." Empirical experiences tell a different story. In Canberra and Hong Kong, for example, despite the fact that the two city governments hold all land titles, there exist vibrant private markets that facilitate the transactions of leasehold rights among private entities. Lessees are free to sell or transfer their land rights to other parties and use their leasehold land as collateral to obtain mortgage loans. These arrangements are far from the types of public land ownership found in the previous communist regimes. Owing to the negative experience of bureaucratic control over land resources in the past, the false impression of public leasehold as absolute state land ownership may have obstructed the establishment of a public land leasing system in some former socialist countries. Based on the comments from the Polish analysts, the passage of legislation promoting public leasehold in Poland will not be smooth.

There are also situations in which parties perceive the adoption of public leasehold as an intermediate step toward freehold. Public officials in some former socialist countries have deployed public leasehold as a means only to elude the constitutional restriction on private land ownership. When the constitution is amended, replacement of public leasehold—an option considered by many private property advocates as only second best—by freehold will be the inevitable outcome. This projected trajectory of the development of public leasehold systems is premature. Although experiences in Canberra, Sweden and Israel seem to indicate an increasing demand from lessees for converting their public leaseholds into more freehold-like arrangements, the leasing systems in Finland, the Netherlands and Hong Kong do not face the same degree of public pressure for any drastic transformation. In other words, the case studies here suggest public leasehold is not necessarily a precursor of a freehold system.

Oversimplification of public leasehold as absolute state ownership and the incorrect view that leasehold ultimately must lead to freehold have at best led to halfhearted acceptance or at worst outright rejection of public land leasing by both reformists and conservatives in some transitional economies. It is therefore desirable to define the principles behind public land leasing carefully, to differentiate this land tenure form as much as possible from other alternative arrangements.

At an abstract level we can treat property in land as a bundle of rights (often referred to as a "bundle of sticks" in the legal literature). Each element of the bundle can be assigned to and controlled by different parties. Using this logic we can treat public leasehold as a system that allows government (as the representative of the public) and private parties to negotiate the delineation and assignment of multiple land rights through contractual arrangements. For instance, a government that is the owner of public land can retain the title of land and lease the right to use, develop, transfer, inherit and benefit from land to private entities. These private lessees can enjoy the assigned land rights only for a specified time and as stipulated in their land contracts.

For comparison purposes, a perpetual leasehold that imposes no restriction on the transfer or use of land and requires a lessee to pay only an up-front payment for leasing land at its fair market value would be very similar to fee simple because the lessee possesses almost all elements of the bundle except the title of land. In this case, we assume government would not resume land ownership without fair reparation, just as fee title would not be taken away from private property owners without just compensation. Conversely, if a government holds all land rights except for temporary use rights assigned to private parties, such a leasehold system would more closely resemble absolute public land ownership. Hence, if we conceptualize fee simple and public land ownership as two ends of a wide spectrum of multiple combinations of public and private ownership of land, public leasehold can be defined in relative terms only. The characterization will depend largely on how the involved parties negotiate and enforce the contractual arrangements stipulated in land leases. As discussed later, existing institutions and organizations will determine the design and enforcement of lease conditions, which delimit the parties' property relations.

One can apply the same argument to the definition of private property rights and state ownership of land, because in reality, no individual or government has absolute control over all elements of the bundle. Even under a freehold system, such as the one in the U.S., private landowners' ability to develop land as they desire is always restricted by land use regulation, and government always retains the right to resume ownership of land for some public purposes. Similarly, when Ukraine was under the control of the communist regime, the use rights of land were assigned to existing private landholders or tenants with restrictions only on the right to transfer their interest to other parties. In other words, even under such a typical case of state land ownership, the "control right" of land might still be in the hands of private individuals.

Land tenure arrangements under most public leasehold systems are not static, because provisions in land contracts are subject to interpretation and renegotiation, which can be triggered by changes in relevant statutes and regulations or other unanticipated developments. There is always the possibility of events that the contracting parties could not foresee. Hence, they may fail to specify in advance the method for dealing with contingencies when they arise. Depending on the political and economic contexts within which the parties practice land leasing, a government lessor may compromise with lessees by giving up some of its abilities to demand payments from lessees. The public leasehold systems in Canberra, The Hague, Israel and Hong Kong have gone through similar changes (see Chapters 2, 3, 6 and 7). Under certain circumstances, renegotiations injected new features into these land leasing systems that made them look more like freehold systems. It is possible that lessees may give up some of their rights, and a government may gain greater control over land, making property rights arrangements more closely resemble state ownership. Hence, public leasehold can be seen as a set of malleable land tenure arrangements. The system may allow the government and private entities to renegotiate the allocation of land rights to balance the public and private interest in land whenever new situations emerge.

PUBLIC POLICY GOALS

The review of different public leasehold systems in this book focuses on the ability of governments to achieve policy goals by leasing public land. Because conditions of individual countries are varied, different governments will set different priorities for what they want to accomplish. For example, while the Hong Kong government emphasizes the use of land leasing to raise public funds for financing public infrastructure investment, officials in Canberra formerly relied on their system to reserve land for building the Australian capital. Thus, it would be unfair to judge the Canberra leasehold system based on the amount of money it generated. Instead, we should focus on whether its public lease-hold system could assist the city to reserve land for building public facilities and allow Canberra to serve as the capital of the country. In each chapter in the second and third sections of the book, the author states the government's goals in implementing a public leasehold system and then evaluates the extent to which public officials can achieve their objectives.

Although the governments in our case studies have different priorities, they all aim at achieving a set of common goals:

» Retain the public's share of land value increments for infrastructure investment.

» Facilitate urban development (or redevelopment).

» Manage urban growth.

» Reserve land for public purposes, such as government buildings and green areas.

» Stabilize land and housing prices.

Other goals are country-specific:

» Avoid selling fee titles of land at low prices when a land market for determining land values and the "optimal" timing of disposal is still underdeveloped.

» Provide a transitional mechanism for raising public funds when an effective system of property taxation is not in place.

» Facilitate investment in property by foreign entities when a country's constitution prohibits ownership of land by foreigners.

» Speed up transfer of property from federal (or central) authorities to local governments for land development.

» Promote economic development and job creation.

» Protect national security by maintaining state ownership of land.

» Encourage use of environment-friendly building materials by incorporating special lease purpose clauses in land contracts.

These are hardly exhaustive lists of the objectives that can be accomplished by leasing public land. There are certainly other attainable goals not thought of by the governments in these case studies.

Judging from the above goals, public land leasing, in theory, could be a very flexible land management tool. It may allow a government to reach multifaceted policy goals by incorporating a set of relevant and enforceable contractual agreements into land leases. The assumption behind this statement is that policy makers and analysts have the foresight to predict how they can structure lease conditions to achieve their policy goals. In reality, that is done mostly by trial and error. Negotiation and political maneuvering may dictate whether government aims can eventually be materialized. It is therefore important to repeat that most governments among these case studies seem incapable of realizing all their desired goals simultaneously. The accomplishment of one goal may have to be at the expense of another. For instance, Needham describes the dilemma that the municipality of The Hague faced when the government was under public pressure to abolish its land leasing system (see Chapter 3). To maintain the public leasehold system as an additional mechanism for controlling land use, the city had to abandon its objective of using land leasing to raise significant amounts of revenue.

Hong provides another example in Chapter 7. The Hong Kong government's intention to collect the maximum amount of revenue at the beginning of the lease term ran into conflict with its objectives of creating affordable housing for the population in the late 1990s. In a market where affordable housing was becoming increasingly scarce, collecting a large sum of money up front for leasing public land would certainly not help lower land costs for housing development. Although the government had reinvested a large portion of lease revenues into public housing programs for the poor, many middle-income families still found buying their own homes impossible. When the government tried to stabilize escalating housing costs by gradually increasing supply, powerful developers and interest groups opposed the plan and forced the government to abandon its initiative.

A government that wants to reserve land for public uses or open space may have to forgo the potential revenues it could have generated were the land leased to private parties for commercial or residential development. In developing countries where economic development is still at a low level, governments that intend to promote industrial growth may grant development rights to foreign and domestic investors at concessionary prices. Unless public officials incorporate enforceable lease conditions that allow them to renegotiate land rent or other lease payments with lessees in the future, the potential cost of achieving the goal of economic development today could be government inability to retain the potential increases in land values in the future. These points imply that there can be tradeoffs among the objectives that governments may want to achieve through public land leasing. Policy makers must find ways to balance these tradeoffs by setting realistic expectations and priorities for what they can achieve, and at what cost. Keeping this issue in mind may at least prevent officials from establishing unrealistic goals or making unattainable promises to their constituents. In the concluding chapter we discuss the experiences of using leasing to achieve public policy goals and explain why some governments succeeded in certain situations, while others failed.

INSTITUTIONS AND ORGANIZATIONS

Priorities for public policy goals are shaped by institutions. For instance, if there is a mandate that local governments must find ways to finance their own public infrastructure and social services, public officials may make raising public funds the top priority for leasing public land. Again, Hong Kong is an example. Not only do institutions dictate the priorities for policy goals, but they also determine if these objectives are obtainable. Hence, it is important to study the institutional influences on the performance of public leasehold systems. We asked the chapter authors to examine how institutions in their case studies affect land leasing. They have discussed three sets of rules that govern the leasing of public land. It is helpful to distinguish them as constitutional, collective decision and operational rules (Ostrom 1990).

Constitutional Rules

In general, the constitutional rules in a country define who has the right to participate in the legislative process, how public representatives are chosen, and what procedures elected public officials must follow to pass proposed bills or modify existing laws. They are normally considered the rules or principles for making legislation. In other words, these rules shape the politics of determining the collective decision rules and in turn the operational rules. More important, the constitution also defines property relations in society and the level of protection the state will provide to private, communal and other types of property.

Among the case studies, Israel, Hong Kong, Ukraine and Beijing began their leasehold systems with their constitutions stating explicitly that the state should own most if not all land and, with subsequent constitutional amendments, may lease other land rights to private entities. The other cases, including the Netherlands, Sweden, Finland and Poland, have less restrictive constitutions that allow the coexistence of public leasehold and freehold. The country-specific constitutional rules set the parameter for land tenure choice or the subsequent development of unique leasing features in each situation. For example, because there is no constitutional restriction on private land ownership in Sweden, local governments could sell off leasehold land to lessees as fee simple when the political ideology shifted in favor of freehold. In facing a similar ideological change, the Israeli government could only modify lease conditions to make public leasehold look more like freehold. The state still holds the title of land as stipulated according to the Basic Law: Israel Lands—described by Alterman as the Constitution in Israel (see Chapter 6).

Constitutions do not always confine land tenure arrangements. Rather, they may be revised to meet the need of a new legal framework for facilitating and protecting land and property transactions in rapidly changing political and economic environments. For example, Strong (Chapter 8) argues that selling public land to private enterprises by the Ukrainian municipalities is not a case of officials trying to disobey laws. Rather, there is confusion about which legal doctrines—the Constitution or other legislation—they should follow. Many laws enacted before 1996 have provisions inconsistent with the Ukrainian Constitution, because recent reforms in Ukraine had totally overhauled its political and economic systems. All legal doctrines are subject to challenges and reinterpretations. Unless government reconciles the differences between the Constitution and legislation, conflicting provisions stated in these two legal doctrines will impede public land leasing and the development of a land market. The Ukrainian situation shows the importance of paying special attention to a country's constitution in adopting public leasehold systems.

The constitution of a democratic country also guarantees the public's right to elect their representatives to government. In Chapter 2 Neutze raises an interesting question in regard to this constitutional rule: can public officials achieve their policy goals by leasing public land when lessees are also the constituents who elect a government lessor? The abolition of residential land rents in Canberra, discussed by Neutze, provides a good example of how public officials who wanted to fulfill their ambitions would forgo potential lease revenues to solicit support from lessees. Another case was the softening of the government's intention to use land leasing to capture land value increments in The Hague because of public pressure (see Chapter 3). Similarly, the Israeli leasehold system is moderated by the government's need to maintain public support of the system. The Israeli Basic Law does not separate land from buildings and offers no distinct provision to delineate and protect the legal entitlement to the two types of property. This implies that, at least according to the law, if the state owns the title of land it also legally possesses all buildings erected on it. Under this legal framework the government would have the legal right to retake both the land and buildings when a lease expires. Yet, as Alterman explains in Chapter 6, with more than 70 percent of Israeli housing units built on public leasehold lands and the remaining on the quasi-state-owned land, the political parties elected by universal suffrage to be the governing body would never take an action that would undermine its ability to stay in power. Even in Hong Kong, where lessees traditionally have very limited right to elect the government, the possibility of instigating social unrest in the early 1970s deterred officials from asking lessees to pay a higher land rent for renewing their land contracts (see Chapter 7). These chapters provide a detailed account of how public pressure could affect public land leasing in countries where government lessors must be accountable to the public.

Collective Decision Rules

The making of collective decision rules (or legislation) is guided by national constitutions. These collective decision rules dictate the standards for establishing and enforcing lease conditions. The example related to public land leasing is the leasehold legislation found in almost all public leasehold systems. In democratic countries leasehold legislation represents collective decisions made by publicly elected officials on behalf of their constituencies. These laws form the legal framework for contract negotiations and enforcements, which in turn increase the level of certainty in public land leasing. They also enhance the security of public leaseholds by legally defining and recognizing the rights of both the lessor and lessee through land registration. Major changes to the features of public land leasing, such as the abolition or revision of annual land rents, will require formal amendments to the laws that must be debated and approved by the legislative bodies.

Almost all contributors to this volume assert the importance of establishing leasehold and other related legislation, such as mortgage and bankruptcy laws applicable to situations under a public leasehold system. Some also discuss in detail how politics and court battles can change the legal framework within which the lessor and lessees interpret, negotiate and enforce lease conditions. Indeed, as Strong (Chapter 8) and Deng (Chapter 10) argue, in situations where enforceable legal rules and an impartial court system are absent, the security and creditability of a public leasehold system will be in jeopardy. According to Needham (Chapter 3), Strong and Deng, the key question all investors ask regarding investment in leasehold land is: if a local government is responsible for leasing public land and at the same time has the sole authority to issue building permits, what legal rights and channels do lessees have to challenge the public lessor if it abuses its power? This issue appears particularly problematic in emerging systems where the necessary legislation is not fully developed. Strong and Deng show that the underdevelopment of legal institutions in Ukraine and the People's Republic of China has led to corruption. This problem is the major obstacle for developing a land market in general and a public leasehold system in particular in these two countries.

Collective decision rules do not always pertain to legislation. They also include informal rules, including generally recognized practices, customs, tradition and other common beliefs. Informal rules may sometimes play a more prominent role than formal legislation in influencing public land leasing. According to Strong, the Land Code of 1992 in Ukraine explicitly confines local governments to granting only a temporary or permanent use right of land to private enterprises. Although the president of Ukraine issued a decree in 1995 to authorize the state to sell or lease land to private enterprises, Parliament rejected the presidential decree and refused to amend the Land Code. Although the Ukrainian government has not resolved the legality of selling industrial land, local public officials act on the presumption that selling land within their jurisdictions is permissible. In this situation, the prevailing informal practices of local governments based on their own policy and fiscal needs are the determining factors of the land assignment method. Formal rules do not seem to play a dominant role.

There are also examples in which culture affects the adoption of the public leasehold system. As stated earlier, local tradition and an attitude of "socially bounded land ownership" in older Finnish towns have supported public leasehold for many years. Virtanen argues that the recognition of land as a resource to serve primarily the interests of the community as a whole, aids local officials in Helsinki in maintaining its public leasehold system despite the increasing popularity of freehold in other smaller Finnish towns.

Social attitudes and political ideologies, however, do not always favor public leasehold. As described by Neutze (Chapter 2) and by Mattsson (Chapter 4), the increased popularity of neoliberalism in Australia and Sweden during the 1980s led to the downsizing of government. Consequently, the roles of public leasehold in allocating and managing public land were also curtailed. Some Swedish municipalities even sold public leaseholds to lessees as freehold interests.

These case studies show that both formal and informal rules established at the collective level are important for understanding different international experiences in leasing public land.

Operational Rules

Operational rules allow investors and the government to make day-to-day decisions on how to use, invest in and profit from land. Lease conditions are examples of operational rules that specify what the lessee can and cannot do with the leased land rights for a specified time; how much money and at what interval (or on which occasions) the lessee must pay the lessor to maintain the land rights; and what penalties the lessor will impose on the lessee if the latter breaches the land contracts. These lease conditions are the most basic rules for delineating the property relations between a government lessor and lessee under a public leasehold system.

Table 1 summarizes the general lease conditions and structures of the public leasehold systems analyzed in this book. Lease conditions are constructed in diverse ways. For instance, lease terms range from five years (England Air Force Base in Louisiana, U.S.) to infinity (Sweden). The most common term is 50 years. All systems allow lessees to renew their land contracts for at least another term if there is a term limit. If we include renewable terms, only the American case (which is unique) has a leasing period shorter than 98 years. The term of leases and the possibility of their renewal will affect lessees' decisions regarding investment in buildings and other improvements and maintenance. It will certainly affect the timing and planning of a public lessor's investment in public infrastructure and urban development. As mentioned by Baxter in Chapter 9, one potential function of public leasehold is to allow the government to allocate land for private uses for the duration of time when the land is not ripe for development. By setting the expiration of the lease to coincide with the commencement date of planned development, the government will be able to take land back from lessees when it is time to undertake the development project. Certainly, whether the government can actually retake land is a political issue that depends largely on the institutional context of a specific system.

Another lease condition that differs among the selected case studies is the lease payment method. There are generally two kinds of lease payment—the land premium and annual land rent. The land premium is a lump sum that lessees pay to the government to obtain, modify or extend their land rights. Analysts refer to a leasehold system as a *premium* system if a government relies mainly on land premiums to collect lease revenues. Examples include the public leasehold systems in Canberra, Israel and Hong Kong.

Not all land-leasing systems are structured as a premium system. For instance, the Dutch, Finnish and Swedish systems require lessees to pay only an annual land rent. Analysts call these *land rent* systems. In The Netherlands municipalities also allow lessees to pay in the beginning of the lease term all yearly rental payments in one lump sum discounted to their present values. This option, if available, blurs the distinction between the premium and land rent systems.

These dissimilarities are not just a matter of technicality. Rather, different lease terms and payment methods can significantly affect property relations between a government lessor and lessees. In Chapter 2 Neutze argues that the shift from the land rent system to a premium system in Canberra during the 1970s allowed lessees to acquire equity in land. The acquisition of equity altered lessees' perceptions of what they owned and what they could claim to do with their lands. With an additional change to the lease renewal clause that guaranteed all residential lessees' rights to renew their contracts at any time during the last 30 years of the term, land contracts in Canberra became de facto perpetual leases. With no payment of rent and no significant fees for lease renewal, public leasehold in this city, Neutze concludes, began to look more like freehold. As the government's equity in land declined, officials encountered great difficulties in requiring lessees to make additional payments for modifying lease conditions for land redevelopment. A similar evolution of property relations was found in the Israeli and Hong Kong leasehold systems, as described by Alterman and Hong (Chapters 6 and 7, respectively).

Interconnections Among Constitutional, Collective Decision and Operational Rules

The three sets of rules are closely intertwined. No single set can adequately determine property relations in a public leasehold system. For example, case studies reveal clearly that lease conditions are in constant flux. Parties involved in public land leasing will renegotiate continually at the operational level for revisions of lease conditions when they fail, due to the emergence of a new situation, to delineate and divide land rights and land value increments between a government lessor and lessees. The general guiding principles for the reconstruction of lease conditions are collective decision rules, namely leasehold legislation and other informal conventions. When these collective rules also become ineffective in providing a legal or nonlegal framework for the disagreeing parties to resolve their problems, changes in legislation and/or informal rules will be deemed necessary. As the Hong Kong experience in the early 1970s showed, although the general characteristics and enforcement of lease conditions were defined by leasehold legislation, conflicts over the conditions that governed lease renewal at an individual level gradually escalated into major political and legal challenges at the collective level for revisions of the laws (see Chapter 7).

In some situations, such as in the Netherlands, Finland, Sweden and Israel, legislation related to public leasehold reflects and is reinforced by the constitution; but in Ukraine and Beijing the two legal doctrines were in conflict with each other during the period of dramatic changes. Similarly, the formal and informal rules can be complementary as well as contradictory. As the experience of the Finnish systems indicates, local tradition is consistent with leasehold legislation, helping some municipalities preserve their public leasehold system. Conversely, in Sweden and Israel, the increase in the popularity of freehold forces government to modify their leasehold legislation to make leaseholds look more like freehold rights. The complex relationships among these rules

TABLE 1 ——
LEASING FEATURES FOR SELECTED COUNTRIES (OR CITIES)

	Canberra, Australia	The Netherlands
Lease term	99 years	50 years or indefinite
Right of renewal	All residential leases are renewable for nominal fee.	Leases with a 50-year term usually are renewable. Level of payment is reviewed during lease renewal.
Ownership of leasehold improvements	Lessee owns improvements to land at the end of lease.	If lease expires or is terminated prematurely, lessee is compensated for the value of improvements to land.
Lease payments	Before 1971 an annual land rent was payable, with adjustments to any increases in land value over time. In 1971 the government abolished all residential land rents and adopted a premium system.	Lessee pays government an annual land rent through the term of lease. Yet, lessee also has the right to convert all annual rental payments into a premium paid at the beginning of lease.
Using lease conditions to control land use	Government includes a purpose clause that defines permissible land uses. Land development must commence and be completed within the time specified in the lease.	Lease conditions are used to control land use only if they complement the land use plan and other existing regulations.
Additional requirements for redevelopment	Lessee must pay a betterment charge of 75 percent (50 percent between 1971 and 1990) of the increase in land value caused by redevelopment.	If lessee wants to redevelop land, permission must be obtained from lessor. Lease payment will also be revised.
Transferability of land rights	Lessee has the right to transfer leasehold rights to another party. For new leases, transfer must be done after completion of development.	Lessee can sell leased land rights in the open market or transfer them to another party.
Government's right to repossess land	Government never repossesses land so as to ensure security of tenure. Government had retained enough land for public purposes, thus chose not to repossess land for redevelopment purposes as the city grew.	Although government can repossess land, lessee rights are quite well protected by law. Procedure of "reentry" may be quicker than compulsory purchase. Lessee will be compensated if land is repossessed.
Public attitude toward public leasehold	Public leasehold was well founded in Australia's history, from the declaration of Crown land in 1788. Freehold was later permitted in all areas except Canberra. Although retention of public leasehold in Canberra remains controversial, the system has survived several public inquiries.	Government lessors often are seen as using land leasing to collect more money from their citizens.

Sweden	Finland	Israel
60 years for residential leases; minimum 20 years for other purposes. Only landowner (lessor) can cancel land contracts.	50–60 years for residential land leases; 50 years for commercial land leases; 20–30 years for industrial land contracts	Basic term is 49 years; for residential use it is usually multiples thereof.
Residential leases are automatically renewed for another 40 years if lessor does not cancel them (minimum 20 years for other leases).	Leases for housing are renewable if lessor does not need the land for other public purposes. For industrial lots, land contracts are not automatically renewable.	In recent decades, new or renewed contracts for residential use are for 2 automatically renewable terms and lately, for 4 such terms, totaling 196 years.
If government lessor cancels contract, it must pay compensation to lessee for buildings and other fixtures erected on land. Lessor does not have to pay compensation if contract is for nonresidential purposes, and it is stipulated in contract that compensation shall not be paid.	Land improvements belong to lessee. If the contract is not renewed, lessor will compensate lessee for improvements to land. The exception is industrial leases that land improvements will not be compensated.	Israeli real-property law does not allow for the separation of ground from buildings so legally all land improvements belong to the state. But most leases state that if a lease expires or is terminated prematurely, lessee must be compensated for the value of improvements to land.
Lease payment to government is in the form of an annual land rent. Rent is adjusted every 10 or 20 years.	Lessee pays annual land rent to government equal to 4–5 percent of estimated land value. Land rent will be adjusted every 30 years according to real increase in land value and also annually according to any change in cost of living.	Lessee is encouraged (in new leases, required) to pay the entire lease value in one lump sum in advance (discounted to present value). Upon sale of leasehold, lessee is then exempt from a "consent fee" (about half the increase in market value) for the transfer permission. To redevelop the leased land, all lessees must pay a "permit fee" (about half the added value) to government lessor.
Land use was controlled to some extent by lease conditions until 1953. Now, detailed plans are the major instruments for controlling land use.	Lease conditions play no role in controlling land use. Land use is controlled by the detailed plan.	Lease conditions usually are not used as a direct mechanism for regulating land use.
If redevelopment is for new purposes or increased use, a new lease must be signed between lessee and government lessor. Payment of land rent will be revised.	The lessee needs to establish a new contract with the government and pay a new land rent.	Lessee is required to submit an application to the lessor for approval (beyond planning-law approval). If approved, lessee will pay a "permit fee."
Site leasehold can be transferred freely.	Land rights (freehold and leasehold) are freely transferable. Subleasing is not permitted.	Lessee can sell, sublease, or bequeath state-owned property at will (with only a notice given to the state), but leases on land owned by the Jewish National Land can be transferred to Jewish persons only.
Lessor can cancel lease at specified periods. The first chance is after 60 years for residential leases, the next chance is after 40 years. For other types of leases, lessor may cancel after a minimum of 20 years.	Government has the right to repossess land with just compensation to lessee for fair market value of any leasehold improvements.	In cases of expropriation for public purposes, the law treats urban leaseholders as equal to freeholders. Full compensation is due for the fair market price of improvements as well as land (the value is usually almost identical to freeholds). Compulsory dedication rules are also identical.
Leasehold rights are being sold as freehold to lessees, especially leases for single-family houses. Homeowners do not like leasehold as land rents increase frequently. Yet, industrialists may prefer leaseholds as they do not need to raise large upfront capital for land acquisition.	Attitude is mainly positive among public authorities and municipalities. This is strengthened by the Parliament's Leasehold Act. Smaller municipalities, however, prefer freehold as leasing incurs high administration costs.	Long-term public leasehold is widely perceived as the normal, almost undebated, state of affairs, especially since a gradual process of quasi-privatization has provided for security of tenure, and market values almost identical to freehold.

continued

TABLE 1 ——
Leasing Features for Selected Countries (or Cities) *(continued)*

	Hong Kong, China	Ukraine
Lease term	50 years (75 years before 1997) for most residential and commercial land leases	5–49 years
Right of renewal	The Basic Law—the mini-Constitution of Hong Kong—does not specify if leases, extended for 50 years in 1997 or after 1997, will again be renewable after 2047. Yet, lessees assume under normal circumstances their contracts will be renewed based on government's past practice.	Most leases are renewable for another 49 years.
Ownership of leasehold improvements	Lessee possesses all improvements to land.	Lessee owns improvements to land. For farm collectives, shares were awarded based on what the member contributed, including land, chattels and labor.
Lease payments	Lessee will pay lump sum premium for leasing land at beginning of lease. When lessee wants to modify lease conditions for land redevelopment, a modification premium is required. Lessee also pays annual land rent, calculated at 3 percent of estimated rental value of land and building. Government revises estimated rental values annually.	Government collects land rent equal to 1 percent of estimated land value.
Using lease conditions to control land use	Government uses lease conditions to specify the land use. Yet, the enforcement of land use regulations still relies heavily on the Planning Department and Buildings Department.	Municipalities do not use lease conditions to control land use. Most controls in urban areas are through the plan, which is highly specific.
Additional requirements for redevelopment	For land redevelopment initiated by lessee, government approval is needed, along with payment of a modification premium.	N/A
Transferability of land rights	No restriction on any transfer of leased land rights.	Lessee must obtain permission from lessor to sublet land.
Government's right to repossess land	Government has legal right to repossess land for public purposes. It must, however, compensate leaseholders for any improvements to land.	If land use plan is violated, government can repossess land lease.
Public attitude toward public leasehold	Public attitude toward public leasehold is pragmatic. There has been no public demand that government should change public leasehold to freehold.	Attitude toward public leasehold is mixed. Many fear giving government too much power, after decades of total government control. Others are indifferent as to whether land is sold or leased, as long as land transactions are transparent.

Source: Compiled by the authors

England Air Force Base, Louisiana, U.S.	Beijing, China	Poland
55-year master lease from DOD to England Authority allows it to acquire fee ownership in increments. The Authority now owns 51% of the land. It leases individual parcels to private entities by short-term leases of various durations.	70 years for residential land leases; 40 years for commercial leases; 50 years for industrial contracts	40–99 years
N/A	Lessee has the right to renew land contract.	Leases can be renewed unless the lessor serves notice not later than 5 years prior to the expiration of the term.
Authority owns the improvements when the leases expire.	Lessee owns all leasehold improvements during the term of lease. Yet, when lease expires, improvements will revert back to government if the lease is not renewed.	Lessee owns land improvements under separate ownership.
DOD does not charge rent for the master lease to the Authority. The Authority collects annual rents from tenants for leasing them both land and buildings.	Lessee makes several upfront payments, including land premium, and community and urban infrastructure fees. Other fees may include an urban renewal fee, as required. Lessee also pays annual land use fee (sometimes called tax).	Highest public bid for land is used to calculate initial installment payment for leasing land, which total ranges 15–25 percent of land price. Lessee also pays a fixed percentage annual ground rent (usually between 1–3 percent) of land price or value depending on use.
The Authority uses lease conditions to control the use of the leased properties.	Lease usually has list of separate land use conditions; enforcement of conditions is lax. There is also a requirement for development of a certain portion of land within 2 years. Some local governments may charge vacant land fee if land is not developed after 2-year limit expires.	Lease conditions state that land development must be compatible with land use zoning regulations, which may be made more specific in contract.
N/A	N/A	N/A
The Authority does not need permission from the DOD to sublease individual sites.	Lessee can sell, mortgage or transfer land rights.	No restriction on transfer of leasehold rights.
Both DOD and the Authority are governmental entities. DOD did not retain rights to repossess the land.	Government can terminate leases and retake land for public purposes.	Upon expiration of lease, land reverts to government ownership, free and clear of leasehold rights.
Master lease was a means to expedite the transfer of federal government properties from the DOD to the Authority for redevelopment to minimize negative impacts of military base closure on local employment.	In the late 1980s there was opposition to public leasehold, especially leasing public land to foreign investors. Public land leasing is now generally accepted by the public.	Planners and investors favor public leasehold as it provides an additional instrument for facilitating land transaction and development. Lessees and lawyers do not like leasehold, for it prevents lessees from enjoying the full capital appreciation of land. They also believe government adjusts land rents too often.

create unique institutional environments that shape individuals' behaviors and investment decisions differently in distinct periods and across spaces. Thus, a comprehensive understanding of their relationships in terms of how these institutional rules were established, enforced and revised could provide important clues for explaining the diverse structures and performances of public leasehold systems—a matter we deal with in the concluding chapter.

Organizations

All institutional rules require organizations to implement and enforce them. Organizations include political, economic, social and educational entities, such as political parties, regulatory agencies, firms, trade unions, churches, social clubs and associations, schools and universities. They are composed of groups of individuals bound by common purposes to achieve certain objectives. Redesigning institutions is another function of organizations in society. It is therefore important to examine what organizations are needed for the adoption and enforcement of institutions, and how they should be structured according to varying circumstances. The authors have identified three types of organizations that are necessary to support public leasehold, and how the governments in their case studies have structured them.

First, responding to his concern about the politics of public land leasing, Neutze (Chapter 2) suggests that governments should establish two separate organizations to manage the public leasehold system and plan for the use of land, respectively. Like most planning agencies around the world, the latter would be an integral part of the government apparatus and be directly accountable to the community. The former is more like a custodian or trustee of public land, focusing on the management of public assets. Like any other private trustees, this agency has to uphold the interests of its beneficiaries by maximizing economic returns in investing and allocating land resources. It should publish an annual report stating the level of available land reserve; the amount of land assigned to private parties; and estimated returns obtainable from these assignments. Segregating the planning and leasing functions of public land would create a system of checks and balances that would clarify the separate objectives of public land management and planning. In the concluding chapter we analyze the extent to which such organizational structures may minimize problems associated with the politicization of leasing public land.

The second type of required organization comprises experts who can appraise the value of leasehold rights and assist the government to create and maintain a cadastral system. In Chapter 8 Strong argues that the absence of assessment techniques and a registration system for leasehold rights (as well as for all other real and intangible property) has impeded the development of a property market in Ukraine. Without a set of generally agreed upon standards for assessing property rights, and a comprehensive record of past transactions, banks will not accept leased land rights as collateral. In developing countries where incomes are low, the lack of credit may mean that only a small segment of the population can afford to lease land and purchase properties, thus hindering the development of a real estate market. Indeed, some governments, especially those in transitional economies, have overlooked the importance of developing essential professions, such as property appraisal, estate surveying and real estate management, that could assist the public to invest in land and housing by defining, valuing and recording leasehold rights. Chapters 2, 4, 5 and 8 illustrate how professional organizations, or the lack of them, affect the performance of different public leasehold systems.

Third, Neutze, Needham and Virtanen argue that the implementation and preservation of public leasehold require organizations that can educate policy makers and the public about the pros and cons of leasing public land (see Chapters 2, 3 and 5). In essence, the form of land tenure is a political decision. The adoption of a public leasehold system would therefore require the acceptance of policy makers and, in democratic countries, the public. Even in undemocratic countries the development of land and property markets will depend on investment decisions made by individual domestic and foreign investors. Their understanding of the utility and operations of public leasehold will affect the sustainability of the system. In Canberra and Israel, public officials who are under the political influence of their constituencies or who have acted out of their own convictions have converted public leaseholds into freehold-like arrangements. Municipalities in the Netherlands and Sweden have even sold leased land rights as fee titles. These actions, according to our authors, may not have relied on careful examinations of what public leasehold can and cannot do for the community as a whole. Rather, ideology and special interests are the driving forces behind these "freehold movements." With the confusion regarding the definition and functions of public leasehold discussed earlier in this chapter, how can we ask citizens to decide if their governments should adopt or retain public leasehold? Educational and research organizations are needed, especially in democratic countries, to inform voters about the advantages and disadvantages of leasing public land. This would in turn allow the population to make well-informed decisions concerning the future of their public leasehold system.[2]

OVERVIEW OF THE CHAPTERS

The book presents ten case study chapters in two major sections. The first section describes the leasing experiences in countries or cities where public leasehold has been established for a long time. These cases include Canberra, Finland, the Netherlands, Sweden, Israel and Hong Kong. The second section focuses on emerging leasing systems. Although they are mainly from transitional economies, namely Ukraine, the PRC and Poland, we also include one study from the U.S., where various federal and county agencies used leasing to facilitate military base conversions. In summarizing the many ideas presented

---

[2] Certainly, the same questions about institutions and organizations should be raised regarding the adoption of private property rights systems, and there are numerous excellent studies that have dealt with the issues (Barzel 1989; Coase 1937, 1960; Demsetz 1967; Libecap 1989; North 1990; Williams 1985).

in individual chapters, we focus primarily on the experience of each case study in achieving policy goals by leasing public land.

Experiences from Developed Systems

We begin with Neutze's assessment of the Canberra public leasehold system. Although public land ownership allowed the government to control land uses in Canberra for building the Australian capital, development around the end of the 1970s and early 1980s led to a major erosion and subsequent poor performance of its public leasehold system. Neutze asserts, "The potential of public leasehold on a publicly owned site to contribute to very good public planning and public finance has not been fully realized." The primary cause was poor management, which in turn created opportunities for special interest groups to influence policy making related to public land leasing. In challenging the government's practice in leasing public land, Neutze expresses two major disappointments.

First, he argues that the government failed to distinguish between rates and lease revenues. Rates are charges imposed on leaseholders for their enjoyment of services provided by public infrastructure, such as roads, water and sewerage, parks and other public facilities. Lease revenues, including annual land rents and lease premiums, are returns to the government lessor on its land assets. The former revenues are land taxes, whereas the latter should be recognized as reasonable investment returns on public land that belongs to the community at large. Combining the two sources of land revenues together in government analyses, Neutze argues, undermined the objective of treating public land as investment capital that could bring significant income to the community. Further, there was no accounting system for recording the amount of money that leasing brought into the public coffers. Since voters never realized the potential financial benefits of leasing public land, the public leasehold system began to give way to pressure from special interest groups, such as nonresidential leaseholders and developers. Public officials who did not appreciate the possible fiscal impacts of public leasehold also gave up their chances of capturing land value increments when they failed to charge lessees land rents that were properly adjusted according to general increases in land values. The 1971 abolition of land rents for all residential leases and the decision to levy less than a 100 percent Change of Use Charge represented the loss of opportunities for the public to use land leasing as a long-term source of substantial government revenue.

Second, the erosion of the financial benefits of public leasehold also undermined the possibility of using lease conditions to regulate urban growth. Unable to treat public land leasing as a profitable undertaking, the government retreated from its role as the lessor who, in a private market situation, would have taken back land, redeveloped it, then leased the development rights again to private entities, to capitalize fully on the development potential of these public assets. Yet, as a public lessor the government was reluctant to take land, partly due to its intention to ensure security of tenure to lessees. In addition, the conversion of the lease payment method from annual land rents to initial premiums in

1971 allowed lessees to acquire substantial equity in land. With only one lump sum payment in the beginning of the lease and no subsequent rental payment, leasehold rights looked increasingly like freeholds. This perception in turn made government repossession of leased land for redevelopment difficult. Since then the government in Canberra, like most governments in other freehold systems, has taken a reactive role in shaping land development and redevelopment of the city. Owing to the failure to achieve these two important goals of public leasehold, Neutze concludes that the land leasing experience in Canberra has not lived up to its potential.

Needham's assessment of the performance of the Dutch public leasehold systems in Chapter 3 is as skeptical as Neutze's. According to Needham, the major objectives of leasing public land in the Netherlands are twofold: to allow municipalities to have more control over land development and to secure a source of revenue for local governments. The first motivation emerged during the second half of the nineteenth century when the municipal governments of Amsterdam, Rotterdam and The Hague faced increasing inflows of workers who put tremendous pressure on the housing stock. The quality of housing also was poor. To deal with these planning issues, the municipalities asked the national government for stronger statutory planning power to regulate housing development and building standards. When the national government refused, they began to regulate development through other alternatives, such as the deed of conveyance for freehold land and lease purpose clauses for long-term leasehold. Needham points out that lease conditions have given the munici- palities additional means to control development besides the "police power" given to them by the state. In Dutch law this is referred to as the "doctrine of the two ways."

In the past, leaseholders brought legal challenges to the use of lease purpose clauses to regulate property development. Currently, the courts require munici- pal governments to prove that the use of lease provisions does not contradict public policy goals, and that statutory powers are "inadequate" to achieve planning purposes. The ambiguity in the law regarding use of lease conditions to control land use may have led some municipalities to be choose caution in exerting both their public and private legal rights. A study cited by Needham found that municipalities that leased public land paid little attention to setting lease conditions for land use control. This study and others illustrate the uncer- tainty of using lease conditions for planning purposes in the Netherlands.

Furthermore, revenues generated from land leasing do not appear significant in the Netherlands. Needham uses Amsterdam as an example; the net income of 113.5 million Dutch guilders (US$43.8 million) from land leasing accounted for only 1.3 percent of the city's 1999 budget. Although the fiscal impact of lease revenues seems minimal, Needham indicates that the possibility of future increases in land rents represents a source of revenue for local governments.

Needham concludes that local governments appear unable to use lease con- ditions to regulate land development and at the same time require lessees to pay land rents at market value. He cites The Hague to illustrate how that city had to retreat from its financial objective for land leasing to prevent voters from demanding that the government abolish the whole system. If the municipality dismantled its public leasehold system, it would have lost both the potential lease revenues and the ability to regulate land development through lease purpose clauses. Needham's analysis fully reveals the policy tradeoffs discussed earlier in this chapter.

The Swedish leasehold system described by Mattsson in Chapter 4 is undergoing an even more dramatic transformation than those experienced in the Canberra and Dutch systems. Due to public pressure, some municipalities in Sweden have been selling off public leaseholds at a sizable discount beginning in the early 1990s. Even Stockholm, which is considered by many as the pioneer of the Swedish leasehold system, began to sell to lessees the freehold rights of land used for single-family housing in 1993. Mattsson offers two reasons for the conversion. First, there has been a growing demand from the nonsocialist majority in local governments to grant citizens the freedom to decide on their tenure choice. Second, local governments have also been attempting to release capital tied up in land.

The Swedish case raises two interesting questions. First, why would the revenue-hungry municipalities believe that selling public leasehold for a one-time payment is financially preferable to maintaining a continuous stream of income through the collection of land rents? Second, if the municipalities want to maximize potential land revenues, why would they sell off public leasehold at a large discount? Mattsson explains that the determination of annual land rents is technically complex and controversial in Sweden. Although legal precedents are available for resolving disagreements, there are always unforeseeable factors that may trigger different interpretations of the rules. If disputes arise, they often lead to costly and time-consuming litigation. Thus, some municipalities prefer to sell land or leasehold sites as freehold to avoid high administration costs associated with negotiating and collecting land rents.

More important, another policy goal of leasing public land is to provide affordable housing to the population. Because of this objective, some municipalities set land rents at below market value. Stockholm discounts land rents for single-family housing by up to 33 percent of fair market value. These land rents will stay the same as long as the original lessees remain in place. The subsidized land rents explain the need for a large discount when selling freehold rights: low land rents discourage lessees from converting their leasehold rights into freeholds unless the lump sum method for buying land is less expensive than the alternative. Once again, the Swedish case illustrates a potential tradeoff between different policy goals of leasing public land. In this case, the intention of maximizing lease revenues is incompatible with the goal of providing affordable housing to the population.

In Chapter 5 Virtanen explains that the experience of leasing public land in major Finnish municipalities contrasts significantly with the experiences found in Canberra, Sweden and the Netherlands; not only are the public leasehold systems in major municipalities such as Helsinki and Lauritsala alive, they are thriving. Virtanen reflects, "Based on my experience as a city surveyor in Lauritsala…both landowners and lessees were satisfied with public leasehold….

[W]hen municipalities have given lessees the option to buy their land, lessees have not been keen to exercise that option." He offers four reasons for this hospitable experience.

First, many local residents view public land leasing as a tradition and believe in "socially bounded land ownership," which advocates that land resources must first serve the interests of the community. Interests of private landowners are treated as secondary. Virtanen explains that this attitude in Finland results from a long history of public land ownership and leasing. The Helsinki local government owns 68 percent of all land within the city, a portion of it received from the Swedish King in 1550, when Finland was still part of Sweden. Laws prohibited the sale of donated land and other public land to private entities until these legal restrictions were lifted after 1943. Between these periods, public leasehold was the only option available to the city for assigning land to private parties for housing and industrial development.

Second, Virtanen argues that Finland has well-established leasehold legislation that can mediate potential conflicts arising from land leasing. The legislation appears to be adequate to protect the rights of both municipalities and lessees concerning the determination of land rents; ownership of leasehold improvements when leases expire; compensation for the resumption of land leases; and legal actions against the lessor or the lessee for any contract noncompliance. The legal framework for guiding negotiation in land leasing in turn enhances the security of public leaseholds in Finland.

Third, unlike Canberra's land administrative system, the public agencies that administer public land leasing in Finland seem successful. Leasing is conducted only in major municipalities where qualified and competent administrators are available. Lease payments from lessees are in the form of annual land rents, with yearly adjustments according to the cost of living and adjustments every 30 years to the real increase in land value. All public agencies must pay an internal land rent to the city's Real Estate Department to lease public land. This payment allows government agencies to recognize land costs of their operations, which reduces the amount of idle land held by public agencies. The Real Estate Department also publishes all leasing-related activities in an annual report in three different languages for public scrutiny.

Fourth, municipalities set their policy goals of leasing public land realistically. They do not employ lease conditions to govern land use planning. Rather, the planning tasks are left to a separate yet complementary planning system. The two major goals of leasing public land are to recoup the public's share of land value increments and promote urban development. Virtanen asserts that Finnish local governments have established enforceable lease conditions in land contracts for achieving these goals with reasonable flexibility in negotiating with lessees for variances if special circumstances arise. The realism and flexibility in leasing public land demonstrate why major municipalities in Finland have maintained the popularity of public leasehold.

In Chapter 6 Alterman describes the evolution of the Israeli public leasehold system, portraying the unique rationale of leasing public land in her country. Unlike Canberra, the Netherlands, Sweden, Finland and Hong Kong, Israel did not design its public leasehold system simply to help local governments achieve their fiscal and planning goals. Instead, the key function of leasing public land is to accommodate a private property market within the context of a land tenure system dominated by public land ownership.

Alterman asserts that long-term public leasehold has resolved the paradox between the geopolitical and ideological needs of public land ownership and the increasing popular demand for private property in land. While most authors in this volume consider public land leasing as a means to extend government involvement in land development and planning, Alterman sees an opposite purpose of the Israeli system: to increase the private property rights in land to expand the role of the market in land resource allocation. For years, the Israeli land tenure system has undergone incremental changes, described by Alterman as *gradual privatization*, which transformed property rights arrangements into something almost tantamount to a freehold system. She details these transformations by focusing on 10 property rights dimensions of leasehold rights in Israel. Here we highlight some of the dimensions.

Using the concept of real property as a bundle of rights as an analytical framework, Alterman shows that land contracts in Israel are in essence perpetual leases, with property rights arrangements analogous to those of fee simple. At present the lease term is 49 years with four automatic renewals totaling 196 years. With a lease term of nearly two centuries, the state could hardly expect lessees to give up both land and buildings when the lease expires. Besides, the payment for lease extension is minimal; lessees do not have to pay the full market value of the lease, they just pay a new land rent equal to one-fifth of the annual rent charged for their initial lease. More important, the new land rent for the entire new term would not exceed 5 percent of the property value at the time of renewal, if a lessee chooses to pay all future rental payments in one lump sum. Similar to Canberra, the Israeli leasehold system has evolved from a land rent system into a premium system. For new leases the entire value of the lease is paid up front in one lump sum, allowing lessees to acquire the full equity in land from the government, which is similar to buying land freehold. The government does not use lease conditions to control land use and rarely refuses applications from lessees requesting extra development rights. Lessees may transfer their leasehold properties to a third party. Although they need permission from the Lands Administration, the government grants its consent almost automatically with the payment of a *consent fee*. The government tries to use the lease condition to require lessees to finish land development in a timely manner, yet, the enforcement of this contract, like most cases discussed in this book, has been ineffective due to public opposition. Owing to these land tenure arrangements, the property rights and obligations of leaseholders, Alterman argues, are almost indistinguishable from those of freeholders in Israel.

The only difference between leasehold and freehold in Israel is that the former provides an additional lever for the government to capture the public's share of land value increments, although it is unclear whether the government can take full advantage of this feature. It does so by levying a consent fee as well as a *permit fee*. The administration calculates the consent fee based on the percentage of the unpaid lease value; thus, if a lessee possesses a fully prepaid lease—all lease payments are made up front in one lump sum, there will be no consent fee. Since the Israeli government encourages (and in the case of new leases requires) lessees to make their lease payment in full, the consent fee will eventually be phased out. The permit fee is a levy on the increase in land value after lease restrictions are lifted for redevelopment, set at 50 percent of the increment caused by lease modification. In addition to the permit fee, local planning authorities also impose a 50 percent betterment levy on leasehold properties. In some cases the national government may also charge an Added Increment Tax. Leaseholders may pay all three charges, whereas owners of freehold properties will pay only the betterment levy and Added Increment Tax. Under these arrangements the government should be able to recoup a larger portion of land value increments from leaseholders than from freeholders. The Israeli case study reveals the malleability of its public leasehold system in allowing the government lessor and lessees to renegotiate property rights arrangements to facilitate land and property transactions in a rapidly changing socioeconomic and, to some extent, politically unstable environment.

The assessment of the Hong Kong public leasehold system is mixed. In Chapter 7 Hong examines the opportunities and risks of using land leasing to achieve public policy goals. He found that among all the objectives, the government could indeed raise substantial funds for public infrastructure investment by auctioning land leases. It could also subsidize public housing development by granting city-owned land to quasi-public agencies at below market value. However, according to Hong these accomplishments are not risk-free. One problem of relying on lease revenues to fund public expenditures is that the government might have lost its ability to reformulate housing policy to accommodate the changing needs of the population.

In substantiating his claims, Hong analyzes how the Hong Kong government uses four mechanisms—initial public auction and tender, lease modification, contract renewal and the collection of land rents—to recoup land value increments. Based on data from 1970 to 1995 he discovered that the government collected 75 percent of all lease payments, totaling US$67 billion, from lessees by public auctions and tenders. The remaining 25 percent came from the other three mechanisms. In Hong Kong a lessee who wins the bid at public auction must pay the initial land premium in full within 30 days. The amount of the initial premium is determined by competitive bidding at public auction.

Hong then raises potential issues regarding this approach to raising lease revenues. In Hong Kong, where developable land is limited, asking that developers pay artificially high initial land premiums up front will certainly not help lower housing costs. Before 1997 when housing demand was strong, land premiums were mostly converted into high property prices, thus transferring a major portion of the financial burden from developers to homebuyers. In addition, collecting land premiums in one lump sum enabled major developers who had the financial resources or backing from banks to compete successfully against their smaller counterparts at the public auctions. As only a handful of developers were able to lease land from the government and build their own land banks, they became increasingly influential in determining the timing, as well as the quantity of housing units supplied to the market.

In view of the high returns on real estate investments, a large proportion of Hong Kong investment capital poured into the housing sector, making the financial health of the economy depend on property prices. As long as housing prices kept rising, public officials, developers and property owners who profited from capital appreciation of their assets never questioned the validity of government land leasing policy. Yet, when the Asian financial crisis struck Hong Kong, property prices began to crumble. To make matters worse, the implementation of a new government initiative to increase housing production in order to expand homeownership coincided with the occurrence of the 1997 financial turmoil. These two changing conditions quickly revised the expectation that property prices would continue to rise. When housing demand decreased because of the anticipated drop in future prices, property values plummeted. Within just one year (1997–1998), developers and private homeowners saw the market value of their assets decrease by over 50 percent. The sharp reduction in property values eventually magnified itself into an economy-wide recession.

Suffering from a major decline in corporate profits or personal wealth, developers and the propertied class accused the government of triggering the collapse of the property market. In the face of public criticism the government halted all land auctions and abandoned its proposed target for future housing production. Despite these compromises there has been no sign of recovery of the housing market from its drastic price decreases since 1997.

The Hong Kong episode, Hong argues, exposes the risks of government reliance on land leasing to raise public funds. In Hong Kong the decision to capture all land value increments at the beginning of the lease has fostered the formation of powerful interest groups composed of developers and the propertied class whose economic wellbeing depends heavily on the performance of the real estate market. Any government attempts to make housing affordable, no matter how well-intended, will be opposed by these special interest groups for such proposals may lower property prices and put their investments in jeopardy. Like Neutze, Needham and Deng, Hong raises the question regarding the intricate roles or identities of the government in leasing public land; he states, "To what extent can a government, acting as a custodian of public land on behalf of its citizens, maximize the financial returns on land leasing without impairing its duties or legitimacy as the protector of public interests?" Obviously, careful consideration of what role or roles the government should play in public land leasing is called for. We will discuss this issue in detail in the concluding chapter.

Experimenting with Public Leasehold Systems

The second section of the book presents four case studies of experimentation with public leasehold systems in Ukraine, Louisiana, Beijing and Poland. In Chapter 8 Strong raises five fundamental impediments to land tenure reform in Ukraine that are applicable to all former socialist countries or transitional economies: the absence of a system of title registration; the lack of mortgage and bankruptcy laws; a poor cadastral system; an insufficient judicial response to conflicts between existing laws; and corruption in governments.

In short, all major obstacles that Ukraine must overcome in reforming its land tenure system are related to building and rebuilding its institutions. These institutional matters do not pertain only to the development of a public leasehold system, they are also critical for any land tenure system, including freehold. This casts doubt on the primacy of the current debates over land tenure in Ukraine. Strong interviewed foreign investors who stated that their investment decision was not based solely on whether their clients held fee title or leasehold. Rather, the important factor was the probability of obtaining a reasonable return that justified the risk involved in investing in real estate. Such an assessment would require the availability of a reliable, stable and transparent system for land transactions. The specific nature of property rights was secondary, from the investors' point of view.

According to Strong, the interviewees who preferred fee simple to leasehold did so based on their opinion that leasehold interests could not be mortgaged. As Strong and other authors argue in this book, no inherent problem appears to deter bankers from granting mortgage loans to borrowers who only hold leasehold rights in land. Public leaseholds in Canberra, the Netherlands, Sweden, Finland, Israel and Hong Kong are as secure as fee simple and have been accepted as collateral for mortgage lending for many years. In other words, it is not because of public leasehold that lessees cannot use their leased land rights as collateral. Instead, the possibility of mortgaging leasehold rights depends on the availability of the above-mentioned institutions to delineate and enforce leasehold interest. Only through clear delineation and effective enforcement can government enhance the security of lessees' land rights, which enable them to use these rights as collateral for financing their land investments.

As institutional changes cannot be brought forth overnight, what can the Ukrainian governments do, during the transitional period, to facilitate land resource allocation? Strong recommends that during a time of great uncertainty it is preferable to use short-term leases to allocate land rights in Ukraine. Her argument is based on an important yet overlooked feature of public land leasing—its flexibility—which, Strong argues, comes from two sources.

First, if land rights are assigned to private individuals (either existing occupants of land or new users) for temporary uses, land resources will continue to be utilized by landholders until a more productive alternative use emerges in the future. As government is the landowner, it can in principle repossess land and allocate it for new development. This is particularly important for Ukraine, where the government may need a lot of land for public infrastructure development to accommodate anticipated urban growth. If land is sold, the government may have to pay a huge amount to private landowners for reacquiring land to undertake public construction. Although none of the case studies indicates that land repossession at the end of a lease term is politically tenable, these experiences are mainly related to long-term leases (50–99 years) with the option to renew for another term. Retaking land under these long-term leasing arrangements has indeed proved infeasible. Yet, if a government lessor can limit the term of the lease to, say, five years with the option to renew only when land is not needed for public use, repossessing land by the lessor is still conceivable. The short lease term and frequent renewal requirement may help remind leaseholders that they are not the owners of land. This may allow lessees to set the appropriate expectations of their property rights in land and minimize the potential problems associated with land repossession in the future.

Second, Strong believes that short term leases may also provide financial flexibility to the government. At a time when supporting institutions and organizations for land transactions are not fully developed, the government will have to sell land or assign long-term leasehold at low prices to attract investment in a highly risky environment. Short-term leases can facilitate interim land allocation to the private sector. The government can then renegotiate with lessees for additional payments when leases expire, or it can retake lands and sell them at higher prices when land values increase, as the country makes progress in building the necessary institutions.

The arguments postulated by Baxter (Chapter 9) for using leasing to facilitate military base conveyance in the U.S. are similar to Strong's for Ukraine, although the two cases are situated in quite distinct social, political and economic contexts. Both authors believe that under conditions of constant flux the flexibility of public land leasing represents a better short-term land tenure system than other property rights arrangements, at least from the government lessor's point of view. Baxter describes how the U.S. Department of Defense (DOD) transferred control over property at England Air Force Base in Louisiana to its local redevelopment authority (England Authority), and from the local authority to private users, all through the use of short-term leases. The complex public land conveyance process mandated by the U.S. Congress, and the expensive cleanup requirements imposed by the National Environmental Policy Act slowed the procedures for converting this former military base into civilian use. Local officials and community groups, however, wanted to find alternative uses for the land immediately after the close of the military base, to minimize employment impacts on the local economy. There were tremendous uncertainties as to who should gain control over the property and what types of land use would be most suitable for the available land when the conveyance was completed. Financial resources were also lacking for any comprehensive redevelopment.

To address the situation, the DOD leased the property to the England Authority, which then subleased part of the property to interested parties under short-term leasing arrangements that gave the England Authority two types of flexibility. First, subleasing allowed the England Authority to put the resources immediately into use and generated a stream of revenues to finance facility redevelopment and operating costs. Second, the England Authority deliberately timed lease expirations to coincide with planned redevelopment and incorporated into lease conditions the right to move tenants to equal or better spaces, to gain the flexibility of shifting uses around as the cleanup and conveyance progressed.

Based on this leasing experience, Baxter asserts that the flexibility available under short-term leasing arrangements may enable other former military bases to expedite the process of normalization before their lands and assets become suitable to be placed in the private market. This process is needed because changing the status of military bases from federal holdings to private property can generate numerous claims from community groups and public agencies to take control of the public land. When the delineation of property rights and future uses of the assets are unclear, selling prices for land at former military bases are certain to be lower than under circumstances of greater certainty. Interestingly, this situation parallels the Ukrainian condition reported by Strong. Both Baxter and Strong conclude that short-term leasing appears to be the best arrangement for the public lessor under this condition.

Deng's discussion of China's public land leasing in Chapter 10 reaffirms Strong's arguments for paying special attention to supporting institutions and organizations in implementing a public leasehold system. Deng describes land reform in China as gradual, partial and dual track—an approach that emphasizes flexibility and the inherent trial-and-error nature of reforming institutions. Before the reform, land was assigned to users, such as state-owned enterprises and collective farms, through an "administrative allocation" system. Deng calls it the Three No system, meaning that users could obtain the right to use land from the government with no payment, no termination date of occupancy and no right to transfer property to other parties. One purpose of establishing a public leasehold system is to correct some of the problems associated with this land allocation system, including land resource misallocation and corruption. Fiscal considerations play a key role as well.

Using Beijing as a case study, Deng argues that the city's public leasehold system led to two positive outcomes in the 1990s. First, based on his estimates, lease revenues seemed to play an important role in financing urban infrastructure investment in Beijing. Second, housing production and the number of urban renewal projects increased dramatically after the city government launched its leasing program in 1992. In Deng's view, leasing created the opportunity for private developers to acquire development rights at a time when real estate prices in Beijing rose rapidly.

Deng cautions, however, that underneath these positive results lies a major threat to the current development of public leasehold in China: the multiple government roles in managing and allocating land can create conflicts of interest within the government and confusion for investors. Moreover, lack of reform in China's political institutions creates the opportunity for corruption. Although the central government has encouraged all city governments to auction land, the administrative allocation system continues to be the predominant mechanism for allocating land resources in most cities, including Beijing. Under this system the city government will allocate land to state-owned real estate companies free of any charges. These companies can then benefit from the allocated land rights by leasing them to private users or developers at high prices. Because local officials have discretion to decide when allocating land administratively is appropriate, bribery may sometimes allow private entities to obtain land at very low cost for profitable undertakings. When the city government leases land rights directly to end users, private negotiation, not public auction, is the preferred method for establishing a price. As private negotiation does not involve any open bidding, this leasing method may also lead to corruption.

When the state acts as both regulator of land use and lessor, the policy objectives of the planning bureau and the leasing department within the same government apparatus may not always coincide. According to Deng, land use planning in China remains largely the same, albeit the country has gone through many economic reforms since 1984. Many areas in Beijing are still restricted from development even though the leasing office likes to lease as many sites as possible in these districts to private developers, due to their high development potential. When conflicts emerge, resolution is based on the power relations between agencies, not by rule of law. This can create confusion as to which agencies or which set of rules private developers should follow in making decisions regarding their land investments. Deng argues that political reforms are indispensable to making public land leasing functional in China.

The case studies discussed so far were examined primarily from a political economy perspective, focusing on public policy issues; but there are other approaches. In Chapter 11 Dale-Johnson and Brzeski analyze land leasing in Poland from the standpoint of private investors and economic efficiency. The inclusion of this approach here provides readers with the opportunity to appreciate the examination of public leasehold from a different lens. Readers who are comfortable with technical analysis will find this chapter particularly interesting.

In analyzing the various leasing options for the Polish public leasehold system, Dale-Johnson and Brzeski used a model to simulate potential economic outcomes of different lease structures. Specifically, they studied how the inclusion of provisions that guarantee lessees' right to renew their leases, and the ownership of leasehold improvements may affect the timing and intensity of land redevelopment. They assumed that fee title would derive the "optimal" redevelopment decision, and used the investment behavior of freeholders as the benchmark for comparing other leasing arrangements. Their view is that, to encourage lessees to redevelop their leased land as if they were owners of fee simple, there must be certainty about their ability to extend the lease and possession of the improvements to the land if the lease is not renewed. If the two contractual elements are present in long-term public leaseholds, lessees would invest in high-density property redevelopment that maximizes the development potential of the land—an investment decision that is close to the freehold outcome.

Owing to their different emphasis and assumptions, Dale-Johnson and Brzeski arrive at a recommendation that differs from that suggested by Strong and Baxter. While Dale-Johnson and Brzeski advocate long-term public leasehold with the option to renew and the residual claim to leasehold improvements, Strong and Baxter believe that short-term leases would provide the flexibility for the government to repossess land for potential fiscal and/or planning purposes in the future. These different recommendations, we believe, are based on the distinct assumptions about future government roles in land development. If it is believed, because of a specific institutional setting of a country, that the private lessees should play a dominant role in land and property development, then the proposal of Dale-Johnson and Brzeski appears to be sensible. Conversely, if the public thinks that active government involvements in the allocation of land resources and distribution of future land value increments are necessary, the suggestion provided by Strong and Baxter may be more appropriate. As we have argued here, this is a political decision that can be made only in consideration of the institutional environment of a country at a specific time. We will let the reader decide which assumptions appear more realistic for dealing with their unique situations at hand.

The concluding chapter summarizes the case study experiences in accomplishing designed public policy goals through land leasing. We explain differences in performance in the context of the institutional settings and organizational structures of these public leasehold systems, and we reflect on important lessons for adopting public leasehold in other situations.

REFERENCES

Barzel, Yoram. 1989. *Economic analysis of property rights*. New York: Cambridge University Press.

Bourassa, Steven C., Max Neutze and Ann Louise Strong. 1996. Managing publicly owned land in Canberra: Rural to urban change of use. *Land Use Policy* 13:273–288.

_____. 1997. Assessing betterment under a public premium leasehold system: Principles and practice in Canberra. *Journal of Property Research* 14:49–68.

Coase, Ronald H. 1937. The nature of the firm. *Economica* 4(3):386–405.

_____. 1960. The problem of social cost. *Journal of Law and Economics* 3(October):1–44.

Demsetz, Harold. 1967. Towards a theory of property rights. *The American Economic Review* 57(2):347–359.

Farvacque, Catherine and Patrick McAuslan. 1992. *Reforming urban land policies and institutions in developing countries*. Washington, DC: The World Bank.

Hallowell, Irving A. 1955. The nature and function of property as a social institution. In *Culture and experience*, Irving A. Hallowell, ed., 236–249. Philadelphia: University of Pennsylvania Press.

Hong, Yu-Hung. 1995. Public land leasing: Flexibility and rigidity in allocating the surplus land value. Ph.D. dissertation. Cambridge, MA: Massachusetts Institute of Technology, Department of Urban Studies and Planning.

_____. 1998. Transaction costs of allocating increased land value under public leasehold systems: Hong Kong. *Urban Studies* 35(9):1577–1595.

_____. 1999. Myths and realities of public land leasing: Canberra and Hong Kong. *Land Lines* 11(3): 1–3.

Jacobs, Harvey M. 1998. Conclusion: Who owns America? In *Who owns America? Social conflict over property rights*, Harvey M. Jacobs, ed., 245–252. Madison, WI: University of Wisconsin Press.

Lai, Lawrence Wai-Chun. 1998. The leasehold system as a means of planning by contract: The case of Hong Kong. *Town Planning Review* 69 (3):249–275.

Last, Donald. 1998. Private property rights with responsibilities: What would Thomas Jefferson say about the "wise use" movement? In *Who owns America? Social conflict over property rights*, Harvey M. Jacobs, ed., 45–53. Madison, WI: University of Wisconsin Press.

Libecap, Gary D. 1989. *Contracting for property rights*. New York: Cambridge University Press.

Marx, Karl. 1978. Capital, vol. 1. In *The Marx-Engels Reader*, Robert C. Tucker, ed., 294–442. New York: W. W. Norton & Company.

Neutze, Max. 1988. The Canberra leasehold system. *Urban Law and Policy* 9:1–34.

North, Douglass C. 1990. *Institutions, institutional changes and economic performance*. New York: Cambridge University Press.

Ostrom, Elinor. 1990. *Governing the commons: The evolution of institutions for collective action*. New York: Cambridge University Press.

Stein, Paul, Patrick Troy and Robert Yeomans. 1995. *Report into the administration of the ACT leasehold*. Canberra: Australia Capital Territory Government.

Tideman, Nicolaus et al. 1991. Open letter to Mikhail Gorbachev. In *Now the synthesis: Capitalism, socialism and the new social contract*, Richard Noyes, ed., 225–230. London: Center for Incentive Taxation.

Williams, Oliver E. 1985. *The economic institutions of capitalism: Firms, markets, relational contracting*. New York: The Free Press.

Yeh, Anthony G.-O. 1994. Land leasing and urban planning: Lessons from Hong Kong. *Regional Development Dialogue* 15(2):3–21.

PART II

EXPERIENCES FROM DEVELOPED SYSTEMS

Leasing of Publicly Owned Land in Canberra, Australia

2

Max Neutze

This chapter concerns Australia's experience of leasing public land for urban use in Canberra, the national capital.[1] The first section describes Australian land policy more generally in the period leading up to the federation of the British colonies in 1901, and the decision to build a new national capital. Land policy had been a major staple of politics since the 1830s. There was widespread criticism of the control of huge rural areas by squatters who paid little if anything for their land. Urban land speculation also was rife, especially in the 1880s (Cannon 1966).

Much that is good about Canberra, especially its planning, has been facilitated by public leasehold and by the public ownership of land prior to urban development. Notwithstanding this overall assessment, this chapter pays a lot of attention to its failures. The potential of public leasehold on a publicly owned site to contribute to very good public planning and public finance has not been fully realized. In recent decades, in particular, public leasehold has been corrupted in many ways.

HISTORICAL BACKGROUND

When Colonel Arthur Phillip landed in Sydney Cove in 1788 to establish a penal colony, he proclaimed British sovereignty and, acting on British precedent, claimed all of the land on behalf of the crown. This claim of ownership by the crown was justified much later by the doctrine of *terra nullius*, which asserted that the land was unoccupied in 1788 and therefore belonged to no one. It was not until 1992, through the High Court judgment in *Mabo v Queensland*, no. 2, that native title was recognized to have existed before European invasion.[2] This section of the chapter sketches some of the reasons

---

[1] Canberra is the only significant urban area in the Australian Capital Territory (ACT). The remainder of the ACT is largely natural bush, which serves as water catchment and open space.

for the privatization of land ownership in rural Australia that had parallels in urban areas. By the end of the nineteenth century, most land in Australia was held privately in an estate of freehold.

From Settlement in 1788 to Federation in 1901

In retrospect, in spite of the heroic attempts of early governors of New South Wales (NSW) (Bonyhady 2000), an opportunity to ensure that land was used to benefit all Australians was missed. Instead, the first settlers saw a mostly infertile land covered with eucalyptus and acacias that were so hard they blunted the settlers' axes. The greatest threat to the infant settlement was starvation, so food production was encouraged. Until 1830 land was allocated by grants of leases: each emancipated convict received 30 acres, or 50 acres if married, with an additional 10 acres for each child. Larger grants were made to soldiers and free immigrants. The land was rent-free for 10 years and thereafter cost a shilling per year for every 10 acres. Grantees were required to live on, clear and farm their land, but these conditions were widely ignored and the land grants became the subject of speculative purchase. By 1830 less than 10 percent of the nearly four million acres granted had been cleared and less than a quarter of the cleared land cultivated.

From 1831 land sales became an important source of income for the colonial governments. Landholders were becoming increasingly powerful politically, but there were shortages of labor and relatively few women. In NSW land was sold at auction with a reserve price of five shillings an acre, rising to 12 shillings in 1839 and £1 in 1842, and the revenue was used to assist migration. By 1851 less than two million acres had been sold. No attempt was made to limit how much land could be purchased. Speculative purchases were again a problem and little of the land was cleared for agriculture. A new phenomenon, squatting, emerged outside the defined settled districts in each colony. Squatters generally had no title to the land. From 1847 a small number of squatters were permitted to lease their land for 14 years with the option to purchase any part of it for £1 per acre. They used this provision to purchase strategic areas with access to water, which then gave them control over much larger areas.

By the 1850s some squatters were powerful enough to prevent more intensive use of the land and were demanding leases (Gollan 1960). During the gold rushes of the 1850s there had been very rapid immigration and the colonial governments were concerned about the possibility of mass unemployment as the gold was worked out. Universal adult male suffrage was introduced in the 1850s. The numbers working in the gold fields fell late in that decade. Opening up the lands, against the opposition of the squatters, became politically popular. Attempts to break up the large land holdings failed, largely as a result of "[f]aulty legislation, poor administration and human greed" (Brennan 1971, 7). A NSW Royal Commission in 1883 described the operation of the relevant act as "tarnishing the personal virtues of veracity and honest dealing by the daily

---

[2] 175 CLR, pp. 51–53.

habit of intrigue, by the practice of evading the law and declarations universally made in defiance of fact" (Roberts 1924, 307).

Deep antipathy to large landowners continued in Australia for generations, so that radical ideas in relation to land were widely held, even among people who were conservative in other respects. Moves to unlock the land that began in the 1850s were greatly influenced by the ideas of classical economists, most notably John Stuart Mill (1870). They took two forms that were seen as achieving similar objectives: perpetual government ownership of all land or progressive (with respect to value of land owned) land taxes.

In 1870 William H. Gresham founded a short-lived Land Tax Reform League with the following objectives: the immediate cessation of sales of all Crown land; the fee simple of the public domain to vest in perpetuity in the state—that is, in the people in their corporate capacity; occupancy, with fixity of tenure, subject to rental for revenue purposes; alienated land to be repurchased with no resale to individuals but permitting transfer of rights; and the gradual abolition of all indirect taxes, the revenue of the state to be derived solely from the rental of land (Mayer 1964).

Although Gresham's League soon disappeared, others took up its agenda, including George Harker and James Mirams who were elected to the Victorian Parliament on a land nationalization platform. In 1872 the newly formed Land Tenure Reform League of Victoria adopted similar proposals for land management not long after the publication of Henry George's *Our Land and Land Policy* (George 1871; Else-Mitchell 1993). In Australia, Henry George's program for a single tax on land was seen as consistent with land nationalization. Following his visit to Australia in 1889–1890, single tax leagues were formed in many places. His ideas were embraced, particularly by the supporters of free trade, but had less support among the protectionists, including the Labor Party, which was wedded to customs duties. Partly for this reason, the free trade colonies of NSW and Queensland adopted taxes on the unimproved value of land as the main source of funds for local government, while the protectionist colonies of Victoria, Tasmania and South Australia relied on taxes on improved value. The free trade colonies also had more land and more revenue from land sales.

Support for land taxation and nationalization peaked during the 1890s depression, the decade of the debates about the formation of the Australian federation and its Constitution, and about the new national capital. The excesses of the 1880s urban property boom were fresh in people's minds, and some of the chickens came home to roost in the early 1890s in the form of bankruptcies and foreclosures (Cannon 1966). Section 125 of the Constitution states, in part, that

> [t]he seat of Government of the Commonwealth shall be determined by the Parliament, and shall be within territory which shall have been granted to or acquired by the Commonwealth, and shall be vested in and belong to the Commonwealth, and shall be in the State of New South Wales.... Such territory shall contain not less than one hundred square miles, and such portion thereof as shall consist of Crown lands shall be granted to the Commonwealth without any payment therefor.

There has been much discussion about whether this section itself prohibits the sale of land by the Commonwealth. The majority of legal opinion is that under this section the Commonwealth acquired territorial rather than proprietary rights. However, Section 9 of the Seat of Government (Administration) Act 1910 was clear on this matter, stating that "no Crown lands in the territory shall be sold or disposed of for any estate of freehold." Together the Act and the Constitution ensure a monopoly public supply of urban land and public leasehold of developed land.

The Century Since Federation

The recent Report into the Administration of the ACT Leasehold (Stein, Troy and Yeomans 1995) summarizes the reasons for the initial establishment of public leasehold in the Australian Capital Territory (ACT) as: avoiding speculation in undeveloped land; allowing unearned increments in land value to be retained by the Australian people; defraying the expenses of establishing the national capital; and ensuring orderly planned development through lease purpose clauses. In regard to the latter objective, a contract between a lessor and a lessee was believed to be a more effective and positive measure than making decisions on applications to develop under a statutory plan.

The first two of these objectives can be read as applying to undeveloped and developed land, respectively. Thus, public leasehold aims to avoid private capture of unearned increments in land value that result from government or collective actions such as population and economic growth both before and after urban development. A new objective is that public land ownership aims to reduce the cost of land for housing, open space, roads and other public facilities. The objectives are interrelated. For example, avoidance of private capture is necessary to allow unearned increments in value to accrue to the Australian people and, by removing an incentive to obtain variations from plans or amendments in zoning, is of great assistance in ensuring that planned development actually occurs. The third of the above reasons was very important in the 1890s because some saw federalism itself and the federal capital as extravagances. That objective has become much less important over time.

The means are as important as the ends. The policy measures introduced to achieve these objectives, many of which have subsequently been compromised, are: Commonwealth ownership of all land suitable for urban development or redevelopment; land leased to private users rather than sold; land rent adjusted over time with changes in its value; leases include a purpose clause, which is the instrument of land use control; the development required on a newly granted lease must be commenced and completed within specified times (for all but very large developments, commenced within one year and completed within two); a new lease cannot be transferred to another lessee before the required development has been completed; and any change in lease purpose will result in an adjustment of land rent to reflect changes in the value of the lease.

One major change in Canberra has been from a Commonwealth government construction camp with a population of 2,000 in 1921 to a self-governing city of 297,000 people in 1996. Even at the end of the 1920s there was a very small population and the overwhelming focus of administration was on planning and building the future city. Most of the growth occurred after the Second World War; the population in 1947 was only 15,000. In 1989 the new ACT government became responsible for most planning and land management. As a result those functions became much more responsive to the priorities of and pressure from local business and to a lesser extent the local population. Some argued that with a few minor exceptions the building of the national capital had been completed.

Most work on Canberra ceased during the First World War, though by 1920 water supply, sewerage and electricity were available. In addition, a large number of trees had been planted. Work recommenced after the war, the "temporary" Parliament House in Canberra was opened in 1927 and Parliament moved there from its first home in Melbourne. But it was the late 1960s before all the major government departments followed. The permanent Parliament House was not completed until 1988.

The first leases were short-term renewable leases of rural land granted under the Leases Ordinance of 1918. In 1924 the City Area Leases Ordinance (CALO) empowered the minister to offer leases for up to 99 years at auction. The annual rent was set at 5 percent of the unimproved value (as bid by the purchaser), with provision for the value to be reappraised after 20 years and then at intervals of 10 years. The purpose clauses of the leases specified that they were either for residential purposes or a particular class or classes of business or community use. Over time increasingly detailed permissible uses and development conditions were included in new lease contracts.

The Federal Capital Commission (FCC) was responsible for development of the city from 1925 until 1930. Following its abolition, the planning and development of Canberra was placed in the hands of government departments, primarily Works and Home Affairs. Yet, from the late 1920s to the late 1940s there was not much growth. An advisory council was set up in 1930 comprising four occupants of designated public service positions and three elected residents of Canberra.

Following the Second World War, there were shortages of housing and other accommodation throughout Australia. The Federal (now known as the Commonwealth) government became much more important as a result of its role in the mobilization of resources for the war and the states giving it their income taxing powers. Political pressures from other states to end Melbourne's position as de facto national capital increased the rate of transfer of functions to Canberra and the demand for both office and residential accommodation during the 1950s. There was growing dissatisfaction with the delays caused by the division of responsibility between different departments.

A 1955 Senate Inquiry (McCallum 1955) resulted in the establishment of the National Capital Development Commission (NCDC) in 1957 with a broad remit to "plan, develop and construct" the city of Canberra. It did not, however, have responsibility for land administration. Adequately funded with the support of Prime Minister Menzies and anxious to dampen interstate tensions, the commission planned and developed and—in the case of public buildings and facilities—constructed the city as it grew from a population of about 36,000 in 1957 to about 275,000 in 1989. Like the FCC in the late 1920s the commission was accused at different times of restricting supply or of wasting resources by supplying too much serviced land when demand was slack, often because of failures in the program of transferring Commonwealth departments from Melbourne. Neither public nor private developers could foresee demand accurately enough to avoid such problems.

As a result of the increasing importance of serving the established population and businesses relative to catering for much lower growth in Commonwealth employment, and the opportunity for it to reduce its cost, there was a change from Commonwealth administration to self-government in 1989. The NCDC was abolished and a spatial division of responsibility for land administration and planning was established. National land, used mostly by the Commonwealth government and its authorities, was administered by the new National Capital Planning Authority, subsequently renamed the National Capital Authority (NCA). Territory land was administered by the ACT government. The NCA is responsible for planning areas designated as being of national importance. Although the Commonwealth remained the formal lessor of territory land, the ACT government became the beneficial lessor. Since self-government, most raw land has been serviced and subdivided by private developers granted development leases via auction, rather than by contractors directly responsible to the government. While the NCDC was responsible for detailed planning, the ACT government planners determine where development is to occur and its broad parameters, and approve the detailed plans of new subdivisions proposed by the private developers that are successful in bidding for the development rights. The important implications of these institutional changes are discussed later in the chapter. The next section assesses how far the means to achieve the objectives of public leasehold have been followed.

POLICY GOALS

Public Land Ownership

Land purchases began in 1911, and by 1917 more than 200,000 acres had been acquired. Little was purchased in subsequent years, even after development accelerated in the 1960s. In 1967 the owners of some of the 97,500 acres of the remaining freehold land applied for permission to subdivide their rural holdings and develop them for urban use. This resulted in a decision by the Commonwealth to buy the remaining freehold, and all but 670 acres had been purchased by 1985 (Sparke 1987). Publicly owned rural land may be leased for short terms for rural uses only.[3]

There has been significant development close to Canberra in NSW, where land can be purchased freehold. The town of Queanbeyan, NSW, eight miles

---

[3] The ACT government, however, has announced its intention to grant 99-year rural leases in locations where urban development is not expected.

from the center of Canberra, has grown to a city of more than 25,000. Nevertheless, the great majority of the development associated with the national capital has occurred on leased land in the ACT. By ensuring an adequate supply, government ownership of the site has been largely successful in preventing private capture of unearned increments in the value of undeveloped land. Although no detailed study has been carried out, much of the resulting reduction in the cost of developed land appears to have benefited the buyers of developed land. Public leasehold has also been successful in ensuring orderly planned development of the city. This favorable judgment on the effectiveness of public ownership however must be qualified in three respects:

1. There is not much more land suitable for urban use in the ACT without compromising environmental quality. It is likely that in the relatively near future there will be private proposals for large-scale urban development of freehold land across the NSW border to serve the Canberra market.[4]

2. While the nonurban land in the ACT remains in government ownership, proposals have been made recently to expand the rights of rural lessees. It is likely that a rural lessee might apply for a change in lease purpose that would permit urban development. A development-oriented and revenue-hungry ACT government could accept such development proposals even if they were contrary to an adopted plan.

3. More important, the government's equity in leased land has been progressively eroded as a result of changes in the leasehold system. The three most important changes have involved the change in the basis for determining land rent from 1935, abolition of land rents in 1971 and failure to charge lessees the full value of changes in use. These changes are discussed in turn in the following paragraphs.

From 1935 government equity in leased land was reduced when the base for the initial land rent was shifted from the price bid at auction to a reserve price equal to the government valuation. Any amount bid in excess of the valuation was paid as a premium in cash, giving the lessee some equity in the land.[5]

Other Australians have always envied Canberrans because they live in a pampered city. Canberra is criticized as a symbol of and often as shorthand for the resented Commonwealth government. During the 1960s questions began to be asked about the extent to which Canberra, considered a local government, was paying its way. Municipal property taxes (known as *rates,* and levied on the unimproved value of the lease) had been kept at a low level to attract people to live in Canberra (Brennan 1971). Meanwhile, land rents had become unpopular partly because they appeared to be inequitable: in a period of rapid

---

[4] During the early 1970s, when the city was developing rapidly, a proposal was floated that the ACT borders should be expanded to provide for future expansion. The NSW government quickly vetoed the idea, and it has not subsequently been reconsidered. Since that time, Canberra's rate of development has become much slower.

[5] According to Brennan (1971), the direct reason appeared to be a desire of the government to get some cash revenue from the sale of leases for two hotels in a market where demand was very slack.

inflation, rents on similar properties could be vastly different depending on where they were on the 20-year revaluation cycle.[6] In 1970 during a by-election campaign for the seat of Canberra, Prime Minister Gorton announced that land rents would be abolished from January 1971 and municipal rates increased to bring in about the same total revenue, though not necessarily the same for individual leases.[7]

Financially, it was the failure to set and maintain municipal rates at a reasonable level, rather than the abolition of land rent itself, that reduced the government's financial equity in land. Nor were the legal rights of the government as lessor reduced by the change. Politically, however, rates are seen as payment for municipal services, rather than charges for the use of land. Abolition of land rents was a major erosion of the leasehold system. The move to a fully premium-based leasehold made it look very similar to freehold from the point of view of the lessee. Furthermore the abolition of land rents made it impossible for the government to automatically capture increases in the value of land by adjusting rents, as lease purposes were changed as the city developed or as land value increased due to inflation.[8]

An amendment to CALO, adding a new Section 11A in 1936, provided for the first time, a mechanism by which lessees could apply to the Supreme Court to vary their lease purpose clauses. Under the new Section 11A, only variations that would not "be repugnant to the principles for the time being governing the construction and development of the City of Canberra" could be granted. This amendment facilitated and rewarded privately initiated redevelopment that began in the 1980s. Since self-government, applications for variations under the 1991 Land Act, which replaced CALO, have been considered by the ACT Planning Authority.

While the rental leasehold system prevailed, change of purpose clauses for leases within the urban area would attract a revaluation and hence a change in land rent. Under the purely premium leasehold system introduced in 1971, some other mechanism was required. If the precedent set by conversion of leased land from rural-to-urban use had been followed, the lessor would initiate redevelopment, negotiate to buy the lease at its existing-use value and sell it at its value for its new use. In Canberra, however, the NCDC and its ACT government successors have not taken such initiatives. As happens under freehold tenure with planning implemented through land use controls, the government lessor responds to proposals for redevelopment from private lessees.

In such a system, the additional premium for the increased development rights should equal the market value of those additional rights, as it does when rural land is converted to urban use. Otherwise, speculation in redevelopment sites will occur, and redevelopment will be favored relative to development of

---

[6] This problem of inequity was compounded because revaluations of the first leases that became due in 1944 were shelved because of the Second World War.

[7] This generous gesture was not enough for the Prime Minister's party to win the seat.

[8] A premium leasehold system is one in which development or use rights are sold for a capital sum rather than leased on payment of an annual ground rent. Any increases in the rights of the lessee are similarly paid for by a betterment charge rather than an increased ground rent.

greenfield sites (Bourassa, Neutze and Strong 1997). Instead of requiring a full premium, an amendment to CALO in 1971 required successful applicants for a change in lease purpose clause to pay a betterment charge of 50 percent of the increase in the value that resulted from the change. This betterment charge is now known as a Change of Use Charge (CUC). Since 1990 (under self-government), there have been a number of changes in both the rate of charge, which has varied between 50 percent and 100 percent, and in the definition of betterment (Nicholls 1999). Between 1990 and 1992, the increase in value was calculated from a base of the *market* value of the lease before approval of the application rather than its value assuming that its *existing use* would continue. Under this definition, owners of leases suitable for redevelopment would likely anticipate the capital gains developers could make, and to increase their asking price to get as much as possible of the 50 percent that would otherwise go to the developer. This would raise the market value and hence the base for calculating the charge, so that the betterment charge would become 50 percent of 50 percent of the increase and, with successive iterations, vanishingly small.

Subsequently, however, the policy was changed to address this problem by requiring the "before" value of the lease to be based on the rights the lease contains at that time. Thus, anticipated increases in value cannot be capitalized into the before value. The current policy requires a betterment charge of 75 percent of the increase in the value of the lease, in most cases.[9]

In summary, the change from a rental system to a premium leasehold system that began in 1935 and was completed in 1971 precluded the government from automatically receiving rent increases as a result of increased values of existing urban leases. It has not replaced this mechanism with an adequate CUC. The government still owns the decreasing areas of nonurban land suitable for conversion to urban use. In relation to the increasingly important changes from one urban use to another, and increasing density of use, the government lessor has failed to take full advantage of its ownership of all new or additional development rights. First, it has failed to be active in initiating redevelopment and change of use even where that could be profitable; second, it has failed to charge the full market value of increased development rights that are specified in variations in the lease purpose clauses.

Land Is Leased Rather Than Sold

From a legal point of view, land for private use has been leased in Canberra since it became the national capital, but over time, as described in the previous section, the rights of the lessee have increased and the rights of the lessor correspondingly decreased. There have been some additional causes of erosion. In 1935 the timing of revaluation of the lease for the purpose of setting land rent was changed from "after twenty years and thereafter every tenth year" to "each twentieth year." While long periods between revaluations may have been appropriate during the depressed interwar period, they were a serious

---

[9] Information on current betterment policy in Canberra was obtained from *http://www.palm.act.gov.au*; the information on the Change of Use Charge was updated August 8, 2002. Bourassa, Neutze and Strong (1997) analyze in some detail the way betterment should be defined in a premium leasehold system.

problem in the more-buoyant period after the Second World War. No private lessor would countenance such long periods. From 1938 lessees were given rights to the value of improvements at the end of a lease.[10]

In 1980 the responsible Commonwealth Minister announced that residential lessees would be guaranteed the right of renewal of their leases at any time during the last 30 years of the lease term, on paying a nominal administrative cost. The change was incorporated in legislation in the 1991 ACT Land Act. The same act made a similar provision for nonresidential leases as long as the land is not required by the ACT or the Commonwealth government for a public purpose. In effect, leases in the ACT have become leases in perpetuity.

Since the 1920s there has been opposition to the leasehold system that continues even following the change to de facto perpetual leases. Although public leasehold was and is common in extensive grazing areas of Australia, where it is justified as a means of preventing overgrazing and environmental damage, it has been uncommon in Australian cities since the 1830s, and urban public leasehold with a monopoly lessor is almost unknown outside the ACT.[11] Partly as a result, lenders have had reservations about the security of leases as collateral. Both lenders and property developers appear to have a psychological distrust of leases, though most of Canberra's residential and nonresidential lessees seem scarcely aware that they have a lease rather than freehold title. The pressure for freehold appears to be coming from the developers and investors. There have been several public inquiries into the leasehold system in Canberra and all have recommended that it should continue.[12]

Adjusting Land Rent According to Increases in Land Value

Prior to the abolition of land rents in 1971, the long intervals between revaluations and the rapid rate of inflation reduced the lessor's equity in land.[13] This was one reason for the abolition: had land rents been adjusted at least once every five years they may have appeared more like commercial rents and less like a tax. After abolition, only two opportunities remained for the lessor to receive at least part of the increase in the value of leases. The first was when leases expired. This was never a realistic option for residential leases. The second was when there was a change in land use. The first opportunity disappeared once all leases could be renewed at the administrative cost; we now turn to the second.

Arguments for the abolition of land rent did not recognize the political and economic significance of the different purposes for which land rents and rates

---

[10] This was a desirable change, though in the light of subsequent policy changes it has had little effect on rights.

[11] Darwin, the capital of the Northern Territory, was built on leased land, but much has been converted to freehold. Residential land leased from churches occurs in some cities.

[12] They are summarized in Stein, Troy and Yeomans (1995).

[13] It is arguable that the change to a premium leasehold system had no impact on lessor equity in leases granted after the change. Buyers of premium leases will incorporate expected changes in the net returns from their leases in the premiums they are prepared to pay. The 1971 change did, of course, give a significant windfall to existing lessees.

were levied. While rates are a means of funding services, land rent or premium income is a return to the lessor on its land assets. Considering all revenue from land together ignores the important effects of land rents in discouraging the purchase of land with the objective of securing unearned increments and then exerting political pressure to have land use controls changed to achieve that objective. Similarly, the most important impact of the CUC in a premium leasehold system is to discourage land holding that aims mainly to privatize increments in value. Also, the responsibility of developers to provide services gives desirable allocative incentives but may be regressive in its impact on the price of housing. As recently as 1999 this failure to distinguish the different purposes is reflected in Nicholls (1999). He adds together the revenue gained from rates, CUCs, land rents (mainly on rural land) and land taxes (on land used for business purposes and rental housing) as if they were simply alternative ways of getting public revenue from land. He implies that the small revenue from the CUC does not matter very much because more revenue is received from other charges on land. At one stage the cost of any required infrastructure supplementation was deductible from the CUC.

Purpose Clauses as Instruments of Planning and Land Use Control

There has been, and still is, much confusion about the relationship between the functions of planning and lease administration, similar in some respects to the confusion between planning and land use control of freehold land.[14] It had always been intended that Canberra would be a planned city and the early years of the twentieth century were a period of grand plans (e.g., New Delhi). The 1911 international competition for the design of a new capital city was won by the Chicago landscape architect, Walter Burley Griffin. Criticisms that his plan was too elaborate and too costly resulted in delays in its implementation as well as some changes to the plan. However, most of its structural aspects have been implemented through public works and buildings, reservation of extensive areas of open space and the regulation of land uses through "lease purpose" clauses. The terms of the competition required a plan for a city of about 27,000 people. The later incorporation of garden city ideas resulted in lower residential density than Griffin envisaged, so only the inner areas of Canberra—including inner suburbs, Lake Burley Griffin, the public areas, the undeveloped hills and the street pattern—follow his plan.

As Canberra approached the limits of the Griffin plan, further extensions were planned and developed. As long as the city's development consisted mainly of conversion of rural land for urban use, statutory land plans were not needed: there were no private owners to be controlled since the government was the owner of both rural and urban land, planner and developer. The plans gave residents of Canberra information about how the city might grow in the future and provided the justification for the lessor to resume rural leases, provide

---

[14] There is frequently confusion between land use planning, which is a forward-looking activity designed to address the wide range of impacts of future development, and land use controls that convey development rights and are designed to implement plans and take account of the impacts of particular development proposals.

infrastructure and subdivide land. When, in the late 1960s, development applications were received from owners of remaining areas of freehold, a metropolitan plan was produced to show where, in the public interest, development should be permitted.

Once lessees began to seek changes in lease purpose clauses, plans for future land use were needed so that the government could certify whether the proposed change was consistent with those plans. This would not have been necessary had the government (the lessor) negotiated the purchase of leases suitable for redevelopment and resold them with new lease purpose clauses. There would have been far less incentive for lessees and developers to redevelop. In any event, plans for the future development of Canberra would have become necessary once redevelopment became significant, if only because redevelopment typically affects the amenity of neighbors. As things stand, redevelopment in Canberra causes as much dispute over much the same issues as it does under freehold title.

Ideally, in a mature urban public leasehold system, there should be a land use planner within government that is charged with protecting amenity on behalf of the residents and businesses guided by the mixture of political and professional considerations that guide planning everywhere. In addition, there should be a statutory land management authority at arm's length from political control and acts as a government business enterprise. Its development proposals, like those of a private developer, should be subject to planning controls. In Canberra no new lease can be issued with conditions contrary to those in an adopted plan, and only leases that are consistent with adopted plans can confer development rights; plan adoption itself does not convey those rights. The objectives of land management should be to maximize the value of and income from the public estate subject to, first, planning approval and, second, controls that prevent monopolistic restrictions on the supply of land. Accountability of the land management authority would be achieved through a set of land management accounts. Despite many promises since the later 1980s that such accounts were being developed, they have never been produced (Stein, Troy and Yeomans 1995).

Planning and land management in Canberra were separate prior to self-government, but planning was the responsibility of a statutory authority (the NCDC) while land management was carried out by a government department subject to direct ministerial control. The opportunities that this gave for the use of land management to encourage kinds of developments chosen for political and short term financial reasons (revenue from premiums) may help explain why accounts were never produced. Since self-government the two functions have been carried out in a single department of the ACT government. Both functions have been subject to interest group pressures and used (some would claim misused) to pursue the government's aim of encouraging early development at the expense of long-term revenue from land ownership. As a result, developers promising to bring investment and jobs to the city have been given discounted premiums and CUCs. No official estimates of the cost of these concessions have been published. Land use zoning, rather than lease purposes, have become the main instruments for the control of land use, further reducing the salience of the leasehold system.

As subdivision and servicing of rural land have increasingly become functions of risk-taking private developers (Bourassa, Neutze and Strong 1996), the planning role of government has become more significant and more similar to where land is held under freehold. The lease administration issues and markets short-term development leases for raw land to developers, and subsequently issues 99-year leases to owner-occupants and investors. Since redevelopment and change of use are almost entirely a function of risk-taking private firms, the main public control over them is through planning. Lease administration does little more than provide a lease consistent with a permissible land use and assesses and collects any premium or CUC.

Time Limit on the Completion of Land Development

Requiring building on a long-term lease to be completed within a specified time has limited the opportunities for speculative holding of building sites and, subject to market demand, has enabled the lessor to control the supply of sites and hence the rate of development. This has always been a condition of leases of newly serviced urban land, but it can as readily be imposed if publicly owned land is sold rather than leased. Since the ACT government transferred most servicing and subdivision of rural land to the private sector, however, it has lost much of its control over the rate of development. When the lessor took the risk of investing in subdivision and servicing, it was able to control the rate of development subject only to demand. But when private investors became responsible for subdivision and servicing they were able to tailor the rate of production of lots to their judgment of the market requirements. The lessor can specify some rate of development in the development lease but can scarcely enforce it if market demand falls. And since it is difficult to know whether slowing the production of lots is in order to meet an unexpected fall in demand or to make speculative profits, the lessor loses control over supply. The requirement that development must occur within a limited time has not been enforced with respect to granting of rights to redevelopment.[15]

To summarize, the lessor's requirement that lessees develop within a specified time is a way of ensuring that land for housing is brought to the market at a rate that keeps the prices of building sites close to their opportunity cost: rural value plus the cost of subdivision and services. This was achieved as long as the lessor ensured there were enough serviced sites to meet the demand at that price, but partially lost where raw land was leased to private developers for subdivision, servicing and sale, and never attempted with relation to increasingly important redevelopment.

No Transfer of Leases Prior to Completion of Improvements

To prevent holding of serviced sites to gain unearned increments, the lease could not be transferred before completion of the building. The first building

---

[15] The experience of Hong Kong in this respect has been similar.

sites—fully serviced—were auctioned in 1924. The importance of the no-building-no-transfer requirement can be seen from the effect of its removal in 1926, allegedly to increase revenue to the government from sale of leases. The change ushered in a period of highly speculative purchases. The FCC was accused of limiting the supply of building sites in order to increase its revenue. But, following the change, all but one of the leases sold at an auction in 1927 were surrendered within the first year, before the lessees were required to commence building, demonstrating that most were bought to make capital gains on resale rather than for home building or long-term investment purposes. Price increased at the auction in 1927 because of increased speculative demand rather than restrictions of supply. These events were one of the reasons for the FCC's demise four years later. To add insult to injury, these inflated prices influenced the valuation of properties for property rates and land rents paid by lessors and tenants in government-provided housing (Brennan 1971). The requirement was not reinstated until 1959, but for most of the intervening period demand for serviced land was low. Leases could be bought over the counter at reserve prices, and opportunities for profitable speculative holding were very limited.

Adjusting Land Rent with Changes in Lease Purposes

There were no substantial changes in lease purpose clauses prior to the abolition of land rent from January 1971, when the requirement to adjust land rent was replaced by a betterment charge of 50 percent. The several changes in the definition of betterment during the 1990s and the changes in the proportion of it collected have been summarized. Since 1970 it has proved to be a much less significant source of revenue in Canberra (Nicholls 1999) than in other cities, such as Amsterdam, where public leasehold tenure has been widely used. For the reasons just outlined, revenue from Canberra leases has made little contribution to the cost of building the national capital.

MANAGING PUBLIC LEASEHOLD

This section begins to explore the reasons that, for all of its successes, Canberra's public leasehold system has fallen short of its full potential and to ask whether these reasons are endemic to public leasehold systems. If not, does Canberra's experience suggest ways in which the same problems could be avoided elsewhere? Three areas of performance are given below as examples.

Return on the Capital Value of Public Estate

It must be recognized that there are two possible uses for the saving in land costs that results from avoidance of speculation in a public leasehold system: increased public revenue or the replacement of other taxes and lower cost land for housing and for public use. Even when there is no speculation, the smaller the margin between urban land prices and their opportunity cost, the less revenue can be collected. A revenue-maximizing public monopoly landowner in a city with a captive market, such as Canberra, can make a lot of money by restricting supply, but that is scarcely in the broader public interest. Policy in Canberra has been to direct the savings into lower cost land rather than public revenue, especially at the time of rural-to-urban conversion. The overall failure has been that the equity of lessees in Canberra leases has increased at the expense of the lessor. As a result, private profits from unearned increments have increased in the Canberra land market in the many ways described above.

Relatively little public revenue has been obtained from publicly owned land, and certainly not enough to defray a considerable part of the cost of building the national capital as was hoped in the 1890s.[16] The best results have been obtained during rural-to-urban land conversion with revenue produced from land rents in the early years and more recently from premiums. The main direct reasons are (1) the failure to adjust land rents frequently prior to 1970 and their abolition (absorption into municipal rates) from 1971; and (2) the failure to recover the full market value for the increased development rights granted when lease purpose clauses were varied. But why did the public lessor fail in these two respects?

Canberra has collected little revenue from CUCs. Loosely drafted lease documents resulted in ambiguity about the development rights of lessees. This ambiguity made it difficult to decide if a change of use rendered the lessee liable for a CUC and to estimate the value the lease would have if its existing terms and conditions remained the same until it expired. Legislation that was unclear in its definition of betterment, and which has been amended no less than six times in the decade since self-government, has added to the confusion by requiring a determination of which legislative definition should be applied in each case.

Such ambiguity served the interests of the property lobby and, without a set of land accounts, no one knows how much it has cost the ACT taxpayer. Property owners object and appeal when they believe the assessment of betterment is too high; the ACT government rarely, if ever, appeals when it thinks it too low. The ACT government itself has done little to support the legitimate operation of the leasehold system, despite the financial reward it could have received from doing so. On the contrary, it has pursued a "whole of government" approach in its pursuit of development, using both its land use planning powers and its position as lessor to provide incentives to developers and to facilitate approval of their proposals. There has been no education program to inform residents and businesses about the nature and advantages of leasehold, and no set revenue objectives or required rate of return on investment in leasehold land.

Valuation of land under hypothetical conditions is always difficult. How can the value of a redevelopment site be assessed "assuming the current lease conditions continue," when all similar nearby sites exceed that value because a significant percentage of any increase in their value as a result of getting

---

[16] An underlying reason is that land now forms a much smaller proportion of the total capital in advanced economies, relative to buildings, equipment and knowledge and information, than it did when the constitution conventions were debating the building of a national capital in the 1890s.

permission to redevelop accrues to the current lessee? Valuers never solved that problem in Canberra. As Bourassa, Neutze and Strong (1997) showed, it is a problem only because the rate of CUC was 50 percent (now 75 percent) rather than 100 percent. Many assessments of the existing use value were reduced on appeal. The bizarre ad hoc solution was for betterment to be negotiated between the ACT government and the developer, and the negotiators knew that the government would not support an appeal.

The problem had two origins. The first was the decision of the public lessor, which owns all the development rights except those sold to the current lessee, not to initiate changes in use or redevelopment of leased land—no private lessor would act in that manner. The second problem is the decision to charge less than the full market value for any increase in development rights. The government, under pressure from the property lobby, justified the policy on the basis that it would encourage redevelopment. But not only did it have the effect of subsidizing redevelopment and change of use relative to development of new sites, it also resulted in market values of sites with redevelopment potential exceeding their value in their existing use. Paradoxically, by introducing an incentive to redevelop by permitting speculative gains, the discounted rate of CUC may well have resulted in redevelopment being delayed by owners keen to maximize those gains and discouraged by the high prices of property with redevelopment potential.

Control over Land Use to Achieve Planning and Environmental Objectives

Lease conditions frequently were not enforced during the long period from about 1928 to the mid-1950s, when growth was slow and the market slack. As demand increased during the 1950s there was also increased demand for cheap space for nonresidential use around commercial centers and in residential areas. Section 10 of CALO permitted the government to approve limited non-residential activity in residential areas (e.g., a doctor with consulting rooms in his or her home). But there have been numerous complaints about residential leases being used solely for nonresidential purposes (e.g., offices of various kinds, vehicle repairs, car retailing and storage) and industrial land used for more valuable retail and commercial purposes.

Some of these problems arose in the older parts of the city where leases were granted before and soon after the Second World War. These leases commonly specified land use in quite general terms such as "business" or "residential." Business lessees argued that they were entitled to engage in retailing, manufacturing, services or office activities and residential lessees argued that, since the lease did not define residential, they had the right to redevelop at a higher density. Leases granted from the late 1950s defined the permissible uses more precisely (Neutze 1988).

The ultimate sanction against a continued breach of a lease purpose clause was termination of the lease. Partly because of an alleged desire to reassure lessees that their leases were as secure as freehold, the lease administrators seldom enforced lease conditions, even in the face of complaints from neighbors. Perhaps what was most lacking was what Stein, Troy and Yeomans (1995, 194) called a "culture of compliance" in lease administration both before and since self-government. The lack of such a culture was more understandable when all revenues from land went to the Commonwealth consolidated revenue; it is more surprising that it persisted after self-government, when land revenue went to the ACT government.

Poor Administration

A series of public enquiries have attributed much of the poor performance of the ACT leasehold system to poor administration; the most recent was by a Board of Inquiry into the Administration of the ACT Leasehold (Stein, Troy and Yeomans 1995). Two of the most prominent complaints about poor administration have been described above. In evaluating them, it is necessary to recognize several important reasons for administrative shortcomings.

First, during much of the twentieth century there was no established profession of estate management in Australia. The public servants charged with land administration in the ACT had no professional qualifications and no profession that could provide guidelines and criteria for good administration.

Second, by the time the first leases were issued in Canberra, many of the federal members of parliament who were enthusiastic supporters of land reform had left public life. During the twentieth century, interest in and commitment to the leasehold system among politicians at all levels of government has waned. With that has gone a loss of knowledge and understanding of the objectives of public leasehold and how they can be achieved. Public land came to be seen, as it was in the mid-nineteenth century, as a source of short-term revenue rather than a long-term endowment. Selling public land freehold or leasing it for as large a premium as possible were more popular than measures to maintain the public equity through long-term leases with adjustable land rents. Governments at both Commonwealth and ACT level and of all political persuasions have used Canberra's land endowment to encourage development by providing sites at less than their market value or collecting less from CUCs than the legislation permitted. Whether sold or leased for a long term, disposal of rights in land is largely irreversible and therefore unsuitable for the short-term assistance needed to encourage development. The property lobby was a persistent opponent of leasehold and supporter of policies that made it as much as possible like freehold. National and territorial politicians have been receptive to that lobby's views.

THE POLITICAL ECONOMY OF PUBLIC LEASEHOLD

There are parallels between rural Australia in the decades following 1850 and urban Canberra in the decades following 1970. In the first case, rural land was first leased then converted from leasehold to freehold tenure at prices that were derisory relative to the value of the property rights transferred, and opportunities for public benefit were forgone. In the second case, the public equity in Canberra leases was greatly eroded, and opportunities for both a long-term flow of revenue to the government and for more effective public land use planning were forgone.

Another parallel relates to self-government. In the middle of the nineteenth century the Australian colonies were making the transfer from direct rule from London to self-government in matters other than external affairs. Between 1855 and 1890 all colonies became self-governing. Also, beginning in 1857 in Victoria, universal male adult suffrage was introduced. Land policy and administration were firmly under the control of the governments of each colony. Although there was a partly elected advisory council in Canberra from the 1930s, the Commonwealth was responsible for government of the territory until 1989. In both cases, then, the transition from a remote, authoritarian government not responsible to local electors coincided with erosion of the leasehold system. In the case of Canberra, this is particularly surprising. Before 1989 all revenue from land became Commonwealth revenue, though anticipation of self-government was one of the reasons for changes in land policy.

A rhetorical question that has been asked about Canberra is: can a leasehold system be stable when the lessees elect the lessor? And, does that apply with greater force the more democratic and responsible the government is to local lessees? The erosion, even corruption, of the leasehold system under self-government suggests that the answer is *no*. But this does not explain much of leasehold policy. Much of the erosion occurred before self-government and when Canberra had only one or no elected representative in the Commonwealth parliament. One could as well ask whether a public finance system can be stable when the taxpayers elect those who collect taxes. There are, however, two reasons why leasehold systems are more vulnerable.

First, taxes are justified because they permit governments to provide public services, but the same does not apply directly to rents or premiums from public land. Indeed, when land revenues are seen as taxes rather than rents, they become more vulnerable. To some extent, however, the same arguments apply to taxes. The more democratic a government, the greater the tendency to engage in asset stripping in order to have lower taxes and charges in the short run, even at the expense of long-term public wealth.

Second, the sustained opposition to leasehold has come from nonresidential lease owners and developers rather than from the general population. With about two-thirds of households owner-occupants, many people are lessees, but in terms of the value of leases, ownership is very unequally distributed. Owner-occupants are largely unaffected by whether they own or lease their site. But long-term risk-taking investors in property are much more affected and much more active in opposing leasehold.

CONCLUSION

Many of us who are interested in the interface between the urban land market and land use planning have argued that the public as planner will always have difficulty regulating the use of land where development rights are privately owned and unearned increments accrue to private owners. The large capital gains that can result from permission to use their land for more profitable purposes give private owners large incentives to manipulate land use controls. We have noted the success of planning in the British new towns where the new town corporation was both planner and landowner, and in American new towns where large private corporations both owned the land and had detailed control over land use. Canberra is another example of public planning of public land. In many respects it lives up to the high expectations of those who were responsible for deciding to build the capital of a new nation on publicly owned land leased, where appropriate, for private use. In other respects, it does not.

Both public ownership of all land for urban development and maintaining that ownership through a public leasehold system have been essential for achieving the planning and financial objectives of public leasehold in Canberra. Public ownership before development may be more important in this respect than whether the land is sold or leased for private urban use. Public purchase of leases prior to redevelopment has not been attempted in Canberra and in part explains the lack of success in achieving the planning and financial objectives as the use of established urban areas have changed.

Canberra has a reputation as one of the most successful planned cities in the Western world. This is partly because the Commonwealth government was willing to invest heavily in its development. But it is also because the public ownership of land allowed the government to control development to implement its plan while still ensuring supply was sufficient to avoid land price inflation. There was no need to release a lot of land to accommodate demand from buyers wanting to privatize increments in land value. By and large, the government was able to anticipate the need for land for different uses and to provide an adequate supply. Land for housing and for public facilities could be provided at about its opportunity cost. From being a remote hardship posting for public servants, Canberra has become a pleasant and popular place in which to live and work.

Around the end of the 1970s and early 1980s, the situation changed. There was a reduction in the city's growth rate, as the neoliberal program of reducing the size of government cut the rate of growth of the Commonwealth public service. As a result, planning and land management became less a matter of building for future residents and more of providing for the changing demands of the existing population. The decision to abolish land rents was an early harbinger of that change. The NCDC was formally a single Commissioner appointed by the Commonwealth. It did not have to consult with the local population. The same was true of the Commonwealth Department of Interior, responsible for land administration.

Another very important "sin of omission" was that when the demand for redevelopment and changes of use emerged in the 1980s, the government did not take the initiative in resuming leases to provide sites for it. Public education about leasehold ceased around the 1960s, and a development industry that had been supportive of leasehold was forced by competition to take advantage of poor legislation and administration of betterment charges.

Around the world, public leasehold systems within market economies require continual support from committed advocates to ensure their advantages are kept before voters, as they were in the 1890s.[17] A well-established profession of estate management that understands urban leasehold is also important. Without strong political support, the pressures of the property market and the interests of those who profit from the private ownership of land are likely to result in the steady erosion of public leasehold. Well-designed, publicly available land accounts and performance indicators for land administration help local voters to see how much or how little is earned on their public land assets. A government lessor with a commitment to encouraging development and a body politic that is poorly informed and uninterested in the gains from public leasehold, provide the conditions most likely to lead to erosion.

---

[17] A Commission of Inquiry into Land Tenures set up during the 1972–1975 Labor government, when there was a renewal of interest in public leasehold, recommended that it should be retained in Canberra and also used in growth centers elsewhere in Australia (Else-Mitchell, Mathews and Dusseldorp 1974; 1976). Growth centers disappeared from the policy agenda following a change in government in 1975 and the end of the long postwar boom.

REFERENCES

Bonyhady, Tim. 2000. Governor Phillip's legacy. In *Equity, environment, efficiency: Urban Australia*. Patrick Troy, ed. Melbourne: Melbourne University Press.

Bourassa, Steven C., Max Neutze and Ann Louise Strong. 1996. Managing publicly owned land in Canberra: Rural to urban change of use, *Land Use Policy* 13(4):273–288.

———. 1997. Assessing betterment under a public premium leasehold system: Principles and practice in Canberra. *Journal of Property Research* 14:49–68.

Brennan, Frank. 1971. *Canberra in crisis*. Canberra: Dalton.

Cannon, Michael. 1966. *The land boomers*. Melbourne: Melbourne University Press.

Else-Mitchell, R. 1993. Land taxation in Australia: The influence of Henry George. Address delivered to international conference convened by the Georgist Council of Australia and the International Union for Land Value Taxation. Melbourne (26 September–2 October).

Else-Mitchell, R., R. L. Mathews, and G. J. Dusseldorp. 1974. *Commission of inquiry into land tenures: First report*. Canberra: Australian Government Publishing Service.

———. 1976. *Commission of inquiry into land tenures: Final report*. Canberra: Australian Government Publishing Service.

George, Henry. 1871. *Our land and land policy, national and state*. San Francisco: White and Bauer.

Gollan, Robin. 1960. *Radical and working class politics: A study of Eastern Australia*. Melbourne: Melbourne University Press.

Mayer, Henry. 1964. *Marx, Engels and Australia*. Melbourne: Cheshire.

McCallum, John A. 1955. *Report of the select committee on the development of Canberra*. Canberra: Government Printing Office.

Mill, John Stuart. 1870. *Principles of political economy*. New York: D. Appleton.

Neutze, Max. 1988. The Canberra leasehold system. *Urban Law and Policy* 9:1–34.

Nicholls, Des. 1999. *A study of betterment and the change of use charge in the Australian Capital Territory*. Canberra: Australian Capital Territory Government.

Roberts, Stephen H. 1924. *History of Australian land settlement*. Melbourne: Melbourne University Press.

Sparke, Eric. 1987. *Canberra 1954–1980*. Canberra: Australian Government Publishing Service.

Stein, Paul, Patrick Troy and Robert Yeomans. 1995. *Report into the administration of the ACT leasehold*. Canberra: Australian Capital Territory Government.

ONE HUNDRED YEARS OF PUBLIC LAND LEASING IN THE NETHERLANDS

3

Barrie Needham

Around the beginning of the nineteenth century, the largest cities in the Netherlands started to buy land and dispose of it for building on long-term ground leases. They took this step to obtain more power to control development and influence how that development was subsequently used, with the expectation that these leases would be a source of income "for the community" as land values increased and were captured by the municipality. Other municipalities followed this practice but only a handful have consistently disposed of land leasehold rather than freehold. Moreover, this practice of public land leasing is declining. This is the story told and analyzed in this chapter.

The first section describes how land leasing is legally regulated, and reports how many municipalities supply building land that way rather than freehold. The second section analyzes the planning reasons for public land leasing and the third section the financial reasons. The third section is supported by a technical appendix about determining the price and value of ground leases. The fourth section places public land leasing in the context of legal principles about limiting the powers of public agencies. The fifth section looks at recent political debates about the fairness of the way some municipalities use public land leasing, in particular the way they determine and increase the price of ground leases. The decline in the number of municipalities that practice land leasing can be explained partly by those political debates. The conclusions drawn in the final section concern the lessons to be learned from the experience of more than 100 years of public land leasing in the Netherlands.

The author wishes to thank the City of Rotterdam, the City of Amsterdam and professor Dr. George de Kam for comments on and information for this contribution.

PUBLIC LAND LEASING IN THE NETHERLANDS: THE LEGAL REGULATIONS

The way land leasing is regulated in the Netherlands derives from the Napoleonic Code, which in turn derives from Roman Law. So, the general principles are shared with other countries that have a Napoleonic legal system.[1] Under this system the owner of land (in Anglo-Saxon terms, the owner of a freehold interest, or fee simple, in land) may, while retaining legal ownership, transfer to another the right to use that land under certain conditions.

There are various sorts of rights the owner of the freehold interest may split off in this way. Some of these are material rights (a right in rem: the owner of the right may assign it to someone else); some are personal rights (a right in persona: the exercise of the right is limited to the person who has acquired it from the owner of the freehold right). Examples of material rights are use of the land for agriculture *(pacht)* or for short-term use (e.g., for a temporary building—*opstalrecht*).[2] We are interested in the right that makes it possible and financially feasible to erect, use and sell a permanent building on the land. The right of *erfpacht* (referred to henceforth as a *ground lease*) is the only sort of right that is suitable for this. This is the right "to hold and to use landed property owned by another" (Civil Code, book 5, title 7, article 85). Erfpacht is a right in rem, or a material right, which means it exists independently of who the owner is. This means that it is a right that can be traded and which, therefore, has a monetary value. Clearly, the freehold owner of land who grants a ground lease on it limits what he himself can do with that ownership during the period of the lease.

WHO CREATES AND SELLS GROUND LEASES

Anyone who owns the freehold of undeveloped land in the Netherlands may create and sell a ground lease on it. The terms (including the price) are agreed on jointly by lessor and lessee, but must meet certain requirements. The Civil Code (book 5, title 5) specifies the conditions that apply "unless the contract specifies something else."[3]

In the Netherlands very few landowners, besides municipalities, create ground leases.[4] In 1981 a survey was made of the use of ground leases by municipalities (De Jong 1984). This survey was repeated in 1994 (De Jong,

---

[1] These countries are France, Italy, Spain, Portugal, the Netherlands, Belgium and Luxemburg (Newman and Thornley 1996).

[2] The Civil Code (book 5) gives a limited list of material rights in landed property.

[3] The Civil Code can, in this respect, be used as a sort of default lease contract. Also, the Association of Municipal Estates Departments *(Vereniging van Grondbedrijven)* has written a model leasehold contract, which smaller municipalities tend to follow.

[4] In the south of the country the Catholic Church leases out some of its land this way. Recently, some housing associations in Rotterdam, when they sell a dwelling they previously rented, do not sell the freehold of the land. These, however, are exceptions.

TABLE 1
HOW MUNICIPALITIES DISPOSE OF BUILDING LAND

Method of Disposing of Land	1981 (1)		1994 (2)	
	Number of Municipalities	Percent of Those Responding	Number of Municipalities	Percent of Those Responding
Freehold only	9	8	28	24
Freehold mostly	80	75	70	59
Ground lease mostly	13	12	7	6
Ground lease or freehold, depending on circumstances	5	5	13	11
Total	107	100	118	100

Sources: (1) De Jong (1984); (2) De Jong, Pluijmers and de Wolff (1996)

Pluijmers and de Wolff 1996) (see Table 1). In both surveys all municipalities with more than 25,000 residents were included. The response rate in 1981 was 78 percent; in 1994, 84 percent. The results can be regarded as giving a true picture of all municipalities in this size range.

Clearly, the number of municipalities that dispose of building land mostly on ground leases (that is, as a general rule they do not sell it freehold) has decreased from 12 percent to 6 percent, and the number of municipalities that never use ground leases has increased from 8 percent to 24 percent. In this sense public land leasing as an absolute rule has lost ground. Yet, more municipalities now use both ground leases and freehold, depending on the circumstances (an increase from 5 percent to 11 percent).

The survey also found that the few municipalities that dispose of land mostly by ground leases are almost all large municipalities in the west of the country. The municipalities that never use ground leases are all small. Nevertheless, most of the smaller municipalities do sometimes use ground leases, if special circumstances seem to justify it. For example, in the 1970s the municipality of Nijmegen rebuilt a rundown area between the city center and the river. The municipality first acquired the land, then issued it on ground leases. Normally, the municipality of Nijmegen does not practice land leasing, but in this case it expected that the redeveloped area would gradually increase in value. The municipality wanted to recover some of its costs this way.

Before someone can create and sell a ground lease on land, that person must first own the freehold interest in that land.[5] So, a municipality that practices public land leasing must first own that land. If we first investigate this—why municipalities own building land—it will help us understand the practice of public land leasing.

Most municipalities have no reserves of land to be used for building.[6] So, if they are to sell ground leases they must first buy development land. This is

---

[5] Once a building lease has been created and sold to the first lessee, it can be resold by that lessee. That is not our concern here. Moreover, there is no evidence of a widespread trading of building leases, apart from when they are sold in connection with the transfer of the building on the land.

[6] They own, of course, a lot of land within their boundaries. This is for roads, parks, etc., estimated at around 1.5 percent of the land area of The Netherlands (Giebels, Koopmans and Moolhuizen 1985).

a very widespread practice. For several decades now, almost all building in the Netherlands (apart from on small individual plots) has occurred on land acquired from the municipality. On sites and locations where development or redevelopment is to occur, the practice is that the municipality acquires the land, then services it and sells building plots (Needham 1992). Until recently this practice was uncontested simply because the development gains on land (the difference between value without and value with planning permission) were too small to compensate a private developer for the risks of land development. As a result, most municipalities could buy land amicably, hardly ever having to use their powers of compulsory purchase. Land prices have risen since the beginning of the 1990s and so have development gains. This practice is now increasingly being contested by private parties (for the law gives municipalities no monopoly over the supply of building land). Nevertheless, it is still widely expected (and even desired by some private developers) that municipalities supply serviced building land (Needham 1997; Needham and Faludi 1999). This active land policy by municipalities is characteristic of planning and development in the Netherlands and has attracted much attention from practitioners and academics in other countries (see Lefcoe 1978; Badcock 1994).

The survey reported above contains a rather surprising, hidden message: all of the municipalities surveyed in 1981 and 1994 supplied building land! Although those municipalities could have disposed of building land by ground leases, only a minority chose to do so.

PLANNING REASONS FOR PUBLIC LAND LEASING

Municipalities have been given powers specifically for carrying out spatial planning within their boundaries: we call these "statutory planning powers." The most important of these is the power to grant or withhold a building permit, whereby that permit must be refused if it is not in conformity with an approved land use plan (Needham 1999). Dutch municipalities want the land use development within their boundaries to meet high standards, and in this the local politicians are supported by the local voters. If a municipality thinks that the statutory powers the national government has given it for doing this are inadequate, then it seeks additional powers. This is the main explanation why some municipalities began an active land policy, including land leasing.

In the second half of the nineteenth century, the municipal governments of Amsterdam, Rotterdam and The Hague were appalled at the poor quality of housing being built for the workers flooding into these cities. These city governments held that the powers, given them by the national government for improving housing and building standards, were inadequate, and wanted stronger powers. The national government disagreed, so the municipalities took steps independently. If they owned development land they sold it and imposed through the deed of conveyance additional requirements on the developer. Further, they started to acquire potential building land, precisely so as to be able to impose those requirements more widely. The cities of Amsterdam, Rotterdam, The Hague and Utrecht were the first to go even further, by disposing of serviced land by ground leases rather than freehold.[7] Amsterdam started in 1896; The Hague in 1911. As a result, nowadays, most of the land in those cities is owned by the municipality: in Amsterdam about 80 percent and in The Hague about 65 percent (with the central government owning another 12 percent there). The attitude of the municipalities can best be described as pragmatic rather than ideological (Needham 1993).

Even now, when the statutory powers for spatial planning are much greater than they were 100 years ago, many municipalities still feel that those powers are inadequate, and want to provide building land so as to have additional powers. Moreover, this view still has much political and social support, from the local as well as from the national government. Those additional powers are included in the deed of conveyance (the *grondakte*) to which both parties agree when land is sold. This can include conditions a municipality is not permitted to regulate under the statutory powers for spatial planning. The additional conditions concern such matters as: the type of housing to be built (for rent, for sale); the price at which that housing will be sold or rented; the type of shops to be built in a shopping center; the type of firms on an industrial estate; obligations to contribute to the maintenance of certain shared facilities; the use of environmentally friendly building materials; the date on which construction should start and the date on which it should be completed.

In addition, when disposing of the land, the municipality can use the proceeds to include a contribution by the developer toward the provision of certain facilities (e.g., local open space and infrastructure services outside the development site); a contribution to the costs of the municipality in making the plan and supervising the construction process; and a contribution so that land for social housing can be sold below market value. Of course, this is possible only if the disposal price is not set above its market value and if there is sufficient surplus between the acquisition and servicing costs on one hand, the income from disposals on the other. Dutch municipalities may not use the statutory powers for spatial planning to demand these contributions from developers, so they are glad to be able to use land sales for this purpose.

Some municipalities go even further. They have statutory powers for spatial planning; they supplement these by providing building land, but they want even more powers. So, they choose to dispose of the land not freehold but on a long-term lease, which enables them to regulate even more matters relevant to planning. The additional planning powers land leasing gives to a municipality are as follows:

---

[7] This practice has been described by Van der Valk (1989) for Amsterdam 1850–1900; by Delfgaauw (1934) for Amsterdam up to 1930; by Van der Werf (1977) for Amsterdam up to 1975; by Ottens (1996) for Amsterdam 1896–1996; and by Werkgroep Nota Grondbeleid (1986) for The Hague from 1900. A much earlier example is provided by Morris (1985), who describes how, as early as 1609, the City of Amsterdam took compulsory purchase powers so as to be able to buy land it then sold subject to covenants.

» *Regulating the use of the land over a longer period*. The conditions in the conveyance deed when land is sold freehold are agreed to by the first buyer and can if necessary be enforced through a court of law. However, it is not easy to oblige subsequent owners of the freehold to follow those conditions. If it is not the freehold but a ground lease that is sold, the continuation of the conditions can be enforced easily, because the lessor still has a material interest in the land (the lessor is what is called a *naked owner* but nevertheless still the owner of the land). This is used for such matters as contributing to the upkeep of shared facilities and regulating the type of retail or business activity that may be conducted.[8]

» *Obliging the lessee to maintain the buildings on the leased land*. This can be important in older urban areas if they begin to deteriorate, and it is very difficult to achieve under statutory powers.

» *Assembling land for redevelopment schemes*. If the municipality wants to redevelop an area, it must have the unencumbered freehold of all the land. If amicable acquisition does not succeed, the municipality can use compulsory purchase. If it has retained the freehold, selling only ground leases, then assembling the land is quicker, for it is easier to terminate a lease against the wishes of the lessee than to acquire a freehold compulsorily. (It is not necessarily cheaper, however. The municipalities that practice land leasing usually include a clause in the lease that, if they want to rescind the lease before the end of its term, they will pay a price near the price that would be paid were the property purchased compulsorily.)

It will be seen that the planning powers given by public land leasing, additional to those given by selling the freehold of building land, are powers for exercising some control over land and buildings after they have been developed.

These matters usually are included in the contract regulating the ground lease by two sets of conditions: general conditions for the matters the municipality regulates the same way in all contracts (e.g., the length of the ground lease, method of payment, terminating the lease), and conditions specific to each ground lease (e.g., the price of the land and the use to which it may be put).

FINANCIAL REASONS FOR PUBLIC LAND LEASING

When the larger cities started to dispose of building land by ground leases rather than freehold, they were quite explicit that one of the reasons was, unequivocally, to benefit from expected rises in land values and to capture increases in land values for the community (Delfgaauw 1934).

---

[8] The City of The Hague has used its powers as ground lessor to prevent the spread of the red light district into certain areas. This could be regulated at the moment the municipality first sold the land, but it would not continue if the first buyer then resold the land. This was not something that at the time could be regulated through the statutory planning system, although it now can be.

This was to be done, principally, by revising the ground rent at the expiration of the ground lease. Initially, the leases were for 50 years, later for 75 years. An annual ground rent was set, based on the estimated freehold value of the land.[9] Later, it was made possible, partly at the request of businesses that leased land, to capitalize those annual rents over the period of the lease and pay them as a premium at the beginning. At the expiration of the lease, the ground rent or premium was revised in line with current land values.

In order to set the value of the ground rents at the beginning of the second or subsequent terms it is necessary to estimate the value of the site separately from the value of the existing building on it, and that is a disputable assessment. Moreover, the increase in ground rents after 50 or 75 years can be high. These points, together with the fact that it is a body of the public administration (the municipality) that is the financial beneficiary, have generated much opposition to public land leasing.

Rapid rises in land values in the 1960s and 1970s were the occasions for some municipalities to introduce additional ways to capture those through public land leasing. Under the first way the ground rents remained constant for 50 or 75 years, even though the land value was increasing. Some municipalities started to index-link ground rents: the initial ground rent was set as before, but instead of remaining constant for the period of the lease it was adjusted every five years in line with inflation. Once again, a lump sum premium could be paid instead of the annual rents; but setting the value of this was disputable (one does not know how inflation will change during the lease period). There has been even more opposition to this form of land leasing. The municipality is the clear winner, and it is cold comfort to say to the lessees, "but when the ground rent is revised after 50 years, you will not be faced with a huge increase." This issue is discussed in more detail in the appendix.

There is another way the municipality, as lessor, can benefit from rises in land values. If the owner of the ground lease redevelops the site (increases the intensity of use or changes to a higher value use), this can increase the value of the land. Under the terms of the lease, the lessee must obtain permission for this from the lessor (the municipality) and the value of the ground rent is revised accordingly, as soon as the change had been made. There is little opposition to this practice: it is obviously felt to be fair. It can be argued that this practice deters privately initiated urban renewal, because the lessee does not gain from the increased land value. In practice, most urban renewal is carried out jointly by landowners, developers and the municipality.

For some municipalities land leasing is an important source of income. For example, in 1999 the City of Amsterdam had a net income of HFl 113.5 million from this source (exchange rate at November 2000: HFl 2.59 = US$1).[10]

---

[9] The usual practice was to take that value and multiply it by the market rate of interest, with a supplement for administrative costs (see the appendix).

[10] This is the sum of *meerwaarde afkoopsom* and *saldo erfpachtbedrijf* (Amsterdam 2000b, 46).

This can be compared with the income the city raised from property taxes in that year—HFl 263 million. To put this in perspective, it should be added that property taxes finance is only a small part of the current expenditure of a Dutch municipality: in Amsterdam only 3 percent in 1999. The net income from land leasing was equivalent to 1.3 percent of the current expenditure (Amsterdam 2000b). What makes land leasing a particularly attractive source of income is that, as ground rents are revised (always upwards), the income increases but the costs remain the same. In 1980, for example, the City of The Hague had a gross income from ground rents of about HFl 26 million, which was expected to rise to HFl 42 million in 2000 and HFl 62 million in 2025 (constant 1983 prices), while costs were expected to remain at around HFl 26 million a year (Werkgroep Nota Grondbeleid 1986, 88).

The two reasons for municipal land leasing—planning and financial—can influence each other. If the planning reasons produce obvious benefits for the citizen, the public will be more ready to accept the price they must pay for the ground leases. And if the income to the municipality is used to ensure better maintenance of the urban infrastructure and better redevelopment schemes, as Carey (1976) argued was the case in Amsterdam, and as the municipal council of Amsterdam has recently promised to do (Amsterdam 2000a, 19), then once again, the citizens will be more ready to pay the price.

LEGAL RESTRICTIONS ON PUBLIC LAND LEASING

How can a public agency be prevented from abusing its powers as ground lessor when it has, in addition, all sorts of other powers over land and buildings? To discuss this we use the distinction made in the Netherlands (and in other countries with a legal system based on the Napoleonic Code) between two sorts of powers available to a public agency: powers under public law and powers under civil law.

Powers under public law (similar to "police powers" in the U.S.) are given by legislation that empowers a public body to impose obligations on others. The statutory powers for spatial planning are clearly of this type (e.g., that one is not allowed to build without a permit, which is issued only under certain conditions). Clearly, a private body does not have these powers. Civil law regulates obligations freely entered into by two parties (as distinct from obligations imposed by one party on the other). All legal persons can use the civil law. The issue arises because a public body is also a legal person and can therefore use not only public law but also all the powers under civil law available to other legal persons.

This point can be illustrated with the example of a municipality acquiring land. It can buy land amicably under the conditions of the civil law. In addition, it can buy land compulsorily using public powers. More generally, when a municipality carries out spatial planning using its statutory powers, it is using powers under public law. When it sells land as an instrument of spatial policy it is supplementing its public powers with powers under civil law. If, in order to be able to sell that land it first acquires compulsorily it is using powers under public law. If it can buy that land amicably it is using powers under civil law. And if it chooses to dispose of the land by ground leases rather than freehold it is using civil law to strengthen its position even more.

This possibility of using both public and private powers can be abused by a municipality (or any other public body) which is empowered to act in the public interest. Suppose, for example, that a municipality has made a land use plan for a location on which it owns some of the land. The municipality has an interest in selling its own land quickly in order to reduce interest charges. So, it could use its powers of issuing building permits to give priority to an applicant wanting to build on municipal land. This situation is particularly topical now that many municipalities have entered into public-private partnerships for carrying out large-scale developments.

We shall describe two cases of the tension between public and private powers that can arise in public land leasing. The first comes from the City of Rotterdam. Here, when the municipality sold a ground lease on a parcel of land for industrial use, it included in the contract that the firm (as the lessee) should follow certain employment codes (the *Besluit inzake sociaal vestigingsbeleid*). A developer who wanted to acquire land from the municipality appealed against this rule and won the case in 1984. The court explained that obligations were being imposed on a firm that had nothing to do with its specific location, and which, therefore, were different from obligations on other firms in other locations (not on leased land) in the municipality. The municipality suspended the practice.

In the second example—*Kunst en antiekstudio v Lelystad BV*, HR 8 July 1991, NJ 1991–691—the municipality was the lessor of land on which there was a building used as an art studio. The lessee wanted to rent the studio to a discount furniture store. The municipality refused permission because the use of the building for retail purposes was not mentioned in the ground lease. The lessee appealed against this refusal, arguing that such matters—if they were an important part of municipal policy—should be regulated in the land use plan (public powers) and not by the private powers of a landowner. The appeal was dismissed. Many municipalities breathed a sigh of relief: if the appeal had been allowed, it would have undermined one of the bases of public land leasing.

This issue is clearly important and has a wider implication beyond public land leasing. In Dutch law, this issue is known as the *doctrine of the two ways (tweewegenleer)*, where the two ways are public law and private law. The current state of jurisprudence on this matter is that a public authority may use private powers to pursue its public responsibilities, only if the public powers for this are inadequate, but not if this would contradict the established aims of that public policy. This is called the *doctrine of thwarting (doorkruisingsleer)*. Jurisprudence specifically on the application of this legal principle to public land leasing is scarce (Geertsen 1999). Nevertheless, the principle was the basis on which the company of notaries (Velten, Snijders and Huijgen 1995) argued that public land leasing should be stopped altogether. That legal argument has not won support. Certain social and political arguments are more influential.

THE SOCIAL AND POLITICAL ISSUES

Dutch municipalities dispose of land on ground leases for financial reasons. However, the financial advantages for the municipality are not obviously translated into advantages for its citizens; on the contrary, some see no benefits, only that the municipality uses land leasing to raise money from the lessees, who are the citizens. As a result, most people in the Netherlands prefer to own land freehold rather than lease it from a municipality under the current lease terms. One possible financial advantage to the lessee of land leasing is that acquisition requires less capital outlay. Lessees buy the structure (capital) and pay for the costs of the land annually as a ground rent, so they do not tie up capital in the land. However, the advantage is small: to buy the land as well as the building they simply take out a larger mortgage.[11] Moreover, most lessees prefer to pay the ground rent up front as a premium because the risk of having to pay index-linked ground rents is reduced or avoided. In Amsterdam, 95 percent of all lessees pay the ground rent in the form of lump sum premium (Amsterdam 2000a, 15). Also, although one might expect it to be slightly cheaper to buy a building on leased land rather than on freehold land, that difference can hardly be observed in practice.[12] The financial advantages are, therefore, small or nonexistent. However, the financial disadvantages of owning a ground lease rather than the freehold can be great under some land leasing systems.

Dutch municipalities lease land for property management reasons also, but here again the citizen sees no advantage, for municipalities rarely use their powers as lessor for this purpose. The survey by De Jong, Pluijmers and de Wolff (1996) explicitly asked about this. One finding was that municipalities that used land leasing did not pay more attention to setting conditions on land disposals than municipalities that used freehold. The survey found also that only half of the municipalities using land leasing had any system for monitoring observance of the lease conditions.

Generally, citizens see public land leasing as a sort of tax paid to the municipality—they do not see it as resulting in better property management in their town or city. It is no wonder that public land leasing is unpopular. This explains the selective use of public land leasing: municipalities do not apply it if they fear it will make them unpopular. The smaller local authorities do not use it for they fear that households and firms will choose to locate elsewhere.

---

[11] In the Netherlands a house buyer usually can take a mortgage for 90–100 percent of the value of the land plus buildings. Interest payments on the mortgage are deductible against income, but so are annual ground rents. On the other hand, a business may not want to tie up capital in land ownership.

[12] In the City of The Hague the sales prices were compared between dwellings on freehold land and on leasehold land: no difference could be found that was attributable to the form of land tenure. The City of Amsterdam wanted to conduct a similar study but could not find data on sufficient dwellings that were on freehold land. The study was therefore made of the sales prices of dwellings on leasehold land where the lease still had a long period to run, where the ground rent had been paid in the form of a premium (this price approximates the price of a dwelling on freehold land) and where the ground rent was still being paid yearly. In all, 75 sales prices were compared. In 70 percent no difference could be found to be attributable to the difference in land tenure, and in the remaining 30 percent only a part (60 percent) of the expected difference in value was reflected in the sales prices (Amsterdam 1996).

It is the larger local authorities that issue land by ground leases, for they know that demand to locate within their boundaries is so strong that they can afford to deter some of it. Some local authorities sell ground leases for industrial use because firms have no local vote, but not for housing because the local council does not want to antagonize its electors. Some municipalities sell land lease-hold rather than freehold only to local housing associations, because those are committed to building locally. This selective use is shown in the results of the survey by De Jong, Pluijmers and de Wolff (1996).

The tensions to which this gives rise can be seen in how the City of The Hague revised its land leasing policy in 1986. The rules for land leasing were changed in 1977: instead of ground rent being held constant for 75 years, it was revised every five years in line with inflation. At the beginning of the 1980s the effects of these changes were felt. At the same time, the leases issued under the rules of 1923 (ground rents unchanged for 50 years) were coming up for renewal and there had been some highly publicized cases of huge increases. A large number of residents lived on land leased from the municipality, and started to pressure the local politicians. The politicians representing the Liberal Party (VVD) in particular became very critical of public land leasing.

The City of The Hague was at that time in severe financial difficulty and stood to benefit from the expected increase in income from ground rents (see the figures above for the expected increase in net income from land leasing). The irony was that the member of the municipal executive responsible for finance (the *wethouder financiën*) was a member of the Liberal Party. From the party's point of view he wanted to abolish public land leasing, while his responsibilities for the city's finances led him to want to retain it.

The political discussions lasted for several years, and finally the following was formally adopted (in the form of a new set of regulations in 1986). The land leasing rules would be changed so that the financial position of the lessee would be closely equal to the position of a freeholder. When the ground lease was issued for the first time, it was to be valued as the same as the freehold right. The lessee could pay either a premium or an annual ground rent. This was calculated as the capital value multiplied by the current rate of inter-est, with a small addition for administrative costs. The leasehold was for an indefinite period and the ground rent, once fixed, remained constant (apart from revisions every five years in line with changes in the interest rate). Lessees who chose to pay the premium were financially in the same position as those buying the land freehold. A choice to pay the ground rent was financially the same as taking an indefinite loan to buy the freehold interest, with the interest rate revised every five years. There is only one difference between the financial position of the owner of the ground lease and that of the freehold: if the use of the site is changed or the site is redeveloped, so that the initial conditions of the lease are no longer met, the lessee must obtain permission from the lessor (the municipality) and the payment for the lease can be increased.

All ground leases now issued by the City of The Hague follow the new rules. Owners of leases issued under the regulations of 1911 and 1923 (ground rents held constant for 75 years) can, on expiration of those leases, apply for a new lease under the regulations of 1986 (perpetual leasehold and constant ground rents). The price for the renewed ground lease is to be based on land prices at the time of renewal. So, the municipality can still expect a large, once only increase in income as the old leases expire and are reissued. Owners of leases issued under the regulations of 1977 (ground rents linked to inflation) can apply to have their leases converted according to the new 1986 regulations. Thereafter, land leasing will cease to be a source of (net) income to the municipality. Land value increases can no longer be captured except when they are caused by redevelopment.

Recently the City of Amsterdam has undertaken a similar policy review. Under pressure from some of the local political parties and from some local pressure groups, the municipality has revised the rules of its land leasing system. The financial disadvantages to the lessee (when compared to the financial position of a freeholder) have been reduced but the changes have not gone as far as in The Hague (Amsterdam 2000a).

These experiences can be analyzed in terms of the two main reasons a public landowner might decide to dispose of land leasehold rather than freehold. If the public authority uses land leasing as a source of income, it risks antagonizing the voters, who will pressure the politicians to change the system. If this pressure is great enough the politicians might even decide to abandon land leasing totally. In that case, they lose not only the income but also the planning (property management) powers that land leasing can give. The dilemma is sharpened by the way most Dutch municipalities organize their functions into departments: the estates management function (which includes land leasing) is in one department, planning (and/or housing) in another. So the heads of departments and the political chairmen often have conflicting interests. The politicians of the city council of The Hague wanted to keep the planning powers, so they stopped using land leasing as a source of income. Public land leasing was saved in The Hague.[13] It is noteworthy that there was little resistance to the clause that the ground rent could be revised in the event of changes in the use of land. Clearly, this way of capturing increases in land values is politically acceptable.

It must be added that the municipality of The Hague had until then not made much use of the property management powers given by its land leasing. There was no active monitoring of lessees to see whether they were complying with the terms of the ground lease. If someone complained of nuisance from a neighbor, or if a tenant complained of poor maintenance by the landlord, the

---

[13] This analysis also can be applied to private landowners who sell ground leases on their land. Recent history of leasehold enfranchisement in Britain (the Leasehold Reform, Housing and Urban Development Act 1993) can be seen in this light. Some of the old landed estates used their freehold interests to manage large areas of central London and also parts of Birmingham. However, ground rents increased so much that the lessees wanted to acquire the freehold. They put pressure on Parliament. The landed estates did not have the option that the Dutch municipalities have of unilaterally changing the rules. Parliament passed legislation to allow lessees to acquire the freehold in some circumstances. The landed estates lost both the income and the property management powers (Needham 1993; Young 1993).

land leases gave the municipality the means to intervene. But the municipality did not actively monitor the ground leases unless someone "blew the whistle" to attract attention. Nor was there evidence that the municipality was using its income from land leasing to benefit the public. This sheds a rather different light on what happened in The Hague. The politicians argued that they would give up the financial benefits in order to retain the property management powers, but perhaps the whole political conflict was symbolic rather than substantive.

Elsewhere also, there is little evidence that any of the municipalities that use land leasing take active advantage of the planning powers of land leasing. It would seem that financial reasons are important. There are, for example, cases of housing associations wanting to redevelop some of their older housing on land leased from the municipality. The municipality could have taken advantage of its land ownership to stimulate good development. In practice, however, there were acrimonious debates about money between the housing association and the municipality. The municipality wanted to raise the ground rent, and the housing association threatened to drop all plans for redevelopment if this occurred. The outcome was that the municipality sold the freehold to the housing association for a lump sum greater than the value when the ground lease was first issued (the municipality had captured some land price increase) but smaller than current market value. The municipality realized the capital value of the land it had owned, the housing association bought its freedom. The fact that the municipality had given away one of its planning powers in an area needing redevelopment played no role.

CONCLUSION

It is difficult not to be cynical about public land leasing in the Netherlands. It is practiced by some municipalities, which say that they do it for the extra planning powers. However, there is little evidence that they use those extra powers systematically. The municipalities know that their land leasing is unpopular, mainly because it puts the lessee at a financial disadvantage compared to the freeholder. So, municipalities do not practice land leasing if they think that firms and households might locate elsewhere (to municipalities that sell land freehold).

The City of The Hague was heroic. In effect, it said, "we don't do it for the money, but for the planning powers, and to prove it we will give up all future financial gain so as to be able to retain the planning powers" (the minutes of the council meeting of 4 November 1985 support this statement). But The Hague is not using those planning powers! Other municipalities, in particular, the cities of Amsterdam, Rotterdam and Utrecht, do not want to give up the income they enjoy from land leasing. If they are pressured to abandon it altogether, they respond by softening some of the financial disadvantages to the lessee while retaining land leasing as a source of income.

This story of more than 100 years of public land leasing in the Netherlands contains lessons that can be used by other countries. The lessons can be described under five points:

1. *How strong is the planning reason for public land leasing?* This depends on the rules and regulations available under public law in that country (e.g., powers under statutory planning, under building regulations, under local ordinances for preventing public nuisances and under environmental health). The powers given by public land leasing are additional and supplementary. If all other powers are comprehensive and detailed there might be little reason for wanting to supplement them with public land leasing. If the other powers are weak or cannot tackle some important matters, public land leasing can be a useful addition.

   In that case it is important to do so consistently and openly, which requires systematic monitoring of the constructive way in which the land leasing is being used; and publicity to show citizens they are benefiting from that active use.

2. *What are the financial consequences for the lessee?* What the citizen buys is not land but a right in land. The choice is between buying a freehold right and a leasehold right. The value of a freehold right is greater because it includes more than a leasehold right. So, the capital value of a freehold right is greater than the capital value of a leasehold right. This argument is unchanged if one acquires the ground lease not by paying a premium but by paying annual ground rents: the capitalized value of the annual ground rents should be less than the capital value of the freehold right. How this works out in practice depends on the financial terms of the lease; but the principle remains (for further details, see this chapter's appendix).

   There can be one exception to this, namely, when there is a change in use on leasehold land, a change that can decrease or increase the value of using that land. This can be difficult to foresee and therefore difficult to include in the financial terms of the ground lease when it is first issued. There is a strong argument for saying that the market does not take into account such changes, when the market value is determined initially. In that case the price paid for the lease can be adjusted when the change is made, even though that can result in the leasehold right being priced higher than the freehold right at the beginning of the lease.

3. *What are the financial consequences for the public lessor?* If the public lessor wants to use public land leasing for capturing value increases, a distinction should be made between value increases caused by changes of use and value increases caused by general rises in land value. The first cause can legitimately be captured by raising ground rents or premiums (although in some countries, there are alternative instruments for capturing that sort of betterment).

   It is more difficult to work out a justifiable method of capturing land price increases caused by a general rise in land values, because the initial value of the ground rent (or the value of the premium) is usually set by reference to the market price of the land at the beginning of the ground lease. It is reasonable to assume that the market price at the beginning of the lease period incorporates an allowance for expected land value increases. So, if the public land lessor wants to raise ground rents in line with increasing land values, the *initial* ground rent should be set *below* the market value at that moment. That way the capitalized values of increasing ground rents will not necessarily be greater than the freehold value at the start of the lease.

Further advice: let citizens see what the financial consequences are for the public lessor. If the leasehold system generates income for the municipality, let the citizens see how this is being used for the good of the community.

4. *The effects in both the short and the long term must be considered.* The experience in the Netherlands is that the financial consequences to the lessee of public land leasing become clear only in the longer term. In the short term, people (including the electorate) are inclined to think that it is perhaps a good thing. For example, it allows one to obtain land without committing capital reserves to it.[14] The crunch comes in the longer term, when the ground lease comes up for renewal or when the ground rents are revised. Then it becomes very obvious that one is not the owner of the freehold: one might even lose the right to renew the leasehold. If one does get the chance to take out a ground lease for a second term, it will be seen that the asking price is much higher than for the first term. And it will seem that the valuation of the leasehold right on developed land is arbitrary. Valuing the leasehold of developed land for lease renewal is indeed very difficult (Needham 1996; also, see the appendix). If the citizen is against public land leasing, no politician will introduce or retain it. So, the public authority should think the whole proposal through into the long term. Is it building up problems for itself?

5. *How can municipalities balance the tradeoff between planning and financial objectives?* Finally, if one wants public land leasing for both planning reasons and financial reasons, one should not be so greedy for financial gains so as to provoke a political reaction against public land leasing so great that public land leasing has to be scrapped. Then, the planning benefits are lost as well.

At press time for this book, newspapers (November 2, 2002) reported that the municipality of Rotterdam had decided to scrap its public land leasing as of 2003. A new municipal council was elected in 2002, and it has taken this action in view of the unpopularity of leasehold among the voters. There are also financial reasons: selling the ground leases to the existing lessees will raise Euro 900 million in the short term.

---

[14] Some housing associations in Germany use leasehold precisely for this purpose. They dispose of land leasehold to people who want to build their own houses, for then those people do not have to spend part of their borrowing power—the amount they may borrow on a mortgage—on land acquisition.

REFERENCES

Amsterdam. 1996. *Erfpacht, een onderzoek naar de invloed van erfpacht op verkoopcijfers in het kader van de Wet WOZ*, Amsterdam: Gemeentebelastingen.

———. 2000a. *Gemeenteblad afd.1, n2.19, Eindrapportage 100 jaar erfpacht: operatie Groot onderhoud*. Amsterdam: Gemeentebestuur.

———. 2000b. *Jaarverslag 1999*. Amsterdam: Gemeentelijk Grondbedrijf.

Badcock, B. 1994. The strategic implications for the Randstad of the Dutch property system. *Urban Studies* 31(3):425–446.

Carey, G. 1976. Land tenure, speculation, and the state of the aging metropolis. *Geographical Review* 66:253–265.

De Jong, J. 1984. *Gemeentelijke gronduitgifte*, proefschrift Rijksuniversiteit Utrecht. Deventer.

De Jong, J., Y, Pluijmers and H. W. de Wolff. 1996. De praktijk van de gemeentelijke. gronduitgifte, in *Weekblad voor privaatrecht, notariaat en registratie*, 9 September, 546–551.

Delfgaauw, G. Th. J. 1934. *De grondpolitiek van de gemeente Amsterdam*. Paris, Amsterdam.

Geertsen, S. R. J. 1999. *De juridische toelaatbaarheid van stedelijke erfpacht als ruimtelijk ordeningsinstrument*. Nijmegen: Vakgroep planologie, Nijmegen School of Management, University of Nijmegen.

Giebels, R., C. C. Koopmans and F. Moolhuizen. 1985. *De risico's voor gemeenten op de markt voor bouwrijpe grond*. Amsterdam: Stichting voor Economisch Onderzoek.

Lefcoe, G. 1978. When governments become land developers. *Urban Land and Policy* 1:103–120.

Morris, A. E. J. 1985. Historical roots of Dutch city planning and urban form. In *Public planning in The Netherlands: Perspectives and changes since the Second World War*. A. K. Dutt and F. J. Costa, ed. Oxford: Oxford University Press.

Needham. B. 1992. Long leases: A biblical stewardship? *Estates Gazette* 9325:114–116.

———. 1993. Amsterdam under construction. In *Dutch strategic planning in international perspective*, A. Faludi, ed. Amsterdam: SISWO publicatie 372:127–132.

———. 1996. The valuation of building leases on developed land. Paper delivered to the Third Annual Conference of the European Real Estate Society, Belfast 26–28 June 1996.

———. 1997. Land policy in the Netherlands. In *Tijdschrift voor Economische en Sociale Geografie* 88(3):291–296.

———. 1999. The EU compendium of spatial planning systems and policies: The Netherlands. Luxembourg: Office for Official Publications of the European Communities.

Needham, B. and A. Faludi. 1999. Dutch growth management in a changing market. *Planning Practice and Research* 14(4):481–491.

Newman P., and A. Thornley. 1996. *Urban planning reform, housing and urban development act* 1993. Cambridge: Granta Editions.

Ottens E. S., ed. 1996. *Een eeuw erfpacht in Amsterdam*. Amsterdam: Gemeentelijk Grondbedrijf.

Rust, W. N. J. 1996. Erfpacht: en financieel-economische beschouwing. In *Een eeuw erfpacht in Amsterdam*, E. S. Ottens, ed. Amsterdam: Gemeentelijk Grondbedrijf, 95–102.

Valk, A. van der. 1989. *Amsterdam in aanleg*. Planologische Studies nr. 8, Het Planologisch en Demografisch Instituut, University of Amsterdam.

Velten, A. A. van, G. M. F. Snijders and W. G. Huijgen. 1995. *Erfpacht: pre-advies van de Koninklijke Notariële Broederschap*. Lelystad: Koninklijke Vermande.

Werf, S. van der. 1977. De grondpolitiek van Amsterdam. In *Spiegel van onroerend goed*. G. Bolle and C. A. Snepvangers, ed. Deventer: Kluwer, 193–246.

Werkgroep Nota Grondbeleid. 1986. *Discussienota Grondbeleid*. Gemeent 's-Gravenhage, Den Haag.

Young, P. 1993. *Pyrrhic victory: The leasehold reform, housing and urban development act 1993*. Cambridge: Granta Editions.

DETERMINING THE PRICE AND VALUE OF GROUND LEASES

1. PRINCIPLES FOR DETERMINING THE MARKET VALUE OF A GROUND LEASE ON UNDEVELOPED LAND

Suppose ground leases were auctioned. The price could be either a capital sum (a premium, no further payments for the duration of the lease), or an annual sum (to be paid every year for the duration of the lease, where the agreed price could include arrangements for varying the annual payments during the life of the lease). Were the lease auctioned, it could be assumed that the price would vary according to the terms of the lease (e.g., restrictions on the use to which the land can be put), and according to expectations about inflation and about real changes in the value of the lease. Such a method would result in a price being paid equal to what the market considered the value of the ground lease.

Using some fictional inputs we can work out what the results of this method would be.

» Suppose that using a parcel of land produced a net income in the first year of 100 units (realized at the end of the first year). (Note: this is the income after subtracting all costs, including the construction costs.) Suppose that the lease is for 50 years, there is no inflation and no risk. The real rate of interest (i.e., abstracting from loss in the real value of money caused by inflation) is 4 percent. Suppose it is not expected that the real net income from operating on this site will change during the life of the lease (no increase or decrease caused by changes in adjacent uses, by changes from competitors, etc.). The net present value of this income stream is 2,134 units.

$$= \sum_{t=0}^{50} \frac{100}{(1.04)^t}$$

» Suppose the current rate of inflation is 2 percent per year. It is expected that the net annual income will rise accordingly. But then the rate at which this is discounted must be increased to take account of inflation: the discount rate is then 4 plus 2 percent. The net present value of this income stream is 2,163 units.

$$= \sum_{t=0}^{50} \frac{100 \, (1.02)^t}{(1.06)^t}$$

This is almost the same as without inflation: the annual increase in the money value of the net annual income is cancelled out by the higher discount rate.

» Suppose the real net income from operating on the site is expected to increase, because of improvements in the area, an increase estimated to be 1 percent per year. We can ignore inflation as long as we do so not only for the effects on the money value of the net income but also for the effects on the discount rate. So, we take account of the real increase of 1 percent per year in net annual income and use a discount rate of 4 percent. The net present value of this income stream is 2,564 units.

$$= \sum_{t=0}^{50} \frac{100\,(1.01)^t}{(1.04)^t}$$

2. How the Price of a Ground Lease on Undeveloped Land is Set by Municipalities in the Netherlands

Determining the price of a ground lease by auction is not practiced in the Netherlands, nor are there any signs that this will develop. The asking price is set by the lessor (in practice, a municipality) and although there is room for negotiation, this room is small, for a municipality does not want to risk the suspicion that it is acting arbitrarily or favoring some lessees above others. How does this work in practice?

For Commercial Properties

The asking price is set as follows:

» The stream of net income from using the developed land (land + buildings) during the period of the lease is estimated and the net present value of this is calculated (A).

» The capital cost of developing the land (construction cost of the building) is estimated (B).

» The difference (A–B) is the capital value of the right to use the land during the period of the lease.

In practice, the net present value of the income stream is calculated as if the lease had an infinite duration: but the difference between this value and the value of the income stream for 50 years is small, because of the effect of discounting. Sometimes account is taken of what will happen to the built structure at the end of the lease. If the lessor is obligated to pay compensation for any remaining value, this will increase the value of the lease. But, again, the effect on the net present value will be small when this compensation is discounted over 50 years.

The ground rent is then set:

» either a premium equal to (A−B) is paid at the beginning of the period.

» or an initial annual ground rent is set by multiplying the capital value (A−B) by a percentage equal to the current (money) rate of interest. (There might also be a small supplement to cover administrative costs: we shall ignore this further, although at the moment the municipality of Amsterdam sets this supplement at 1.5 percent of the capital value!)

How do the results of this practice compare with the results if the principles for determining the market value (see Section 1) were followed?

» Suppose that the net annual income from operating the developed land was 100 units (first payment received after the first year, duration of lease 50 years). (Note: this is the net income from the land and the building. In the fictional cases worked out in the first section, it was assumed that 100 units was the net income from the land alone.) Suppose the real rate of interest is 4 percent, there is inflation of 2 percent and the real income from the developed land increases by 1 percent per year. The money value of the net annual income increases by 3 percent a year and the discount rate is 6 percent. The net present value of this stream of income (A) is 2,592 units.

$$= \sum_{t=0}^{50} \frac{100 \ (1.03)^t}{(1.06)^t}$$

» Suppose construction costs (B) amount to 1,500 units. Then the net present value of using the land (A−B) is 1,092 units. A perfectly operating market would put this value on the ground lease. But what is the price that the lessor asks for the ground lease? If the ground rent is paid in the form of a premium, set at the price (A−B), this is the same as the market value of the ground lease. If the ground rent is paid annually, the municipality would set the price in the following way. The value (A−B: in this case 1,092 units) is multiplied by the money rate of interest (in this case 6 percent), giving an annual rent of 65.52 units. If this remains constant, the net present value when discounted at 6 percent is 1,029 units.

$$= \sum_{t=0}^{50} \frac{65.52}{(1.06)^t}$$

This (1,029 units) is 5 percent less than the market value of the ground lease (1,092 units).

» Suppose the ground rent is paid annually, the price in the first year is set as described above (65.52 units), but the price is increased in line with inflation (2 percent a year). The net present value of the annual payments is 1,417 units.

$$= \sum_{t=0}^{50} \frac{65.52\ (1.02)^t}{(1.06)^t}$$

This is clearly much more than the market value (1,092 units).

The reason the net present value of the indexed annual ground rent is more than the market value of the lease is that the initial ground rent is derived from the market value of the land, and expected inflation has already been incorporated in that market value. As a result, indexing the ground rent takes inflation into account a second time. If the initial ground rent is to be indexed in line with inflation, the initial ground rent should be set lower. For example, if the initial ground rent was set at 50 units (4.6 percent of the market value of the ground lease) instead of 65.52 units (6 percent of the market value of the ground lease) the net present value of the ground rents when indexed at 2 percent per year and discounted at 6 percent is 1,081 units, around the same as the market value.

This conclusion is based on the assumption that the market—when valuing at the beginning of the leasehold period the net present value of the income stream—assesses the future rate of inflation correctly. Whether this future rate of inflation has, in fact, been assessed correctly can be quite easily tested later, by comparing the assumed cash flow with the actual cash flow. If the future rate had been assessed higher than turns out to be the case, then the ground rent should be revised downwards. If the future rate had been assessed lower than turns out, the ground rent should be revised upwards.

For Residential Properties

The practice is to first estimate the capital value of the land. This is done by estimating the market value of a house built according to the specifications in the ground lease (A) and subtracting the estimated construction costs (B). The ground rent is then set:

» either a premium equal to (A−B) is paid at the beginning of the period

» or an initial annual ground rent is set by multiplying the capital value (A−B) by a percentage equal to the current (money) rate of interest. (There may also be a small supplement to cover administrative costs. We shall ignore this.)

It will be seen that the principle is the same as with commercial properties. The difference is in how the capital value of the developed land is estimated. With commercial properties this is derived from estimates of cash flows, which are then capitalized; with houses this is derived from an estimate of the selling price on the market for comparable houses on leasehold land.

If the lease is paid as a premium, this will be the same as the market value of the lease. If the lease is paid annually and remains constant throughout the period of the lease, the net present value of the annual rents will be nearly the same as the price of the premium and thus the same as the market value of the lease. If the lease is paid annually and is revised in line with inflation, the net present value will be higher than market value. (The calculations made for commercial properties can be repeated here and would show the same results.)

The reason the net present value of the annual ground rents (when these are revised in line with inflation) is higher than the market value of the ground lease is the same as for commercial properties. Namely, that the initial ground rent is based on the market price of the property, and that expectations of inflation are built into this market price. However, the market for housing does this implicitly when houses and apartments are sold, not explicitly as does the market for commercial properties. This makes it difficult to check afterwards whether the housing market assessed the future rate of inflation correctly. And that makes it difficult to know whether it is justifiable to revise annual ground rents to take account of changes in the market value of land.

3. A NOTE ON THE VALUATION OF GROUND LEASES ON DEVELOPED LAND

It is necessary to put a price on a ground lease on developed land at the end of the lease term, or if either lessor or lessee wants to renegotiate the lease before it terminates. The latter can happen, for example, if the lessee wants to sell the building plus ground lease to someone else and the lease is near the end of its term. The property will fetch a higher price if sold with a long lease period remaining. Thus, the seller will ask for a lease renewal before offering the house for sale. The question then is, "How does one value a ground lease on developed land?" The methods described above for undeveloped land do not apply here.

It is not even certain that auctioning the lease would be the best way: one of the interested buyers will usually be the existing lessee. If so, the buyer will have a much stronger reason for wanting to buy the ground lease than others, because for the existing lessee a ground lease on another site is not as good a substitute as for a potential buyer who does not occupy the land. The existing lessee will be prepared to pay a higher price.

The valuation method, which can best be justified theoretically, is the following:

a. If the land were undeveloped, with what use and at what density would development be allowed? In estimating this, the limitations on redevelopment imposed by the planning regulations for that site are applicable.

b. What would be the value of a building lease on that undeveloped land? This can be estimated as described above.

c. What would the potential owner of the leasehold on the developed land have to do before being able to make the developed land undeveloped, and what would that cost? The difference between (b) and (c) is the value of the ground lease on the developed land. This is worked out further in Needham (1996).

The practical difficulty with this method is step (c). The costs can be regarded as being the compensation due to the owner of the building works on the land. If the lease is about to expire and the terms exclude compensation to that owner for the value of the works, then step (c) has a zero value. If the lease is about to expire and the owner of the building is entitled to compensation for the works, this is equal to the depreciated value of those works (not easy to estimate). If compensation is to be paid before the end of the leasehold period, more should be paid than the depreciated capital value of the works, for the lessee still has the right to occupy the land for a number of years.

What methods are used in the Netherlands? Some argue that the value of the ground lease on developed land is the same as on undeveloped land (Rust 1996). This can be shown to be absurd, as follows. Suppose there are three plots of land next to each other, of the same size. Two plots (A) and (B) are vacant, on the other (C) there is a house built 30 years ago. Three rights are offered for sale: the freehold right of plot (A) under the condition that on that plot a house must be built with the same size, design, etc., as the existing house on (C); the leasehold right on (B) under the condition that on that plot a house must be built with the same size, design, etc., as the existing house on (C); and the leasehold right on (C) under the condition that the existing house is maintained. Most buyers would prefer to have the freehold right on (A) rather than the leasehold right on (B), and would prefer that latter rather than the leasehold right on (C). And most buyers would be prepared to pay for those preferences. That is, the value of the leasehold right on undeveloped land is less than the value of the freehold right on undeveloped land (argued above), and the value of the leasehold right on developed land is less than the value of the leasehold right on undeveloped land.

Once again, the practice is illustrated by the City of The Hague. First, the freehold value of the land is estimated as if the site were undeveloped, but subject to the same use restrictions as the developed land. Then this value is reduced by 45 percent. This method was tested in the Court for Taxation Matters, which ruled that the leasehold value of developed land is 60 percent of the leasehold value of the land if undeveloped and with permission to use the same way. The court also gave a justification for the reduction (but not for the size of the reduction):

» There are building works on the land, which, because they are old, cannot be used as efficiently as if they were new;

» Transforming developed land into undeveloped land would cost money.

The City of Amsterdam is reviewing the method it uses for assessing the value of ground leases on developed land, pending judgement by the courts on this matter (Amsterdam 2000a).

Two conclusions can be drawn from this. First, there are no fully satisfactory methods of valuing a ground lease on developed land. Second, anyone contemplating introducing public land leasing will soon face the necessity of carrying out such valuations, and will have to be prepared to accept the political unpopularity caused by the difficulties in justifying the valuation method.

SITE LEASEHOLD IN SWEDEN

A TOOL TO CAPTURE LAND VALUE

4

Hans Mattsson

According to Swedish law, the right to use land for a specific purpose can be leased to private individuals for an indefinite period with a payment of an annual ground rent. This is done through the form of tenure known as *site leasehold (tomträtt)*. A grant of this kind may be made only for a property belonging to the state or a municipality, or otherwise publicly owned. With government permission, site leasehold also may be granted by a foundation.

Site leasehold was introduced in 1907 and was the subject of a major review in 1953. To begin with, interest in using this land-tenure arrangement was confined to the Swedish capital, Stockholm. It was not until the 1930s and 1940s that the use of site leasehold spread to other municipalities. At least since 1953, site leasehold in Sweden has been used for capturing land value and sometimes for reasons of housing policy. Unlike leasehold systems in some other countries, site leasehold in Sweden has rarely been used as an instrument of planning. In 2001 Sweden had 105,000 site leaseholds, 85,000 more than in 1950. Yet, over the past five years, the number dropped by 3,000. Expansion has given way to a slow phaseout, which is likely to continue in the future.

A site lessee is free to use the property within the conditions specified in the lease contract. Tenants may not cancel leasehold agreements with the municipality, whereas the latter may do so after 60 years for residential leasehold and after 20 years for other types of site leases. Buildings and other facilities normally must be purchased by the lessor should they cancel the agreement. By the right to revoke the site leasehold agreement, the legislature would like to safeguard the interests of the public to repossess land, should the government need land for any public purpose. By increasing the ground rents, municipalities may also retain the increased land value.

Site leasehold has been given characteristics otherwise reserved for freehold tenure. In establishing special legislation for site leasehold, lawmakers have acknowledged not only the interests of lessees in their investment in land, but their need to treat leased land rights as collateral. Lessees can assign, mortgage and sublease all or part of their leased land rights to a third party.

This chapter has four sections. The first section provides a brief overview of the planning policy in Sweden as a background. The second section gives a historical perspective of the development of site leasehold, describing its origins and current features.[1] The third section describes the formal procedures for setting ground rents. The final section discusses the previous growth period and the current phaseout of site leasehold in Sweden.

PLANNING POLICY

Sweden's housing production peaked between 1950 and 1975, when 2 million of today's 4.1 million housing units were built (Kalbro and Mattsson 1995). This was a period of high internal migration and rapidly improving living standards. The expansion was a breeding ground for rapid land value appreciation. It was deemed politically unacceptable for the gains to benefit landowners and developers only. Instead, the gains should accrue to housing tenants or be captured by the municipality. One way of recapturing the increased land value was by granting land in site leasehold.

Site leasehold, however, had never been used to control urban growth. That control was instead exercised through three mechanisms: (1) municipal monopoly power over planning; (2) public land banking; and (3) conditions attaching to the award of government subsidies. Municipalities decided whether the adoption of a detailed development plan for urban development was necessary, and their rejection of such a plan was final. This put municipalities in a strong position when they negotiated with developers on issues related to land development. Necessary areas for infrastructure and green spaces could be reserved in the plan, and developers had to transfer land for streets and parks free of charge to the municipalities. Charges could also be levied on developers for public services such as streets and water and sewerage. If the developer was required to construct these public facilities according to the provisions of development agreements, the facilities would be transferred free of charge to the municipality after their completion.

Municipalities also made extensive purchases of land. As major landowners, they could sell land to developers, which further strengthened their negotiating position. The position was equally strong if land was transferred to private entities in site leasehold. Between 1970 and 1990, 70–80 percent of all housing construction took place on land sold or leased by municipalities, which demonstrates the extent of municipal land holdings (Boverket 1991; Vedung 1993).

The planning monopoly, like the extensive municipal land holdings, was intended to facilitate the implementation of public housing programs and ensure a low cost of providing high quality housing to the public. The instruments of

[1] Importantly, other Swedish leasehold titles *(arrenden)* will not be described here because they are not used in urban areas. They also differ fundamentally from site leasehold, as they can be contracted, though not mortgaged or subleased, by a private landowner. That site leasehold can be granted for an indefinite period is another distinguishing feature, as other leases in urban areas can be granted for 25 years only.

housing policy also came to govern other construction activity. In addition, the state made loans available with terms favorable for housing production. Yet, it made certain that government subsidies would not raise land costs by setting a maximum land price at which national subsidies would be payable. This system was based on the awareness that very few citizens could afford to own homes without public subsidies. The monopoly power over planning and the extensive public landownership allowed municipalities to regulate land prices.

Regulated land prices, however, could encourage developers to collect windfalls through high rents or selling prices for housing. This potential problem was minimized by prohibiting developers or property owners to set rents higher than those charged by nonprofit housing organizations. Price controls were also set over the initial sale of tenant-owned flats in multifamily houses and freehold single-family dwellings.

The planning and housing policies of the 1970s remain essentially intact. The state, however, has gradually withdrawn from housing policy by phasing out the subsidies system. Besides, current building output is small: between 10,000 and 15,000 dwellings annually, as compared with the 1970 annual output of 110,000. One burning political issue, therefore, is how to increase housing production in a system with no subsidies and a planning structure designed for a subsidized housing market.

In Sweden local governments do not need site leasehold to regulate land uses. The mandatory detailed development plans perform this function, as they are binding. There is no requirement in the planning regulations for landowners to receive equal treatment, even if their lands are adjacent or in close proximity. Instead, land must be used in the best possible way, and it is the municipality's role to ensure that this goal is foremost.

The sole purpose of site leasehold is to harvest the appreciation of land values and to some extent to subsidize housing costs, by setting ground rents below their fair market values. It has no primary function in controlling urban growth and land uses. Because of this unique characteristic, the next section discusses the historical development of the legal institution for capturing land value under the Swedish site leasehold system.

LEGAL INSTITUTION FOR SITE LEASEHOLD

Before 1953

Although private land had existed in Swedish towns since medieval times in the form of freehold plots *(fria tomter)*, the main part of town land remained as collective property. As such, land that belonged to the town could only be granted in the form of nonfreehold plots *(ofria tomter)*. The title to these plots was hereditary and of indefinite duration. As a rule, the tenant had to pay a charge for the plot. When the land came up for sale, the town had the right of first refusal. Collective ownership was prompted by the principle of land use being ultimately determined by the town, not by individuals (Améen 1964; Prawitz 1954; Westerlind 1965).

The law was gradually changed when more and more town land passed into private ownership, a result of the conversion of nonfreehold plots into freehold due to the impact of nineteenth century liberalism. Grants of nonfreehold plots were abolished in 1907, as its supporting legal system became obsolete.

In 1907 site leasehold (tomträtt) entered Swedish law. The new leasehold right was based partly on the previous method of granting nonfreehold plots. Another model was the German *erbbaurecht*, and elements were also derived from Henry George's ideas in the United States (Westerlind 1965; Sidenbladh 1981). More important, the power of granting site leaseholds was vested in public bodies only.

Introduction of site leasehold had two essential motives (Westerlind 1965). The first was social. Larger towns and cities had a severe housing shortage. Housing production was low in relation to demand, and less well-to-do members of society were especially hard hit, in part, due to high land costs. By supplying land cheaply through site leasehold, the cities encouraged developers to build without incurring the cost of acquiring freehold title to the land. The municipalities also intended to incorporate land use regulations into the terms of the contract, so as to use leasing as a planning tool at the time when planning instruments were weak.

The second motive was fiscal. If long-term leases could be used instead of freehold, the city could reap a considerable profit by reclaiming land in the future and reselling it when land value increased. Besides, by raising ground rents successively, a considerable share of the appreciation in land value would accrue to the public. This way, developers would be prevented from pocketing the land value increments created by public investments in streets, water and sewerage and other infrastructure. Through their power of repossessing land at lease expiration, municipalities also assured the collection of the increased land value on behalf of the community. Finally, widespread municipal grants of leases might discourage land speculation and exert a regulatory influence over land prices and rents.

Legislators assumed, albeit incorrectly, that use of site leasehold would be temporary. The system was used in suburban areas to lease public land for building single-family houses. As cities grew, municipalities could have retaken land when leases expired and sold it to private parties at higher prices (SOU 1952). In practice, however, this intention never materialized.

When first introduced in Swedish law, conditions incorporated in site leasehold contracts were fairly open-ended. Municipalities and lessees were free to negotiate on the conditions of their contracts. The term of site leasehold, however, had to be fixed between 26 and 100 years (Westerlind 1965).[2]

Despite the latitude permitted, site leaseholds usually were granted for 60 years (although the term of leasing industrial sites could vary considerably). The term of the site leasehold normally was supplemented by a clause requiring

---

[2] Information about the pre-1953 development of site leasehold is from Westerlind (1965).

the plot to be built within a certain time. The ground rent was usually kept constant for the duration of the site leasehold, although provision could be made for adjustments at certain intervals. In some exceptional cases the ground rent also could be set as a percentage of the annual sales of a business.

When site leaseholds were registered, buildings and other permanent facilities automatically became fixtures pertaining to it. This enabled lessees to use site leaseholds as collateral. More important, from a credit viewpoint, the same rules of attachment procedure applied as with real property.

When the term of a site leasehold expired, the leased land rights reverted back to the municipality. There was no legal requirement for a government lessor to purchase leasehold improvements. Yet, the existence of a duty to purchase leasehold improvements upon expiration of a site lease made a difference to its economic value, which in turn affected its value as collateral for securing a mortgage loan. This point was fully appreciated by the municipalities. Hence, at the beginning of the 1950s, a rule was almost universally applied that a government lessor would purchase leasehold improvements if it did not renew an expiring site lease. Site leaseholds for industrial purposes were the only exception.

It was understood from the outset that the practical usefulness of site leasehold would depend on the possibility of its use as collateral. But the discretion given by law to the involved parties to negotiate land contracts had negative repercussions on the mortgage value of site leasehold. Private lending institutions doubted the creditworthiness of site leasehold and were unwilling to treat it as collateral. Only specialized institutions, such as the City of Stockholm Site Leasehold Credit Institute *(Stockholms stads tomträttskassa)*, would accept site leasehold as a form of security. Although the attitude of private credit institutions toward site leasehold had changed, the growing prominence of credit questions related to site leasehold led to a review of related legislation in 1953.

1953 and Beyond

The law was amended in 1953. Security of tenure and certainty of retaining the value of the lessee's investments were reinforced, as was the credit value of the title. Banking legislation was then altered to facilitate the use of site leasehold as collateral (Westerlind 1965). The aim of these amendments was to make site leasehold a genuine alternative to freehold. The new rules made site leasehold look more like freehold than ever before. In principle, municipalities should possess the value of the land and nothing else. Site leasehold was to become a long-term source of revenue, with municipalities collecting rising land value through periodic increases in ground rents. This way, the new rules would encourage municipalities to retain land ownership.

A government commission, which proposed the new 1953 law, observed that municipalities were not always interested in repossessing site leaseholds for either land redevelopment or resale when leases expired. Instead, their preference was to renew the site contracts whenever possible. The commission also dealt briefly with planning and housing policy, declaring that planning and other related legislation for governing the development of private land and site leaseholds were adequate. It was thus unnecessary for site leasehold to be seen as a tool for controlling land use (SOU 1952). This argument was upheld by a later government commission, which stated that using site leasehold as a planning tool should be withdrawn from public discussion and legal examination (SOU 1980). The content of the 1953 legislation remains unaltered, though in 1970 the statutory rules were transferred from a special enactment to the new Land Code, as described below:

1. Only a public body and foundation can grant site leasehold, unless the government allows for an exception. This makes site leasehold an exclusive public instrument.

2. Site leasehold is granted indefinitely for an annual ground rent only. The law does not permit any lump sum payment.

3. The legislation safeguards the transfer of ownership of any buildings and other fixtures on the property to the lessee. If payment is to be rendered for the transfer, a special agreement must be made to this effect. Because buildings and other fixtures on the site, as well as all land rights, pass from the lessor to the lessee, the lessor retains only the freehold title to the land.

4. The lease agreement must be in writing and recorded legally in the land register. Alterations and transfers of the agreement are of no effect unless they, too, are put in writing and registered. Since the land register in Sweden is public domain, land registration and lease documents are accessible to purchasers, creditors, appraiser, lawyers and other interested parties.

5. The site leasehold contract shall contain the purpose of the lease and the amount of the ground rent. The deed of grant shall also contain detailed provisions concerning the use of the land and building. It may also contain provisions applicable to the site leasehold. Restrictive covenants on land use, however, are unusual because planning relies on other legislation (SOU 1980). All regulatory provisions to the building contained in a detailed development plan at the time of the grant will, failing agreement to the contrary, automatically apply to the development without being specially mentioned in the agreement. The result is that a strong planning system makes unnecessary the use of lease agreements for planning control. The reference to land use in site contracts is mainly to protect lessees from increases in ground rent. These increases could arise from changes of a detailed plan that open up an opportunity to more intensive land use than what is originally specified in site leases. If lessees do not wish to redevelop their property into more intensive use, they will not have to pay additional land rent.

6. The commencement and duration of the site leasehold may not be conditional. Nor may any restriction be imposed on the right of the site lessee to transfer the site leasehold or to grant a mortgage title or usufruct in it. It is not possible to prescribe in the lease that rents for flats are to be kept

below a certain level. Consequently, site leasehold may not be treated as a tool for rent control. The restrictions on the right of agreement are aimed at ensuring the full credit value of site leasehold.

7. The ground rent and its future increases affect the value of site leasehold. The initial ground rent is a matter for negotiation. Yet, subsequent adjustments shall reflect the yield of the land or fall short of it, which further guarantees the economic value of the title. (Ground rent problems will be considered more closely in the next section.)

8. Site leasehold agreements do not automatically expire at a given point in time. Rather, only government lessors can terminate site leases at the end of certain periods. The first period is 60 years; subsequent periods are 40 years. This way, possession is guaranteed for a long period. Shorter periods, though not less than 20 years, may be applied to site leasehold granted mainly for industrial development. The reason given for the public right of cancellation is that municipalities may need the land for other purposes, in which case they must have a smooth procedure for repossessing it. But, it is apparent that municipalities rarely reclaim land in this way, if ever.

   Lessees can contest cancellation in the land court, if they consider the municipality's claim to need the land to be unfounded. The reason for using court procedures in this situation is to strengthen the confidence of both lessees and creditors in site leasehold. If a site leasehold is terminated the landowner must purchase any buildings or other fixtures on the site. If, however, the grant of site leasehold refers to a purpose other than that of housing development, the parties may agree that buildings and other fixtures are to be purchased to a limited extent only, or not at all. Discretion of this kind mainly applies to industrial enterprises because legislators were concerned that municipalities would otherwise lease land under ordinary leasehold, which is easier to regulate but impossible to mortgage.

   If the parties can not agree on a purchase price, the matter must be brought before a land court. Both parties can file proceedings of this kind. When a purchase takes place, only buildings and fixtures are paid for. There is no compensation for moving costs and damages to a business, nor for any part of the land value. Legal costs are, in the first instance, borne by the landowner. If a case goes to a higher court, the losing party will pay the legal costs.

   A government lessor who wishes to recover a site leasehold before its term expires has two choices. Like any other private party, it can purchase the site leasehold from the lessee. Alternatively, the site leasehold can be expropriated the same way as privately owned land, provided that land is needed for urban expansion or public uses.

9. For tax purposes, site leasehold receives essentially the same treatment as freehold. The tax base and rate for taxing land and buildings are determined regardless of whether the property is leasehold. Site lessees pay their property taxes based on the total value of land plus buildings. Yet, they

are entitled to deduct the ground rent from their taxable income, just as a property owner is entitled to deduct interest payments on loans for land purchased. Tax on properties obtained from inheritance and gift are determined solely with reference to the value of the building (SOU 1980).

GROUND RENT CALCULATION

As mentioned earlier, the primary purpose of site leasehold is to keep the value of land in public hands. It must be emphasized that the main objective is not to produce an immediate financial return for municipalities, but to capture increasing land values through periodic increases in ground rents. The calculation of ground rent, therefore, is critical to the success or failure of this endeavor.

The legislation, however, does not clarify how the ground rent for site leasehold is to be calculated, nor has there been any uniformity in municipal practices (SOU 1980). One common principle is for the value of the land (the ground rent base) to be multiplied by an interest rate (ground rent interest) to give an annual ground rent. Since neither base nor interest rate is easy to determine, a host of different methods have been presented over the years for working out these two factors. Gradually, a large volume of legal cases has led to an increasing uniformity in ground rent calculation, especially in the determination of ground rent interest. Even so, difficulties associated with the calculation of ground rent base persist and frequently lead to litigation. A short description of certain methods of calculating ground rent will not be out of place here.

The initial ground rent, once determined, remains unchanged for a period of 10 years, unless a longer period has been agreed on. This rent is decided entirely by the involved parties through negotiation, with no special guideline for determining either the base or the interest rate. Yet, in some situations, there are general principles for calculating first-time ground rent.

In grants of site leasehold for housing purposes, the base has been determined with reference to municipal development costs including the costs for land. The base often is defined according to standardized costs of municipal development. In other cases, municipalities take the assessed value of the land as their starting point. Costs of installing water and sewerage are not normally included in the base; these costs are recouped as a one-time payment levied on site lessees.

Where grants are made for nonhousing purposes, the base often has been based on municipal ground preparation costs. In the case of commercial site leaseholds in urban centers the base is calculated at the fair market value of land. In many municipalities, however, the base has fallen short of the full development costs or the market value of land, because of policy considerations related to either social housing or business development and location (SOU 1980).

Principles for defining the interest rate for calculating ground rent vary from one municipality to another. Guidelines include, for example, the average rate of interest on 10-year municipal loans, the interest on national housing loans or the interest on special site leasehold loans from the state. In addition, some municipalities add 0.1 percent to the interest rate for covering administrative overheads (SOU 1990).

The practice of ground rent adjustment also varies from one municipality to another, although the same method is used for the first-time grants in calculating the base and the interest rate by all municipalities. In practice, case law has narrowed the variety in interest rate calculation. In 2001 the most commonly used interest rates were 3.75 percent for 10-year leases and 4.5 percent for 20-year leases, assuming that land value would increase at the rate of inflation.

If an agreement can not be reached on a new ground rent, proceedings can be filed with a land court no later than one year before the term for the existing ground rent expires. The court procedure aims to protect lessees and creditors from excessive rises in ground rent and also makes it possible for the municipality to obtain the full ground rent. The court must determine the ground rent according to the land value at the time of reassessment. In doing so it will consider the purpose of the grant and the detailed provisions imposed on the use and development of the property.

Basing the ground rent on land value is intended to protect both site lessee and mortgagee against rental changes that would reduce the value of site leasehold. But this approach has created problems, as reflected by the rulings of the Supreme Court and other courts, on a series of disputes between municipalities and site lessees over the adjustment of ground rents. The most important decision was a case tried by the Supreme Court in 1986 (NJA 1986, 272).

The case concerned the determination of both the interest rate for calculating ground rent and the estimation of land value for a commercial property in the center of Stockholm. The court judged that the real rate of interest should be 3 percent. Because land value was expected to rise more than the real interest rate, the rate used for ground rent calculation was fixed at 5.3 percent of the land value. The land value was calculated based on an estimated return on the full development of the site at the time of rent adjustment. The court decided that 7 percent was a reasonable return on land plus building. This rate of return was then applied to a hypothetical calculation containing gross yield, operating and administration expenses and depreciation of the property to derive an estimated land value.

The court, however, observed that calculation of the base and interest rates could not be precise, especially when they were based on several components of varying certainty. In the ultimate analysis, the court ruled that an assessment be made of what was equitable for both the municipality and the site lessee.

The large number of court cases shows that the methods used are complicated and not always widely agreed on, although a body of case law is gradually emerging. In addition, owing to the number of uncertain factors, the parties in court proceedings normally have differing opinions about land value. They are compelled to present large quantities of evidence to support their views.

Litigation is expensive and time-consuming to involved parties and society (SOU 1980), and creates uncertainty in predicting how the court will decide on ground rents. This complex process may encourage negotiated agreements, but it also can lead to frustration.

Two government commissions have tried to solve the problem, but their proposals have not led to new legislation. This reflects the difficulties in creating simple but acceptable principles. The last commission was appointed in 1988 to simplify the rules in order to reduce the number of court cases. One of it's main proposals was to set the nominal ground rent for single-family dwellings to 3.5 percent of the assessed land value. Because property reassessment occurs every six years, the assessed land value would be adjusted either up or down during the intervening years, based on a property price index.

For other site leasehold grants, land would be valued individually every five years. During the intervals, land value would be modified according to the consumer price index. In these cases, the ground rent interest was set at 3 percent. However, freedom of negotiation would be accepted concerning other principles of adjustment (SOU 1990).

This proposal has not led to new legislation, but the government is working on the proposal, albeit in modified form, with higher ground rents (around 4 percent). The proposal will eventually be put before Parliament *(Riksdag)*. The controversial point is whether it is reasonable to apply a predetermined interest rate generally.

One way of settling ground rent problems is for the parties to take a test case to court and, through voluntary negotiations, resolve their disagreements according to the court's ruling. This procedure requires other adjustments to be kept pending in court. The procedure is normally applied to valuable commercial site leaseholds; disputes over ground rent increments for single-family dwellings are usually not taken to court. The political process will decide if a municipality could opt for a full or partial increase in ground rents.

As mentioned earlier, detailed development plans govern what may be built in Swedish towns and cities. This applies both to the intensity and use of building development. Building rights determine land value. If land is privately owned, any increases in land value would accrue to the property owner. If land is held as site leasehold the municipality will charge a ground rent according to the building rights. If there is a change in land use, a new detailed development plan must be adopted by the municipality.

In the site leasehold case, an amendment to the original contract must be made to coordinate any changes in building permission. Under the current law, a lessee who continues with the old use will not be charged for the higher potential value of the land. If the municipality insists on a change of use, it must purchase the lease from the lessee. If the lessee accepts the new use, there will be an increase in the ground rent. An amendment will also be put into the original site contract. Currently, new constructions are rarely the subject of negotiation. Amendments to existing plans and building alterations are more common. These modifications of site leasehold sometimes lead to complex negotiations between the lessor, the lessee and planners.

One advantage of site leasehold is that if the municipality improves public infrastructure (e.g., streets, squares and parks), it can recover the investment costs by requesting lessees to pay a new land rent calculated based on the increased land value. It is generally more difficult to recover money from private landowners, even if arrangements are in place for special charges and development agreements.

Development of Site Leasehold: Past and Present

The original site leasehold legislation established in 1907 was inspired by the City of Stockholm, which applied the legislation immediately. Other Swedish towns and cities showed little or no interest. The second and third largest cities, Göteborg and Malmö, did not begin making more general use of site leasehold until the 1930s and 1940s. A number of medium-sized towns also began using site leasehold in the 1940s, mainly for housing purposes. Despite a wider use of site leasehold in the early 1950s, Stockholm still had two-thirds of all site leaseholds in Sweden. Also, there was extensive discretion concerning the way lease documents were framed, but the Stockholm practice influenced the rest of the country. Gradually, a fairly uniform practice evolved (Westerlind 1965).

Early Growth Period

Initially, site leasehold was a Stockholm phenomenon intended to stimulate owner-occupied housing development. Stockholm also used its extensive land holdings in outlying areas to accomplish its home ownership program. This resulted in the creation of many large garden cities. Gradually, it became clear that the rapid demographic expansion of the city demanded rental, multifamily housing construction. As a result, the use of site leasehold for rental housing and commercial development expanded rapidly from the 1930s onwards in outlying urban areas. Site leasehold for industrial purposes, however, started much later than site leasehold for residential development, because for a long time entrepreneurs had free choice between freehold and site leasehold. Owing to difficulties of mortgaging site leaseholds, businesses usually opted for free-hold (Westerlind 1965). Site leasehold, therefore, was used mainly for leasing public land in outlying areas.

After the Second World War, site leasehold for rental housing development became very much a part of housing policy. Site lessees with rental properties were often obliged to accept only tenants referred to them by the Municipal Housing Exchange. Rents also could be controlled (Westerlind 1965). As discussed earlier, the 1953 amendment of the site leasehold legislation elimi-nated rent control, so the creditworthiness of site leaseholds would not be jeopardized.

It was not until the 1940s that Stockholm began granting land in the inner city on site leasehold. Between 1950 and 1975 the city also pursued a very active policy of land purchasing in the central district for purposes of urban renewal and construction of underground railways and traffic arteries.

The assembled land was then granted to developers by site leasehold. The land purchasing policy was vigorously supported by means of expropriation (Sidenbladh 1985).

Beginning mainly as a big city phenomenon, site leasehold gradually spread to smaller communities, especially when the government initiated the great post-war housing construction programs. By 1950 a total of 18,000 site leaseholds had been granted in Sweden, including 85 percent for single-family dwellings and 13 percent for rental blocks. An additional 74,000 site leaseholds were granted between 1950 and 1977. Among these site leases, 87 percent were granted for single-family housing, 7 percent for multifamily housing, and the remainder for commercial and industrial development. Between 1977 and 1995 another 16,000 site leaseholds were granted. Unfortunately, there is no record to show the breakdown of different uses.

In 1995 there were a total of 108,000 site leaseholds. Five years later the number had fallen to 105,000 (SOU 1980; CFD 1995; LMV 1999). The decline following the 1970s could also be reflected by the following figures. During the 1970s 15 percent of all new plots for single-family housing development in Sweden were granted in site leasehold, and 25 percent of all new dwelling units were constructed on site leasehold land. The corresponding figures for the 1980s declined to 2 percent and 10 percent, respectively (SCB 1992). These figures indicated a decrease in the total number of site leasehold granted after a period of rapid growth between 1950 and 1977.

In 2001 roughly 25 of Sweden's 300 municipalities had more than 1,000 site leaseholds each. Site leasehold also occurred, to a notable extent, in another 25 or so municipalities, and to a slight extent in about 50. Yet, site leaseholds in these municipalities seldom exceeded 10–15 percent of the total number of properties (SOU 1980; LMV 1999). The number of site leaseholds in Sweden also can be compared with the total number of properties in urban communities. The estimated total number of freehold properties is 1.8 million, so site leaseholds make up 6 percent of total urban properties (Kalbro and Mattsson 1995).

The City of Stockholm, with 58,000 properties, had 28,000 site leaseholds at the beginning of 2000, or about half of all properties. Stockholm's site leaseholds make up a quarter of the national total. Göteborgin has 10,000 site leaseholds out of 65,000 properties. In Västerås, a medium-sized city, 35 percent (9,000 out of 25,000) of all properties are held by site leasehold. Stockholm, Göteborg and Västerås have the largest numbers of site leaseholds among all municipalities in Sweden (SOU 1990; LMV 1999).

Although proceeds from site leaseholds can be considerable, they account for only a small percentage of total municipal revenues. They amounted to MSEK 1,500 (approximately US$170 million), roughly 5 percent of the total revenues for the City of Stockholm in 1999. Although site leaseholds for single-family dwellings make up more than 80 percent of the total number of grants, they generated only 10 percent of total site leasehold proceeds. The large earnings from site leaseholds came from inner city land and commercial properties in outlying areas (USK 1999).

From 1953 onwards, site leasehold has become very much an instrument for keeping the appreciation of land values in the municipal hands. The original social housing motive from the beginning of the twentieth century also lives on as evidenced by the City of Stockholm's policy on ground rents. Stockholm ground rents for single-family housing sites are discounted by up to 33 percent. The municipality finds it unreasonable to raise ground rents to their full market values in the course of rent adjustments. Yet, the city has decided to scale down the discount on ground rents over a 10-year period (Stockholm City 1999).

Phaseout of Site Leasehold

The main appeal of site leasehold has been to the left, with the social democrats as the biggest supporters. At the beginning of the 1990s, when the Municipality of Västerås elected a nonsocialist majority and began selling site leaseholds for single-family housing development to tenants, the action sparked a widespread political debate. The majority argued that site lessees should be allowed to decide if they wanted the freehold of land. The municipality also wanted to release the capital that was tied up in the land.

The legality of selling site leaseholds was challenged because the municipality was asking tenants to pay only 30 percent of the assessed land value. In relation to the market value of land the discount appeared even larger, because *assessed land value* in Sweden is, at most, 75 percent of market value. The court, however, found that the municipality had not disposed of land improperly, because only a marginal increase in wealth would have been obtained by the government, were the site leaseholds valued as freehold properties. In the course of a few years, 10 percent (1,000 out of 10,000) of the site leaseholds in Västerås were sold at a sizable discount (Mattsson 1998; Stockholm City 1999).

An investigation has shown that the market value of land for single-family housing development increases by 25 percent once the land tenure is converted from site leasehold to freehold (Stockholm City 1999). Thus, the selling price is an important factor in explaining the success of the selloff. The current widespread selling of site leaseholds for single-family housing development is a good example. The state of affairs can be illustrated with announcements culled from the Stockholm Metropolitan Press in November 1999. At the beginning of the 1990s, the Municipality of Nacka tried to sell site leaseholds as freehold rights at their assessed values. Only one site leasehold was sold in the initial year. The municipality is currently contemplating a price reduction.

In Södertälje a decision was made to sell site leaseholds at 65 percent of their assessed values. After four years, less than 100 out of 1,200 site leaseholds were sold. In the Municipality of Upplands-Bro site lessees have been able to acquire their plots freehold for 40 percent of the assessed values. About 27 percent (400 out of 1,500) of site leaseholds have been sold since 1996. The interesting thing is that decisions to sell site leaseholds in Södertälje and Upplands-Bro were made by social democrats, not nonsocialists. In Danderyd, an affluent neighborhood, all site leaseholds were sold for 55 percent of their assessed values.

The City of Stockholm, which was a pioneer in introducing site leasehold, began selling off site leaseholds for single-family housing in 1993. The asking price was 75 percent of the estimated land value, and less than 1 percent (130 out of 25,000) of site leaseholds were sold during 1993. The political majority at that time was nonsocialist. In the second round of the selloff implemented between 1997 and 1998, another 800 site leaseholds were sold at a price averaging just above 50 percent of their assessed values. This time, the social democrats were in power (Mattsson 1998; Stockholm City 1999). In the summer of 1999 the city had a new nonsocialist majority in office. For ideological reasons, city officials decided to sell site leaseholds for single-family housing purposes at an average selling price of below 50 percent of assessed values (Stockholm City 1999). Approximately 15,000 property owners signed up as potential buyers of the freehold of their plots. In 2000, 1,000 purchases were completed.

The remarkable thing is that demand for freehold purchase has risen distinctly since 1997–1998, even though the price reduction has been marginal. Low interest rates, the realization of imminent increases in ground rents and the reduction of rental subsidies may have stimulated interest in buying. The impact of psychological factors can not be excluded: site lessees believe that conditions of sale offered by a nonsocialist government are more favorable than those offered by a social democratic authority.

The City of Stockholm is also selling commercial site leaseholds. City officials are expecting full compensation for the future loss of lease revenue. Consequently, the selloff has been marginal. However, the municipality has ordered its own public agencies currently holding site leaseholds to purchase the freehold of land at full market value. This has resulted in many forced sales.

Municipalities are less interested in retaining site leasehold because they do not want their capital tied up in land. Due to the early-1990s economic crisis, straitened public finance and a slow rate of land value appreciation partly explained why municipalities sold site leaseholds. Neoliberal tendencies also at work were presumably the foremost reason for selling site leaseholds in some municipalities, especially in Stockholm. Although the phaseout of site leasehold is the trend, municipalities do sometimes create new site leaseholds to assist industrialists who are either unwilling to tie up capital in land or financially incapable of raising the initial startup capital for their businesses.

Municipalities rarely repurchase site leaseholds from existing tenants when they have the opportunity, because as an institution site leasehold is barely a century old. Consequently, building development on site leasehold lots is acceptably modern and not yet ripe for redevelopment. Although land may be needed for public purposes, that need is unlikely to coincide with the expiration dates of site leases.

Municipalities may, under exceptional situations, use site leasehold to restrict land use to one specific purpose. For example, the site leasehold for a private daycare center may not be transferred to a different use if the existing operation goes out of business. Only another daycare center can take over the site leasehold. Besides, a municipality may wish to dispose of a historic property. If it does so by site leasehold, the grant would include provisions concerning the conservation and management of the historic building. Nevertheless, other legislation could allow the municipality to accomplish similar land use and conservation purposes.

CONCLUSION

Site leasehold was originally prompted by the consideration of social housing, although land value capture also played a part. The motives changed at the beginning of the 1950s, when capturing land value became the prime objective. That change was underpinned by new legislation, which at the same time did everything possible to sustain the creditworthiness of site leaseholds. Plots were to be developed with modern buildings that could be used as collateral for obtaining mortgage loans. Only the rise in land value was to be retained by municipalities.

Site leasehold creates two problems for municipalities. First, city governments will have capital tied up in land, and will be able to collect ground rents only. Second is the uncertainty surrounding changes in ground rent. The determination of ground rent could be both complex and controversial under current Swedish legislation. In turn, these issues make future leasehold revenues hard to predict. Like private individuals, municipalities also risk involvement in expensive, time-consuming court battles. However, this rarely happens with ground rents for single-family dwellings, because rental increases are usually too small for site lessees to justify the cost of taking legal action if disputes arise. On the other hand, ground rent adjustments for downtown properties usually involve large sums of money, so site lessees and municipalities are willing to enter expensive judicial proceedings to settle their disagreements.

Two government commissions have recommended changing ground rent computations by multiplying the market value of land by a fixed interest rate. This proposal has not yet produced new legislation, but a bill may be presented to the Riksdag in the near future.

Site leasehold, therefore, has been used in Sweden as a means of ensuring that land value increments accrue to the public lessor. It has also been prompted by the motive of housing policy. Rarely has it been used to influence urban development. Instead, other tools have been employed to facilitate city planning and provide citizens with subsidized housing loans under prescribed circumstances.

A number of Swedish municipalities have been phasing out site leasehold since the 1990s for both fiscal and ideological reasons. By selling site leaseholds to lessees, these municipalities can release tied-up capital. The phaseout is also prompted by neoliberal persuasions.

REFERENCES

Améen, L. 1964. *Stadsbebyggelse och domänstruktur.* Lund, Sweden.

Boverket. 1991. *Studie av markvillkoret och dess tillämpning.* Karlskrona: Boverket.

CFD. 1995. *Fastigheter i Sverige—Registrerade och avregistrerade enheter.* Gävle: Centralnämnden för fastighetsdata.

Kalbro, T. and H. Mattsson. 1995. *Urban land and property market in Sweden.* London: UCL Press.

KTH and LMV. 1998. *Swedish land and cadastral legislation* (Translation of Swedish Acts). Stockholm: KTH fastighetsvetenskap.

LMV. 1999. *Antal levande registerenheter i fastighetsdatasystemet 1999-07-01.* Gävle: Lantmäteriverket.

Mattsson, H. 1998. The Swedish system of landownership and use. In *Ten paradigms of market economies and land systems,* Cho, L. J. and Kim, Y. H., eds. South Korea: Korea Research Institute for Human Settlements.

NJA. 1986. Nytt juridiskt arkiv. Case from the Supreme Court in Sweden.

Prawitz, G. 1954. *Tomter och Stadsägor—om fastighetsindelning i Sveriges städer, 2nd ed.* Stockholm.

SCB. 1992. *Bostads och byggnadsstatistisk årsbok.* Stockholm: Statistiska Centralbyrån.

Sidenbladh, G. 1981. *Planering för Stockholm 1923–1958.* Stockholm.

———. 1985. *Norrmalm förnyat 1951–1981.* Stockholm.

Smith, N. 1979. Towards a theory of gentrification: A back to the city movement by capital, not people. *Journal of American Planning Association* 45:538–548.

SOU. 1952. *Lagberedningens förslag till ny lagstiftning om tomträtt m.m,* Statens Offentliga Utredningar, 1952:28. Sweden.

———. 1980. *Tomträtt.* Statens Offentliga Utredningar, 1980:49. Sweden.

———. 1990. *Tomträttsavgäld.* Statens Offentliga Utredningar, 1990:23. Sweden.

Stockholm City. 1999. *Översyn av friköpspriser för småhustomträtter mm.* Tjänsteutlåtande från Stockholm stads gatu-och fastighetskontoret, 1 March 1999. Stockholm.

USK. 1999. *Statistisk årsbok för Stockholm 1999,* Stockholm utrednings-och statistikkontor. Stockholm.

Vedung, E. 1993. *Statens markpolitik, kommunerna och historiens ironi.* Stockholm.

Westerlind, P. 1965. *Studier över tomrättsinstitutet.* Stockholm.

PUBLIC LAND LEASING IN FINLAND

5

Pekka V. Virtanen

This chapter discusses the Finnish public leasehold system, where land leases for housing, business and industry in the urban areas are most important. Public land leasing is operated mostly at the municipal level. State authorities and the church play only a minor role in public leasehold. This chapter has three sections. The first section provides the background information concerning the land tenure arrangements and urban land policy in Finland. The second section describes the characteristics of the Finnish public leasehold system. The final section evaluates the experience in leasing urban land.

BACKGROUND

Finland is a parliamentary democracy with multiple political parties. Although there is a rightist majority in the Parliament, the largest single party is the social democrats. Members of this party occupy 51 of the 200 seats in the Parliament. Different agencies of the national government are normally coalitions of several parties.

Finland was part of Sweden until 1809. From then until 1917, when it became independent, it was an autonomous Grand Duchy of Russia, with its own language, legislature and government. It has been a member of the European Union since 1995.

Finland is sparsely populated (about 5.1 million) and a land area of 305,000 square kilometers, and an average density of only 16 persons per square kilometer. Urban districts occupy only 1 percent of the total land area. Finland is

I received valuable information from representatives of Real Estate Departments in five cities. They are Jussi Eerolainen of Espoo; Kauko Juhamäki of Mikkeli; Tom Masalin of Kotka; Kaija Puhakka of Oulu and Matti Rytkölä of Helsinki. I also received useful information about leasing activities from state authorities or state-owned firms. I would especially like to thank Merja Julin of the Kapiteeli; Antero Luhtio of the Forests and Parks Service; Eino Piri of the Finnish Forest Research Institute and Erkki Vaalasranta of the State Real Property Agency.

divided into five "normal" provinces plus one semi-autonomous area *(Ahve-nanmaa)*. There are 448 independent municipalities, and 109 of them are called towns. All municipalities have the same power. Most of them are rather small, and three-quarters of them have less than 10,000 inhabitants. These small municipalities usually do not have their own planners or real estate officials.

In Finland, as in other Nordic countries (Sweden, Norway and Denmark), municipalities occupy a central position in the country's administrative system. The position is accentuated by the ability to levy municipal income and property taxes. Municipalities also play a key role in land use planning and urban land policy.

Planning in Finland consists of three different statutory plans: a regional physical plan for each province, composed of a group of municipalities; a master plan for each municipality; and detailed town plans for dense urban development. Municipalities have the monopoly power over planning. They can also influence the making of regional physical plans because municipalities nominate provincial governments that formulate and approve regional plans. For master and detailed town plans, municipalities have the power to design and approve these plans themselves.

Land Ownership

At the beginning of the 1990s, 60 percent of land in Finland was privately owned. If we include ownership of wood processing companies partly owned by the state, the percentage of private ownership would increase to 68 percent. The state owned 29 percent of all land and municipalities possessed 2 percent. The main part of the state's possession consisted of the wilderness in northern Finland (Virtanen 1995). The remaining 1 percent of land belonged to the church.

Municipal land ownership typically is more prominent in towns than in rural areas, although there are marked differences between municipalities. For example, the City of Helsinki owns 68 percent of all land within its boundaries. Due to extensive municipal land ownership in towns, public land leasing is conducted mainly in urban areas.

Private land ownership in Finland is well protected. According to the 1919 Constitution (renewed in 2000), any expropriation of private property for public purposes must be based on law, and compensation must be paid in full (that is, the property's market value). If there is no compensation or the compensation is below market value, a municipality must justify its action according to the special legal procedures regulated by the Constitution.

Land ownership has a special sentimental value in the mind of the Finnish population. Many found public leasehold less appealing than freehold, even though leasehold interests are well protected. However, this attitude toward land has changed. Some citizens believe in "socially bounded land ownership," which means that land, as a special and unique resource, must first serve the community's interests; the interests of private landowners are secondary. In addition, this attitude toward land ownership encourages the use of public leasehold.

The legal basis for this attitude was first founded in the 1920 Neighborhood Act *(Laki eräistä naapuruussuhteista)*. This act forbids landowners to use land in any way that would harm their neighbors. Since then, the freedom to use one's land has been limited by an increasing number of laws, which are often related to the prevention of environmental hazards. Despite disagreements among legislators in the Parliament, this trend continues because these land use regulations protect the majority's interests.

Public leasehold is very popular in many towns, due to a local tradition. According to custom, in older towns where public land ownership arose from the Crown's past land donation, local officials could lease land to private parties only. For municipalities that do not own land or have expertise in managing public leasehold, selling land prevails over leasing.

Urban Land Policy

Urban land policy in Finland is, for the most part, based on some general goals and guidelines associated with land use planning and environmental preservation. At the national level several laws address these concerns: the Neighborhood Act *(Naapuruussuhdelaki)*, Land Use and Building Act *(Maankäyttö- ja rakennuslaki)*, Nature Protection Act *(Luonnonsuojelulaki)*, Building Protection Act *(Rakennussuojelulaki)*, Soil Act *(Maa-aineslaki)*, Antiquities Act *(Muinaismuistolaki)*, Wilderness Act *(Erämaalaki)*, Water Act *(Vesilaki)*, and Waterfalls Protection Act *(Koskiensuojelulaki)*.

There are also tax laws related to land policy. In most cases, the main purpose of these laws is to empower the state and municipalities to collect tax revenues. For instance, the 1992 Real Estate Tax Act *(Tuloverolaki)* enabled municipalities to impose an annual tax on most building sites and improvements. An amendment to that act in 1999 also allowed municipalities to levy a special penalty tax on vacant lots.

Another tax legislation with a clear connection to land policy is the 1992 Income Tax Act, including rules about the taxation of sales profits. An amendment in 1999 allowed a special exemption when land was sold to municipalities between November 15, 1999 and June 30, 2000. The goal was to encourage landowners to sell land to municipalities for urban development.

In addition, the national government had designed special programs to protect the environment, including the Development Program for National Parks and Nature Parks, the Swamp Protection Program, the Bird Sanctuary Program, the Ridge Protection Program, the Leafy Grove Protection Program, the Shore Protection Program, the Protection Program for Old Forests and the Protection Program for Nationally Valuable Landscape Areas. These special programs have little connection with public leasehold. Although there is no restriction on using land leasing for environmental protection, the national government has relied mainly on special programs and laws to accomplish the objective. At least at the national level, public leasehold has never been an important instrument for environmental protection.

Municipalities may have their own land policy goals shaped mainly by local traditions. These objectives may not be stated explicitly in official documents.

Only a minority of municipalities have prepared and approved their own land policy programs. Some common goals are to facilitate land use planning; stabilize land prices; recapture increased land values; prevent land speculation; and promote industrial development (Imatran kaupunki 1987; Lappeenrannan kaupunki 1988; Porin kaupunki 1999). How public leasehold helps municipalities achieve these policy goals will be discussed later.

PUBLIC LAND LEASING IN FINLAND

Finnish towns established before 1906 (35 in total) received donated land from the former sovereigns. Currently, these townships account for approximately one-third of all towns in Finland. The donations included built-up areas and vacated land. The vacated land could either be used as pastures or kitchen gardens or reserved for future construction. Sale of the donated land was prohibited. Private entities could only lease the right to use land (dominium utile) on payment of an annual land rent.

The restriction on selling urban land was first partially removed in 1943. The government passed a law that allowed the sale of land located outside the town's planning areas. In 1962 a second law was passed that extended the municipalities' right to sell land in all areas (Jokiperä 1988).

As mentioned earlier, residents in old towns have accepted public land leasing as a normal practice because of its long tradition. The attitude toward public leasehold in rural areas and new towns, however, is different. In new towns, where municipalities never received land donations, people often prefer owning land to leasing.

In the rural areas, special laws allowed lessees to buy their leasehold interest with the help of the government. In 1962 some lessees in urban areas sought similar rights. The Parliament immediately passed the Act on the Organizing of Leased Land in Towns (Laki vuokra-alueiden järjestelystä kaupungeissa ja kauppaloissa) to extend the term of all urban leases for another 50 years. The justification was that most leased land sites were in municipalities where leasing had been the tradition. If a government lessor refused to extend the lease term, a lessee would have the right to buy out the leased land rights. If lessee and lessor could not agree on the renewed land rent, the court would determine the amount according to the local rent level (Virtanen and Halme 1983).

The State's Role in Public Leasehold

As stated earlier, the state owns approximately 29 percent of all land in Finland. Nearly all of that is wilderness located in northern Finland.[1] The alienation of state-owned land is tightly regulated by the Act on the Right to Alienate State Owned Land and Income Bringing Rights (Laki oikeudesta luovuttaa valtion

---

[1] The largest manager of state-owned rural land is the Forest and Park Service (Metsähallitus). It possesses about nine million hectares of land plus three million hectares of water area. The Forest and Park Service does not operate in urban areas. This information was received in a letter to the author, from Antero Luhtio, director of the Forests and Parks Service, on December 7, 1999.

maaomaisuutta ja tuloatuottavia oikeuksia) that deals with selling and leasing public land. One principle is that the state can only sell or lease public land at market value, the only exception being the sale of land to municipalities at favorable terms. In addition the Wilderness Act *(Erämaalaki)* forbids selling or leasing land inside special wilderness areas that amount to 1.3 million hectares of land.

The state has leased out approximately 14,000 land sites, about 4,000 of which are for building purposes. A small number of these leased building lots are for housing while the majority are for recreational purposes. The annual income generated from leasing these properties was, in 1998, about 15 million Finnish markka (FMK), equivalent to US$2.2 million.[2, 3]

The State Real Property Agency *(Valtion Kiinteistölaitos)* is the primary organization that manages all state-owned urban properties. Its main task is to lease the facilities to different agencies within the government, including, for example, public universities and civil service departments. In leasing land to public universities, negotiation between the contracting parties will determine the amount of land rent. Land leased to universities for student housing is normally granted at zero land rent.[4]

In 1999 the National Government established a real estate investment company known as *Kapiteeli*. Although the company is founded by the state it is legally a private entity. Its tasks are to own, develop, sell or lease state-owned properties not needed for public purposes. The company has received improved and unimproved properties from various state agencies as capital contributions.[5]

Most state authorities are not interested in leasing. For instance, the Kapiteeli has been trying to get rid of its leasehold sites by selling them at favorable prices. The only exception is the Forest and Park Service, which is still actively marketing new lots for recreational purposes in rural areas, and gives its customers the option to either lease or buy land. One reason state authorities prefer selling land to leasing land is that the latter requires continuous monitoring and administration of land rent collection.

Leasehold Legislation

Before the Second World War there was no legislation for public leasehold in Finland (Hallituksen Esitys 1965). Because all urban land belonged to the towns, leasing encountered no challenges. After 1926 a new law, the Act on the Changing of Municipal Division *(Laki kunnallisen jaoituksen muuttamisesta,* no. 180/1925) allowed the incorporation of privately owned land into urban

---

[2] This information is from Antero Luhtio (see footnote 1) and from Eino Piri, director of the National Forest Research Institute *(Metsäntutkimuslaitos)* in a letter to the author dated December 2, 1999.

[3] The exchange rate is US$1 = FMK 6.85.

[4] The information was gathered from personal interviews with Erkki Vaalasranta, division head of the State Real Property Agency, December 1999 and May 2000.

[5] This information is from Merja Julin, Research and Development Manager, Kapiteeli, in a letter to the author dated December 3 and 10, 1999.

municipalities. Consequently, starting from the 1930s the amount of private land in urban areas increased rapidly. During this period many rural munici-palities developed into towns. As land tenure arrangements became complex and the leasing of private land began, new legislation was deemed necessary.

After the Second World War the government started working on a new leasehold legislation. Not until 1966 did the government enact the new Lease-hold Act *(Maanvukralaki*, no. 258/1966). According to the explanations of this law, land uses in Finland would be based mainly on the freehold in land. However, legislators should also treat leasehold as a useful alternative to add flexibility and options to land markets.

At present, the Leasehold Act governs all land leases. It prescribes the dura-tion of different types of land contracts. In general, lease terms for housing sites range from 30 to 100 years. The maximum lease term for farmland with buildings is 15 years. For unimproved agricultural land the maximum term is only 10 years. Lease terms for industrial land, holiday camps and antenna sites are determined by negotiation.

The Leasehold Act contains no restriction on the timing of development. Yet, municipalities usually incorporate a special condition in leases that requires lessees to complete construction within a specified period. If a lessee fails to fulfill this condition, the municipality may cancel the land contract. The municipality will have the right to take back land and lease it to another party. In some cities, government lessors may also impose a penalty on lessees. The two purposes of this lease condition are to encourage timely land development and prevent land speculation.

Land Rent

Negotiation between the lessor and lessee determines the rent. There is no legal restriction on the maximum rent, but the law contains a section about the arbi-tration of rents and other rental terms to protect the interests of both lessees and lessors. Although the law does not prohibit total or partial prepayment of rent at the beginning of the lease, lessees seldom make such a prepayment to municipalities (Kartio 1983).

The Leasehold Act permits periodical adjustments of land rents. These adjustments must be made according to the criteria specified in land leases. In practice, rental adjustments normally are tied to the living cost index (LCI) in Finland. In the past, there were disputes over the applicability of index clauses to rental adjustments. In 1968 the Parliament enacted a law that prohibited officials from using index clauses in all land contracts. The government soon realized that this legislation was detrimental to housing construction. Subse-quently, the ban on the use of index clauses was repealed in respect to leasehold contracts (Wirilander 1981; Kartio 1983).

The prevailing index legislation allows the use of index clauses in land leases with terms longer than 10 years. Since the mid-1990s it also makes pos-sible rental adjustments based on indexes other than the LCI. If, for instance, there is a reliable index of land prices, it can be used as a basis for increasing land rents. Currently, this alternate method is used for some leases in Helsinki

(Suomen Kuntaliitto 1997).[6] The amendment of index legislation has given municipalities a better chance to recapture the land value increments.

In most cases, lessees pay their land rents diligently. Financial losses caused by a lessee's default in land rent payment are minimal. For example, in Helsinki the share of unpaid land rents was only 0.07 percent in 1999 (Helsingin kiinteistövirasto 2000).[7] Low land rents cannot explain this outcome. Land rents are moderate but not insignificant. The Real Estate Department and the Building Inspection Department have been enforcing lease conditions scrupulously.

Public agencies must pay an internal land rent to the proper government for using public land. The use of internal rent is a new phenomenon whose application began in the mid-1990s. In 1999, 60 percent of the cities with more than 50,000 residents collected internal land rents, and the rest of the large municipalities have planned to do so in the future. The goal of implementing internal land rents is to enhance land use efficiency in the public sector. The internal land rents are designed to help public agencies recognize land costs of their operations; reduce the amount of idle land; encourage agencies to save money by "optimizing" land allocation; and direct land costs to appropriate users (Leväinen 1999).

Lease Termination and Renewal

The Leasehold Act contains provisions that make the cancellation of leasehold agreements difficult. A lessor has the right to cancel a land contract only if a lessee fails to pay rent; neglects land maintenance; uses the property in a manner contrary to the contractual agreements; or does not develop the land within the specified period. If the government has to terminate leasehold agreements due to compelling public interests, it can either negotiate with the lessee for a transfer of land rights or use compulsory purchase. Rules that govern compulsory purchase are included in the Land Use and Building Act *(Maankäyttö- ja rakennuslaki)*. Compulsory purchase is extremely rare in Finland. The municipal officials interviewed could not remember any compulsory purchase of leasehold rights in recent years. Rather, lease terminations are usually conducted through negotiation. Even the number of negotiated purchases is small. The lessee has the right to cancel the contract if the possibility of using the leased area has diminished (if, for example, the natural conditions have changed).

When a lease expires, the lessee may renew the land contract. If the contract is not renewed the lessor will compensate the lessee for improvements made to the land. In a model contract designed by the Finnish Association of Local and Regional Authorities (FALRA), lessees are given the right to renew their contracts when housing continues to be the land use. On the contrary, industrial leases are not renewed automatically, though the option is available (Suomen Kuntaliitto 1997).

---

[6] The information is based on written and oral communications with Matti Rytköla, division head of the Real Estate Department of Helsinki City, in November 1999 and June 2000.

[7] I obtained similar information from an interview with Kauko Juhamäki, city surveyor of Mikkeli, in 2000.

Compensation and Transferability

The law and special lease agreements govern the compensation for leasehold improvements. The rule is that a lessor must pay compensation to the lessee for the improvements. In general, compensation is set at 60–70 percent of the "technical value" of the building, which takes depreciation into account. For industrial estates, compensation will be available only if the contracting parties have specified this right in the lease. FALRA's model contract has no provision for compensation for leasehold improvements. If there is no special agreement in advance, the lessee must demolish existing buildings and structures from the site when the lease expires (Suomen Kuntaliitto 1997).

The leasing of industrial land differs from residential land because industrial buildings usually are built for special purposes. Valuation of these unique buildings can be arbitrary, though not impossible, because they have no unequivocal market value. Besides, many industrial premises in Finland are rarely useful beyond their land contracts. In special cases the lessor agrees to pay the lessee compensation for improvements on industrial land. The method of determining the amount of compensation will be specified in the lease on a case-by-case basis.

Lessees have the right to transfer their contracts. They can also use their leasehold rights as collateral to secure a mortgage loan. According to the Basic Code of Land Laws (*maakaari*), lessees must register their land contracts in court to secure their leasehold rights.

Popularity of Public Leasehold

Although public leasehold is popular in numerous municipalities, freehold is also employed to dispose of public land. On one hand, selling land is common in small rural municipalities where land allocation relies on the private land market. On the other hand, rapidly growing large and medium cities are generally active in public land leasing. Land values in these cities are higher. These cities have competent staff for the acquisition, disposal and appraisal of land. Their key personnel usually are well-trained real estate surveyors. Municipalities that do not use leasing usually lack the necessary expertise in land management.

In most municipalities, ideology does not play a role in public land leasing. Rather, leasing is treated as a policy instrument for accomplishing certain public goals, such as promoting affordable housing, creating employment and capturing increased land values. The use of public leasehold does not depend on the political structure of the city. It is widely used in very conservative cities, like Helsinki, as well as in leftist urban neighborhoods, like Kotka. The popularity of public leasehold is due in part to a local tradition, and in part to positive experiences with this land tenure system. Some urban municipalities offer builders the option to either buy or lease land. According to the information gathered from the author's interviews with public officials, only a few builders have chosen the option to buy. This may indicate that lessees feel secure about leasehold rights. They also realize that leasing requires a lower initial capital investment than the investment in buying land.

This author is aware of no statistics on the amount of leased building lots in Finland. Kartio (1983) found that in 1975 Finland had 85 towns and leased out more than 40,000 lots during that time. The 400 rural municipalities leased only 3,000 lots at the same time. Holopainen (1999) estimated that the total number of leased land sites in 1998 was 48,900.

In his study on the land policy of 94 towns between 1986 and 1991, Eerolainen (1992, 10–11) found that municipalities leased more housing lots than it sold. The number of leased sites for single-family houses was 13,161, whereas municipalities sold 12,639 land lots to private entities. The leased lands generated 13.4 million square meters of total floor areas. Lands that were sold created 12.4 million square meters.

In 1998 municipalities generated from leasing public land FMK 1.135 billion (US$190 million) of rental revenues. Income from land sales was only FMK 636 million, and 67 million of that income came from the conversion of leased lots into freehold lands. Because leasing experiences among municipalities are diverse, the above information cannot be generalized for all cities. Hence, it would be useful to examine the experience of the case of Helsinki.

Land Leasing in Helsinki

Helsinki is the capital of Finland and its largest city. In 1999 the city had 550,000 inhabitants. It received 24 square kilometers of land in 1550 from the Swedish King, and later the city bought additional land. At present, Helsinki owns 68 percent (127 square kilometers) of all land within its borders, and possesses 78 square kilometers of land in other municipalities. It has a long tradition as a city with strong land policy. Leasing has been the main method of conveying land to developers. Yet, the city government also has sold land recently.

Helsingin kiinteistövirasto (2000) estimated that the total number of lease contracts in Helsinki was about 7,000 in 1999. Revenues generated from leasing land for the same year was FMK 734 million, of which 244 million was from leasing land to the state and municipal agencies. The latter portion of the lease revenues accounted for 5 percent of total tax revenues in Helsinki. Income from selling commercial land was FMK 370 million.[8]

Lease terms in Helsinki vary depending on land uses. For housing lots, lease terms range from 50 to 60 years. Since 1995 the city has also been using the 100-year term. Not only does the government revise land rents annually based on the LCI, but it also makes rental adjustments according to real increases in land value. For instance, the government revises land rents for all 100-year leases every 30 years, to reflect changes in the market value of land. For commercial sites the common lease term is 50 years; for industrial land the terms range from 20 to 30 years. Land rent adjustments for these two types of leases are conducted every year only.

---

[8] Information related to land leasing in Helsinki is mostly from Matti Rytkölä, the former division head of the Real Estate Department of Helsinki City in 1999 and 2000. Other sources will be indicated separately.

Land rents for the best housing sites, which are leased through public auctions, are set at 4 percent of the market value of land. This type of land accounts for less than 1 percent of all housing sites. For housing sites leased through negotiation, rents are set at 4 percent of the "moderate land value," about 5–10 percent below market value. If the land site is leased for subsidized housing, the municipality will negotiate a land rent equal to 4 percent of an estimated land value, 20 percent lower than the market value of land. Land contracts that charge market land rents account for 40 percent of all leases. The majority of these contracts are for commercial and industrial purposes. Land rents for commercial and industrial sites are calculated at 5 percent of their market values (Helsingin kaupunki 1994).

In Helsinki some lessees pay nominal or zero rent. These lessees are non-profit organizations that provide public services or charitable functions to the community. The city recently sought to recognize these subsidized land rents as government expenditures. In the budget these rents were treated as expenses for the Social Welfare Department and as potential returns on leasing for the Real Estate Department. This policy change has no impact on the balance of the government budget or the allocation of land for public uses. The only difference is that political leaders and nonprofit organizations can now recognize the true costs of subsidized land rents.

The Real Estate Department of Helsinki reports its activities to the public annually. The annual report has been written in three different languages, Finnish, Swedish and English. One function of the annual reporting is to make the operations of the department transparent to the public.

Because the number of willing lessees in Helsinki is larger than the number of sites available for leasing, the local government needs some systematic methods to assign land to private entities. For instance, the government leases land sites for single-family houses according to a point system based on the potential lessees' family size and wealth. Sites for apartment or housing complexes are normally leased at rents negotiated between developers and the Real Estate Department. The very best or special sites are sold or leased through public auction. The leasing or selling based on bidding does not concern larger areas because the city wants to avoid development that may lead to segregation. Unlike other cities, Helsinki does not offer lessees the option to buy the fee simple of land. There has been no political pressure toward the conversion of public leasehold into freehold.

EVALUATION OF PUBLIC LEASEHOLD IN FINLAND

In Finland the main goal of leasing public land is not to maximize lease revenues. Rather, it is to promote municipal development and public housing. Public land leasing plays a minor role in environmental conservation and land reservation for public purposes. Table 1 summarizes the advantages and disadvantages of public leasehold that may be founded in some Finn-

TABLE 1

THE PROS AND CONS OF PUBLIC LEASEHOLD

For Municipalities	For Lessees
Pros	
Municipalities may be able to recapture a portion of the unearned land value increments by adjusting land rents regularly.	Developers may not need to raise huge initial investment capital to buy land for real estate development.
Public leasehold may restrain rises in land prices and thus keep housing affordable to the population.	Leasing may reduce property tax liability.
Public leasehold may discourage land speculation.	
Leasing may generate a stable stream of rental revenues for municipalities.	
Leasing may allow the government to repossess land for redevelopment after leases expire.	
Cons	
Lessees may neglect the maintenance of leasehold improvements when the lease term is approaching its expiration.	Lessees may lose their properties when leases expire.
	Contract may include irksome conditions.
Administering public leasehold requires government lessors to have a high level of integrity and land management expertise. Small municipalities usually do not have the political autonomy and experienced staff to manage public leasehold.	Leasehold may not give lessees the same psychological satisfaction as freehold.
	Credit worthiness of expiring leasehold rights may be less than freehold.
Income accumulation is slow if the prepayment of annual land rents is not used.	Land rent will change periodically and this increases uncertainty.
	Lessees may not profit from increments in land value.

Source: Compiled by the author

ish municipalities. These pros and cons are discussed from both lessees' and municipalities' perspectives.

The foremost advantage of public leasehold for lessees is that the initial investment capital needed for land development is smaller if private individuals lease rather than buy land (Archer 1974). Housing loans granted by the Finnish credit institutions cover about 70 percent of the transacting price of the property. Potential homebuyers must pay the remaining 30 percent as down payment for their purchases. Many families in Finland may not have sufficient money to make the downpayment. Leasing the land allows homebuyers to lower their initial downpayment. More important, if a government lessor uses a discounted market value of land to set annual land rents, leasing could give lessees a real saving in the total costs of land and housing development.

In Finland land speculators appear uninterested in leasehold properties. Leases often include a clause that requires lessees to complete land development within a specified period. As mentioned earlier, municipalities may cancel the land contracts or impose a penalty on lessees, if land is left idle.

Table 1 indicates that public leasehold has more pros than cons for munici-palities, whereas the situation for lessees is the opposite. This may not be true, because leasehold interests in Finland are well protected. The state and local governments have taken important steps to minimize problems associated with tenure insecurity (discussed below). Both lessees and lessors in many munici-palities appear to be satisfied with public leasehold. As stated earlier, some municipalities have offered lessees the option to convert their leasehold rights into freehold; however, few lessees have accepted the offer.

Security of Land Tenure

To deal with the perceived insecurity of public leasehold, municipalities have taken three actions. First, lessees are allowed to renew their contracts before expiration. Although the Leasehold Act says nothing about the lessees' right to renew their contracts, FALRA has incorporated this right into its model contract for land leased for the development of single-family houses and flats. The model contract for industrial land, however, does not include the right to renew. The incorporation of this right will depend on the negotiation between the contracting parties on a case-by-case basis. Second, municipalities also grant perpetual leases to private entities. Third, as discussed earlier, the Leasehold Act prohibits any arbitrary termination of land contracts by the government. These actions have been able to reduce lessees' fear of losing their properties at the end of the lease term. It has also minimized problems associated with the negligence of building maintenance when leases are expiring.

The Leasehold Act also protects the lessor's rights against damage or abuse of the leasehold property. The lessor may cancel a land contract if a lessee contaminates the soil or uses the land in a way disallowed in the contract or by law. The Leasehold Act allows the lessor to seek compensation if damages are made to the leased land.

Compensation for leasehold improvements at lease expiration can also enhance tenure security (Douglas 1976). Again, FALRA has recommended, in its model land contract for housing lots, that compensation for leasehold improvements should be equal to 60 percent of the estimated value of the buildings. For industrial leases, the recommendation is that no compensation will be paid (Suomen Kuntaliitto 1997).

Psychological Satisfaction

Some people in Finland do not think freehold is important. Based on this author's experience as a city surveyor in Lauritsala and interviews of several municipal real estate officers, both landowners and lessees are satisfied with public leasehold. As described earlier, when municipalities have given lessees the option to buy their land, lessees have not been keen to exercise that option.

One way to lessen the psychological disadvantage of public leasehold is to grant lessees the right to sell and bequest their leasehold interest and improve-ments to other entities (Douglas 1976). If these rights do not exist, lessees are bound to the land. It would be unacceptable in today's society where people often move from one place to another because of employment. Free transfer of leasehold rights has been secured in the Leasehold Act. Lessees can sell, donate or leave as inheritance their leased land rights and the buildings to other parties.

The question of lessees' right to buy their leased land is not covered in legislation. FALRA's model contract reserves the possibility of inserting a buyout clause. If there is a buyout clause it may allow the lessee to buy the leased land after the development is completed. The lessor will fix the price. The clause also limits the period within which the buyout option is available. There is a vast difference between municipalities in the use of the buyout option; in Helsinki the option does not exist. In theory, the buyout option could reduce the significance of public leasehold if the prevailing social or political attitudes change to favor freehold. So far, such a situation does not emerge.

Potential Rent Increases

Adjustments to land rents should not become a problem if the contracting parties can establish a mechanism to ensure the "fairness" of calculating land rents. Certainly, the definition of fair rents varies according to different economic, social and political circumstances. When disputes over the fairness of calculating land rents occur, a third party—preferably the government or a court of justice—should be involved in resolving disagreements. One method of avoiding unnecessary conflict is to stipulate the basis of rent and its subsequent adjustments clearly in the land contract.

In Finland the goal of ensuring fair rents is reached in two ways. First, the Leasehold Act includes statutes about the arbitration of inordinate terms to which parties involved in a disagreement can resort. Second, actions taken by public authorities are open to public scrutiny and criticism in Finland. This in turn may discourage government lessors from imposing unreasonable rents on lessees.

Disputes over the fairness of rents are rare in Finland. Only once in Helsinki have lessees objected to the calculation of land rents. Rents established during the 1989 boom market appeared unreasonably high when land prices fell 40–50 percent between 1990 and 1991. In response to the objection the city government admitted the rents were exorbitant and unfair.

The Leasehold Act protects the municipalities' right to collect land rents from lessees, as specified in land contracts as well. Nonpayment of rent usually is the strongest cause for a cancellation of a land lease. This right could protect public interest in land because the government is collecting land rents on behalf of the community. For municipalities, rental income generated from public land leasing has been an important source of revenue for financing public infrastructure and social services. The law also allows future adjustments of land rents according to the LCI and other relevant indexes.

LESSONS FROM THE FINNISH EXPERIENCE

All countries are unique. Thus, lessons learned from the experience in Finland may not be transferable to other countries. There are, however, common factors that policymakers who are experimenting with public leasehold systems should consider: (1) good leasehold legislation; (2) a competent and noncorrupt administration; (3) clear policy goals supported by enforceable lease conditions; and (4) a complementary planning system.

First, the Leasehold Act in Finland secures the interests of both lessees and lessors. Leasehold rights of lessees are so secure that there is no fear of eviction. FALRA's model contract also provides local authorities with a good uniform basis for practicing land contracting with the flexibility of allowing small variations according to varying circumstances.

Second, one may think public leasehold systems can be unstable because lessees elect the lessor. Under political pressure, a government lessor may favor lessees by converting public leaseholds into freehold rights at bargain prices. Such a phenomenon does not occur in Finland. The national government and municipalities are composed of members from several parties, none of which usually has the majority. This multiple party system in turn creates a system of checks and balances for administering public leasehold.

An effective administration is also needed to collect land rents and reevaluate property values in a timely manner. These requirements demand many resources from local governments. Hence, public leasehold may be unsuitable for small municipalities where financial and human resources are limited.

Third, because one central goal of leasing land is to promote urban development, municipalities include a building clause in all leases. If a lessee does not complete the land development on time, a government lessor can cancel the contract and impose a penalty. Local governments have enforced this lease condition rigorously. They grant an extension for completion time only if the lessee has legitimate reasons.

Another objective of leasing public land in Finland is to ensure housing affordability. The option to lease land lightens the financial burden of raising the initial downpayment for housing consumption. In some cases, municipalities use discretionary prices or rents in leasing public land to lower the cost of housing development.

Fourth and finally, conflicts do not emerge from the use of both lease conditions and regulation to control land use in Finland. Statutory land use plans always have priority over contractual agreements stated in the leases. The Building Control Authority will ensure all building projects follow the regulations of the land use plan. In fact, the existence of land use plans in Finland eases the implementation of its public leasehold system. The lessee and lessor do not have to negotiate lease conditions for governing the use of the leased land. Rather, they can just refer to the existing land use plans legislated and enforced by the municipality. Contract negotiation could have been complicated had the statutory land use plans not existed.

REFERENCES

Archer, R. W. 1974. The leasehold system of urban development: Land tenure, decision making and the land market in urban development and land use. *Regional Studies* 8:225–238.

Douglas, Roy. 1976. *Land, people and politics: A history of the land question in the United Kingdom, 1878–1952.* London: Allison and Busby.

Eerolainen, Jussi. 1992. *Kaupunkien maapolitiikka vuosina, 1986–1991* (Land policy in towns 1986–1991). Helsinki: Suomen Kaupunkiliitto.

Hallituksen Esitys. 1965. Maanvuokralainsäädännön uudistaminen, vp. no. 126 (Government bill for the New Leasehold Act).

Helsingin kaupunki (City of Helsinki). 1994. *Alennukset maan, kiinteistöjen ja huonetilojen vuokrauksissa,* A18/1994 (Discounts in the leasing of land, real estate and apartments). Helsinki: Kaupunginkanslian julkaisusarja.

Helsingin kiinteistövirasto (Helsinki City Real Estate Department). 2000. *Toimintavuosi 1999 (Annual report 1999).* Helsinki.

Holopainen, Matti. 1999. *Kiinteistö- ja mittaustoimen tilastot vuodelta 1998* (Statistics on surveying and real estate administration in Finnish towns in 1998). Helsinki: Suomen Kuntaliitto.

Imatran kaupunki (City of Imatra). 1987. *Maapoliittinen ohjelma 1987* (Land policy program 1987). Imatra, Finland.

Jokiperä, Hannu. 1988. *Kaupunkien lahjoitusmaat ja niiden käyttö 1900-luvulla* (Donated lands in towns and their use in the 1900s). Institute of Real Estate publication, no. B55. Espoo, Finland: Helsinki University of Technology.

Kartio, Leena. 1983. *Asuntoalueen vuokra* (Lease of housing land). Vammala: Suomen Lakimiesliiton Kustannus Oy.

Laki kunnallisen jaoituksen muuttamisesta (Act on the redistribution of local authority areas), 1925.

Lappeenrannan kaupunki *(City of Lappeenranta).* 1988. *Maapoliittinen ohjelma 1988* (Land policy program 1988). Lappeenranta, Finland.

Leväinen, Kari. 1999. *Sisäisen maanvuokran perusteet* (Foundations of the internal leasehold: A case from the City of Espoo). Institute of Real Estate publication, no. B88. Espoo. Finland: Helsinki University of Technology.

Porin kaupunki (City of Pori). 1999. *Maapoliittinen ohjelma 2004* (Land policy program 2004). Pori, Finland.

Suomen Kuntaliitto (The Association of Finnish Local and Regional Authorities). 1997. *Kiinteistökauppa, Maanvuokra; sopimusmallit 1997* (Model Agreements for Selling and Leasing Land 1997). Helsinki.

Virtanen, P. V. and P. Halme. 1983. *Land reforms in Finland.* Helsinki: Ministry of the Environment.

Virtanen, P. V. 1995. *Maankäytön perusteista* (Principles of Land Use). Helsinki: Otatieto.

Wirilander, Juhani. 1981. *Maanvuokraoikeus* (Leasehold Legislation). Vammala: Suomen Lakimiesliiton Kustannus Oy.

THE LAND OF LEASEHOLDS

6

ISRAEL'S EXTENSIVE PUBLIC LAND OWNERSHIP IN AN ERA OF PRIVATIZATION

Rachelle Alterman

Israel is known to many as The Holy Land. Those interested in land policy may well also call it "Leaseholds Land." Today it is the only democratic, advanced-economy country where state or quasi-state agencies own the vast majority of the land area, and where government leaseholds predominate the land system. An estimated 93 percent of the country's total land area is owned by the state or by quasi-state agencies.[1] (Here and throughout this chapter, *Israel proper* is referred to without the occupied areas of the West Bank and Gaza.) Quantitatively, this percentage of nationally owned land is the largest amount in any nation, outside a few remaining communist countries and city-states such as Singapore and (formerly) Hong Kong. Most formerly communist countries are in the process of privatizing the major part of their publicly owned land (Bonneville 1996; Limonov and Renard 1995; Renard and Acosta 1993; Reiner and Strong 1995). In advanced-economy countries public land usually is allocated for distinctly public purposes. Leasing out public land for private development is the exception not the rule (see for example, Gordon 1997; Kalbro and Mattsson 1995; Needham, Koenders and Kruijt 1993).

This chapter analyzes the Israeli land policy system as it has evolved to its present stage. In view of the breadth of the topic, discussion in this chapter is restricted to *urban* land policy; the currently highly complicated and contentious issues regarding Israel's rural land policy will not be discussed. This chapter's purpose is to view Israel as a unique opportunity to study a land system where public leaseholds are the main form of tenure for the majority of the country's residents. It will be argued that Israel's overwhelmingly large public leasehold system has resulted in special policies tailored to accommodate it to the private market. This has been done incrementally rather than

---

[1] In the absence of confirmed data from the Israel Lands Administration, I asked Dr. Nahman Oron, the officer in charge of data there, to verify this widely cited figure. In his April 1996 letter he noted that currently 93.6 percent of Israel's land area is managed by the administration. However, a small area of land still is in dispute and undergoing the legally mandated examination procedure. It is estimated that once the status of such land is resolved the figure will be about 93 percent.

strategically, through a process termed *gradual privatization*. This persistent process has gone further than in most other cases covered in this book.

The first section of the chapter presents two introductory sections to provide some background to Israel's demographic, geographic and economic context, and to outline its key urban and regional policies. The second section provides information on Israel's land policy context, to enable the reader to understand the unique circumstances for the evolution of Israel's system of leaseholds. Israel is in many ways an extreme case—what theorists sometimes call an *ideal case*—that holds lessons for other less extreme leasehold systems. The third section is the heart of the chapter. It presents the evolution of the public lease-hold system through the prism of property rights. This evolution is viewed as an odyssey along the path of reconciliation between public ownership of land on one hand, and the desire to reduce public intervention in the development market, on the other. The chapter is concluded with the one million dollar question, "What public policy goals are achieved by Israel's public leasehold land system?" This question has many answers, depending on one's ideology and values, so it will be discussed in brief only. It deserves a separate chapter.

BACKGROUND TO ISRAEL AND ITS PLANNING POLICIES

As a background to understanding the reasons for the emergence, change and perseverance of Israel's unique land system, this section looks at several key indicators of Israel's geography and demography, and introduces its key urban and regional policies.

Background Geographic, Demographic and Economic Characteristics

Israel's population in 2001 was 6.4 million, approximately 80 percent Jewish and 20 percent Arab (within Israel proper).[2] At the time of independence in 1948, Israel's Jewish population was approximately 670,000 and the Arab population (that remained in the area after the 1948 war) approximately 160,000 (Israel Central Bureau of Statistics 2001). The rate of growth in over 50 years has been extensive, in the early years through mass immigration, and in later years through a higher natural growth rate than other advanced-economy countries. Israel's population is 92 percent urban (compare with the United States, 74 percent; Canada, 77 percent; Britain 89 percent; Sweden, 84 percent and the Netherlands, 89 percent) (United Nations 1996). Israel's land area is approximately 21,000 square kilometer, meaning that population density is approximately 300 persons per square kilometers. Although this density level is currently not the highest among the advanced-economy countries (the Netherlands and Japan being two of the highest), Israel is expected to overtake most of these countries in the future (for a comparative perspective,

---

[2] The Golan Heights, a small area in the northeast, has undergone quasi-annexation by Israel from Syria through Israeli domestic legislation, but its international legal status is contentious. In any event, virtually the entire area of the Golan was offered to Syria in 2000 (and possibly earlier) as part of a prospective peace treaty.

see Alterman 2001a.) And since more than 50 percent of Israel's land area is in the inhospitable southern desert, the effective density is much higher. Good land management should therefore be a major national challenge.

Today, Israel is the only country in the West that is ideologically committed to taking in mass immigration (of Jews and family members). Having taken in close to one million former Soviet-block citizens since 1990, Israel has held the western world's record in immigrant intake, proportionate to population size (Alterman 2002). Since 1948 Israel's economy has grown steadily. It began from a level of GDP per person typical of developing countries (not much higher, for example, than Jordan today). By 2001 the GDP per person, despite a deep recession, was up to $17,000, on the lower end of the group of advanced-economy countries. This remarkable economic growth has taken the form of a steep rise in demand for land and built-up space.

To this cocktail of needs and constraints one should add that Israel is the only country represented in this volume which, for most of its history has been at war with its neighbors. Despite the peace treaties with Egypt in 1978 and Jordan in 1994, the 1993 Oslo peace accords with the Palestinians and the pullout from Lebanon in May 2000, hostilities with the Palestinians broke out again in October 2000 and peaceful coexistence has again receded from sight. Issues of security still dominate public policy and probably are the latent under-pinning for the perseverance of the large-scale public land ownership system.

This combination of factors—Israel's small geographic size; its demographi-cally growing population; its policy favoring mass immigration; its accelerated economic growth; and its geopolitical and security needs—has encouraged Israeli policymakers to harness urban, regional and land policies in order to achieveme national goals (Alterman 2001a). Like most countries, Israel has marched along the path of decentralization, deregulation and privatization; but its starting point has been different (Shefer 1996; Alterman 2001a; 2001b).

National Urban, Regional and Housing Policies

Before delving into Israel's land policy and the details of the leasehold system, it would be appropriate to provide a brief outline of Israel's key urban, regional and housing policies.

Israeli cities and towns are quite compact and are more typical of cities and towns in Europe than in North America. Most Israelis live in medium or high-density apartment buildings, mostly in condominium tenure. Until the 1980s there was very little construction in urban areas of land-consuming "ground-attached" (Israeli professional jargon for single- or double-family low-rise) housing. This mode of living was reserved for rural and exurban areas. However, since the 1980s consumer demand on the upmarket side has shifted to new construction of ground-attached housing in towns and cities. The 1990s saw the proliferation of land-gobbling shopping malls on the outskirts of urban areas. Yet, the majority of Israelis still live in apartment buildings whose densities and heights have been steeply increasing in recent years. Furthermore, the new ground-attached houses, though viewed by Israelis as low-density, typically are planned at 35 or more to the net hectare (13 to the acre).

This information may be seen as paradoxical: in a small country with a growing economy, a strong natural growth rate and an open-gate policy toward potential immigrants, one would expect a policy of careful stewardship of land reserves. Yet, until the 1990 mass-immigration crisis, the concern with land as a depletable resource was not very strong (Mazor 1993). The reasons for this paradox lie with the nation-building ideology and goals that prevailed during most of Israel's history. These explain the prominence of the ideology of national land ownership, and deserve a closer look.

During Israel's incipient years and still to some extent today, public land ownership was seen as a key instrument for achieving the country's territorial and demographic stabilization (Brutzkus 1988). In the years following the 1948 War of Independence, Israel sought to establish its legitimate standing within its international borders, some of which were (and still are) officially only armistice lines in international law.[3] This geopolitical agenda yielded a strong focus on population distribution as widely as possible to Galilee in the north and the Negev desert in the south. The goal was to create a Jewish presence in most areas of the country (Yiftachel 1992, 95–98). State control of land ownership was one of the major tools that enabled the achievement of population distribution and Jewish presence goals.[4]

Population distribution and territorial presence were viewed as being best achieved by planning many small, rural villages widely dispersed rather than through urban concentrations. This population distribution goal was reinforced by an ideological emphasis on rural development as a utopian form of living, to symbolize the return of the Jewish people to the Holy Land and to agriculture (Cohen 1970). This two-pronged ideology led to the establishment of several hundred cooperative or communal rural settlements, distributed as widely as possible within Israel. Some were established prestate (on land owned by the JNF, see below), others after 1948 and into the 1970s (on both JNF and state land). This massive effort was the focus of considerable attention by planners and received generous land, water and budget allocations.

The prorural policy was, however, at odds with the factual reality. At all times the vast majority of Israel's residents preferred to live in urban areas. To bridge this disparity, some 30 small new towns were planned and established by central government on nationally owned land during the 1950s and 1960s (Alterman and Hill 1986).[5] Retention of most of the country's land area in national ownership was a major instrument that enabled central government

---

[3] A reminder: this refers to the international law status of the borders of Israel proper, without the areas occupied in the 1967 war.

[4] The population distribution policy has been implemented in many ways, not only through state control of public land and stimulation of construction. The Law for the Encouragement of Capital Investments offers differential loan, writeoff and tax perks to anyone wishing to locate an industry in a peripheral area. Households of young couples, new immigrants or needy families are offered preferred mortgage terms. Employees are offered reduced income tax.

[5] As in many other countries (Alterman and Cars 1991) the housing then was characterized by uniform blocks of apartments designed by government architects with little regard for consumer diversity, and little attention paid to the differing landscapes. A new town in the green hills of the Galilee might be planned at a density similar to a neighborhood in Tel Aviv.

to control the timing, location, size and type of new villages and towns. By contrast, in the older, prestate cities and towns there was not much public land. But since these cities were at the time already built up, this fact was not viewed as meriting intervention, especially since concentrations of public land holdings were usually available on the outskirts of these cities, enabling the government to construct housing for immigrants there.

During Israel's early years, preservation of open spaces was not a prominent part of the politicians' agenda and was *not* one of the reasons the public land ownership system was instituted. The fact that the major national parks were declared in the 1960s and 1970s, on both public and private land, was a feat of conviction of a few leading planners rather than a reflection of the priorities of the politicians (Brutzkus 1988).

Despite the deep-rooted changes in Israeli demographics and geopolitics, the population-distribution doctrine was not challenged until the mass-immigration crisis of the 1990s (Shachar 1993). Leading national-level planners working for the Ministry of Interior in charge of statutory planning and the Ministry of the Environment used the crisis as an opportunity to challenge this "sacred cow," and offered a doctrine more befitting Israel's current objective conditions.

The new doctrine promoted by the statutory planning and environmental agencies and by nongovernment organizations (NGOs) revolves around the new awareness that land and natural resources in densely developed Israel are extremely scarce and vulnerable. This doctrine encourages the preservation of enough open spaces for future generations and the intensification of use and reuse of urban land. Since the late 1990s the planning bodies have been promoting multiuse, higher urban densities and urban redevelopment.

However, at the same time the statutory planning bodies are still called on to approve contentious land-gobbling projects, and they often find it difficult to withstand these pressures. The Ministry of Housing and the Lands Administration have not given up on their traditional development agendas. The construction of the Cross-Israel Highway is proceeding despite extensive criticism (Alexander 1998). During 2002 these powerful agencies, supplemented by the Prime Minister's Office and the Ministry of Finance, spearheaded a cabinet decision to initiate several new towns and scores of new exurban neighborhoods (within Israel proper). These proposals are propelled by the same mixture of geopolitical and security goals that have always been behind Israel's population distribution policies. But today these goals have new partners—the growing number of Israeli households who seek the lifestyle offered by lower-density communities. These proposals must receive the approval of the statutory planning bodies, where the environmental agencies and NGOs have a voice. The debate promises to be intensive.

A few words about housing policy. Until the mid-1970s the overwhelming majority of housing starts were classified as public: some 80 percent of the annual housing starts in the 1950s and 60 percent in the 1970s. During that period some housing was constructed by the Ministry of Housing with public funds, but gradually, public housing has come to mean housing planned by the Ministry of Housing but financed and constructed by private developers.

In Israel this second type of housing is called public-program housing; Europeans might call it social housing. (For a comparison with The Netherlands, see Needham and Verhage 1998.) The share of social housing subsequently declined sharply during the 1970s, and by the late 1980s was only 17 percent of the annual housing starts (Israel Central Bureau of Statistics 1988). The share of public rental housing is very small and declining further due to a policy of encouraging long-term residents to "buy" (i.e., long-term lease) their unit.

In the early 1990s when mass-immigration from the former Soviet Union commenced unexpectedly, state-built housing was resumed. Yet, from the time the crisis ebbed out, the share of public housing has gradually been returning to precrisis levels and is once again concentrated in the peripheral areas. Since private home ownership (or long-term leasing) has always been the consumer preference and public policy has actively encouraged this trend, more than 70 percent of Israeli households own a long-term lease for their housing unit (usually in condominium tenure).

THE ORIGINS AND LEGAL BASIS FOR ISRAEL'S PUBLIC LAND OWNERSHIP

In order to understand the evolution of Israel's public leasehold system, it would be useful to survey its origins and its key legal attributes.

The Origins of National Land Ownership

The sources of national land reflect Israel's special history and raison d'etre. Israel's public land should by no means be viewed as a land bank, as understood in other countries, because the essence of a bank is that there is a turnover of land holdings. In contrast, under the Israeli system the total stock has remained almost static for decades. This fact arises from the special manner in which Israel's public land holdings emerged.

For the purpose of this chapter, a detailed historical account about how Israel's mammoth presence of public land emerged is unnecessary. This issue will be left to historians and political geographers (and, of course, to politicians) who will undoubtedly continue to discuss it for many years to come. It will suffice to say that there were three main routes whereby the state and quasi-state land holdings came about. These parallel the three types of national landowners who constitute national land, as defined in Clause 1 of the Basic Law: Israel Lands (of 1960). It defines "Israel Lands" as owned by one of three agencies: the State of Israel, the Jewish National Fund (JNF) or the Development Authority. Henceforth these three categories together will be called *national land*.

The JNF is not a state agency. It is a nonprofit worldwide organization of the Jewish people, established at the end of the nineteenth century as part of the Zionist Movement, and registered in London. Its major goal was to purchase land from local landowners to prepare the ground for a hoped-for Jewish State in the region then called Palestine. Until the early 1960s the JNF managed its own land holdings, its own leasehold contracts and levied the rent on them. In 1960 it signed a treaty with the State of Israel as part of a package of legal arrangements whereby the JNF agreed to place its land holdings, without transferring title, under the administration of a state agency to be established for that purpose. The treaty and the concomitant set of legislation stipulated that the JNF would have equal representation in the joint statutory decision-making bodies, and that the proceeds from transactions carried out on JNF land would accrue to it after deduction of the costs of management.

The 1960 Israel Lands Administration Law establishes the statutory agencies that would manage Israel Lands. It states that all three categories of national land are to be administered by the Israel Lands Council (the policy-making body) and the Israel Lands Administration (the managing body). The JNF appoints half (less one) of the members of the Council, while the government appoints the other half (plus one).

Three types of landowners represent the historic sources of national land, and will be discussed in their historic order: JNF land, state land and Development Authority land.

The first source of public land holdings was the purchases made by the JNF, which today owns some 13 percent of the total of nationally owned land. The JNF saw itself as a land trust for Jewish settlement and development in the Holy Land, and to maintain as much land as possible in "Jewish hands." The Fund began purchasing land from local Arab landowners at the beginning of the twentieth century. With the establishment of Israel in 1948 and the changed geopolitical situation in the Middle East, the Fund's land purchases have almost ceased.[6] Arab landowners were no longer willing to sell land to Jewish government or quasi-government institutions.

Because the JNF, in prestate times, had focused its efforts on buying arable and vacant land suitable for building housing, most of its land holdings are now located in relatively attractive areas that carry a considerably higher value than its proportionate share of the total public land holdings. The JNF thus receives hefty annual proceeds from rent payments and other fees on its land. The JNF uses these funds for two major purposes: first, to undertake certain types of public works not routinely funded by government, such as regional water reservoirs,[7] rock clearing and soil erosion and conservation works; second, to steward open spaces through large-scale afforestation, development of parks and installation of open space recreation facilities for the general public. Today the JNF can be counted among the "green" agencies on most issues.

---

[6] The Fund, through a subsidiary called *Himanutah*, still occasionally carries out small-scale, pin-pointed land purchases from private landowners, for the usual Jewish-Arab demographic reasons.

[7] The JNF, as an agency of the Jewish People rather than the Israeli Government, sees its role as promoting Jewish towns and villages in Israel, especially in areas such as the Galilee, where there is demographic competition over which sector—Jewish or Arab—will become the majority in the area. Some view this as a defense issue, citing the danger of secession from Israel if an Arab majority is achieved. Others view this as phobia and criticize the JNF for being a quasi-government body that carries out a distinctly discriminatory policy. However, the investments in forests, parks and waterworks is to benefit the general public and is equally accessible to all. I predict that at some point in the near future, the High Court of Justice will rule that the JNF is, in many ways, a quasi-government body and cannot continue its policy of investing only, or mostly, in the Jewish sector and ignoring the Arab sector.

The second source of public land goes back to land registered under the British Mandate over Palestine, the rulers of the region until 1948. These large holdings were transferred to the State of Israel upon its establishment. This category of land constitutes about 75 percent of all total Israel Lands. Because the British Mandate government could not be choosy in its land holdings (it, too, inherited much of it from the Turkish-empire regime), state-owned land represents a broad range of types in terms both of geographic location and development potential. So, while the state owns extensive tracts of land within and near cities, towns and agricultural villages, it also owns the entire uninhabitable desert area in the south of Israel, which constitutes about 50 percent of the country's total area.

By now, most state land reserves within cities and towns are exhausted, having been used for the construction of housing, industry and public facilities. Beginning in the 1950s state-owned land, at times supplemented by JNF and Development Authority land, was used to house hundreds of thousands of immigrants. It was also a major instrument for implementing the population-distribution policy by enabling the construction of cooperative and communal villages in outlying areas.[8] Most of Israel's 30-odd new towns were built on state-owned land. Today, most remaining land reserves in national ownership are classified as agricultural and are attached to cooperative or communal villages. Private undeveloped land is even scarcer than national land, so most land available for future development is likely to be in state ownership.

The third source of national land pertains to the remaining 12 percent, the most politically sensitive type of national land. A statutory body established in 1950, the Development Authority, received its holdings from the Custodian of Absentee Property. This is a government officer charged with registering the land owned (mostly) by Arab residents who left or were expelled from their place of residence during the 1948–1949 war. Most of these land holdings have been leased or sold, but continue to be listed in the Registry of the Custodian of Absentee Property.

Not a Land Bank: The Static Nature of the Public Land Holdings

The total amount of public land holdings in Israel has been almost static over time since 1948, when the state was established; this arises from three factors. First, as will be explained later, there are strong legal and ideological constraints to the transfer of title to national land into private hands. Very little land leaves the pool. Second, most sources of national land refer back to a particular historic context that no longer exists, so there are few opportunities for new sources of public land.[9] New land acquisitions by the state or quasi-national

---

[8] These were established by the state in collaboration with quasi-state agencies: the JNF and the Jewish Agency.

[9] The last major increments to national land holdings occurred in the 1960s as part of the last major expropriations of land owned by Arab villagers for the purpose of constructing new (Jewish) towns (Yiftachel 1992). Such action encountered increasing criticism and sharply declined in subsequent years. Authorities are now more careful, that where needed for projects like the current Cross-Israel Highway, expropriations be done equally from both Jewish landowners (or long-term leaseholders) and Arab landowners.

agencies (as distinguished from municipal acquisitions; see below) do occur on occasion, for example, where there are pockets of private land within an area designated for a public facility, such as an airport or major road, or for a new state-initiated new town or village. But this is done only on an as-needed, small-scale basis, and is not part of a land banking policy.[10] Third, municipal land acquisitions, while common on the local level for the purpose of supplying neighborhood and urban public services, are not a significant quantitative addition to the total public land holdings.

The Weak Role of Municipalities and Municipal Land

Unlike most countries represented in this book, the vast majority of public land in Israel is owned or managed directly by the state, and not by municipal or regional agencies. (For a comparison with The Netherlands, see Needham and Verhage 1998.) Municipalities in Israel are legally and financially quite weak (Alterman 2001b). The Basic Law: Israel Lands does not even include municipally owned land under the definition of "Israel Lands" (Weisman 1993, 231–232).[11] Israeli municipalities have never practiced land banking to any significant degree (Alterman 1990a; Alexander, Alterman and Law Yone 1983). The municipalities do have some land holdings, but these vary from almost none, as typical of "development towns," to around 10 percent in older cities (Alterman 1997).

As in most U.S. cities, the major sources of municipal land in Israel are dedications or expropriations for roads and public buildings, carried out incrementally as necessary for each new development approved (Alterman 1988a; 1988b; 1990b). Land designated for public services may fall on nationally owned land or on private land, depending on the land use plan's designations. The Planning and Building Law ostensibly expects planning bodies to be "ownership blind." Often, the land necessary for local public infrastructure and services is owned by the state. In the past, the Lands Administration used to transfer title to the municipalities voluntarily. For legal and administrative reasons this practice has been phased out since the 1980s. The Lands Administration increasingly has been acting as a private landowner. It prefers that the municipalities exercise their legal powers and exact the land through compulsory dedication under the same legal conditions that apply to private property, or through negotiated exactions (Alterman 1988b; 1990b).[12] In

---

[10] The chronologically last source of national land—expropriation by national agencies—is, happily, no longer practiced on a significant scale, having ceased in the 1970s in response to political protest by the Arab sector (Yiftachel 1992). The current controversy concerns the expropriations planned for the new Cross-Israel Highway. Public protest is so strong that I estimate the Lands Administration will not succeed in most cases, except if state-owned land is offered elsewhere in exchange.

[11] Weisman (1993, 231–232) notes past distinction between national and municipal land was somewhat foggy. It is uncertain the fog is entirely cleared. The question would arise when a local authority wanted to expropriate land for public services from the Lands Administration. This may seem curious to non-Israelis but is indeed the widespread procedure. Local authorities in Israel do routinely *expropriate* land for public services from the national Lands Administration—it does not just *give* the land over to local authorities. Legally and administratively, this makes excellent sense in the Israeli land and legal system (see Alterman 1990).

these cases, there would be a reduction in the stock of nationally owned land, through its transfer to the municipality. Only where the land taken for roads or public services was privately owned would there be a net addition to the public land pool (in state or municipal ownership, depending on the type of land use). Although very important at the local scale, at the national scale such land transfers are quantitatively negligible.

The Unlimited Range of Uses Located on National Land

A unique characteristic of Israeli public land is the literally unlimited range of land uses that are located on it. About 70 percent of Israel's households live on nationally owned land, and a good portion of its industrial production is undertaken on such land. And of course, the majority of public services and utilities (airports, power plants, universities, hospitals, cemeteries) are located on Israel Lands. It is the capacity of the leasehold system to adapt to the country's changing economic and social conditions that has made it possible to undertake all these activities on public land.

Another striking difference makes the Israeli land-policy system unique: in most countries (even during the lifetime of the Soviet regimes[13]), there is, in general, more publicly owned land in urban regions than in the agricultural sector. In Israel the picture is reversed: the majority of agricultural land is in national ownership. About 83 percent of all agricultural production is conducted on nationally owned land. Indeed, of the 7 percent of private land, most is found in urbanized areas. Due to strong conversion pressures, most agricultural land in private ownership has already been converted, and the balance is fast disappearing.

The Legal Prohibition to Privatizing National Land

In the past, Israel's national land holdings were strongly bolstered by ideology. Today, the ideological basis is receding, and the near-monopoly of the Israel Lands Administration no longer is immune from challenge (Alterman 1997). At the same time, the support for continuing the national ownership of most of the land has by no means dissipated. In other countries, this issue, with its extensive economic and social repercussions, would likely have become a key item on the national party–political platforms and would have enticed electoral interest. However, in Israel's special political climate, issues of security, the controversy over the occupied areas and conflicts between the religiously non-Orthodox majority and the Orthodox minority usually occupy the public agenda. Thus, no major political party has as yet placed land policy issues in a prominent place on its political platform and there is little public interest

---

[12] The common legal opinion—and practice—is that local authorities are fully authorized to expropriate state-owned land under the same conditions as private property. Recently, some legal experts have cast doubt on this approach, but the High Court has not had the opportunity to rule on this topic.

[13] In the countries of Eastern Europe (e.g., Poland, Yugoslavia and, to a lesser extent, Hungary), in Soviet times, some types of land remained in private ownership. These were first and foremost located in the rural sector.

to debate this issue (except lately regarding the rights of farmers in cases of conversion to urban use).

The commitment to maintain the existing national land holdings is enshrined in a basic (constitutional) law—the 1960 Basic Law: Israel Lands. In strict legal terms, the fact that we are dealing with a basic law rather than a regular law means little because this particular basic law has no special procedure for amending or repealing it.[14] But, significantly, the Knesset elected to set the country's key land policy in a law titled "basic." It says that the legislators of the time viewed national land ownership and its protection as one of the basic tenets of the State of Israel. However, that intention has very little legal import today, and has declined ideologically as well. Yet, despite the major changes made in land policy, the Basic Law has, to date, never been amended, not even slightly. These changes have been made by means of hundreds of incremental regulative decisions made by the Lands Council. These have not, or not yet, infringed directly on the principles set out by the Basic Law.

The Basic Law has only three clauses: the first two are discussed here, and the last in the section on property rights. The first clause defines the three categories of "Israel Lands" (see above), and states that the "[o]wnership [of Israel Lands] will not be transferred through sale or any other way."

The second clause indicates that the above principle will not apply to particular types of real property or transactions that have been explicitly excluded by law. Here, *law* means any Knesset legislation, not necessarily a basic law. (Subsidiary legislation, however, does not qualify.) If another law explicitly permits, transfer of full title could be allowed. Otherwise, transfer of rights in land would be allowed through a mechanism short of transfer of title, for example, through long-term leaseholds or short-term rental.

The 1960 Israel Lands Law, legislated as a package together with the Basic Law, sets the main exceptions to the transfer-prohibition clause in the Basic Law. This law specifies a finite set of situations whereby it allows the transfer of title. The majority of these situations refer to highly specific, small-scale situations, for example, where national land is exchanged with nonnational land in order to complete a plot of land, or where a swap occurs between the state and the JNF in order to solve a specific problem.[15] The only general allowance for the outright sale of land is the enigmatic clause that allows the transfer of title of up to 10,000 hectares (approximately 25,000 acres) of *urban* land. The law does not specify any use limitations or any additional conditions. The ceiling is cumulative, not annual, and that number has not been amended since

[14] The concept of using basic laws was proposed in the 1950s, when it became clear to politicians and legal scholars that the Knesset was not likely to muster a majority in the foreseeable future, for legislating a full-scale constitution. They proposed a modular compromise—to incrementally legislate those constitutional elements for which a majority can be mustered from time to time. Each element was to be included in a special law, titled "Basic Law." Only in subsequent years did the Knesset develop more sophisticated tools to assure that basic laws will have a special status.

[15] The latter sometimes is used by the Lands Administration to solve site-specific problems where Arab-Israeli citizens wish to live or lease commercial-industrial property located on JNF land.

originally enacted. According to official Lands Administration figures, the cap is still far from being exhausted.[16]

The Israel Lands Law applies equally to all Israel Lands. But during negotiations with the State of Israel about the joint management of all national land, the JNF had set up an additional set of restrictions on the transfer of its own land. By means of a *treaty* signed in 1960 between the State of Israel and the JNF, the latter prohibits any transfer of title to its land (except against swaps of land where necessary). The treaty requires that title to JNF land may never be transferred through sale, inheritance, gift or the like. That means that the 10,000 hectares of urban land, which the Israel Lands Law allows to be sold, would in fact apply to state and Development Authority land only.

Viewing itself as a custodian of land for the Jewish people, the JNF incorporated into the treaty with the State of Israel a further and highly controversial condition. The Israel Lands Administration would be allowed to *lease* JNF land to Jewish people only, whether to those living in Israel or residing abroad.

The set of laws about Israel Lands thus makes it clear that the majority of land in Israel, once released for development or use, must be governed through a legal tool short of ownership and transfer of title. It is here that Israel's extensive public leasehold system comes into view. For decades, it has been used as the primary contractual tool regarding national land in the urban sector. While long-term leaseholds were the intended mode in the rural sector as well, this did not materialize. Most of that sector is in fact governed by three-year automatically renewable contracts.[17] Nonetheless, almost everyone in Israel and outside (for example, most literature on Israel's land system) speaks of rural land—erroneously—as if it is governed by long-term leases for 49 years.

Leaseholds and Land Use Law

How do land use planning controls apply to all this public land? The answer can be found in the 1965 Planning and Building Law, which replaced the 1936

---

[16] However, the Lands Administration has never clarified which types of title transfers it regards as falling within this clause (Weisman 1993). This fog may have emerged because, in the initial years, it was unclear whether the transfer of title to local authorities when land is dedicated for public services—probably the single largest category of transfers—should be counted against this ceiling. Current prevailing legal opinion is that it should be, but I have seen no figures that report on these and other types of transfers. The Israel Lands Council has not developed a general set of policies regarding the application of this clause to outright sale, rather using this clause to solve special problems ad hoc. The amount of land sold outright is likely quite small.

[17] This situation arose not by design but by default, for technical reasons pertaining to a backlog in cadastre preparation and land registration, and a syndrome of procrastinating that typified all agencies involved, including the residents. Until recent years this legal situation bothered no one, since the agricultural sector on public land (the cooperative and communal villages) was characterized by very stable social-economic organization and a high degree of tenure certainty despite the "funny" contracts. However, with the decline of agriculture as an economic base, and a chronic socioideological crisis that beset the communal mode of living, pressure to allow urban development in some of the rural land has intensified in recent years, especially since the mass-immigration crisis of the early 1990s. The legal status of occupants of rural public land became a hot economic and political issue. In recent years residents of the cooperative and communal villages have been promoting the gradual replacement of the three-year perpetually renewable contracts with long-term leasehold.

Town Planning Ordinance, enacted by British Mandate over Palestine.[18] Until 1965 planning controls did not apply to government-initiated development, such as by the Ministry of Housing or the Public Works Department. The Planning and Building Law abolished the distinction between private and public developers. All government developers—national or local—must abide by planning regulations and procedures, just like private developers, and no concessions are allowed (except for defense-related development, which is governed by a special procedure). The relationship between the particular attributes of the Israeli leasehold contracts and planning controls will be one of the issues discussed later in this chapter.

The Legal Status of Private Land and Its Influence on Public Leaseholds

Ironically, despite the quantitative dominance of national land and the fact that the private land sector is only about 7 percent, Israel is today very much a country where the ethos of private property dominates both legally and politically. I argue that the concept of private land ownership has become so dominant it has gradually encroached into the very idea of public land owner-ship. Israel thus presents an interesting, probably unique, hybrid that enshrines public ownership on the one hand, but at the same time places private land ownership on a legal and economic pedestal.

The above statement—which may seem counterintuitive to most readers—is very much the reality of Israel's land market, land law and land policy. To justify this ostensible anomaly, let us discuss the conclusion that the weight of private land ownership is many times its quantitative weight. There are six reasons:

1. The small percentage of freehold land has de facto always played a much more significant role than its numeric size implies, because it happens to be located in areas where development pressures are high, either economically or demographically. These include core areas in the older, prestate cities that today are economic centers; and towns along the high-growth coastline that originally were private-sector Jewish agricultural villages where each household-owned title to its land (a tenure rare in Israel). Conversion to urban development occurred in these areas much sooner than to publicly owned farmland, and most of these areas are now cities undergoing further land use intensification. Private land also is concentrated in Arab villages and towns where most land is privately owned and where development pressures are high due to a very high natural growth rate.

2. Most real property taxes apply equally to private land and to long-term leased land, as shall be explained later in detail.

3. A 1992 constitutional law provides an extremely high degree of protection to property rights. The Basic Law: Human Honor and Freedom constitu-tionally enshrines property owners' right to have authorities refrain as much

---

[18] Laws of the State of Israel, 1965. (Official translations were available in English until the early 1980s only, and thus did not cover many later amendments.) For a detailed description of the law and the plan-ning bodies, see Alterman (2000).

as possible from incursion into a person's property rights. The trend in court decisions in recent years is to further bolster these rights. This trend spills over into the interpretation of public leasehold tenure rights.[19]

4. The share of publicly initiated development has greatly declined over the years and most development on public land is currently carried out through the private sector and with private financing. As will be shown, incremental trends in the leasehold system have paralled these changes. Public financing today is offered only for "classic" public services, i.e., roads and schools, and for a small part of the housing sector only. However, in outlying areas the range of publicly financed development is considerably broader.

5. The public has voted with its cash in favor of private property rights. Some 70 percent of Israeli households own or hold a long-term lease on their housing units. This is very high in international comparative terms. Public policy has consistently encouraged home (mostly condominium) owner-ship and most families expect to have the opportunity to own (or lease long-term) their housing unit (Alterman 2002). Real property—mostly as long-term leaseholds—is the highest-value asset held by the vast majority of households and by many commercial establishments.

6. Most important for un derstanding public leaseholds in Israel, the market-place in urban land hardly distinguishes in price between similar properties located on private or public land. As we shall see, the Lands Administration has gradually eliminated most restrictions within the leasehold contracts, thus making them almost tantamount to private land ownership.

ISRAEL'S PUBLIC LEASEHOLD SYSTEM VIEWED THROUGH THE PRISM OF PROPERTY RIGHTS

The stage is now set for analyzing the leasehold system in Israel, which will be presented along the 10 dimensions shown in Table 1. Each dimension pertains to a particular property right—a "stick" in the "bundle" of property rights that compose freehold ownership. The prism of property rights will be used to present the Israeli public leasehold system. Regarding each type of property right, I will ask: to what extent do the terms of the lease limit this right? The argument will be that in view of the special characteristics of the Israeli land policy system, a process of quasi-privatization has occurred, which over the decades has gradually closed most of the property rights gaps between lease-hold and freehold.

Understanding Israel's leasehold system is a bit like composing a picture from a puzzle that contains many rather strange, counterintuitive subele-ments. This puzzle-picture is composed of the 10 property rights dimensions.

---

[19] For example, the demands of the current property rights movement in the U.S. are pale as compared with Israel's current law on compensation rights for what Americans call *takings*.

TABLE 1 ────────────────────────────────
ISRAELI LONG-TERM LEASEHOLD SYSTEM AND PROPERTY RIGHTS

1. Applicability to land and/or fixtures: Does the lease enable the separation of ground from fixtures?
2. Period: What is the term of the leasehold?
3. Renewal: Are there extension or renewal rights?
4. Value: How is the value of the lease calculated (original and extended)?
5. Use rights: Are there restrictions on use? What linkage is there with regulatory land use planning?
6. Development rights: The rights and conditions regarding future development
7. Transfer rights: Are there restrictions on transfer (sale, inheritance)?
8. Market rights: Who benefits from the rise in property value upon transfer? May the land be mortgaged?
9. The right to control the timing of development
10. Tax obligations: Who is responsible for the various property based taxes (e.g., betterment, added-increment, property)

Source: Compiled by the author

To understand the operation of the leasehold system, the reader might wait until all elements of the puzzle (all 10 components in Table 1) have been presented.

Applicability to Land and/or Fixtures

The third clause of the Basic Law: Israel Lands defines *lands* as including all buildings and other fixtures permanently attached to the land. Israeli property law does not enable separation of the ground from the fixtures in property transactions or title registration. This means that the state, the JNF and the Development Authority who own the title to the land will also own whatever anyone builds on it, regardless of who has constructed it and with what capital.

The majority of Israeli citizens, including many planners, do not realize the legal and economic meaning of this clause. In theory, this clause means that if the leasehold is ever terminated the lessee will lose all property rights, not only to the land but also to the fixtures (land, plantings), but will be compensated. To the shocked reader, I hasten to say that this is not likely to occur. The manner in which the Israeli leasehold system has developed reflects to a significant extent the decision makers' desire to prevent the reversion of property rights, along with the fixtures, to the public landowner. But while providing a high (though not absolute) degree of security to leaseholders in the urban areas, the decision makers have at the same time forfeited the opportunity to use the leasehold system as a potential lever to guide or control land use, redevelopment, social balance or other public planning goals.

I will note that in the rural areas, quasi-privatization has not occurred to any parallel degree. Leaseholder security in the rural sector is today much lower than in the urban areas. A High Court of Justice decision, delivered in August 2002, ruled that whenever conversion of public agricultural use is sought (usually because it is no longer economically viable), the lease will revert to the Lands Administration and the farmers will receive compensation for their investments in farming improvements only. They will remain with leasehold rights to the residential house plot only.[20]

The Period of Life of the Lease

In the 1969 Real Property Law, leasehold is defined in Clause 3 simply as rental for more than five years, while long-term leasehold (literally, in Hebrew, *lease-hold for generations*) is defined as leasehold for more than 25 years. However, very few leases around the country are drawn out for only 25 years because the dominant lessor, the Israel Lands Administration, uses 49 years as its basic term. The JNF has been using this term since the 1920s, when it started leasing out the land holdings it had purchased. The period of 49 years was initially chosen by the JNF as a symbolic "citation" (to use postmodern language) of the Biblical Jubilee period of 50 years. After that period, says the Bible, land is to revert to its original owners.

If there was any symbolism in this jubilee-like period, it has evaporated away. Some leaseholds—signed before the late 1970s and not yet altered—may still carry the 49-year term, but incremental policy changes regarding renewal of the lease (discussed below) have, in more recent leases, led to longer time periods, usually as multiples of the 49-year basic term. This trend applies to urban residential leases—the majority of the leases. (Nonresidential leases may still carry only one term of 49 years.)

Today, leases are regularly drawn out for two periods of 49 years (98 years). Furthermore, in 1999 the Israel Lands Council authorized the administration to sign new leases for *two* automatically renewable terms of 98 years (196 years). Two centuries are a long time anywhere in the world, and especially in the turbulent Middle East. Legal scholars might debate the question of whether a lease for that length of time no longer qualifies as leasehold, because it may be tantamount to freehold ownership.[21]

Under most systems of leaseholds, the marketplace assigns differing values to properties under leasehold, depending on how long the lease must "run" before it expires. One of the most interesting aspects of the Israeli leasehold system is that the marketplace has never been sensitive to the duration of time before the lease runs out. A lease may have only a few years remaining, yet the potential buyers will rarely ask about that, nor are they likely to negotiate the

---

[20] H.C.J. 244/2000 Amutat Siah Hadash *(The Association for a New Discourse; RA) v The Minsiter of National Infrastructure, the Israel Lands Adminstration et al.)*. Available in Hebrew at *www.court.gov.il*

[21] Such a debate already has occurred in the mid-1980s between two leading legal scholars in Israel, in connection with the recommendations of the Goldenberg Committee (one of many public commit-tees charged with reviewing the national land policy) to extend the leaseholds to 999 years. Amnon Goldenberg, a leading private-sector lawyer, thought this would still be legally considered leasehold and would not negate the Basic Law: Israel Lands. Professor Joshua Weisman, a leading property law scholar, disagreed. Since the committee finally did not propose the 999-year recommendation, this question has not yet been tested in court. The committee's proposal of 98 years was not adopted until a dozen years later.

price accordingly. Even Israeli lawyers tend to be oblivious to this question. Some may be caught off guard if asked to handle a leasehold contract with a lessor other than the Israel Lands Administration. Being so engulfed by the special leasehold terms of the Israel Lands Administration, some Israelis have been known to mistakenly extrapolate their disregard for leasehold life to real estate transactions abroad, sometimes with perilous results....[22]

Expiration of the Lease and Renewal Rights

What happens upon the expiration of the lease? Does the lessee have renewal rights and if so, under what financial terms? If the lease is indeed terminated, what will happen to the value of the buildings, etc., and other improvements to it, provided they were paid for or built by the lessee? In the past this issue could have been regarded as the soft belly of the Israeli public leaseholds in the urban sector, but a satisfactory policy was developed in time to avoid a crisis.

The first prestate leases with the JNF dating from the 1920s started to expire in the 1970s. Some older leases had no reference to what would happen upon expiration. They were silent about renewal rights, or stated only that renewal would be according to the policy of the lessor at the time (see Weisman 1993, 253). In British-Mandate Palestine of the 1920s and 1930s, the 49-year horizon must have looked very far off. More surprising is the fact that the Lands Administration failed to develop a coherent policy in advance of the first waves of expirations. Lore has it that as the first few dozens of residential leaseholds expired in the 1970s (in one of the suburbs of Haifa), the administrator in charge simply sent a notice to the residents in accordance with the dry language of the lease.[23] According to those leases, upon expiration, the lessee would be obliged to vacate the premises. The lessee would then be entitled to receive from the Lands Administration the value of the fixtures (buildings, trees) that had been added to the land. The notice generously allowed the leaseholders to extend the lease for another period, but only if they paid the full reassessment value of the property for the new period. Given the high real estate prices in Israel relative to average income, the residents were understandably dismayed, and raised their voices.

Although the issue of leasehold termination never made large national headlines (probably because the Israeli news agenda is perpetually occupied with other issues), one can assume the elected politicians realized the danger of leaving the problem unresolved. They probably knew well how to extrapolate the initial small scale problem to the time when a larger number of leases would expire. With time, most Israeli households would encounter this problem. What politician would allow their voters to be required to vacate their homes? What Israeli courts, traditionally very reluctant to vacate residents, would implement

---

[22] I can recount many stories of how Israeli developers, and even their lawyers, misread a rare tender put out by some *private* property holder in Israel, asking for proposals to build on the property while getting a leasehold contract for part of the property in exchange. They would not regard the life of the leasehold as of much relevance, and assume that it would in effect be almost for perpetuity.

[23] This story was recounted to me in the 1980s by the late Mr. Ben Shemesh, former director general of the JNF and subsequently chair of the Urban Committee of the Israel Lands Council.

this requirement on a large scale? Alternatively, what household could afford to pay tens or even hundreds of thousands of dollars to renew their lease? It cannot be imagined how the expiration of residential public leaseholds in Israel could be implemented. I would hazard the guess that few people in Israel have ever actually paid the full sum required under a public residential lease for extending their leasehold contract.

In an attempt to deal with the problem, the Lands Council in 1976 and subsequently in 1986, developed rules regarding expiration and renewal rights that still stand today. The principle is that the lessee does have the *right* to extend the lease for another term without any up-front payment (see below), and for only one-fifth the annual rent payments charged for initial leases (1 percent instead of 5 percent per year for the entire term) (Weisman 1993, 255). Thus, even though the leases may still say that extension will be governed by the policy of the lessor at the time of expiration, the need for payment upon extension will effectively be waived. Furthermore, in its 1999 decision about the double 98-year leasehold periods, the Council went on to say that when the lease expires (in the twenty-second century!), the total extension payment of rent for the extended period would not exceed 5 percent of the value of the property at that time. These decisions have in effect abolished the extension payment requirement. Today, when a lessee comes into the Lands Administration offices to inquire about one of the frequent bonus offers to those who upgrade an existing lease (see below), the lessee will be offered a new lease where the automatic renewal rights will be explicitly stated.

Calculating the Value of the Lease—the Land Rent Charges

To understand the manner in which the value of the lease is calculated, one should understand the manner in which national land comes into the development pool.

The manner in which land is released for development

The Lands Administration regularly releases land from its stock to meet the country's development needs. The land released usually is vacant land or land converted from agricultural use. Commercial developers who win Lands Administration tenders usually "sell" (i.e., long-term lease) the built-up property to the consumers. They try to do so as early as possible in the development process to retrieve their investment in the land (as the market will permit). Transfer to the consumer means that the consumer will sign a long-term lease directly with the Lands Administration.

Until the 1970s the system of price setting by the administration was based on artificial chart prices. These were set by government appraisers for each land use type, and included several levels and types of subsidies and many categories of privileged institutions and groups. Because these prices were not updated periodically, they were usually significantly below market price. This system has been phased out almost entirely (except for a small set of public services). Today, subsidies are set mainly to encourage development in periphery regions, and are made transparent and publicly known. However, a proposal to abolish these subsidies will be placed before the Lands Council by the end of 2002 (*Haaretz* 2002). The current categories of land prices are:

» 100 percent—full market price of the lease. Applicable in the coastal and central regions of the country (where most building starts occur).

» 50 percent of market price in the nondistant peripheries (Lower and Middle Galilee regions in the north, and the Northern Negev region in the south).

» 33 percent of market price in the more distant peripheral areas (Northern and Easter Galilee, the Israeli part of the Jordan Valley, and the Negev Desert).

» Zero charge for the lease in border areas with active hostilities (according to changing security conditions).[24]

Developers are also required to pay fees for infrastructure and, in some cases, schools. In the regions of preference—border or periphery—these fees may be partially subsidized, depending on national-regional development policies in force.

During the mass-immigration crisis in the early 1990s, when Israel was required to take in hundreds of thousands of penniless immigrants from the USSR and post-USSR states, additional subsidies for land and infrastructure costs—which at that time applied even in the country's central regions—were successfully used as a lever to stimulate housing starts (for a more detailed account of how these policies worked, see Alterman 2002).

Since the late 1970s, the major system of price setting gradually came to be based on public tenders. The administration's appraisers usually set a minimum price level for the tender and competitors must make a bid beyond that level. During times of recession, such as since 1997, some tenders do not engender any contenders. If convinced that there is market demand, the administration may then adjust the minimum price and try again.[25]

The alternative system, the lottery system, has not been used in Israel on a large scale but, rather, for very special types of programs. These usually are motivated by a policy of achieving below market prices. When the lottery system is used, the government land appraiser sets the prices. If the prices are indeed below market, there will presumably be more people registered so that allocation can be done by lottery. This system has been used in "development towns" (usually in the country's peripheries) as a means for retaining, or luring, households with above-average incomes. In a popular program called "Build Your Own Home," a limited number of plots of land are offered for single- or double-attached family homes (a scarce commodity in Israel). The households themselves enter the lottery and then act as their own developers. This system

---

[24] Over the last two decades the border with Lebanon was the main conflict zone, but since the October 2000 hostilities with the Palestinian Authority began, other areas may enter this classification.

[25] The minimum-price policy is a point of continuous contention between the Developer's Union and the administration. The administration's rationale is to eliminate any opportunity for illegal price-setting by developers.

has been used in scores of edge towns and has provided their current or future residents with opportunities for upwards mobility and real property equity.

Another type of lottery-based program has been applied on an experimental basis in a few cases since the mid-1990s. This innovative program, called "Build Your Own Apartment" (an obvious attempt to cite the successful upscale program), targets lower-income families. It is intended to provide opportunities for apartment ownership for disadvantaged households by lowering the cost of the land component. The ground area for the condominium is directly registered in the name of each winning household according to their proportionate share in the total floor area of the condominium building. The developer is thus prevented from reaping any profit from the land component in the price of the apartment.

Despite its benefits, the Build Your Own Apartment program has been severely criticized by the state comptroller general as inequitable and open to potential misuse. Critics note that the absolute (as distinct from the proportionate) value of the subsidy in land prices differs greatly between the different regions in the country. In the center of the country the subsidy system can provide a windfall for the lucky households, while in the peripheries the value of the equity provided makes hardly a difference to the leaseholders' future prospects for upwards mobility. Despite this criticism, lottery-based programs are proposed periodically by elected politicians who wish to cater to their potential voters and are likely to resurface on a small scale. But the tender system is likely to remain the dominant allocation method.

Due to government's perpetual fear that land prices would rocket out of control, the administration's policy is to release as much land as feasible. Critics of the public land system argue that the administration's virtual monopoly creates an artificial scarcity and hike in prices that would not have occurred in a freehold and market system. However, within the particular Israeli land context, the extent of the higher price effect is intangible and will likely always remain an unsolved enigma. The administration's tender system is an expression of the desire to come as close to emulating market transactions as any administrative machinery could.

The manner in which the value of the lease is calculated

Now to the value of the lease itself: how is the land rent calculated and how are lease payments made? In some countries represented in this book, the major part of the leasehold charges is based on periodic, usually annual, payments of land rent. Years ago, this was the case in Israel as well. But with time, the system of *urban* leases (as distinct from rural leases) gradually evolved to one where the *entire value of the lease* is to be paid up front.

In prestate leases and into the 1950s, up to 40 percent of the total payment would be paid upon initial signing of the contract, discounted to present value. Later, in the 1950s and 1960s the prepayment portion was gradually increased to 80 percent. The annual rent thus became quite small and insignificant. The administrative costs of handling the annual payments for hundreds of thousands of leases became unreasonably high. The inefficient administrative machinery of the Lands Administration and the hassle to the lessees became a target of public criticism.

In the late 1970s the Israel Lands Council decided that new urban residential leasehold contracts would require full payment in advance of the rental fee for the entire duration of the lease. This type of contract is called a *discounted contract*, because rental payments due in the future are discounted to present value. As already discussed, this type of lease also waives the payment for lease renewal for another term of 49 years. In addition, the up-front payment embodies some other benefits, to be discussed below.

Since the 1980s the policy of full up-front payment has been gradually expanded to cover most categories of new urban leases. Regarding existing leases, the administration's goal is to encourage the lessees to convert them to the new system. When lessees come into the administration's offices for some other purpose, such as to transfer the lease to another party or to receive permission to realize additional development rights (both types of property rights to be discussed below), the administration's personnel will try to entice them to convert to the new type of lease. From time to time the administration takes active steps to lure lessees by offering them special reduced rent rates. Such offers always have an expiration date, but experience shows they are usually repeated.

I regard the up-front payment system as the most important feature of the Israeli system of urban-sector leaseholds. But, like most major land policy decisions in Israel, the decision to transform the leasehold system from one of periodic rental payments to all up-front payments did not trigger public discussion. This decision has greatly accelerated the process of quasi-privatization of public leaseholds, from a crawl to a racing speed. To appreciate the impact of this change, the reader should know the manner in which the up-front payment is calculated.

To calculate the up-front, discounted payment, the administration has adopted two artificial figures: one for the annual rental charge (5 percent), and the other for the annual discount rate (5 percent). These figures have been used for many years, without fluctuation or change, despite the great vicissitudes in the Israeli real estate market and the turbulence of its economy and financial markets. The 5 percent rental charge tends to be higher, and in some periods, considerably higher, than the rent rate yielded by the private rental market.[26] However, the 5 percent discount rate often is well below the market discount rate. These two figures have been used as the uniform basis for calculating the leasehold charge for most urban leaseholds, regardless of the differences in real land rent values among regions and through time. Variation in rent rates is not used as a policy tool during the life of a lease. However, as noted, a lower rent charge is offered from time to time for the purpose of luring existing

---

[26] The private rental market, which is quite robust, is composed largely of owners or long-term leaseholders of condominium apartments (and some single-family homes) who rent out their units on the private market. Technically the leaseholders are subleasing, but no one in Israel ever uses this term or perceives it as such. In the public leases in the urban sector there are no restrictions on renting out the unit and the Lands Administration is not involved.

leaseholders to convert to the fully discounted lease, and this is justified in that it will save the administration in future administrative costs.

If one inserts into the rent formula a discount rate of 5 percent and an annual rental fee of 5 percent for a period of 49 years, the result is 91 percent. This means that the up-front payment is 91 percent of the full market value of the property, assessed by the government assessor as if it were sold in freehold. Up to the 1970s such assessment may have been grossly below market prices, but in recent decades the government assessments have been quite realistic, to the extent that at times (especially when the market is weak) they might be somewhat higher than market prices.[27] My hunch is that the decision makers first selected 91 percent as a favorite figure that signifies "almost 100 percent but not quite," and then "drew a circle" around it, selecting the two figures of 5 percent as convenient for reaching the desired target number.

Thus, most Israeli urban households are asked to pay 91 percent of the assessed value of the property up front, upon signing the lease (unless some subsidy happens to be in force, and this applies to a minority of the cases only). This is a burden on most households because average land values in Israel are high relative to most other advanced-economy countries, and average salaries lower. The typical price of the land component for a modest apartment is $25,000–$60,000 (outside the Tel Aviv metropolitan regions), and the built-up price would be $100,000–$200,000. Mortgages are expensive and usually cover only part of the price. So, signing a lease with the administration is, for most households, the biggest investment to be made in their lifetime, and the lease is the typical household's major capital asset. (Recall that the norm in Israel is that households would own or leasehold their apartment, and indeed some 70 percent do.)

Therefore, it should not come as a surprise that most Israelis have come to view leasehold contracts as tantamount to freehold rights. People who hold an urban lease typically say that they "own" their house or apartment. The more knowledgeable may make the (erroneous) distinction that the land is public but that they own the apartment. They are unlikely to know whether the public land in question is actually owned by the state or by the JNF—they assume that the owner is the Lands Administration. Most development professionals, even the real estate journalists, are not much more aware of the legal conditions of leaseholds. Knowing that the "discounted" leases require an up-front payment of 91 percent, they are likely to say that the leaseholder "owns 91 percent of the property rights while the administration retains 9 percent of the property rights." Of course, this widely heard explanation is a garbled set of legal-economic nonsense.

What property rights does the administration offer the lessees in exchange for the hefty up-front payment at virtually the full market price in freehold?

---

[27] The reader may wonder if there are any real market prices in a country where 93 percent of the land is public. Yes, in built-up regions there are market prices indeed, shown by the existence of private land in significant proportions in many urban areas, and also the huge private market in public leaseholds. The transfer through sale is at uninhibited market prices. As we shall see, these tend to be almost the same as freehold prices.

Do the leases with the full up-front payment offer the lessee a release from some of the conditions and limitations on their property rights? The answers to these questions will be given in the following sections, each covering one of the relevant types of property right that may be addressed and affected by long-term leases. But first, a detour will explain the relationship between the public leasehold system and land use planning and control.

Land Use Rights and Planning Control

One of the justifications for retaining public leasehold often found in the literature on land policy is the potential capacity to control land use. Theoretically, a public landowner could insert into the terms of the lease conditions that add to or substitute for the general land use planning controls.

Given the dominance of public land ownership in Israel, the relationship between the land ownership system and the land planning system is of prime importance. The Cabinet and the Lands Council decided early that the Israeli public leasehold system (in the urban sector) should *not* be used for the purpose of land use planning control. Indeed, there is a definite policy of disengagement between the leasehold system and the planning control system. In one of its earliest decisions, in 1965, the Lands Council issued a policy guideline that land should be released for development only after a statutory land use plan was in place.

In the 1950s and 1960s, Israel's formative years, the Lands Administration generously transferred large tracts of land to the then-all-powerful Ministries of Housing, the Public Works Department and the various infrastructure agencies. These bodies built scores of new towns and much of the country's modern infrastructure. At the time the administration was not very active in initiating development on its own, and its role was mainly to allocate land to other government bodies and private developers.

Until the 1965 Planning and Building Law was enacted, all government agencies were exempt from submitting a land use plan for legal approval and obtaining a building permit. The 1965 Planning and Building Law set up a new rule. All government bodies, including the Lands Administration, would have the same status under the law as a private developer, and would have to obtain approval for all its land use and development initiatives from the statutory planning and building control bodies.

The administration would, however, have an important edge over private bodies through its membership in the main statutory bodies, the six District Planning Commissions and in the National Planning Board. Until 1995 this membership was somewhat tenuous because the administration came under the cap of the ministry in charge of it (Agriculture then Housing then Infrastructure). A major 1995 amendment to the Planning and Building Law (Amendment 43) gave the administration independent membership, thus solidifying this advantage into law.

However, since the 1980s and in an accelerated pace since 1990, the administration gradually changed its policy and began to assume a growing planning and development role of its own. Today, it is responsible for initiating plans for about half of the housing starts on public land (mostly at market prices), for some urban redevelopment tenders, for the Build Your Own House program, and for industrial parks (see Alterman 2001b).

Ironically, the 1995 legislation that gave the administration independent membership in the District Commissions came into effect shortly after a High Court of Justice decision effectively downgraded its status almost to that of any private interest party, despite its membership in the planning commissions.[28] The High Court ruled that the Lands Administration's representatives should be regarded as having a potential conflict of interests whenever a proposed plan pertains to national land, and should not be allowed to partake in key stages in the planning decision process. This decision carries extra import given the fact that at the time the country faced the mass-immigration flow from the Soviet Union (subsequently the post-USSR states). The clause that was the subject of the petition to the High Court was part of a special law enacted for this crisis period, with the specific intention to give central government bodies special powers (for a full legal analysis, see Alterman 2000).

The court's decision parallels and reinforces the growing criticism of the administration, expressed in the media and by many public and voluntary bodies. The crux of this criticism is that the administration is no longer motivated by public interest goals, but by profit maximization. The powerful Ministry of Finance, which is to receive the income for the national treasury (after cost deduction), watches over the administration's shoulders.

The administration's "split personality" regarding its role in initiating planning and development is embodied in the Land Tenders without Planning (LTWP) method, introduced on a small scale in the mid-1990s. The very idea of this system is replete with irony. Frustrated by the long time its own planners take to receive planning approval from the statutory planning bodies for its planning initiatives, the administration decided to experiment with outsourcing the process of obtaining planning permission. The idea was that a large tract of vacant land slated by the administration for possible development would be offered to private developers through a special tender. Under the usual procedure, the tender price would be based on the approved statutory land use plan, that is, one where the use and permitted density would be stated. By contrast, under the LTWPs the winners would be selected on the basis of two criteria: the planning and urban design concept proposed by the contender for the entire tract; and the amount of money offered for the right to receive the leasehold rights for a predetermined percentage of the land, say 25 percent, if and when planning permission is obtained. Once the statutory land use plan is approved, the developer would receive its portion of the tract of land and be allowed to sell the built-up spaces at market prices.

The administration's rationale for this somewhat acrobatic policy was that a private developer would be more "hungry" (to use Wall Street jargon) to have its suggested plan approved and therefore be more effective in pulling the

---

[28] HC 3480/1991 *Uri Bregman v the Housing Construction Commission, Tel Aviv, Piskei Din* 47 (3), 716.

plan through the statutory planning procedure. However, the State of Israel's comptroller general, in its 1999 Annual Report, criticized this system for skewing public planning goals to serve the developers' interests. The comptroller expressed concern that this system would create undue pressure on the statutory planning authorities, which would feel obligated and pressured to approve the plan submitted by a developer who has won a public tender and is being promoted by a major government body. The Ministry of the Environment and green groups join in this criticism, citing the farmland conversions this system has arguably produced. Although the number of LTWPs actually implemented has been small, the idea is not dead. In 2002 the administration decided to reissue the LTWP, this time for smaller land areas and a lower number of housing or other units. Now that the land use planning system has been explained, I shall resume the discussion of property rights and leaseholds.

Development Rights

The lease usually stipulates that it applies only to existing development rights under current planning regulations. But under the Planning and Building Law the lessee has always had at least partial standing to submit to the statutory planning authorities an application for an amendment to an existing statutory plan, or to ask for a building permit to implement new development rights granted by an amended plan initiated by the municipality. Up to 1996 the planning authorities would not consider a leaseholder's planning initiative until the Lands Administration undersigned the plan as the landowner. The 1996 Amendment 43 to the Planning and the Building Law fully equalized the status of leaseholders with that of freeholders. It granted full legal standing to submit amendments or variances to existing plans to anyone "with an interest in the land," a phrase that has been interpreted to include even holders of lesser rights than leaseholds.

Thus, since 1996 the administration has lost the early warning information mechanism it had through the leaseholders' request for the administration's approval prior to submission of amendment plans to the planning authorities. Thus, the administration has had to develop its own system of information, and is gradually learning to rely on its representatives on the local and district planning commissions to bring in relevant plans before they are approved. This way, the administration can check to see whether its interests and policies are adversely affected and, in that case, submit an objection during the plan-deposit stage, like any other holders of interest in the land.

While the lessee has standing to request an amendment to the statutory plan (i.e., to alter the development rights according to the terms of the lease), the lessee cannot implement these rights without the administration's approval. But unless it has a particular reason to refuse, and that is rare, the administration hardly ever refuses permission for the realization of new development rights. It uses the permission requirement as an opportunity to levy a fee for the added increment (to be discussed below). The need to go to the administration for approval of each routine request for replanning or a variance is viewed by many as an unnecessary bureaucratic hassle. The Lands Council recently has considered relaxing this administrative dependence as well. If this occurs, it will be another step in the process of quasi-privatization.

The lessee has independent standing, also, vis à vis the financial aspects of the Planning and Building Law. Under that law a landowner has the right to claim compensation from the local planning commission for decline in property value due to downzoning or externalities expected from an adjacent reclassified use.[29] The lessee has independent standing to claim these rather generous compensation rights (extremely generous in international comparative terms). If compensation is awarded, the lessee would then be the legal recipient!

In fast-growing Israel, upzoning is more frequent than downzoning. There are many cases of replanning for more lucrative land uses or higher densities. Alongside the compensation rights, Israeli law authorizes (rather, requires) the authorities to levy a betterment charge. It is the long-term lessee who pays this levy (see the Tax Obligations section).

Transfer Rights

The secret behind the perseverance of the Israeli leasehold system, despite its massive scale, is its successful coexistence with the market economy and the country's social structure. The key element in this success is the uninhibited right to transfer urban-sector leases at their full market value to (almost) anyone at anytime. A lessee usually can sell, bequeath, rent out or give the property at will, at any time, to anyone.[30] For the majority of transactions in the urban sector, the leases are fully liquid. So, despite the fact that most real property in Israel is under leasehold, the real-estate market is very vibrant and represents about 12 percent of the GDP, even though most of that market is under leasehold.

There is, however, a small additional bureaucratic errand to undertake upon transfer of leaseholds. Because the leases stipulate that the administration must give its consent for the transfer of the lease, the seller must obtain the administration's consent. In the majority of cases the administration grants its consent almost automatically, and this minor administrative intervention apparently does not impact the market.

The consent requirement for the transfer of the lease from one lessee to another does create a problem regarding the equal rights of Israeli-Arab citizens. Here we should distinguish between state-owned and JNF-owned land.

Regarding state-owned land—the majority of the administration's holding—there are no legal differences among Jews and Arabs, so the administration must grant or decline its consent in an ethnically blind manner. Yet, even regarding state-owned land, the consent requirement, as well as other

---

[29] Israel's compensation system for downzoning is unique and interesting beyond the leaseholds issue (see Alterman and Naim 1992).

[30] In rare cases, where some special subsidy in the price of land may have been involved, there may be a minimal period before the lease may be sold without the lessee having to reimburse the administration for the balance of the subsidy. However, programs that subsidize households through the land component are rare.

administration powers, has been used in a discriminatory manner (Kedar 1996; Yiftachel 1992). Such discrimination is on the decline and has been ruled illegal not only in cities, but also where a "community association" neighborhood is concerned. In a revolutionary 2000 High Court decision, *Qaadan v Katzir*, the court ruled that an exurban community, Katzir, cannot exclude an Arab-Israeli family (Qaadan) from eligibility to take out a government lease on a plot of land and build their home (Kedar 2000).[31] Long before this court decision, an increasing number of Arab citizens in cities and towns have been "buying" housing units on the open market from Jewish leaseholders and thus many reside or do business on state-owned land. A current study by this author shows that in recent years the Lands Administration has also begun to allocate an increasing number of tracts of state land for the expansion needs of Arab towns and villages.

In contrast, where JNF land is concerned, the consent requirement is used as an instrument for discriminating between Israel's Jewish and Arab citizens (Weisman 1980). Recall that the treaty the JNF signed with the state in 1960 mandates that land belonging to the JNF should not be transferred into non-Jewish households or businesses. Such cases are much less frequent than transfers of leases on state land because, for historic reasons, JNF land is concentrated in more limited and particular areas. Yet, cases of discrimination do occur occasionally, for example when an Arab household wishes to buy a lease on JNF land within a largely Jewish town. In such cases the administration often tries to find some creative solution to the specific, localized problem. They sometimes swap land parcels between the state and the JNF, thus removing the treaty's restriction. With the growing social mobility of Israel's Arab population and the increasing ethnic mixture of Israeli cities, this problem is becoming more acute and will likely require a general policy solution.

The landmark High Court of Justice decision may have cast doubt on the constitutionality of the differentiation between state and JNF land. Although the High Court decision concerns state-owned rather than JNF-owned land, it is a beacon for likely future court challenges. I expect that before long, a petition will be made to the High Court to give its opinion regarding JNF land too. The High Court will likely rule that the Lands Administration, like any other Israeli official body, is bound by the norms of administrative and constitutional law that preclude discrimination, and that these override its obligations according to the Treaty. One can guess that the administration's legal advisors already are applying the new (surmised) legal doctrine, and instructing their staff to try to avoid discrimination (e.g., by making the practice of land swaps more systematic). Anticipating this type of legal ruling, voices within the JNF have called for the JNF to withdraw from the Treaty and resume self-management of its land.

---

[31] H.C. 6698/95 *Qaadan v the Israel Lands Administration, Katzir et. al.* (Court decisions are delivered and published in Hebrew. For an unofficial English language summary, see *http://csf.colorado.edu/ forums/ipe/2002/msg00516.html*)

Market Rights

Although the administration almost always gives its permission for lease transfer, it may use this opportunity to tax away part of the added land values. The
basic principle in Israel has always been that the market rights to the unearned
increment accrue partly to the lessee and partly to the administration. The
leases allow the administration to capture the added increment in value on
two main occasions (or *tax incidence points*). The first is the transfer of the
property upon sale or gift of the lease (in Israel there is no inheritance tax on
real property, and a recent attempt to introduce it has failed). The fee linked
to this tax point is called a *consent fee*. The second incidence point is linked to
the realization of additional development rights and is called a *permit fee*.

The consent fee applies when the administration gives its consent to a lessee
to sell or gift a lease. The administration has the right to levy about 40 percent
of the unearned increment, compared with the original purchase price (cor-
rected for inflation). The consent fee is assessed on the *undiscounted* part of
the leasehold fee only. That is, if a person holds a fully prepaid lease, there is
no consent charge at all. If, say, 80 percent of the charges have been discounted
up front, the lessee will pay only 20 percent of the added-value fee.

Common wisdom about leaseholds is that the lessor usually retains the right
to the full added value. However, this theory does not and could not hold under
the massive Israeli leasehold system. At no point did the administration issue
leases that entailed both the up-front payment and the consent fee obligation.
The rationale was that a lessee who pays the up-front leasehold rent (which,
as we saw, is very close to market value under freehold) should not be subject
to higher unearned increment fees than a freehold owner. If the consent fee
were to hold, leasehold would in effect be more costly than freehold, and due
to the overwhelming presence of public leaseholds, this might have caused an
artificial hike in already-high real estate prices.[32] Looking at this issue from
another perspective, one could say that since the administration—and the
Ministry of Finance—were interested in promoting the up-front payment leases
over the former annual payment leases, they waived their right, as lessors, to
the added increment.

This is not all. Israel is a country with very high—probably the world's
highest—taxation of the unearned increment (Alterman 1982). There are three
other added increment levies that the administration either did not or could
not waive even when the entire rent charge is paid up front. These include
another levy imposed by the Lands Administration (the permit fee), and two
more taxes that are national and apply to both leaseholds and freeholds—the
betterment levy and the Added Increment Tax.

The permit fee is charged by the Lands Administration when the lessor asks
for consent to implement additional development beyond the development

---

[32] Clearly, in the Israeli system it is difficult to judge what is the market price and what is an artificial
hike in land values caused by extra leasehold charges. This is especially difficult in areas where consumers have no choice because there is effectively no private land for comparison. But, because the country
is so small, one can assume a considerable interregional price comparison by consumers.

rights that were in force at the time of the lease. The permit fee was 50 percent until October 2002, and ostensibly was reduced to 31 percent (but as I will explain, in many cases there will not be a real reduction). The administration applies this fee to all types of urban leases, and does not exempt even the up-front, discounted type of leases. Whenever both the consent fee and the permit fee apply, the administration will offset the lower of the two against the other, so that the lessor will not end up paying the cumulative sum of the two fees, but will pay significantly more than one.

Unlike the consent fee, the permit fee is not likely to be phased out in the near future, even for fully discounted up-front payments. Yet, some of the Lands Council's deliberations have hinted at the possibility of waiving the fee as a selective incentive, say, for controlling the timing of development (to be discussed below). The Ministry of Housing has also requested a waiver of the permit fee in designated urban redevelopment projects, but the administration and the Ministry of Finance have so far refused.

There are also two types of increment-based taxes that apply to all types of properties (unless an exemption holds). The first, called the *betterment levy*, is mandated by the Planning and Building Law at 50 percent of the appraised increment created directly by approval of an amendment plan, a variance, or nonconforming use, to be levied by the local planning authorities (but there are some exemptions for lower-income areas and some other categories). Many owners of leaseholds must pay both the permit fee to the administration and the betterment levy to the local authority. Until October 2002 the administration would offset the lower of the two fees from the total increment value. The offsetting policy has been abolished, along with the reduction of the fee to 31 percent. Thus, under both the old and the new policies the fee to be paid by leaseholders would be considerably higher than 50 percent.

In addition, owners of property rights are subject to the national Added Increment Tax on Real Property of 50 percent—the statutory parallel to the lease-based consent fee. The Added Increment Tax applies to leaseholds as to freeholds. The law specifies that in case of leaseholds, for generations, the tax is to be paid by the lessee, not the lessor. However, this tax rarely is paid by households because the sale or inheritance of a housing unit (or of a lease to one) is exempt every four years, and most transfers by households fall within this generous exemption clause.[33]

One of the common rationales for public leasehold systems offered by land policy scholars is that they do—or should—enable the public agency to capture more of the unearned increment than freehold. According to this rationale, the Israeli leasehold system does indeed deliver the goods extremely well: while freeholders in Israel pay hefty unearned increment taxes by international comparative terms (Alterman 1982), public leaseholders incur an additional layer of fees grounded in the lease.

---

[33] In late 2001 the added-increment tax was cut to 25 percent, but increments in value gained through 2001 are still assessed at 50 percent, so it will take several years until the benefits of the reform reach most consumers.

This common wisdom on land policy has few followers in Israel—among neither consumers nor the decision makers. Once again, the fact that leaseholds pay an up-front market value almost identical to freeholds for the lease undermines the reasonableness of commonly held notions about public leasehold systems, and gives it a reverse twist. In the eyes of typical Israeli leaseholders (those who are aware of the additional charges), an absurdity of the Israeli system would be that they—who hold lesser property rights than freeholders—are burdened by higher betterment or unearned increment charges. As for decision makers, this issue—like most other key issues in the leasehold system—has never surfaced as a public issue.

The Right to Delay Development

One of the sticks in the bundle of property rights is the landowner's right to decide the timing of development decisions. The converse—the power to control the timing of development—is sought by public authorities in charge of development control, usually with futility. In theory, leasehold contracts could provide a good solution to this perennial quest. The leasing authority could easily introduce a clause in the lease or prelease contract stating that if the construction, or some phase of it, is not completed according to a particular schedule, there would be a fine or the lease would be voided.

This last type of property right, too, has proven resistant to control through leaseholds. With time, the administration's capacity to use leaseholds to control the timing of development has weakened. The administration has attempted to introduce conditions into the leasehold contracts to limit the freedom of the developers who have won tenders on public land to make their own decisions on the timetable of the development process. The main instruments introduced by the Lands Council are called *development contracts,* which developers are required to fulfill as a precondition to the leasehold contract. These vary for different types of development, but they share a time-limit clause, whereby developers must finish the construction of the infrastructure or buildings (or both) within the stipulated time period (usually three to five years). If the developer does not keep to the timetable, the development contract is voided, the lease will not be signed and the land must be returned to the administration.

Timing-control sanctions have been difficult to implement with regard to all types of developers: commercial, public or resident owners. Commercial developers have for years complained that the land return requirement is unreasonable. The Ministry of Finance has been attuned to the developers' argument that the requirement causes artificial delays in the development process and a hike in land prices. Recently, the Lands Council adopted a new policy whereby a developer who encounters financial problems in undertaking the development on time, will be allowed to transfer (sell) the prelease contract to another developer, instead of returning the land to the administration, as previously required.

A similar process has occurred with respect to households (resident owners) in the Build Your Own Home program. As that program has grown in popularity, so has the administration's load of cases, where households could not (or did not find it convenient to) keep to the timetable of construction stipulated in their development contract. Since these residents also are voters, it became politically unsavory for the administration to enforce the return-obligation clause in the development contract, recently leading to the official relaxation of the timing-control sanction in these contracts as well. Thus, one of the last hoped-for benefits of public leaseholds—the desire to control the timing of development by private actors—has also gradually eroded away.

Tax Obligations

All real estate taxes in Israel apply equally to public leaseholds and are the obligation of the lessee rather than the Lands Administration. In the Israeli context, where the income from the administration goes directly into the national treasury (after deduction of costs), the Lands Administration has never been treated as a landlord responsible for paying the taxes. Due to the massive scale of public leaseholds, this simply would have meant transfer from pocket to pocket.

This special Israeli situation (or anomaly) is highlighted through a particular clause in the Planning and Building Law, which imposes the betterment levy. That clause does happen to include a rare statement that ostensibly recognizes that the leaseholder should not be obliged to pay the full tax. The clause says that the landowner has the obligation to reimburse the lessee for the difference in the levy as assessed on freehold compared with leasehold. However, the Lands Administration's leases bypass this clause by waiving the lessor's obligation. Since there usually is little difference in market price between similar freehold and leasehold properties, the problem is not very significant financially (and I have never seen it mentioned in academic or public forums), yet I find it worthy of a legal challenge.[34]

As already noted, over and above Israel's extremely high taxes on the unearned increment, that are charged equally on the unearned increment on both freeholders and leaseholders,[35] leaseholders generally pay additional unearned increment fees grounded in the lease.[36] Contrary to common wisdom about leaseholds, had the average leaseholder known about this anomaly, she or he probably would have viewed these lease-based fees as additional—and unwarranted—taxes, rather than as a justified additional recoupment of the unearned increment rightly due to the landowner. They might have argued

---

[34] The public lease could be regarded as a uniform contract that applies to consumers who have little choice but to sign it. The administration is almost a monopoly (in many areas of the country, a full monopoly). Could leaseholders initiate class action against this clause? The catch is, of course, that under the Israeli public leasehold system there is little difference in value between the same property assessed as freehold or leasehold. The legal costs may not be worth the trouble. If, however, the court struck this clause from the contract, the Lands Administration would potentially be swamped with thousands of reimbursement claims for relatively small amounts of money each, which would accumulate to a large sum.

[35] Except where exceptions apply in taxation laws. These exceptions, too, are "ownership blind" and where relevant apply equally to freeholders and leaseholders.

[36] As mentioned above, two types of fees imposed by public leases apply in addition to statutory taxes.

that the income from all these taxes and fees goes to the same address—the national treasury (except for the planning-system based betterment levy that goes to the local authority).

Had the average leaseholder realized that she or he in effect pays higher taxes than freeholders, the leaseholder would likely have asked why private landowners—the minority—are regarded by the taxation system as privileged over leaseholders. After all, leaseholders bear greater administrative and financial burden than freeholders. But the vast majority of leaseholders—and even the vast majority of real estate professionals—has not paid much attention to this anomaly. These questions have rarely, if ever, been addressed in the press or the Knesset (Parliament) as a public policy issue. Indeed, the differences in taxes and fees hardly seem to affect consumers' location decisions. Most householders and smaller businesses will select land or built-up space, not according to taxes that may accrue in the future, but to current locational advantages and prices.

CONCLUSION

The Israeli public leasehold system has been undergoing a process whereby the property rights granted de facto to leaseholders have gradually come to resemble freehold ownership. This trend, which I call *crawling privatization*, has closed almost all remaining gaps between the two types of tenure, leaving only minor controls in the hands of the administration (but capturing even more of the unearned increment than the statutory taxation system). The market in leaseholds is a close simulation to the market in freeholds, as are the prices fetched.

Why has this occurred? When a leasehold system becomes very large, when it becomes the macro, ruling system rather than the exception, it must change gears if it is expected to work. The alternative to quasi-privatization is a land system similar to those in the Soviet bloc countries, whose demise needs no reminder. The absence of a vital market system in those countries had done terrible damage to urban and regional structures, the housing stock and the environment. It is possible that leaseholds—qua leaseholds rather than those masquerading as freeholds—could work as an effective public policy and planning tool only when they constitute an island of special tenure and public policy, in a sea of a private property and market regime. In such cases, leasehold systems will be judged by public opinion and by the marketplace, in what they can offer to the public and private domains, through fair competition with the freehold system.

The Israeli case shows that when the leasehold system becomes the dominant system covering large portions of the population and of businesses, then administrative intervention becomes too cumbersome to manage, and too politically onerous. That is, unless it is altered to become a private property lookalike, and market forces are allowed to work almost unfettered by administrative intervention. This is what has happened over the decades to the Israeli large-scale public leasehold system (in the urban sector), and this is what has made it operate reasonably well.

What is the benefit in maintaining the large and heavy machinery of the Israel Lands Administration? Does it achieve any public policy goals beyond its capacity to capture more of the unearned increment than already captured by the general Israeli taxation system? And do these benefits, if any, counterbalance the damage that this government-heavy system can do? Answering these one million dollar questions is beyond the scope of this chapter, since it requires a systematic exploration into many national policy and planning areas, some of which touch directly or indirectly on the Israel-Arab conflict. However, the savvy reader will be able to draw out partial answers from the various sections here.[37] In politically turbulent Israel, the answer—obviously controversial—will probably depend on one's geopolitical values and views.

---

[37] This key issue has not been tackled systematically by researchers, and is not part of public discourse. Recently, I did attempt such an assessment, the first of its kind, published in an Israeli law journal and already cited by the Supreme Court (Alterman 1998). A summary here would be unfeasible, because it requires the presentation of many planning and public policy topics beyond this chapter.

REFERENCES

Alexander, Ernest R. 1998. Planning theory in practice: The case of planning Highway 6 in Israel. *Environment and Planning B: Planning and Design* 25:435–445.

Alexander, Ernest R., Rachelle Alterman and Hubert Law Yone. 1983. *Evaluating plan implementation: The national statutory planning system in Israel. Progress in Planning* monograph series 20, Part 2. Oxford: Pergamon Press.

Alterman, Rachelle. 1982. Land value recapture: Design and evaluation of alternative policies. Occasional paper no. 26. Vancouver: Center for Human Settlements, University of British Columbia.

———. 1988a. Exactions American style: The context for evaluation. In *Private Supply of Public Services: Evaluation of real-estate exactions, linkage and alternative land policies*, Rachelle Alterman, ed. New York: New York University Press.

———. ed. 1988b. *Private supply of public services: Evaluation of real estate exactions, linkage and alternative land policies*. New York: New York University Press.

———. 1990a. *Municipal land policy in Israel: Does it exist?* Haifa: The Klutznick Center for Urban and Regional Studies. Technion—Israel Institute of Technology. In Hebrew.

———. 1990b. From expropriations to agreements: Developer obligations for public services in Israel. *Israel Law Review* Autumn, 1990.

———. 1995. Can planning help in time of crisis? The response of decision makers to Israel's wave of mass immigration. *Journal of the American Planning Association*. 61(2):156–177.

———. 1997. *Israel's future land policy*. Policy report in the set of final reports of *Israel 2020: A national plan for Israel in the 21st century*. Haifa: The Research and Development Foundation. Technion—Israel Institute of Technology. In Hebrew.

———. 1998. 'Who can retell the exploits of Israel lands'? Assessing the justification for national land ownership in Israel. *Iyunei Mishpat—Tel Aviv University Law Review* 21(3):535–579. In Hebrew.

————. 2000. Land-use law in the face of a rapid-growth crisis: The case of the mass-immigration to Israel in the 1990s. *Washington University Journal of Law and Policy* 3:773–840.

————. 2001a. National-level planning in democratic countries: A cross-national perspective. In *National urban and regional planning in democratic countries: A comparative perspective,* Rachelle Alterman, ed. London: Liverpool University Press, Town Planning Review book series.

————. 2001b. National-level planning in Israel: Walking the tightrope between centralization and privatization. In *National urban and regional planning in democratic countries: A comparative perspective,* Rachelle Alterman, ed. London: Liverpool University Press, Town Planning Review book series.

————. 2002. *Planning in the face of crisis: Land-use, housing and mass immigration in Israel.* London: Routledge, Cities and Regions Series.

Alterman, Rachelle and Goran Cars, eds. 1991. *Neighborhood regeneration: An international evaluation.* London: Mansell Pubs.

Alterman, Rachelle and Morris Hill. 1986. Land use planning in Israel. In *International handbook on land use planning,* Nicholas N. Patricios, ed., 119–150. New York: Greenwood Press.

Alterman, Rachelle and Orli Naim. 1992. *Compensation for decline in land values due to planning controls.* Published jointly: Jerusalem, Land Use Research Institute and; Haifa: the Klutznick Center for Urban and Regional Studies. Technion—Israel Institute of Technology. In Hebrew.

Bonneville, Marc. 1996. Real estate in Russia from socialism to market economy: The case of St. Petersburg. *European Planning Studies* 5(Oct. 4):513–526.

Brutzkus, Eliezer. 1988. The development of planning thought in Israel. *City and Region—Ir Ve'ezor* 18(Nov.):188–198. In Hebrew.

Cohen, Eric. 1970. *The city in Zionist history.* Jerusalem: Urban Studies Series, Hebrew University.

Gordon, David L. A. 1997. *Battery Park City: Politics and planning on the New York waterfront.* Amsterdam: Gordon and Breach Publishers.

Haaretz Daily Newspaper. 2002. September 24:C3. In Hebrew.

Israel Central Bureau of Statistics. 2001. *Statistical Abstracts of Israel 2000,* Table 2.1.

————. 1988. *Construction in Israel 1987.* Table 35.

Kalbro, Thomas and Hans Mattsson. 1995. *Urban land and property markets in Sweden.* London: UCL Press.

Kedar, Alexander. 1996. Israeli law and the redemption of Arab land, 1948–1969. Cambridge, MA: Harvard University Law School.

————. 2000. A first step in a difficult and sensitive road: Preliminary observations on *Qaadan v. Katzir. Israel Studies Bulletin* Fall:3–11.

Limonov, Leonid and Vincent Renard, eds. 1995. *Russia: Urban development and emerging property markets.* Paris: Association des Études Foncières (ADEF).

Mazor, Adam. 1993. The land resource in spatial planning. In *Israel 2020: A master plan for Israel in the 21st century, stage 1, vol. 2.* Co-published by the Israel Engineers' and Architects' Association and the Faculty of Architecture and Town Planning, Technion—Israel Institute of Technology. In Hebrew.

Needham, Barrie, Patrick Koenders and Bert Kruijt. 1993. *Urban Land and Property Markers in The Netherlands.* London: UCL Press.

Needham, Barrie and Roelof Verhage. 1998. Housing and land in Israel and the Netherlands. *Town Planning Review* 69(1):397–423.

Reiner, Tom and Ann L. Strong. 1995. Formation of land and housing markers in the Czech Republic. *Journal of the American Planning Association* 61(2):200–209.

Renard, Vincent and Rodrigo Acosta, eds. 1993. Land tenure and property development in Eastern Europe. Paris: Association des Études Foncières (ADEF).

Shachar, Arie. 1993. The national planning doctrine in Israel. In *Israel 2020: A master plan for Israel in the 21st century, stage 1, vol. 2.* Co-published by the Israel Engineer's and Architect's Association and the Faculty of Architecture and Town Planning, Technion—Israel Institute of Technology. In Hebrew.

Shefer, Gabriel. 1996. Society, politics, government and national-level planning in Israel. In *Towards the implementation of the "Israel 2020" plan: National-level planning institutions and decisions in ten countries.* Rachelle Alterman, ed., 195–200. In *Israel 2020: A master plan for Israel in the 21st century, Phase 3, report no. 9.* Co-published by the Israel Engineers' and Architects' Association and the Faculty of Architecture and Town Planning, Technion—Israel Institute of Technology. In Hebrew.

United Nations. 1996. *Demographic yearbook.* New York.

Weisman, J. 1980. Restrictions on the acquisition of land by aliens. *American Journal of Comparative Law* 28:36.

Weisman, Joshua. 1993. *Law of property: General part.* The Harry and Michael Sacher Institute for Legislative Research and Comparative Law: The Hebrew University of Jerusalem.

Yiftachel, Oren. 1992. *Planning a mixed region in Israel: The political geography of Arab-Jewish relations in the Galilee.* Aldershot, England: Averbury Press.

POLICY DILEMMA OF CAPTURING LAND VALUE UNDER THE HONG KONG PUBLIC LEASEHOLD SYSTEM

7

Yu-Hung Hong

In most countries, governments use property and capital gains taxes to recoup the public's share of increases in land value (Hagman and Misczynski 1978). These tax revenues represent major sources of funds for local public finance. For example, in the United States incomes generated from property taxes account for as much as 30 percent of all revenues, or 75 percent of total tax revenue, for local governments (Ladd 1998). Despite their importance, property taxes are very unpopular (Doebele 1991; Wallis 2001). In some situations public revolts against property tax increases have led local governments in developed and developing countries to search for other sources of revenue. In countries where the majority of land is publicly owned, one possibility is leasing public land.

In theory, if a landowner leases only the use right of land to a tenant, the landowner should be able to profit from all future land value increments by collecting a land rent and taking the land back from the lessee for sale when the lease expires. In practice, however, the logic is not always that straightforward when the landlord is a government. Leasing public land by a government has two distinct characteristics. First, under most public leasehold systems the government is the dominant, if not the sole, landowner in an economy. Because of its monopoly power over the supply of land, the method and timing it uses to allocate land would normally have significant implications for housing supply and costs. Second, owing to the prominent position of a government lessor in the land market, its leasing policy will be under close public scrutiny, thereby, of course, opening the door for political influences from special interest groups. In some democratic countries where public officials must be accountable to or elected by their constituencies, increasing land rents or repossessing land at the expiration of the lease may not be politically feasible or even be considered by the government due to the fear of public opposition. Owing to these unique

I thank Professors Steven C. Bourassa, Max Neutze and Sidney Wong for their comments to the earlier drafts. The usual disclaimer applies.

characteristics, it is sometimes difficult to predict if public land leasing can allow government to capture land value, and how it affects land and housing development. The lack of comprehensive analyses of this subject may have hindered the design and implementation of public leasehold systems in some transitional economies.

Using Hong Kong as a case study, this chapter explores both the opportunities and risks of using land leasing to achieve public policy goals, in general, and to recoup the lease value (or land value), in particular.[1] In examining these opportunities, I focus on the government's ability to raise revenue by auctioning land leases and to subsidize public housing and industrial development by granting land to private entities and quasi-public agencies at below market value. As to the risks, I analyze how requiring lessees to pay a huge up-front land premium at the beginning of the lease has fostered the development of an institutional environment that made Hong Kong a captive of high land and housing costs. The ransom for freeing itself from this development path may unavoidably incur immense political costs.

The presentation of the above ideas proceeds in four steps. The first step is to provide background information about the Hong Kong public leasehold system. A discussion of government past attempts to achieve certain public policy goals through land leasing, which is the second step, will follow. The third step involves a detailed examination of the relationships between public land leasing and housing costs. The final step is to reflect on the Hong Kong land leasing experience, raising a fundamental question for land policy-making in Hong Kong and elsewhere.

The intention here certainly is not to generalize the findings for all public leasehold systems based on a very unique case: not all systems are operating in a real estate market where land supply is as scarce as Hong Kong's. Rather, for those policy makers wishing to experiment with the ideas of capturing land value by leasing public land, there should be value in knowing about some of the potential difficulties as illustrated by the Hong Kong experience.

THE ORIGIN OF THE HONG KONG LAND LEASING STRUCTURE

With a population of 6.8 million people in 2002 and a total land area of 1,070 square kilometers of which 80 percent is too hilly for any development, Hong Kong is one of the most densely populated cities in the world.[2] Despite the lack

---

[1] Lease value and land value are, strictly speaking, not the same. The lease value of a land site should be lower than its freehold value, due to the various constraints attached to the contract. In addition, a lessee must pay an annual rent and other leasehold charges to the lessor for modifying or renewing the lease in the future. The two values will be similar only if: (1) the land rent is trivial or nonexistent and (2) the lease term is long and renewable. These two conditions would make the leasehold rights tantamount to fee simple. Because public leaseholds in Hong Kong fit these two criteria, I will use the terms lease value and land value interchangeably here.

[2] This section provides only a brief description of selected issues related to the historical development of public land leasing in Hong Kong. For a comprehensive account, see Nissim (1999).

of natural resources it was well known for rapid economic growth between the 1970s and the mid-1990s. It was referred to as one of the *four little dragons* in Asia; the other three were Singapore, Taiwan and South Korea. Some argued that the economic success of Hong Kong was mainly because of the British laissez-faire approach to managing the economy. Indeed, the British government maintained a minimum level of involvement in regulating business practices and labor relations. There were no trade restrictions on goods or capital, and corporate and personal income taxes were set at a low level to stimulate private investment. After Britain returned Hong Kong's sovereignty to the People's Republic of China (PRC) in 1997, these principles of economic governance remained intact. Yet, hidden under the label of being the most capitalist city in the world, there is a less recognized fact about Hong Kong. The government owns the most valuable and scarce resource in the city: land. The allocation of land to private entities and quasi-public agencies for housing and industrial development is governed by a public leasehold system.

Owing to the unique historical context of Hong Kong, many current features of its public leasehold system evolved from the original structure established in 1884 when the British first set foot on the island. From the beginning, the British government wanted to retain land ownership so it proclaimed that all land belonged to the Crown. Only with the authorization of the Royal Majesty of Great Britain through the "Letters Patent" could the governor of Hong Kong distribute land to private parties by granting them Crown leases (Wesley-Smith 1983; Bristow 1984).

As the city developed, public officials began to see the potential of public leasehold as a tool to accomplish other policy goals, including managing urban growth, promoting industrial and public housing development and raising government funds for infrastructure investment. Although the government attempted to achieve all of these objectives, its economic policy (minimum government intervention and low income taxes) and its status as a colonial ruler (no financial assistance from Britain) made it set the fiscal considerations of leasing land as the top priority. What follows is a brief historical account of how, by trial and error, the government refined its policy goals of leasing public land.

In 1841 most parts of Hong Kong were steep and uninhabited. Despite this uninviting appearance and the vast amount of undeveloped land available, the British government immediately recognized the importance of controlling land and the possibility of raising public funds through the allocation of land resources. In May 1841 Captain Elliot, the first British official in charge of the colony's affairs, issued a public notice to set the guidelines upon which the government would (1) only lease, not sell, land to the public; (2) grant development rights of land through public auction; (3) set a minimum price for lots put up for auction; (4) grant leases to the highest bidder in the auction; and (5) prohibit any private land transaction without notifying the government (Hong Kong Annual Yearbook 1963). Subsequently, these principles became part of a quasi-constitution that governed land leasing in Hong Kong. Based on these rules, the then-governor of Hong Kong formed a committee to survey boundaries of land and established a land court to settle disputes over land claims. In 1844 the government also legislated the Land Registration Ordinance, requiring all land transactions to be registered in the Land Office.

The implementation of the land leasing policy in the 1840s was not without problems. There were periods of confusion as well as contention. In 1843 lessees complained that the duration of the lease (75 years with no option to renew) was too short. In response to this challenge the governor proposed to extend the lease term from 75 to 999 years in 1848 (Hong Kong Annual Yearbook 1963, 11; Bristow 1984, 27). The secretary of state accepted the governor's proposal reluctantly, due to the possible intensification of discontent among lessees and reduction in the collections of land rents. The governor then granted an extension of 924 years to all 75-year leases with no additional charge. For the following 50 years all land leases in Hong Kong, except a few lots on the Kowloon peninsula, were granted for a period of 999 years. Indeed, some of the most expensive land sites in the central business district of Hong Kong today were granted at that time and had a lease term of 999 years until they were renewed in 1997 for another 50 years.

In 1898 the British government began to recognize that the long lease term would deprive it of the ability to share the increasing land values with lessees, and immediately ordered the governor not to grant any additional 999-year leases. Instead, it would offer lessees 75-year leases with an option to renew for another 75 years with no additional payment. The government only required lessees to pay a new level of rent, determined by the director of Public Works, at the date of expiration. Following these events, 75 years became the standard lease term until Hong Kong reunited with the PRC in 1997. Since 1997 the most common lease term has been 50 years, analogous to the promise of the Chinese government to maintain the status quo of Hong Kong for 50 years after reunification.

This history showed that the lease term—which shifted from 75 to 999 years and then back to 75 years with the option to renew before it settled at 50 years—was determined by politics. Politics, as defined here, was the interplay between the constant attempts of lessees to influence the formation and enforcement of rules for leasing public land and the government's reactions toward these efforts. As will become increasingly clear, some policy changes regarding lease payment and renewal could also be explained by the politics of public land leasing.

Since 1898 the system of land leasing in Hong Kong has evolved into a complex structure. Based on the historical institutional arrangements, the government currently assigns land rights to private parties by land leases. These leases state the amount and type of development rights that the government grants to private lessees. They also identify the period during which lessees can enjoy the granted rights. The government possesses the title to land; and private lessees acquire only specific land rights that last through the term of the lease. Within that period lessees can transfer the development rights to other parties. They also have the right to benefit from all land development and transactions, subject to payments of land premiums, annual rents, rates and a property tax to the government.[3]

The government collects from lessees a land rent every year and land premiums at initial public auctions (or tenders), at the time of lease modifications, and during lease renewals. The government also levies rates on all properties based on the estimated ratable values of both land and buildings. The ratable value is an estimated annual rental income that property owners might have obtained had they rented their property in the market. The liability of paying rates normally falls on property occupants. For the rental apartment, the property owner and tenant sometimes can negotiate an agreement on how to share the responsibility of paying rates. The government sets the level of rates annually, depending on its financial needs. In 2002 the government set the rates at 5 percent of the ratable value of property. It was 11.5 percent in the 1970s.

Property tax is payable by owners at 15 percent of the actual rental income earned from the property, less an allowance of 20 percent of taxable income for repairs and maintenance. If a corporation, which is subjected to corporate income tax in Hong Kong, occupies a building or has income from real properties, there will be an exemption from property tax. Instead, any income derived from property will be payable as corporate income tax. Although a tax rate of 15 percent may seem high, the rate is applied to the rental value, not the capital value, of the property. If we assume that an annual rental income of a property is about 6 percent of its capital value, a tax rate of 15 percent on the rental value will be equivalent to a rate of 0.9 percent of its capital value.

POLICY GOALS AND LEASE CONDITIONS

The government has structured lease conditions in ways that would help it achieve public policy goals. Yet, public opposition to government leasing policy has also influenced the enforcement of lease conditions and led to many policy revisions. Hence, to help readers appreciate the unique features of the Hong Kong public leasehold system, an examination of interactions between officials' attempts to achieve their land-leasing goals and lessees' resistances against their intentions is needed.

Managing Urban Growth

When the government plans to lease a parcel of land to private developers through public auction, it first prepares a draft lease called the Conditions of Sale, in which the government specifies the location and the plot size of the leased land and the other attached restrictions on the use, height and design

---

[3] The separation between rates and the property tax in Hong Kong can be confusing for readers, because rates in the British and other Commonwealth systems are usually equivalent to the property tax in the U.S. context. As will be defined later, the property tax in Hong Kong is a tax on income earned from rental properties, using actual rental income as the tax base and the standard income tax rate (15 percent) as the tax rate. Thus, it is different from the property tax in the U.S., where the tax base is usually the assessed capital value of the property.

of the building. In preparing this document, officials in the Lands Department will circulate a draft contract to different public agencies, such as the Planning Department, Transportation Bureau and Works Bureau. Officials in these government units will then review the proposed lease conditions and recommend appropriate changes. This way, the government can ensure that terms established in the lease will be sufficient to guide the uses of the land according to the general comprehensive plan of the city. Besides, based on recommendations from other bureaus, officials of the Lands Department can negotiate with potential developers for the private provision of, say, streets and parking spaces. This is particularly important for large-scale housing development where the private developer will be responsible for constructing all necessary public infrastructure and facilities for the entire complex.

After the preparation of the Conditions of Sale, the government sends the contract to all interested land developers. Based on the conditions stated in the contract, private developers estimate the leasing price and bid for the development rights of land in public auction. In the auction, competition among bidders determines the premium paid to the government for leasing the land. Normally, the government requires the bidder who gets the lease to pay 10 percent of the premium as a downpayment at the closing of the auction. The lessee then must pay the remaining balance in one lump sum within 30 days.

The government has tried to employ lease conditions to enforce land use regulations for many years (Bristow 1984; Roberts 1975). The Town Planning Ordinance in Hong Kong was enacted in 1939 and brought into effect only after 1949 because of the Second World War. It is not as comprehensive as similar legislation in other countries. It provides the power to the Town Planning Board to prepare and approve Outline Zoning Plans only. Enforcement of the plans must rely on the Building (Planning) Regulations of the Buildings Ordinance and lease conditions. In principle, lease conditions can give the government the ability to control development in detail on a case-by-case basis. Whenever leaseholders want to modify the conditions of their leases, they must apply to the Lands Department and the Buildings Department for permission, which will in turn approve or disapprove these applications. If an application is approved, the government will reassess an additional premium and impose a new set of covenants on the modified contract (Robert 1975).

In the past, enforcement of the Outline Zoning Plans through lease conditions has been problematic. Due to the different processes and periods during which the British government took over various parts of Hong Kong, lease structures varied among districts. The major problem was that before 1949 the use of lease conditions to control land development was not guided by zoning plans. While some post-1949 leases had explicit restrictions on the density and use of the leased land, other older leases had unrestricted development rights (Nissim 1999; Yeh 1994; Robert 1975). Yeh (1994) and Bristow (1984) argue that leases with no restrictions on land use have created environmental problems and incompatible land uses in some old districts in Hong Kong. The government could not incorporate new restrictions on land uses into land contracts because the only opportunity for it to change lease conditions was during lease modification or renewal. As stated earlier, the lease terms in Hong Kong ranged from 75 to 999 years before 1997, hence, lease conditions established, say, 75 years ago might not agree with the development control stated in the recent zoning plans. Given the continuous revisions of the Outline Zoning Plans, a condition allowed in the land contract might suddenly be restricted by a modified plan. Using both lease conditions and the statutory plans to control land uses confused developers as to which planning standards they should follow as they made their investments. In other words, although conditions of long-term leases might provide great flexibility for controlling land development on an individual basis, they were extremely inflexible in adjusting to changes in the overall zoning plans through time, unless, of course, there are provisions in the contract that specify which set of rules will prevail if inconsistencies emerge. To put this observation in proper perspective, the issue is similar to the problem of nonconforming use in a freehold system where a government can only make land uses consistent with changed zoning through condemnation and compensation—an approach that is sometimes controversial, and thereby rarely used.

The current practice in Hong Kong is that all land development must follow the guidelines specified in the statutory plans, even if a lease is unrestricted. All new leases have conditions that identify explicitly the Building Ordinance and Town Planning Ordinance as the ultimate guidelines for governing land use. The government can reject any building proposals that contravene development restrictions with no legal obligation of paying the lessee any compensation, albeit exceptions can still be made on a case-by-case basis. In 1992 a special committee reviewed the issues related to compensation and betterment and concluded that there should be no compensation when impacts of planning on a lessee's rights do not amount to any derogation of the land contract. Conversely, when a modification of a statutory plan increases the development potential of a land site that exceeds the rights specified in a lease, the lessee who wants to redevelop the property must apply to the Lands Department for a lease modification and pay the required premium. Put differently, while the government is eager to capture the windfalls, it is reluctant to compensate lessees for any decreases in lease value caused by changes in zoning. For developers, one advantage of the leasehold system is that the land contract provides certainty about the development potential of leasehold rights. With detailed and explicit land use restrictions specified in land leases, developers can calculate the appropriate premium for leasing land. This will in turn reduce the financial risks due to changes in planning regulations (Yeh 1994). The new approach will undoubtedly undermine this certainty available under the leasehold system. Indeed, many developers feel that the lack of compensation for the loss of preexistent contractual land rights caused by a revision of a statutory plan is inequitable (Nissim 1999). The issue of compensation is far from an agreement between the government and developers, and future legal challenges are looming on the horizon.

The planning profession is also seeking alternative avenues to enforce land use regulations instead of relying on the lease purpose clauses. In those rural districts designated by the government as Development Permission Areas, the Planning Department has the power to issue enforcement and compliance notices to lessees or occupants, requiring them to discontinue any unauthorized development. It is an offence in law if lessees do not comply with government notices. In essence, the government has gradually retreated from using lease conditions to control land development in some areas of Hong Kong.

Developing Public Housing

Not all land leases are auctioned publicly. For land that the government provides to special industries and nonprofit organizations, it normally grants the development rights to these entities using the Conditions of Grant (also referred to as the *private treaty grant*); premiums are determined by negotiation, not public auction. To establish such a land lease, a potential lessee must first submit an application to the government, proposing the type of development and a financial plan for the project. If the government approves the application it will then negotiate with the lessee for the amount of premium and the specific lease conditions.

There are three types of Conditions of Grant: (1) nominal premium grant; (2) reduced premium grant; and (3) full market value grant. Lessees who obtain the nominal premium grants, which have a lease term ranging 15–20 years, have to pay only a small amount of money to the government for leasing the land. Only nonprofit organizations, such as schools, religious associations, childcare centers and hospitals, are qualified to apply. Most important, through the nominal premium grants, the government subsidizes public housing by granting land to the Hong Kong Housing Authority (HKHA) at a low premium. The HKHA is a quasi-public agency responsible for the provision of, mostly, public rental housing to the low-income group in Hong Kong. It also operates the Home Ownership Schemes that provide housing units for the middle-income group to purchase at below market value. It was estimated in the early 1990s that the housing programs of the HKHA covered about half the population in Hong Kong (HKHA 1993). With such rapid increases in land prices it would have been impossible for the agency to build affordable housing for the poor were it required to pay for lands at their full market values.

The government also awards the reduced premium grants to the Hong Kong Housing Society (HS)—another nonprofit organization that operates several rental estates and the Flat for Sale Scheme for the middle- and low-income groups. The government grants land to the HS for rental estates at a premium one third of the full market value of the land. For the land the HS uses for the Flat for Sale scheme, the government charges only half the market value.

Castells, Goh and Kwok (1990) argue that public land ownership in Hong Kong allows the government to operate the second largest public housing program in the world. It reduces the land costs of providing public housing for the poor. If land were freehold, the government would have had to be financially strong or willing to exercise its statutory power to obtain land from private owners for public housing construction.

During the 1970s when Hong Kong was developing its industries, the government's ability to provide subsidized housing to labor prevented wages from rising, which in turn enhanced the price competitiveness of Hong Kong products in the international markets. When the economy developed and incomes of the population grew, the public housing program also provided a refuge for the poor whose incomes, though improved, could not keep up with the escalating housing costs. In this way the public housing program, on one hand, could reduce income disparities created by economic development and, on the other, could minimize criticism of the government's "high land price" policy.

The strategy that worked in the 1970s and the 1980s seemed to lose its magic touch after the new government—the government of the Hong Kong Special Administrative Region (HKSAR)—took over in 1997. As household incomes rose further in the 1990s, some lower-middle-income families, referred to as members of the "sandwich class," began to earn incomes too high to qualify for government housing subsidies, but too low to allow them to purchase their own homes in the private property market. When the size of this sandwich class expanded, complaints about high housing costs became louder and more frequent than ever before. In response to this grievance the new government promised to increase land supply and build additional housing units under its Home Ownership Schemes. Unfortunately, right after the government announced this well-intentioned policy, the Asian financial crisis spread to Hong Kong (to be discussed later). Weak housing demand, along with the proposed increase in land supply and housing production, depressed property prices. Major developers and the propertied class immediately called for the government to stop intervening in the private housing market and halt all land auctions. Suddenly the government had to confront a policy dilemma: the propertied group that accounted for about half of the population wanted the government to maintain its high land price policy. The nonpropertied group wanted the government to relax land supply and increase housing production. As will become clear, the emergence of this dilemma affects the way the government leases public land.

Promoting Special Industries

Industries, including shipping, gas, telecommunications, oil refineries and electricity, are usually land intensive and cannot be operated in multistory industrial buildings. If companies in these sectors were required to compete with other land developers for land at the public auctions, it would have been very difficult to attract these key industries to operate in Hong Kong. To promote the development of essential industries, the government leases land to selected industrialists through the full market value grants. Although lessees of this type of land contract have to pay for land at full market value, they sometimes pay their premiums in installments with an interest charge. Besides, the premiums are decided by negotiation between the government and grantees; thus, it is conceivable that the negotiated premiums are lower than what they would have been had the payments been determined at the public auctions.

Between 1969 and 1981 the government also gave all lessees the option to pay their premiums in annual installments. The payment method was deemed necessary because the banking crisis occurring in the late 1960s made the financing of land development difficult to obtain. In 1969 the government applied the scheme only to valuable commercial land sites in the central business district, where the amount of land premiums was then HK$10 million or more (Hong Kong Annual Yearbook 1970). The government later extended the installment payment method to all leasing of residential, commercial and industrial land, offering lessees the option to pay their premiums in 10 equal installments with an interest fee of 5 percent per annum. With the low interest rate charged to leaseholders, the government subsidized land development by providing low-cost financing. After the Hong Kong economy recovered from the banking crisis, the government continued to offer the installment option to lessees until 1981. In that year the government abolished the method because of the increasing numbers of defaults.

Capturing Land Value

Previous research shows that the government could generate a substantial amount of revenue from public land leasing (Hong 1995; 1998). Between 1970 and 2000 the total lease revenue amounted to US$71.1 billion (in constant 2000 U.S. dollars). Adding the amount of revenues collected from rates and property tax to the total lease revenue increased the balance to US$96.1 billion.[4] The rapid increase of property values in Hong Kong could explain, in part, the substantial amount of revenue generated from leasing public land.[5] Table 1 presents the significance of lease revenues in funding public works in Hong Kong. Between 1996 and 2000 annual revenues generated from public land leasing were more than enough to cover the costs of infrastructure and land development, with only 1998 as the exception, due to the Asian financial crisis. On average, lease revenues accounted for 17 percent of total government revenues—the second most important source of public funds after personal and corporate income taxes—and 18 percent of total expenditures during this five-year period. Based on the information, the Hong Kong government seemed capable of retaining a large portion of land value by leasing public land. The retained lease value also was significant in providing public funds for infrastructure development.

Under the Hong Kong public leasehold system the government has four mechanisms to recoup land value: (1) at the initial public auction or tender; (2) the collection of an annual land rent; (3) at the time of lease modification; and (4) during lease renewal. Analyzing how the government utilized these mechanisms revealed another interesting finding: it appeared to rely on initial

---

[4] These figures are from the Director of Accounting, Hong Kong Government (1970–1996); the Commissioner of Inland Review, Hong Kong Government (1970–1996); the Hong Kong Annual Yearbook (1970–1996); and the China Council for the Promotion of International Trade (2002).

[5] According to both Jones Lang Wootton's Index and the index produced by the government, real property prices increased with a mean annual growth rate of about 21 percent from 1984 to 1995 (Lai 1997, 68).

auctions to capture land value. Figure 1 shows the percentages of lease revenues collected from different mechanisms.

Between 1970 and 1995, 75 percent of the total lease revenues were from premiums generated from initial auctions. Premiums received from lease modifications accounted for only 20 percent. The percentages of payments collected from annual land rents and lease renewals were 4 percent and 1 percent, respectively. These data suggested that the government obtained the largest percentage of its lease revenues at the beginning of the lease. Subsequent collections, in terms of modification and renewal premiums and land rents, were not significant. Because this approach of capturing land value, as will be argued later, has important implications for the development of land and housing markets, it is useful to recapitulate my explanations for the government's reliance on the initial public auction to collect lease value (see Hong 1998).

TABLE 1

SIGNIFICANCE OF LEASE REVENUES IN HONG KONG, 1996–2000, (IN MILLIONS OF HK$)

Item	1996	1997	1998	1999	2000	Average
Lease revenues	29,508	65,931	25,686	39,111	32,183	
% of total revenues	14	23	12	17	14	16
% of total expenditures	16	34	11	18	14	18
% of expenditure on public works	101	229	82	133	105	130
Total revenues	208,358	281,226	216,115	232,995	225,060	
Total expenditures	182,680	194,360	239,356	223,043	232,893	
Total expenditures on public works	29,168	28,772	31,267	29,490	30,577	

Source: China Council for the Promotion of International Trade (2000)

FIGURE 1

COMPONENTS OF LEASE REVENUES FOR HONG KONG: 1970–1995

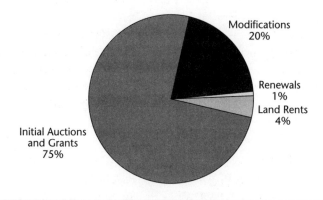

Total Lease Revenues: $67,147
(1995 US$, in Millions)

Modifications
20%

Renewals
1%

Land Rents
4%

Initial Auctions
and Grants
75%

Source: Commissioner of Inland Review, Hong Kong Government (1970–1996)

Lease renewal

One opportunity for the government to capture increases in land value is during lease renewal. Before 1984 there were renewable and nonrenewable leases in Hong Kong. When a nonrenewable lease expired, the lessee had to apply to the government to renew the land rights. Up to 20 years before the lease expired, the lessee could apply for an early renewal. This option was intended to prevent negligence of building maintenance when the lease was approaching its expiration. If the government did not require the land for public use it would issue a new contract to the lessee, specifying the updated building covenants, requirements for public infrastructure, and the additional premium for the renewal. The premium represented the full market value of the land at either the date of expiry or the date of application for the extension. If the government needed the land it could reject the application and retake land with a payment of compensation to the lessee for any leasehold improvements. Similar to the Dutch system described by Needham (Chapter 3, this volume), the government, in principle, could resort to two kinds of legal right to retake land—the right of the lessor to terminate contractual agreements with the lessee when the lease expired and the statutory power of the public authority to repossess land based on the justification of requiring the land for public use. Yet, the process involved in taking back land and determining just compensation was lengthy and complex (Cruden 1986). To make matters worse, the government might risk provoking opposition from the lessee. Thus, there is no evidence to support the assertion that public land leasing has given the government extra power to take back land after the contracts expire.

Procedures involved in the extension of renewable leases were different. As discussed earlier, the government started to grant 75-year renewable leases to lessees in 1898 to replace the 999-year leases. Before 1973, when these leases were up for extension, lessees would only have to pay a new level of rent determined by the director of Public Works. The renewed land rent would then remain the same for another 75 years. Because the government did not explicitly specify the criteria for calculating new land rents in the leases, it could not enforce the rule. In the late 1960s, 5,000 renewable leases were up for renewal, and the government asked leases to pay a new annual land rent based on the full market value of land. In one case the new land rent increased from HK\$76 to HK\$60,764—approximately 800 times higher than what the lessee paid previously (Scholes 1967; Wu 1973). Feeling that he had already purchased the right to renew his lease, the lessee refused to pay the new land rents. He sued the government and the case went all the way to the Privy Council in England. When the lessee lost his legal battle to the government, others organized public protests to fight against the renewal policy. A series of public confrontations, including signature campaigns, rallies and political maneuverings among legislators, occurred within a six-year period (Wu 1973). At the end the government compromised and charged a new annual rent equal to only 3 percent of the ratable value of property, which later became the standardized rule for lease renewal. This series of historical events showed that public resistance made capturing land value during lease renewal politically untenable in Hong Kong, thereby explaining why renewal premiums accounted for such a small percentage of total lease revenues.

Indeed, had the government not been defeated in its effort to recapture land value during lease renewals in the early 1970s, it might have tried again in 1997. That year all leases expired when Hong Kong reunited with the PRC. To maintain the political and economic stability of Hong Kong during the transition, the two governments agreed in 1984 that all land leases would be renewed automatically for another 50 years with no payment of an additional premium. Again, lessees were only required to pay a new level of rent set at 3 percent of the ratable value of their properties. The only difference was that the government would have the right to reassess the ratable value of property annually, which was not done under the pre-1997 system. The next opportunity for the government to retain land value by requiring lessees to pay renewal premiums at full market value will be in 2047. Given that the government will adjust land rents at a regular interval and that there is no precedent for a successful land value capture during lease renewal, it is unlikely that the government will charge lessees any premiums based on full market value of land for renewing their leases in 2047.

Lease modification

When lessees want to redevelop their properties, they may have to apply to the Lands Department to modify lease conditions that impose certain development restrictions on their lands. If the government approves the application it will require an additional premium for relaxing lease restrictions. The premium is based on the potential increases in land value after the development controls are lifted. The rationale for the requirement is that changing the lease restrictions is equivalent to requesting extra development rights from the government. Therefore, the lessee must pay for those newly acquired land rights.

The government has been unable to raise public funds through lease modification, because of severe negotiation problems encountered during the process of assembling land for redevelopment. In Hong Kong multistory apartment buildings are the predominant type of property. With numerous, separately titled apartments erected on a single land parcel, a land contract can have more than 100 leaseholders. When a property has multiple leaseholders, a developer seeking to redevelop the building must negotiate with each individual lessee for the transfer of land rights. The large number of involved lessees increases negotiation costs tremendously. In some instances a minority of lessees might reject the developers' offer and hold up the entire project. Due to high negotiation costs, developers have found it more profitable to obtain land by bidding for new land rights at the public auctions than by purchasing development rights from existing lessees. This is why urban redevelopment conducted by the government or private developers in Hong Kong has not been as active as it should be, given the shortage of land in this city. Low incentives for obtaining land for urban renewal have led to a small number of applications for lease modifications, thus eliminating the government's opportunity to capture land value through lease modification as well.

Annual land rents

In the past, the government did not rely on the collection of land rents to raise public funds. Rather, land rents were fixed, nominal yearly payments that merely symbolized the landlord-tenant relationship between the government and lessees. As mentioned earlier, the government changed this land rent system in 1997. The method of calculating land rents is the same as that used for lease renewal, and officials can now adjust the actual amount of rents collected by reassessing property rental values annually. In theory, this new policy may lower the bidding prices for land leases at the public auctions because part of the payments for leasing public land is now shifted from the initial premium to annual rents, making the latter look more like rates. Indeed, instead of just paying the rates, property owners in Hong Kong now are paying a total of 8 percent (5 percent for the rates and 3 percent for the land rent) of the value of their properties to the government, as land-related levies, every year. So far, there has been no major public outcry about the additional payment of annual land rents since 1997. Certainly, it might be partly because rental values dropped significantly after the Asian financial crisis, which in turn lowered the payments for rates and land rents. This policy shift, however, could still create controversies in the future.

Initial auction

Unable to raise public funds through the other mechanisms, the government has been relying on initial public auction to generate lease revenues. The method of auctioning land rights creates a competitive environment at the public auction. If public officials feel that the bidding price for a parcel of land is too low, they can withdraw the land from the auction. Similarly, if developers think that the bidding price is too high, they can stop competing for the land. Enforcement of the payment of initial premium also incurs low costs. As stated earlier, the government requires the successful bidder to pay 10 percent of the premium as a downpayment at the close of the auction and the rest of the amount in one lump sum within 30 days. If the developer fails to pay the remaining balance in full, the government will confiscate the deposit and auction the land rights again. In general, parties involved in land leasing believe that public auction is more transparent than are other methods based on private negotiation. It also allows the government to generate the largest possible amount of revenue by granting the land contract to the highest bidder.

Although the government's approach to raising public funds has been effective, some people in Hong Kong view its reliance on lease revenues to finance public infrastructure as a primary motivation to create high land prices. Indeed, because the government recoups most of the land value at the beginning of the lease, it must schedule land leasing carefully. Had the government leased all land sites rapidly, at the time when their values were low, it would have lost its ability to capture any future increments because demanding additional payments from lessees for lease modification or renewal had proven either politically controversial or technically difficult. Yet, timing the supply of land rights is tricky, for it is difficult to predict the future demand for land and housing. On one hand, the government does not like to lease land rapidly because of the reason just stated. On the other hand, it does not want to slow land leasing to the extent that housing costs are inflated excessively. This is the balance the government has tried to maintain for many years, and the attempt has been a constant struggle and politically controversial—an issue to which we now turn.

PUBLIC LAND LEASING AND HIGH HOUSING COSTS

There have been numerous debates over the causes of high housing costs in Hong Kong. Certainly, as one of the world's most densely populated cities, it is reasonable to expect properties to be expensive. Yet, scholars and analysts disagree on what other factors may have exacerbated the already very high housing costs in this city. Some assert a causal relationship between land supply (or the supply of land development rights) and property prices, and call for a carefully designed government "land sale" program to stabilize housing production and prices (Peng and Wheaton 1994; Bank of China Group 2001).[6] Others refute any direct link between the pace of land leasing and housing costs. Instead, they argue, the domination of a few developers in the land market is the major problem (Consumer Council 1996; Lai and Wang 1999; Fu and Ching 2001). The remainder of this chapter argues that public land leasing is one of the major causes for high housing costs, describing the process through which institutions for leasing land shape and are shaped by changing conditions in the property market. Before going further it will be useful to summarize several key studies from which the evidence to support the assertion is drawn.

In the mid-1990s Peng and Wheaton (1994) developed an econometric model to test the relationship between land supply and property prices in Hong Kong. They concluded that, prior to the 1990s, the restriction on land supply by the government increased housing prices. The high prices were not triggered by the fall in housing production due to the shortage of land. Rather, they were the outcome of market expectation—a belief that the limited land supply would lead to higher property prices in the future. Anticipation of future price increases led to expanded housing production, encouraging developers to substitute land with capital. Despite the escalating property prices, housing demand remained strong, partly due to the growth in incomes and partly to the homebuyers' fear of having to pay more for their purchases as property prices were expected to rise further in the future. Consequently, restricted land supply increased both property prices and density of development. Based on their analysis, the authors then suggested that the government should not increase

---

[6] The leasing of land rights at the public auction is often referred to as "land sale" in Hong Kong. To be precise, it does not mean selling land as fee simple to private parties.

land supply to stimulate housing development. This action would only create an expectation that property prices may fall in the near term. An anticipated drop in housing prices may then lead to a decrease in investment demand for property and housing production—an effect that can be exactly opposite to the government's intention of boosting housing supply.

Findings of other later studies put forth a different view. Based on their separate reviews of data from 1973 to 1997, Tse (1998) and Lai and Wang (1999) did not discover any significant causal relationship between land supply and housing prices. Instead they found that large developers built their own land banks and developed their landholdings only when they saw a clear sign of increases in housing demand. These researchers argue that developers employed land banking mainly as a means to lower the risk of housing investment. Because private land banks acted as a buffer between any changes of government land supply and housing demand, the pace of land leasing, as they argue, did not seem to have important impacts on housing costs during the study period.

Another study conducted by the Hong Kong Polytechnic University on behalf of the Consumer Council (1996) appeared to confirm the domination of a few private developers in both the land and property markets. In that study scholars revealed that seven developers supplied 70 percent of all new private housing units between 1991 and 1994. More important, 55 percent of these housing units came from just four developers, and one built 25 percent of the units. Although it is obvious that there are a few dominating developers in the housing market, two issues must be resolved before one can conclude whether their domination leads to high property prices. First, analysts who studied the housing market structure of Hong Kong would strengthen their arguments if they could state explicitly how the oligopoly in the property market, if indeed it exists, exerts its influence over prices. For a few developers to agree on delaying land development and housing production so as to manipulate property prices, they must form a collusion to coordinate their production. To make the collusion work, there must be an effective enforcement mechanism that prevents members of the oligopoly from violating the rules. Beside the enforcement issue, delaying land development incurs carrying costs, such as interest expenses and the opportunity costs of capital invested in land acquisition and banking. All these considerations will reduce the incentive for firms to participate in price fixing. To be fair, detecting the practice of collusion is hard because cooperative strategies can persist without any formal written agreements. As the folk theorem suggests, agreements among firms can be sustained for a long time, based on a tacit acknowledgment of acceptable behaviors among group members who interact with each other repeatedly (Fudenberg and Maskin 1986).

Second, new residential units are an additional supply that represents only a small fraction of the total housing stock in the market. It is estimated that new home sales in Hong Kong normally account for no more than 20 percent of all property transactions in a year (Fu and Ching 2001). Thus, even if major developers could control housing production, it is still unclear how much they may influence housing prices, when homebuyers can purchase properties from existing owners.

To deal with the methodological difficulty of measuring imperfect competition, Fu and Ching (2001) designed a method to examine competition in the Hong Kong land market. They hypothesized that if there is free competition, "economic profits"—profits that exceed the normal returns required to compensate businesses for the risk of investment—could not exist in the long run because of new entries into the market. They then estimated the extent to which developers in Hong Kong were able to earn economic profits on land acquisitions between 1986 and 1998.[7] Using the "event-study" method, they showed the existence of economic profits for major developers and concluded that there appeared to be barriers for entry into the land market. Moreover, the economic profits earned by developers increased property prices in Hong Kong.

A few words about how developers could transfer land costs to homebuyers are deemed necessary here. In addition to the suggestions cited earlier, the practice of "trading up" properties may explain why buyers are willing and able to pay high prices for the purchases. In Hong Kong few people can afford their dream homes when they first become homeowners. Property prices are so high that most first-time buyers will normally buy a low-end housing unit. Buying the first (or even the second and third) property is more like an investment in Hong Kong in order to build equity. As property values increase, homeowners will sell their homes to realize the capital appreciation of their assets and then use the proceeds toward a larger, more expensive unit. Through this process, homeowners may move from the lower-tier to the middle- or even the higher-tier housing sector. Because of this system, high land and property prices may not be bad news to homebuyers at all. Quite the contrary, increases in housing prices may enhance their ability to finance the next purchase, as values of existing homes have increased as well. Hence, in some circumstances, as Peng and Wheaton estimated, the demand for housing may not fall significantly when property prices rise. This also explains why the burden of high land costs generally falls on the shoulders of first-time homebuyers in Hong Kong.

The purpose of describing these studies is certainly not to evaluate any technical issues related to the data and models used by researchers to estimate the correlation between land supply and property prices. Instead, the intention is to collect as much evidence as possible to show how public land leasing affects housing costs. A review of the literature revealed that each study provides a missing piece of the jigsaw puzzle that when put together can explain the relationship between land supply and housing costs.

Capturing Land Value at the Initial Auction

The government has relied on the initial land auction to retain land value. This is mainly because the government has encountered fewer problems collecting

---

[7] Fu and Ching (2001) calculated the economic profits of some publicly traded real estate companies that won bids at the public auctions during the study period. They compared the daily returns of these companies' stocks versus the performances of the Hang Seng Index for a period of 100 trading days before and 40 days after the auction.

land premiums from lessees at the initial auctions than through lease modifications and during contract renewals—a phenomenon largely shaped by the
institutional setting of public land leasing in Hong Kong. Facing institutional
constraints, the government does what it must to raise public funds, that is,
to capture as much land value as possible at the beginning of the lease. This
approach will work only if the government regulates the leasing of new land
rights. An example will illustrate why I suspect the government has indeed
controlled land supply, despite its repeated assurances to the public that the
leasing schedule is driven mainly by market conditions.

In 1984 when Britain and the PRC signed the Sino-British Joint Declaration, the Chinese government deliberately incorporated a provision into the
agreement that restricted the pre-1997 government from leasing more than 50
hectares of land annually (excluding the land granted for public rental housing
development) until the return of the sovereignty of Hong Kong to the PRC.
The purpose of the provision was clearly to prevent the British from selling off
all land before the new government took over Hong Kong. If land leasing had
little fiscal impact on the government's budget, the explicit restriction on land
sale would have been unnecessary. Given the fact that lease revenues were (and
still are) important to the government's financial strength, it was possible that
the authority, being the sole landowner, would maintain a regular pace of land
supply to ensure a steady inflow of land premiums into its coffer. Although the
government claimed that it had consistently gone over the 50-hectare limit due
to strong market demand, the data gathered from the Lands Department, which
is presented in Table 2, tell a different story. Between 1985 and 1997, only in
1988 and 1996 did the government lease more than 50 hectares of land. More
important, in each of the two years, the surge in land supply was mainly due
to the assignment of a large piece of nonresidential land to a single company
by private tender—35 hectares in 1988 for the construction of a container port
and 65 hectares designated as "other uses" in 1996. During the 13-year period,
the government leased, on average, 33.5 hectares of land annually, which was
far below the limit set by the Joint Declaration. The supply of residential land
was relatively more stable than that of nonresidential land, with an average
of 20.4 hectares of land sold every year.

Comparing the land sale figures with the real annual changes of the average
property price during the same period revealed the fact that the government
did not increase land sale when property prices increased substantially. Nor
did it reduce the quantity of land supplied significantly when prices dropped.
As shown in Figure 2, the average property price in Hong Kong fluctuated
drastically between 1984 and 1997, with considerable increases of more than
30 percent in 1991, 1992 and 1997, as well as decreases of over 15 percent in
1984 and 1995. Despite the fluctuation, the total quantity of land supplied,
as indicated in Table 2, maintained in general within the range of 20 and 27
hectares each year, when the above-mentioned two special private treaty grants
were excluded from the data for 1988 and 1996. In other words, the government could have auctioned a lot more land than it did in, say, 1991 and 1992,
before it reached the 50-hectare limit, if it were eager to capitalize on the rising

TABLE 2

LAND SUPPLY IN HONG KONG, 1985–1998 (IN HECTARES)

Years	Total Area of Land Supplied	Residential		Nonresidential	
		Amount	Percentage	Amount	Percentage
1985-1986	19.1	11.4	59.5	7.8	40.5
1986–1987	27.1	24.1	88.9	3.0	11.1
1987–1988	27.1	21.4	78.8	5.8	21.2
1988–1989	59.4	21.1	35.6	38.3	64.4
1989–1990	26.6	19.0	71.6	7.6	28.4
1990–1991	27.7	20.3	73.5	7.4	26.5
1991–1992	31.6	26.7	84.8	4.8	15.2
1992–1993	29.7	22.0	74.1	7.7	25.9
1993–1994	19.7	15.4	78.3	4.3	21.7
1994–1995	25.2	21.6	85.7	3.6	14.3
1995–1996	92.5	24.0	25.9	68.5	74.1
1996–1997	15.7	13.2	84.2	2.5	15.8
1997–1998	34.1	25.3	74.2	8.8	25.8
Average	33.5	20.4	70.4	13.1	29.6

Source: Land sale records, Lands Department of Hong Kong, *http://www.info.gov.hk/landsd/lsr/lsr.htm*

FIGURE 2

REAL CHANGE IN AVERAGE PROPERTY PRICE, 1984–1997 (PERCENTAGE)

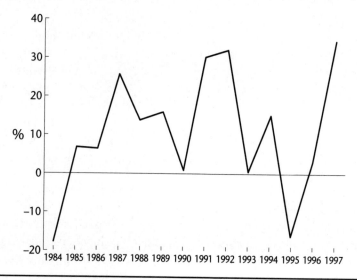

Source: Lai, Neng and Ko Wang (1999)

market to enlarge its lease revenues. Instead, it only increased the total amount of land supplied slightly—from 27.7 to 31.6 hectares.

This information alludes to two government strategies. First, the pre-1997 government seemed to try to maintain a constant land supply disregarding the vicissitudes of property prices so as to minimize its influence over the private housing market. Second, the government's prime fiscal objective was to balance its annual budget, therefore, it might be reluctant to schedule land sale in accordance with the real estate cycles, for this approach would have created a large surplus in one year but a huge deficit in another. These strategies, though sensible, had created an unintended consequence of sending a signal to the public that land supply was regulated, which in turn helped nurture an expectation that property prices would continue to rise in the future. As Peng and Wheaton (1994) demonstrated quantitatively in their paper, this market expectation led to high property prices.

In reality, information is imperfect, hence, the expectation of future movements of property prices could never be precise. When the anticipated price increase is due to artificially inflated land and property prices, projected housing production in response to the price signal may exceed actual demand, especially when an unexpected event suddenly impedes the purchasing power or the sentiment of homebuyers. The Asian financial crisis (to be discussed later) is illustrative of such an event. As an overly optimistic forecast may lead to a huge oversupply of housing units, the adjustment process of eliminating the surplus may take a longer time and incur more financial pain than in a situation where a relatively moderate price increase is expected. In other words, not only could the reliance on the initial public auction to capture land value lead to high land and housing costs, it may also increase the volatility of the property market—a point that has not been discussed in existing analyses.

Land Market Structure

Most analysts seem to agree that imperfect competition in both land and housing markets contributes to high property prices in Hong Kong. I believe the lack of competition has much to do with public land leasing as well. With premiums amounting to millions of Hong Kong dollars at public auctions, developers need either the financial backing from major banks or a large amount of cash on hand to engage in land acquisitions. Certainly, the government could have used the public auction to determine the level of annual land rent, as other public leasehold systems have done, and avoid the need for developers to raise huge up-front capital to pay the initial land premium. But the 1841 decision that set the path for the development of a premium system, and the high default rate of the installment payment method in the 1980s, rendered that option impractical.

Most small developers do not have the financial resources of their larger counterparts. Thus, larger developers dominate the public auctions (Consumer Council 1996; Lai and Wang 1999; Fu and Ching 2001). With only a few large developers obtaining new land leases from the government, they gain control over the supply of land rights for housing development. As stated earlier, Fu and Ching found that major developers were able to earn higher than normal profits from land acquisitions. High returns for these developers, I would add, could further enhance their financial ability to outbid small- and medium-sized firms. Little by little, several dominant firms have emerged in the land market and gained the ability to increase property prices to cover both the land costs and their economic profits.

Two other factors may have reinforced the dominant position of major developers. First, because negotiation costs associated with land assembly for property redevelopment are high, only major developers have the financial resources and scale economies to conduct intricate negotiation with the government for lease modification and with lessees for the transfer of land rights. Thus, activities that can generate additional supply of development rights either from the sales of leasehold rights by existing lessees or through lease modification are also dominated by major developers.

Second, owing to government policy of favoring large-scale, comprehensive housing development where most public infrastructure and facilities will be constructed by private developers, the average size of land lots leased at the public auctions and through tenders has increased tremendously. The increase in both the scale and the scope of housing development further enlarges the capital requirement for companies to enter into the real estate sector.

To promote timely land development the government instigates in all land contracts a condition that obligates lessees to complete their development projects within a specified time, normally 48–60 months. Lessees needing more time must apply to the government for a lease modification and pay an additional premium for deferring the completion date. The government, however, does not impose a heavy enough charge on lessees to discourage them from delaying their projects. Failure to take full advantage of the provision reduces the government's ability to influence housing supply.

The government also publicizes its land sale schedules and projections for housing supply for a five-year interval. By providing updated estimates for the future supply of land and dwellings, public officials hope to help homebuyers make informed decisions about when to purchase their properties. During a general upsurge in real estate prices, however, these government actions seem to have no effect on slowing the escalation of housing demand and property prices.

Overinvestment in the Housing Sector

One reason for the resilience of the expectation of rising property prices was that the government, the business community and banks developed a high financial stake in real estate investments. For the government, lease payments, rates and the property tax amounted to a significant portion of public revenues. As to the economy, land production and financial services related to property transactions accounted for an average of 19 percent of the annual gross domestic product (GDP) between the 1980s and the 1990s. Staley (1994, 27) estimated that

> Hong Kong's property and construction industries represent 45% of the capitalization in the Hong Kong stock market, significantly higher than in Singapore (13%), Malaysia (8%), Japan (under 2%), and the United Kingdom (under 10%). Moreover, over 60% of Hong Kong's investment expenditures are in the form of property and about 30% of all bank lending is to the property and construction industries.

With land-related investments playing such an important role in all economic activities in Hong Kong, a major downturn of the property market could surely have devastating effects on the economy. Due to the prominent position of real estate investments in the public and private sectors, people began to believe the government would use all means to prevent property prices from falling. This expectation, though unfounded, made housing appear a relatively safe investment not just for developers but for the public as well.

The fallacy that housing prices would never fall was finally shattered when the Asian financial crisis spread to Hong Kong in October 1997. The Hong Kong dollar was pegged to the U.S. dollar and was under pressure for a major devaluation. To defend the fixed exchange rate, the government raised interest rates at the time when financial troubles throughout Asia slowed the economic growth of the region almost to a halt. With higher interest rates and an economic downturn, homebuyers started to encounter difficulties in obtaining mortgage loans for their property purchases. As a result, housing demand dropped sharply. Within just one year, property prices plummeted by more than 50 percent from their 1997 peak.

Because investments were highly concentrated in the real estate sector, the dramatic fall in asset values hampered economic activities in other sectors as well. First, consumers cut their consumption after experiencing a 50 percent drop in their personal wealth caused by the decline in property values. When the aggregate demand for consumers' goods decreased, so did profits for general businesses. Second, with the curtailment of property demand and the decrease in housing prices, many real estate companies turned their profits into losses. Shrunken corporate earnings led to a fall in stock prices and lowered the incentive for foreign and domestic investors to invest in Hong Kong. When investment dropped, the whole economy went into a recession, with the real estate and construction industries being the worst hit sectors. The GDP, which had a 5 percent increase in 1997, reversed its trend and declined by 5.1 percent in 1998 (Tsang 1999).

IMPLICATIONS FOR HOUSING POLICY

When the economy was good there was no incentive for the government, developers, property owners or investors to change the systems of leasing public land and financing real estate development, for they all benefited from high returns on their property investments. Only in 1997 did the government of the newly established HKSAR announce that it would like to expand home ownership by establishing a housing production target of 85,000 units per year. The post-1997 government hoped that this housing initiative would alleviate the concern about the never-ending escalation of housing costs. More than half the proposed housing units were supposed to be built by private developers. The rest, about 38,000 units, would be constructed by the HKHA under the Sandwich Class Housing Scheme. Because this housing program targeted the lower-middle-income group, it was perceived initially, even by private developers, as having little impact on the private property market where buyers mostly belonged to the high- and upper-middle-income groups.

Though well intended, the implementation of the housing initiative was derailed by the 1997 financial crisis. As property prices experienced a 50 percent decline, developers and homeowners began to criticize the housing initiative and insist that the government revise its policy. Between 1998 and 1999 the government announced a series of rescue packages amounting to US$7.2 billion, to prevent property prices from falling further (Tang 2000). First, it suspended all public auctions and tenders. Second, the HKHA abolished its target of building 38,000 housing units for the middle-income group. Third, the government allocated special funding for the Home Starter Loan Scheme to increase the number of eligible first-time homebuyers, hoping to improve the demand in the private housing market. Although it is understandable why the government took these actions to prevent an economic catastrophe, tax-payers' money used for the rescue packages might have primarily benefited private developers, investors and property owners. To make matters worse, these government actions seemed unable to turn the depressed housing market around. As of August 2002 there was still no sign of recovery of the property prices that dropped 50–65 percent between 1998 and 2002.

As the new government insists on making affordable housing the number one long-term policy priority, tension has begun to mount between the government and major developers. Some developers openly condemned the government's housing initiative as an unwarranted intervention in the private market (Ho 1998; Gittings 1999; BizAsia 2000). Property owners also organized public protests and accused the government of causing them to lose the life savings they had invested in their properties. This episode clearly indicated that any future policy changes that may dampen property prices would face strong opposition from powerful interest groups. This institutional setting gives the government very little flexibility to modify land and housing policy to accommodate changing demographic and economic conditions. In retrospect, the Asian financial crisis has fully exposed the fundamental weaknesses of the government's decision to raise public funds by collecting a high land premium at the beginning of the lease. The excessively upbeat prospects of the property market, domination of major developers in the land market and overinvestment in real estate have made the recovery of the Hong Kong economy from the Asian financial crisis slow and painful. These trends have also created political controversy surrounding the government's attempt to revise its housing policy to respond to the public's changing needs.

CONCLUSION

Like most public leasehold systems around the world, land leasing has provided the Hong Kong government many opportunities for accomplishing different policy goals. Yet, it has also presented many challenges to the government. Among the opportunities the government is able to raise a substantial amount of revenue from leasing public land. Public land ownership also allows the government to subsidize public housing programs for the poor and the development of key industries. Taking advantage of these opportunities, however, is not risk free. During the past decades, when industrial and commercial development progressed rapidly, collecting a high land premium at the beginning of the lease certainly was not helpful in lowering high housing costs in the private housing market. The government was able to balance the tradeoff between its fiscal considerations of leasing land and the provision of affordable housing for the poor by funding a massive public housing program in 1960s and 1970s. Yet, the method became ineffective in the late 1990s, when property prices increased to such levels that even middle-income families found it difficult to purchase their own homes. When the post-1997 government tried to increase home ownership by setting an annual production target for both public and private housing sectors, its initiative was opposed by major developers and propertied class. This conflict revealed the rigidity of the housing sector—domination of a few large developers in the land and housing markets and overinvestment in real estate—that was encouraged, in part, by the government's leasing policy.

Based on the existing institutional environment in the housing sector of Hong Kong, the possibility of introducing policy changes depends on the government's political will and power to persuade major developers and the propertied class into accepting new rules. If these interested groups refuse to comply with new rules, they will either organize public opposition or invent ways to evade the new regulation that may eventually render the implementation and enforcement of any policy initiative impossible.

For countries that are experimenting with public leasehold systems, the Hong Kong experience unveiled one potential dilemma of leasing land, that is, the tradeoff between raising public funds and stabilizing housing costs. The case study is particularly relevant for cities where the demand for urban land is keen. Depending on individual situations, governments may choose to auction land rights to the highest bidders to raise the much-needed revenues to finance public infrastructure and social services. Yet, as the Hong Kong experience has demonstrated, this approach may promote high land and housing costs. A question that requires a careful analysis on a case-by-case basis is, "To what extent can a government, acting as a custodian of public land on behalf of its citizens, maximize the financial returns on land leasing without impairing its duties or legitimacy as the protector of public interests?" Of course, there is no simple answer to this question, for the solution depends on how politics are played out according to varying institutional arrangements in different times and places.

REFERENCES

Bank of China Group. 2001. The outlook for Hong Kong's property market. *Economic Forum*. Website: *http://www.tdctrade.com/econforum/boc/011001.htm*.

Bristow, Roger. 1984. *Land-use planning in Hong Kong: History, policies, and procedures*. Hong Kong: Oxford University Press.

BizAsia. 2000. Sunday sees growing dissatisfaction with Hong Kong government. June 25.

Castells, M., L. Goh and R. Y. W. Kwok. 1990. *The Shek Kip Mei syndrome: Economic development and public housing in Hong Kong and Singapore*. London: Pion Limited.

Census and Statistics Department of Hong Kong. 1997. *Survey of building, construction, and real estate*. Hong Kong: Hong Kong Government Printer.

China Council for the Promotion of International Trade. 2002. China statistics 2000. Website: *www.ccpit.org/engVersion/cp_tj21/tj2001W.htm*

Commissioner of Inland Revenue, Hong Kong Government. 1970–1996. *Annual review of the financial year by the commissioner of inland revenue of Hong Kong*. Hong Kong: Hong Kong Government Printer.

Consumer Council of Hong Kong. 1996. *How competitive is the private residential property market?* Hong Kong: The Consumer Council.

Cruden, G. N. 1986. *Land compensation and valuation law in Hong Kong*. Singapore: Butterworths.

Director of Accounting, Hong Kong Government. 1970–1996. *Annual report of the director of accounting services and the accounts of Hong Kong*. Hong Kong: The Hong Kong Government Printer.

Doebele, William A. 1991. The interaction of land-based taxation and land policy: A planning perspective. International Conference on Property Taxation and Its Interaction with Land Policy. Cambridge, Massachusetts: Lincoln Institute of Land Policy.

Fu, Yuming and Stephen Ching. 2001. Examining competition in land market: An application of event study to land auctions in Hong Kong. Paper presented at the AREUEA Conference, New Orleans, 2001.

Fudenberg, D. and E. Maskin. 1986. The folk theorem in repeated games with discounting or incomplete information. *Econometrica* 54:533–556.

Gittings, Danny. 1999. Developers' tactics could fall flat. *South China Morning Post*. September 29.

Hagman, Donald G. and Dean J. Misczynski. 1978. *Windfalls for wipeouts: Land value capture and compensation*. Chicago: American Society of Planning Officials.

Ho, Lok Sang. 1998. Policy blunder of the century. *South China Morning Post*. March 24.

Hong Kong Annual Yearbook. 1963. *Hong Kong annual yearbook*. Hong Kong: Hong Kong Government Printer.

———. 1970–1996. *Hong Kong annual yearbook*. Hong Kong: Hong Kong Government Printer.

Hong Kong Housing Authority (HKHA). 1993. *Rising high in harmony: An illustrated summary of 40 years of public housing development in Hong Kong*. Hong Kong: Hong Kong Housing Authority.

Hong, Yu-Hung. 1995. Public land leasing: Flexibility and rigidity in allocating the surplus land value. Ph.D. dissertation. Cambridge, MA: Massachusetts Institute of Technology, Department of Urban Studies and Planning.

———. 1998. Transaction costs of allocating the increased land value under public leasehold systems: Hong Kong. *Urban Studies* 35, 9(August):1577–1596.

Lai, Lawrence Wai-Chung. 1997. *Town planning in Hong Kong: A critical review*. Hong Kong: City University of Hong Kong Press.

Lai, Neng and Ko Wang. 1999. Land-supply restriction, developer strategies and housing policies: The case in Hong Kong. *International Real Estate Review* 2(1):143–159.

Ladd, Helen. 1998. *Local government tax and land use policies in the United States: Understanding the links*. Northampton, MA: Edward Elgar Publishing.

Nissim, Roger. 1999. *Land administration and practice in Hong Kong.* Hong Kong: Hong Kong University Press.

Peng, R. and W. C. Wheaton. 1994. Effects of restrictive land supply on housing in Hong Kong: An econometric analysis. *Journal of Housing Research* 5:263–291.

Rating and Valuation Department of Hong Kong. 1997. *Hong Kong property review.* Hong Kong: Hong Kong Government Printer.

Roberts, Philip James. 1975. *Valuation of development land in Hong Kong.* Hong Kong: Hong Kong University Press.

Scholes, J. 1967. Chang Lan Sheng vs. the attorney general. *Hong Kong Law Report.* June 24.

Staley, Samuel R. 1994. *Planning rules and urban economic performance: The case of Hong Kong.* A Friedman Lecture Fund Monograph. The Hong Kong Centre for Economic Research. Hong Kong: Chinese University Press.

Tang, Connie Pui-yee. 2000. More than housing providers: How Hong Kong property developers grew big? Occasional paper no. 144. Chinese University of Hong Kong, Department of Geography.

Tsang, D. 1999. *Onward with new strengths, the 1999–2000 financial budget.* Speech by the Financial Secretary of the Hong Kong Special Administrative Region. Hong Kong SAR: Hong Kong SAR Government Printer.

Tse, Raymond Y. C. 1998. Housing price, land supply and revenue from land sales. *Urban Studies* 35(8):1377–1392.

Wallis, John Joseph. 2001. A history of the property tax in America. In *Property taxation and local government finance,* Wallace E. Oates, ed. Cambridge, MA: Lincoln Institute of Land Policy.

Wesley-Smith, Peter. 1983. *Unequal treaty, 1989–1997: China, Great Britain, and Hong Kong's new territories.* Hong Kong: Oxford University Press.

Wu, Chung-Tong. 1973. Policy making over land rents in Hong Kong: A case study of the bureaucracy and the pressure groups. Paper presented at the Canton Delta Seminar. Hong Kong: Centre of Asian Studies, University of Hong Kong.

Yeh, Anthony Gar-On. 1994. Land leasing and urban planning: Lessons from Hong Kong. *Regional Development Dialogue* 15, 2(Autumn):3–28.

PART III

EXPERIMENTING WITH
PUBLIC LEASEHOLD SYSTEMS

Tenure Choices for Urban Land Privatization in Ukraine

The Role of Leasehold

8

Ann Louise Strong

The role of leasehold of public land in today's Ukraine is still being determined. The Land Code of 2001, implementing the language of the Constitution concerning property rights, was enacted by Parliament (the *Verkhovna Rada*) in October 2001, signed by President Kuchma in November 2001, and took effect in January 2002. It should prove a major step in determining how leasehold is used in the future.

The choice of tenure for urban land in independent Ukraine has been heavily influenced by the nation's socialist past as part of the Union of Soviet Socialist Republics (USSR). During most of that period the dominant tenure form was state ownership.

During the 1990s there was an evolution in thinking about private tenure and of what it might consist, both for land and structures. There continues to be a demarcation in law and practice between land related to individual housing and land related to enterprises. The former, even prior to Ukraine's independence in 1991, had been granted through a form of tenure denominated as "given in use." The Land Code of 1990 brought the first significant

This chapter is an abridged and revised version of a report prepared for the Harvard Institute of International Development (HIID) Kyiv, "Tenure Choices for Urban Land Privatization in Ukraine," co-authored with Dr. Olexander Babanin, consultant to HIID Kyiv. I would like to acknowledge the financial support of HIID Kyiv for my three-week trip to Ukraine to initiate work on this project. I thank the University of Toronto Press for permission to reproduce Map 1 (page 181). Comments on this chapter received from Thomas Atmer, Steven Bourassa and Yu-Hung Hong have been addressed in revisions to the original text.

Information given in this chapter was provided by interviews in 1999 and 2000 with Louis Faoro, Chief of Party, and Justin Holl, Senior Legal Advisor of the Ukrainian Non-Agricultural Land Privatization Project (UKRels); Michael Holytsia, Deputy Mayor and Head of the Kyiv Housing Department; Volodymyr Nosik of Kyiv Taras Shevchenko University; Valentina Legka, Project Manager, Pavel Strelnikov, Deputy Project Manager, and Larysa Shidlovs'ka, Public Relations Manager of Unfinished Construction Site Privatization in Ukraine, International Finance Corporation; Anton Tretyak, First Deputy Head of the State Committee of Ukraine on Land Resources; Valentina Drugak, Director of the Land Reform Centre; Vitaly Stepanyuk, UKRels; Anatolyi Bondar, Director, and Mykhailo Cheremshynsky, First Deputy Director of the General Administration of Geodesy, Cartography and Cadaster of Ukraine; and Anatoly Yurchenko, Chief Counsel of the State Committee of Ukraine on Land Resources.

expansion of the rights of individuals, authorizing them to own small plots for a home, dacha, garden or garage.[1] Then, starting in 1992, people holding residential land under the terms of given in use were, at their option, entitled to a free grant of fee title by the state. As of 2000, 23 percent of the population, rural and urban, held residential land given in use, while 20 percent held land in fee (that is, freehold). If there is leasehold by the state of residential land, it does not appear in published reports.

Enterprise-related land, as land related to profit-seeking institutions relying on labor force, has been thought to require greater state control for ideological reasons. Privatized enterprises, including owners of apartment buildings, first were authorized to own land or to hold it under a 49-year lease in 1995.[2] However, the law governing disposition of enterprise land remains unclear, although the practice is to offer such land for lease or sale. Also as of 2000, 6,000 hectares of nonagricultural land had been given in use, while 449 hectares had been sold in fee and 60 hectares sold in leasehold. The fragile economy, in which the GDP fell by two-thirds between 1990 and 2000, is a constraint on choice of tenure, since householders and entrepreneurs alike have little access to credit to finance the acquisition of land.

The foci of this chapter are the post-1991 actions of the Ukrainian state and its cities to privatize urban land, and the role that leasehold has been playing and might play in the future in this process. Laws and decrees, fiscal considerations and political perspectives all play a role. The chapter has seven sections: this introduction; a brief history of land ownership from 1917 to 2000; a summary of the legal structure that shapes land privatization; the urban setting in which land privatization is occurring; tenure choices in privatization of land to individuals and enterprises; impediments to privatization; and conclusions about appropriate forms of land tenure, particularly leasehold, for Ukraine now and in the near future. This chapter's appendix lists the principal land use laws and decrees enacted between 1989 and 2000.

At the outset it is important to emphasize that there has been little policy debate about the use of leasehold. It is not being used as a tool to manage land that is likely to be urbanized in the near future, and it is not being used as part of urban residential land privatization. The only area of debate about leasehold has concerned land related to enterprises. Here, the United States Agency for International Development (USAID) consultant advising the government of Ukraine on enterprise land privatization has been adamant that only freehold should be used. The state, for its part, has allowed municipalities to elect to use leasehold and/or freehold. Until 1999 Kyiv (in Russian, *Kiev*), was the only municipality to use leasehold exclusively; now it uses both forms of tenure. All other municipalities used freehold, and many also used leasehold.

It would be beneficial, I believe, for actors at the national and local levels who are participating in privatization of urban land to engage in a debate about how the form of land tenure could influence urbanization costs and outcomes.

---

[1] The Land Code of 1990, #562/90, as amended by #98/91 and by #98/92.

[2] The decree of the president, On Privatization and Lease of Non-Agricultural Land Plots for Business Activity, July 12, 1995.

These actors should include government officials responsible for implementing privatization laws, local government planners and private sector developers, financiers and realtors. Such a debate might facilitate the adoption of policies toward peripheral urban land facing development pressure that differ from policies for urban land facing redevelopment. It is clearly difficult for officials who are accustomed to total, unilateral control over the timing and character of urban development to envision that private ownership will bring new perspectives and pressures that will alter past practices. In this context, it is important to state that the most sought after goal of the private sector is for public transparency in this, as in other matters.

LAND OWNERSHIP, 1917–2000

There was private land holding in Ukraine in past centuries and in this century, until the advent of communism. Memories of the past are one influence on current attitudes toward land ownership. By late in the nineteenth century, most Ukrainian peasants owned small plots of land—over 85 percent of the peasants living on the Right Bank of the Dnipro River (in Russian, *Dnieper*) and over 70 percent of the peasants living on the Left Bank. Much other land was held in large private estates. Attitudes toward land ownership were one

MAP 1

SOVIET UKRAINE DURING THE INTERWAR PERIOD

Source: Subtelny (1988, map 22)

of the causes of twentieth-century conflict between groups seeking to control Ukraine (see Subtelny 1988, for a detailed history of this period).

The decade from 1917 to 1927 saw government transformations in which changes in patterns of land holding were pivotal issues. Ukraine experienced one brief period of independence from 1918 until the close of 1920, marked by turbulence, violence and incessant struggle. In 1917 an autonomous, leftist Ukraine, consisting of nine eastern provinces, was proclaimed, then invaded by Russian Bolsheviks. In January 1918 the Ukrainians proclaimed an independent state and proceeded to nationalize large estates. About a year later, a conservative German-backed government took control with the intention of protecting private property and restoring the land that previously had belonged to the rich. Infuriated peasants soon toppled this government. Simultaneously an independent government was formed in western Ukraine, and it seized the Poles' large estates and gave that land to peasants. The two independent governments united, but in November 1920 were defeated in the west by Poland and in the east by the Bolsheviks.

The Ukrainian Soviet Socialist Republic (SSR) was established. It faced economic hardship and famine but land remained in private ownership for a few years. In 1921, to counter peasant resistance in Ukraine, Lenin temporarily abandoned farm collectivization there, but it was reinstituted in 1928 as part of Stalin's First Five-Year Plan. The *kulaks*—farmers somewhat better off than the peasants—were obliterated as an entity in Ukraine; some were shot and 850,000 were deported to the Arctic or Siberia, where many died. From the perspective of land in the Ukrainian SSR, 1928 was the onset of state ownership, a status that persisted until after the reestablishment of the Ukrainian state in 1991. The years 1932 and 1933 saw the Stalin-induced famine in Ukraine during which between seven and eight million people starved to death (Mace 1984).

Some lands, now part of Ukraine, remained private for some years, including lands held by Poland, Czechoslovakia or Romania from after the First World War until prior to the Second World War. While there are Ukrainians with old land titles amongst their possessions, restitution of land, urban or rural, is not an issue in today's Ukraine. This is in contrast to many countries of Central Europe, where restitution is an extremely thorny problem. Poland, for instance, has yet to enact a restitution law, despite widespread clamor for such action (Strong, Reiner and Szyrmer 1996). The different attitude in Ukraine may be attributed to several factors. It was Stalin's policy to move whole ethnic groups to areas foreign to them, with the intent of creating loyalty to the state rather than to one's native region. Pogroms, gulags and the Second World War killed millions and added further to dispersal from homelands. Denial of permission to move from where one had ended up was another factor.

Starting in 1990 and increasingly after its declaration of independence on August 24, 1991, Ukraine gradually has moved to divest itself of ownership of various types of land. Some lands have been placed effectively, although not yet legally, into the hands of local governments. Steps have been taken to transfer ownership of farmlands to collectives and individuals. Municipalities have been

MAP 2

Ukraine 2000

Source: Adapted from various sources by author

privatizing urban residential lands. As of January 2000, 10.7 million residents of Ukraine held privatized land plots totaling 3.2 million hectares. Much of the privatized land is rural. Few rural residents, though, held a certificate of title, since the heads of collective farms tended to hold all of the certificates. The state, acting through cities, is offering some enterprise lands for lease or purchase at auction or by negotiated sale.[3] Also as of January 2000, over 1,500 plots had been sold in fee or leasehold to enterprises for a sum of 31.6 million Ukrainian *hryvna* (UAH), equivalent to approximately US$6.3 million (the exchange rate was UAH 5 = US$1 during fall 1999. The enterprise plots total 500 hectares and are primarily held by small enterprises, occupying one hectare or less of land.

The Legal Structure for Land Privatization

One major question explored in this chapter is, "Under what circumstances would Ukraine be well advised to lease urban public land for private use rather than to sell it?" The evolution of laws in Ukraine during the 1990s concerning the rights in land that may be alienated reflects changes in social attitudes toward private exploitation of property. Fee title sale, initially limited to

---

[3] Decree of the president, #168/2000, February 4, 2000.

individuals, has been extended to enterprises and has become widely accepted, although with a variety of constraints. There is still dispute as to the validity of the law that authorizes such sales, but many city councils act on the presumption that it is valid. Thus, today it is more public policy and fiscal constraints than law that are the principal forces determining whether land is to be sold or leased, or, as is the dominant practice, given in permanent use. Nonetheless, it is necessary to have a background comprehension of pertinent legislation in order to understand actions being taken to privatize urban land. This chapter's appendix summarizes the key laws and decrees that have shaped the process of privatization of urban land. This section describes the principal issues underlying these legislative and executive actions.

In reviewing the laws that have been adopted, it is also important to understand that many other proposed laws have been rejected by Parliament. Adequate laws do not yet exist that govern title registration, mortgages, cadastres, bankruptcy and division of ownership of public lands between the state and local governments. Such laws, not relevant under state socialism, are essential so that a market system for real property can function effectively.

The context of urban land privatization is some 60 years of a system in which individual or enterprise land ownership was anathema. Under state socialism, all of the people were said to own all of the land with the state acting as manager on their behalf. By the time of Gorbachev and perestroika, the leaders of the Soviet Union had recognized that property ownership by everyone resulted in property maintenance by no one. Several laws were enacted between 1989 and 1991 that created some forms of private property rights in land. These laws have influenced what has been enacted subsequently in Ukraine.

There were three types of private tenure immediately prior to independence: (1) possession, which applied either to plots of rural land for individuals, in which case it was for life and inheritable, or for farms, cooperatives and institutions, in which case it was permanent; (2) use, which was for state, cooperative and social enterprises, and which could be either temporary or permanent; and (3) lease, which was for both individuals and enterprises.

> This form of tenure was conceptually linked to the idea of the "work contract"—the new perestroika form of relationship between an employer and a group of employees (the work unit). By means of a lease, the assets of a large cooperative or enterprise could be subdivided and allocated to semi-independent, self-managed work groups.... [T]he rent payment would insure that a "true" cost of the land and other property inputs was reflected... (Valletta 1997, 61).

Possession and use rights were given by a unilateral grant from the state, while leases were negotiated between the state and the lessee. Holders of land under possession or use paid a land tax, while lessees paid rent.[4] All plots were subject to detailed state plans governing their use. No right was transferable. All rights could be withdrawn by the state, with compensation if the state took the land for another public use, and without compensation if the holder failed to use the plot in accord with the terms of the grant or lease (Valletta 1997).

---

[4] Contrary to the intent ascribed above by Valletta (1997), thus far, land rent and land tax are synonymous, although the law differentiates one from the other.

The many laws and decrees enacted over the period from 1989 to the present demonstrate the ongoing shifts in attitudes toward private land ownership and toward government's role in the management of this resource. From the state as owner of all land, the first step was to allow very limited rights of ownership for small house plots and related lands. Then in 1991 Ukraine moved to acknowledge that public and individual ownership were equal under the law. In 1992 the word *private* was substituted for *individual*, thus bringing legitimacy to property rights for enterprises. However, the 1992 Land Code made clear that such property rights were limited to temporary or permanent use or leasehold. In 1995 President Kuchma went much further. He issued a decree authorizing the state to sell as well as lease enterprise land and authorizing the purchaser or lessee to resell, give away or mortgage such land or, in the case of leases, sublet the land. Parliament rejected this decree, refusing to enact the amendment to the Land Code that would have incorporated it. The Constitution of 1996 includes enterprises, as well as individuals, as those whose right to property is protected. However, uncertainty still exists as to what forms of land tenure rights have been granted to enterprises.

The pervasive use of tenure by gift of use is an expression of the state's readiness to have private rights in property while retaining a greater measure of state control than is likely to exist under freehold or leasehold. The state gives the use rights on its terms and, at least in concept, has greater ability to revoke these rights than under freehold or leasehold. However, the grantee pays the land tax in the same manner, as if holding a fee title. Since 1992 gift of use tenure has been the bridge to fee ownership for individuals holding residential and garden plots. All such individuals are entitled to free privatization of their plots, following which they are entitled to sell the plots as long as the price paid is at least as high as the normative value. In 1999 the maximum size of an individual private plot was increased to two hectares.

The land tax and the land rent remain two different terms for what are essentially parallel charges. Laws enacted in 1992 and 1996 state that the land rent may not be less than the land tax, which does suggest that the rent might be higher, although there is no evidence that it has been. Both charges are deposited in the same account, and there is no differentiation in accounting between them. Under the 1996 Constitution 30 percent of the land tax and the land rent are allocated to the state, 10 percent to the *oblast* or the Autonomous Republic of Crimea and 60 percent to the local government.

A remarkably candid and forward-looking decree was issued by the president in February 2000.[5] The document, On Measures about Development and Regulation of the Market of Lands of Settlements, Other Lands of Non-Agricultural Destination, establishes the goal of creating a legal, economic and organizational climate, in which the urban land market can flourish within the context of "effective and rational land use, promotion of entrepreneurship development, improvement of socio-economic situation in Ukraine." The decree acknowledges that privatization of urban land has not progressed as

---

[5] Decree of the president #168/2000, February 4, 2000.

rapidly as desired, with the effects that investment in this sector has been limited and municipal revenues from private land holding have been insufficient. The decree recognizes the difficulties posed by inadequate enabling legislation:

> In Ukraine…conditions for efficient functioning of market institutions (land exchanges, land banks, land auctions, etc.), which should facilitate development and functioning of the secondary land market, are not created, clear and accessible information on land plots, their value, their market history (information on time value of land plots) and restrictions on their use are absent, as well as mechanisms of facilitation of the full payment of taxes and collections.… Organization of conducting of expert money appraisal…is far from being excellent. Procedures of preliminary approval of conditions of construction,… approval of project documentation and reception of permits on construction…are quite cumbersome.

The decree describes the framework that is needed for the market to function efficiently and calls for rational use of land that takes ecological concerns into account. Among the 32 specific tasks called for are: creation of the state land register as part of the state land cadastre; creation of a data bank relating to land market supply and demand; creation of a system of land appraisal; state regulation of expert appraisal licensing; and establishment of a system that enables prospective investors to obtain information about land rights and limitations on land use.

THE URBAN SETTING

Privatization of urban land in Ukraine occurs in the context of urban demographics and of the division of land-related powers and responsibilities between the state and local governments.

Urban Demographics

How much land will be needed for urban expansion in the next decade? Will cities have sufficient land within their borders, or will annexation be necessary? Factors that could influence expansion include: urban population growth from rural to urban migration and from a rise in the birth rate; changes in composition and size of families; preferences for lower-density housing; and an increase in disposable income.

Population changes

The total population of Ukraine has shown a 3.8 percent decline in the last decade, dropping from 51.5 million in 1989 to 49.6 million in early 2000. The annual population deficit in 1999 was almost 400,000. The U.S. Bureau of the Census (1997) projects a 2020 population of 44.4 million. Since 1995 the birth rate has been 1.3 percent.

Migration to and from Ukraine has not been a substantial influence on population. Over the 1991–1997 period 2.0 million people migrated to Ukraine as compared to 1.9 million who left. However, emigration has exceeded immigration every year since 1994 and by 45,000 in 1999.

The percent of the population that lives in urban areas (defined by the census as towns of the urban type with a population of at least 5,000, plus cities) has remained almost constant recently—67 percent in 1989 and 68 percent in 1998. The percent of people 60 years old or older is considerably less in urban areas than in rural areas. In 1997 these figures were 15.9 percent of the urban population and 24.9 percent of the rural population. If worldwide patterns become true for Ukraine, there will be migration from farms and villages to cities, which would give rise to a demand for further urban development.

City size by population

Cities are defined as having 10,000 or more people, at least 60 percent of whom are not engaged in agriculture. As of January 2000 there were 448 cities, most of which had populations of between 10,000 and 50,000 people; but most people lived in cities of 100,000 or more. Five cities—Dnipropetrovsk, Donetsk, Kyiv, Odessa and Kharkiv—had populations of more than 1 million. Kyiv, the capital, was and still is the largest at 2.6 million.

Chief Architect of Kyiv, Sergey Babushkin, projects that the city's population will reach three million by 2005. He believes that between 30 and 35 square kilometers of land outside the current city limits will be needed for additional development. Others believe that new growth could be accommodated within current boundaries.

Urban areas and densities

As of 1998, 3.9 percent of the land of Ukraine was defined as urban. A total of 1.3 million hectares is within city borders, and another 5.7 million hectares is within town and village boundaries. However, 3.6 million hectares of this land is in agricultural use. Some collective farms near urban centers are encouraging development of low-density, single-family housing for urban commuters.

Kyiv's density is 3,000 people per square kilometer. Density varies with housing type: there is low-density, older housing that was in villages subsequently annexed to the city; there is a diverse mix of moderate-density housing built from late in the nineteenth century until the Second World War; and there are the high-rise, high-density housing blocks typical of post-war Soviet and East European construction. Fifty percent of Kyiv's population lives in this last type of construction, with 800,000 people housed in the three principal satellites and the remainder in other satellites of more than 100,000 people each.

Government structure and city functions

The units of government in Ukraine are the state, the Autonomous Republic of Crimea, 24 oblasts (regions), 486 *rayons* (districts or counties), 448 cities, 894 urban towns and 28,700 villages. Many villages have only 50–100 elderly residents, and there is some expectation that such villages will wither and die.

National and local government structures

Ukraine is governed by the president, the prime minister and the unicameral Parliament of 450 members. Leonid Kuchma, whose block is left of center, was reelected to the presidency in a runoff against a communist opponent in November 1999. Parliamentary elections of March 2002 brought some changes. The Communist Party had been the largest party in Parliament. Now, the communist delegation has dropped to 20 percent but the three parties of the left combined hold 51 percent of the seats, and the parties of the right 49 percent. The strong position of the left has militated against passage of legislation supportive of a free market, including a free market in land. The 1996 Constitution articulates the powers of the legislative, executive and judicial branches of government.

In addition to the Constitution, laws and resolutions enacted by Parliament, there are decrees issued by the president, the cabinet or the council of ministers concerning matters not already covered by law. Presidential decrees must be submitted as draft legislation to Parliament upon issuance. They become effective if, within 30 days, Parliament does not pass a law covering the same matter or does not reject the draft law by a two-thirds majority.

There are several levels of courts of general jurisdiction, with the Supreme Court being the highest of these courts. The constitutional court is the final arbiter of constitutional challenges. It has 18 judges, each of whom serves a single nine-year term. The judges are appointed one-third each by Parliament, the president, and the congress of judges. This court has a particularly important role in Ukraine, since laws enacted prior to 1996, including many of the laws governing property rights, often conflict with constitutional provisions.

Regions and districts elect councils, or *rada*, with powers specified by national legislation. Cities are governed by an elected mayor and council. Cities may elect to establish districts, each of which then has an elected council. The city of Kyiv, for instance, has 14 districts.

Land-related powers and responsibilities of cities

City and town councils may enact the following types of land-related laws: land use regulation; land tax rates; permitting for use of natural resources; establishment of natural, historic or cultural reserves; and approval of construction programs.

Planning for urban land use occurs under the Law on the Principles of Urban Development of 1992, as amplified by various decrees. As in Soviet times, planning is a top-down activity, starting with the state and proceeding downward as far as districts of a city. General plans for a city are accompanied by very specific detailed plans. For instance, footprints for buildings are shown, as well as their prospective uses or targets. For cities in excess of one million people, the number of people to be housed in high-rise apartment buildings as well as the number of stories of these buildings is mandated.

Cities do have zoning ordinances, although much that is conventionally included in a zoning ordinance in other countries—or more—is specified by plan. In Ukraine, zoning typically establishes only two categories of use, residential and nonresidential. Informants say that obtaining a change in zoning usually involves bribery.

A developer who wishes to build must obtain construction approval. This is a complicated, time-consuming process; in Kyiv it takes a year on average. Twenty permits and authorizations must be obtained, after which final approval must be granted by the city development council, a body of six representatives of city agencies chaired by the chief architect. This process also is said to be tarnished by bribery. As of summer 2000 there was no law governing title registration. There is a cadastral system but it is out of date and inadequately maintained.

Disposition of land is a powerful tool for implementing urban settlement policies. The State Committee of Ukraine for Land Resources, with its local administrative units, is charged with responsibility for privatizing land. This includes the determination of what will be sold and under what terms. While the Local Self-Government Law of 1996 granted municipalities the right to sell municipal land, they do not currently own land. Legislation to transfer ownership of some land within municipal boundaries from the state to the municipalities was rejected by Parliament in September 1999.

The salient fact is that the state has effectively transferred to the munici-palities the right to manage or to sell or give away the land if they so desire. Land for enterprises may be offered as leasehold or freehold and may be sold through negotiation or by auction. The sale price for a negotiated sale cannot be less than the normative price for that area, or in some municipalities the appraised value, unless the state grants its approval. The municipalities can offer land at a higher price but rarely do so.

Annexation of land by a city can occur only with approval of Parliament. Kyiv is planning to annex 36 villages to its north and has been working with the local governments for several years to reach accord, following which the proposed new boundaries will be submitted to Parliament for approval.

City revenues from land

Income from sales or leases of public lands is retained by the seller, be it the state or a municipality.[6] An exception is income from sales or leases of land at unfinished construction sites. This income goes to the municipality in which the land is located.[7] As of 2000, 93 percent of such income realized by the state went to the state general fund and 7 percent to the state privatization fund for administrative expenses. Also as of 2000, 90 percent of such local income went to the local budget with 10 percent to the privatization fund.[8]

Land in private ownership and land held in possession or use are subject to the land tax. In many cities the base for this tax is set by a normative approach, using assumed rents. In 1999 the cabinet of ministers enacted a decree requir-ing cities to introduce systems of expert valuation to establish the base value for taxation. As more and more market transactions occur, followed by reg-istration of location and price of sale, there will be a steadily growing pool

---

[6] Decree #32/99, On Sales of Non-Agricultural Land Plots, as amended March 9, 2000.

[7] Decree #591/99, On Privatization of Unfinished Construction Sites.

[8] On State Budget for 2000, articles 5 and 41.

of information that will enable appraisers to develop such systems. The land tax is of particular importance to local budgets. In 1998 it accounted for 8.5 percent of local revenues, but for only 3.9 percent of state revenues.

There is, as yet, no comprehensive real estate tax law that covers structures as well as land. Several drafts have been introduced in Parliament, but none has been adopted. Both state industries and agricultural enterprises have been opposed to the proposals because they would then be subject to taxation.

PRIVATIZATION OF URBAN LAND

At independence in 1991, urban land belonged to the state, in essence, although some land was subject to limited private rights of use, possession or lease. As stated previously, as of January 2000, under the 1992 decree of the cabinet of ministers, On Privatization of Land Plots, 10.7 million people, or around 20 percent of the population, had acquired title to plots totaling 3.2 million hectares. Although data are lacking it is probable that the majority of these people are on collective farms. Few farm residents, however, had certificates of title, thus considerably limiting marketability. An additional 11.3 million people held use rights to land. These totals include urban and rural plots.

As of January 2000, under the 1995 decree of the president, On Privatization and Lease of Non-Agricultural Land Plots for Business Activity, as well as under decrees on privatization of land at gas stations and land under unfinished buildings, enterprises had acquired in fee or leasehold more than 1,500 plots totaling more than 500 hectares, with a value of UAH 31.6 million, or, according to data from the Ukraine Enterprise Non-Agricultural Land Privatization Project (UKRels), in excess of UAH 45 million. In addition, almost 22,000 plots totaling about 6,000 hectares had been given in use.

Privatization of Housing and Residential Land

Privatization of urban residential land has occurred in the setting of the privatization of housing. First, apartments were allocated in permanent use tenure, subject to payment for rent and utilities. Subsequently, tenants were offered the opportunity for free privatization in fee of these apartments.

In 1990 the nation's housing stock totaled 922 million square meters; of this, 53 percent was private and 47 percent was either state-owned, owned by collectives or by housing construction cooperatives. The urban housing stock totaled 574 million square meters, of which only 31 percent was private. By 1999, 57 percent of urban housing was private.

The housing privatization program started in early 1993. Its goal was privatization of 7.1 million apartments and one dwelling unit (single-family) buildings by the end of 1999, or approximately one million apartments per year. These apartments were from the stock of urban and rural state and social housing, 93 percent of which was urban. Their occupants had been given them in use. During the first two years the program results were on track. However, during 1995–1999, the rate of privatization slowed, and on average only 500,000 apartments per year were privatized. Nonetheless, overall this is a creditable 63 percent of the goal of 7.1 million dwelling units. Parliament extended the free privatization program from its prior termination date of January 1, 2000 to December 31, 2000.

Concurrently, cities, acting under the 1992 decree, On Privatization of Land Plots, have been transferring freehold title to plots formerly given in use at no cost other than payment of some administrative fees. These plots may include land surrounding a single family house, land at a *dacha*, gardens and garage sites. This program was to expire on January 1, 2000, but has been extended until January 1, 2004.

In Kyiv there are 51,000 plots available. On the assumption that there are three people per household, 153,000 people, or 6 percent of the city's population, could benefit from receipt of free land. So far, one-third of these plots have been privatized.

Privatization of Enterprise Land

Privatization of enterprise land parallels privatization of the enterprise itself. The State Property Fund is responsible for sale of the structures. Between 1992 and 1999 the Fund privatized 53,000 enterprise structures. The State Committee of Ukraine for Land Resources is responsible for enterprise land privatization.

The committee's early ventures were solely through sale of leasehold. This was in accord both with socialist sentiment that public land should not be sold to those engaged in capitalist ventures, and with Article 4 of the Land Code of 1992. Starting in 1995, in accordance with the decree of the president, On Privatization and Lease of Non-Agricultural Land Plots for Business Activity, some cities offered plots for sale to enterprises, and this practice has become increasingly common. The Bancroft Group report notes reasons many cities prefer leasehold (1997, 15):

> There is a perception that the use of leases ensures a long-term cash flow, whereas the alienation of the ownership from the municipality to private enterprises may not. The use of leases also ensures that the municipality will retain as much of the revenue as possible. Long-term control of the land and the familiarity with principles and procedures involving leases also discourage the sale of enterprise land.

At a meeting with members of the Kyiv Association of Realtors, all present said that their clients were indifferent as to whether they acquired leasehold or freehold. What is vital to the clients is a unified law on privatization and land use that offers security of land tenure.

There have been three types of enterprise land disposition: from 1994 to 1995 the lease by auction of land for various uses in four cities; from 1995 to the present the lease or sale of land under or adjacent to unfinished buildings; and, also from 1995 to the present, the lease or sale of enterprise land throughout Ukraine.

Lease of land in Chernihiv, L'viv, Kharkiv and Odessa

The year 1994 saw land auctions in the cities of Chernihiv, L'viv, Kharkiv and Odessa, each situated in a different region of the country. The local governments of these cities, the State Committee of Ukraine on Urban Development and Architecture, the State Committee of Ukraine for Land Resources, and USAID, through the consulting firm, PADCO, Inc., worked together to develop auction procedures, model documents and hold the auctions (State Committee of Ukraine on Urban Development and Architecture et al. 1995, 16).[9] Among the rationales advanced for auctions were the following:

> Land auctions remove the shroud of secrecy surrounding many land allocation decisions and place such decisions in an open and transparent forum, eliminating to a substantial degree the possibility of improper considerations.

Land auctions create the opportunity to establish and learn market values of land parcels, thus providing crucial information for buyers and sellers as well as for local land valuation efforts.

The auctions involved sales of the leasehold to parcels of land for 49 years, with the lease renewable for an additional 49 years. Leases were fully transferable. Provision was included that, should fee title become legal for enterprises, the lease could be converted to fee. Land was offered with prior approval for specified types of development, such as single-family houses, garages, dachas, gas stations, shops and other commercial uses. The cities set limits on costs that could be exacted for infrastructure, with Chernihiv and Kharkiv stating that these costs would not exceed 30 percent of construction costs and L'viv and Odessa setting a limit of 50 percent of construction costs.

Starting prices at the auctions were intentionally set low—somewhere between 10 and 50 percent of the expected sale price—to encourage bidders to participate. Bidders were required to deposit 10 percent of the starting price and received this money back if their bids were unsuccessful. The winning bid amounts were paid to the city, which then also received annual rents.

The first auction was in Kharkiv, in January 1994. During this year three auctions were held in Kharkiv, with thirty-four parcels offered, some for residential use, some for commercial use, some for parking and one for a garage. Fourteen of the thirty-four leases offered were sold. Parcels ranged in size from 500 to 9,000 square meters. Most lease sales were at prices markedly higher than the starting price, reflecting the intent to encourage bidding. The mean sale price for the six parcels auctioned for commercial use was UAH 785 per square meter. All told, the auctions generated UAH 2.3 million for the city (1994 currency was *carbovanets*).

Chernihiv held one auction of five leases for various commercial uses. All leases sold, again at prices well above the starting prices, and brought the city UAH 245,000.

---

[9] Professor Jerold S. Kayden of Harvard University was senior advisor to the Government of Ukraine on Land Reform and Head of the Ukraine Land Auction Program. Professor Volodymyr Nosik of Kyiv Taras Shevchenko University was Land Auction Program advisor for PADCO.

L'viv held one auction of ten parcels, of which two found lease purchasers. One parcel was targeted for multistory parking, the other for a supermarket and offices. The prices were quite close to the starting prices and brought UAH 25,000. Odessa held one auction of ten parcels. Of the four parcels sold, two were sold in fee title under the unfinished construction program, and two were sold as long-term leases. Prices in Odessa for both types of parcels were quite close to the starting prices.

Following the 1994 auctions of leases in these four cities, some of these cities, as well as others, held similar auctions in 1995. The program then came to a halt, partly because of a lack of initiative for continuation of the auctions, at either the state or local level. For example, the city of Kharkiv experienced a turnover in city council, so that antimarket forces dominated. In part, USAID ceased providing financial and technical support for this project.

Privatization of land under and adjacent to unfinished structures

The presidential decree of 1993, On Privatization of Objects of Incomplete Construction, addressed the serious problem of abandoned, unfinished buildings. There were 62,000 such structures—factories, hotels, schools, hospitals, gas stations and apartment buildings. The presidential decree of 1995, On Privatization and Lease of Non-Agricultural Land Plots for Business Activity, enabled sale of underlying or related land. With the assistance of the USAID-backed International Finance Corporation, the state's Land Resources Committee, acting through its local branches, has been seeking buyers for land. Whether local governments have participated at all in this program, and whether they have offered land for sale or lease, has depended on their political orientation. The International Finance Corporation's position has been that purchasers of land should have a choice between fee title and leasehold, but many municipalities, particularly those with left wing councils, have limited offerings to leasehold. The format for all transactions has been for the Land Resources Committee to engage experts to value the land, and then, in conjunction with the local council, decide whether to proceed by auction or negotiation and whether to offer leases and/or fee title.

Prices sought and prices obtained have varied widely, as have the attractiveness and the condition of the properties. Starting prices have ranged from nominal to one million hryvna, and sale prices have ranged from one hryvna to five million hryvna. In total, only 5,000 of the 62,000 sites have been privatized, with three-quarters of the sales occurring by auction. Of the 5,000 privatized sites, only 60 are now completed projects. Some foreign investors have formed joint ventures with Ukrainians, with such participation in 7–8 percent of all projects. One reason a buyer might bid on one of these sites rather than buy vacant land is that building permission has been obtained and needed infrastructure may be in place.

Fee sales, leases and use rights for enterprises

When the state decides to privatize an enterprise, concurrently, the municipality may decide to privatize the underlying and related land, in which case, the

Committee for Land Resources, through its local offices, assumes leadership. Buyers must be 100 percent Ukrainian, 100 percent private firms. USAID has funded UKRels to assist the Land Resources Committee in this undertaking. According to Chief of Party Louis Faoro, the UKRels policy is to privatize land by fee sale, not lease.

> Land will be managed best if in private ownership. Owners will be more solvent and have a healthier business if they own the fee. UKRels is ideologically opposed to the public sector as lessor. Public ownership is politically motivated, not economically. No one will invest unless the fee is offered; no one wants the state as a partner.

Anton Tretyak of the State Committee of Ukraine for Land Resources, also favors fee sales on the ground that they are more profitable for investors. Note, however, that the realtors interviewed did not agree with this. Justin Holl, senior legal advisor to UKRels, stated that local governments will sell leases, not the fee, if given the choice.

Land to be offered for privatization is valued, and then the local council adopts a resolution stating this value as the offering price. Since January 1999 expert valuation has been used. Initially the program addressed small enterprises seeking less than one hectare of land, but now the focus has shifted to larger tracts. Raw land has been offered for privatization starting in 2000. Currently the only financing available is payment deferrals that may be offered by local councils. These deferrals may be for from three months to three years. Negotiations are underway with the National Bank of Ukraine for that bank to offer loans for land purchase. So far, banks have not acknowledged the value of land as a commodity and so have been unwilling to treat it as collateral for loans.[10]

The Committee for Land Resources (1999) provides a detailed account for each of 24 regions, the Autonomous Republic of Crimea and the cities of Kyiv and Sevastopol. The report covers the years 1993 through 1999, and includes information about plots ready for sale, already sold in fee simple and already sold in leasehold, as well as information about revenues.

In total, 23,246 plots were privatized: 875 (4 percent) by sale in fee simple; 659 (3 percent) by sale of leasehold; and 21,712 (93 percent) by gift of use. An additional 736 plots were in the pipeline being prepared for sale. Municipalities in all regions used sale in fee, while municipalities in 11 regions also used lease sale. Only the city of Kyiv relied solely on lease sales. Following the election of a new mayor in May 1999 the Kyiv council endorsed the use of fee sales as well as lease sales.

Concerning the 1,534 plots sold in fee or leasehold, the total area was 509 hectares, with 449 hectares sold in fee and 60 hectares sold in leasehold. The total sale price was UAH 31,617,000. Fee sales brought an average of UAH 60,000 per hectare, while lease sales brought more: an average of UAH 78,000 per hectare.[11] The total revenue realized from both fee and lease sales was UAH 23 million, while payment of UAH 8.5 million, or 30 percent of the sales prices, was deferred for from one to three years.

---

[10] Comments by Pavel Strelnikov, as reported in UKRels memorandum, Background to Financing of Enterprise Land Sales, March 1998.

The state calculates that 200,000 hectares, or 2,000 square kilometers, which is 10 percent of Ukraine's urbanized land, could be privatized for enterprises. If this calculation is correct, in terms of hectares, Ukraine enterprise land privatization is 0.25 percent on the way to meeting the goal. The yield from this possible privatization is estimated at UAH 50 billion.[12] This sum assumes that the average price of urban enterprise land would be UAH 250,000 per hectare.

Of all fee simple sales, only 14 percent were by auction. Municipalities may prefer negotiated sales to auctions, since they deal with only one prospective buyer. However, this opens the door to opportunities for corruption. Of the purchasers, 41 percent were enterprises engaged in trade; 23 percent, offices and warehouses; 12 percent, gas stations; 9 percent, industries; and 7 percent, restaurants and cafes. The remaining 8 percent of the purchasers bought vacant land. The overall sale price was UAH 26.9 million. The disparity between the valuation and actual sale price was great, with some valuations far below the sale price and some far higher. Small entrepreneurs are said to feel hectored by public officials and believe that they are buffered better from them if they buy fee simple titles.

The 659 plots privatized by sale of leasehold, usually at auction, had a mean size of 0.3 hectare. The total sale price for the leaseholds was UAH 4.7 million, or UAH 78,000 per hectare. Cities are starting to gain annual income from land under lease. Between January and September 1999, such income to the city of Kyiv totaled UAH 2.19 million, 40 percent higher than in 1998 (*Vechirniy Kyiv* 1999).

Of the 21,712 plots, or almost 6,000 hectares, privatized by gift of use, 71 percent were vacant land without a related privatized structure. All of these plots are subject to payment of the annual land tax.

Interestingly, the smaller cities have been most active in privatizing land, with 84 percent of such sales in cities with populations of half a million or less. A market for urban land, as well as for urban offices and apartments, is developing. A recent sale in Kyiv of 0.5 hectare of land under a downtown office building brought UAH 2.19 million to the seller. This is one-third of the going price for urban land in St. Petersburg, although in making the comparison one should note that St. Petersburg's population is 2.6 times that of Kyiv.

IMPEDIMENTS TO AN URBAN LAND MARKET

As the preceding section on land privatization demonstrates, there has been considerable momentum since 1993 to privatize residential land, and some effort to privatize enterprise land, each in parallel with privatization of apartments and business structures. There are active real estate markets, particularly for housing and offices. Yet, much remains unresolved and the lack of

---

[11] This comparison does not control for differences in location and timing of fee and lease sales.

[12] Decree of the president #168/2000, February 4, 2000.

underlying policy accord and of consequent legislation and regulation hamper the market from full development. Investment in real estate by both Ukrainian and foreign investors is deterred. Whether the practice of giving use of land or transfer of fee title or leasehold is preferable is at present largely a theoretical discussion, since the practice is shaped by the particulars of Ukrainian circumstances. The arguments for each form of tenure will be reviewed after discussing the impediments to a flourishing urban land market.

These impediments fall under several categories: lack of necessary enabling laws, conflicts between existing laws, insufficient judicial response, lack of transparency in administration, and public and private corruption. One fundamental, pervasive problem is the lack of reliable information.

Lack of Necessary Enabling Laws

Many government-appointed commissions and many advisors, domestic and foreign, have labored during the 1990s to produce policy recommendations and draft legislation on matters vital to undergird an urban land market. Yet, today, adequate laws providing for systems of title registration, mortgages, bankruptcy and cadastres have yet to be enacted.

Some would assert that the absence of a law authorizing taxation of structures is an impediment. Others would disagree. With the land tax in place and functioning, it is desirable for the government to debate whether reliance on a land tax alone rather than on a real property tax covering both land and buildings is a better choice for Ukraine. Proponents of taxing land and not structures believe that it promotes efficient use of land and does not discourage development. Taxing buildings as well can discourage new construction, rehabilitation and maintenance, because such activities result in higher property value and thus higher taxes (Netzer 1966).

Absence of a sound system of title registration

For a lively land market to thrive, investors need information. They need ready access to accurate and detailed evidence as to land boundaries, prior and current ownership, limitations on use of the land and constraints on alienation. They need security of title.

Today's very limited system of title registration provides little information and less security of title. A buyer can learn some details of the most recent transaction but nothing of prior transactions. Prospective investors who have yet to make a commitment to purchase have no access to such information as exists. Impediments to title, including public and private easements and mechanics' liens, are not recorded. Neither are mortgages. There is no mechanism for searching titles, and the overall lack of title information inhibits lenders from issuing mortgages. There is no title insurance. Buyers who paid more than the normative value are able to state normative value as the price paid, so as to pay a lower land tax.

The repeated failures to pass appropriate title registration legislation illustrate the difficulties surrounding efforts to introduce new measures that support a market system for land. From 1994 through 1997 there was a multinational effort to work with Ukrainian government officials to design a new system of title registration and draft appropriate legislation. Canada, England, Sweden and the U.S., with support from the World Bank and the European Union, set up an advisory group to work with Ukrainian government officials to design a national title registration system. Pilot projects were established in several cities, computer hardware and software recommendations were developed, and real estate assessment techniques were proposed. There were recommendations for legislation.

> Specific language was suggested that called for a single registration system covering both land and buildings under the auspices of a single registration body. The primary recommendations in this regard were that every parcel of real estate be assigned a unique cadastral number and that this be used, not only for identifying parcels in all documents dealing with real estate rights, but that the same number be used for all fiscal purposes.... The value of the real estate would be updated on a regular basis... (Bancroft Group 1997, 13).

Yet, after all this cooperative effort, no law has been passed. Problems cited in the Bancroft Group report include government instability marked by the frequent turnover of senior officials participating in this process, and denial of access to information about real estate at both the national and local levels. According to one draft law that passed its first reading in mid-1999, title registration would be centralized. Two other draft laws have been prepared, and a committee of Parliament is currently charged with preparing a revised draft for further consideration. One obstacle to the enactment of a title registration law is said to be a dispute between the ministry of justice and the Committee on Construction, Architecture and Housing Policy, over which agency will manage the system. Observers believe the latter agency would be more subject to influence by the municipalities, as is the Bureau of Technical Inventory today. A revised draft was submitted in spring 2000; it is part of the package of land laws that passed first reading before summer adjournment of Parliament.

One repercussion of the lack of an open, accurate title registration system is that the mandate of Parliament to apply expert valuation for the purpose of establishing the base for the land tax is generally not applied. This is in part because there are few trained appraisers able to use the method, and in part because of the questionable quality and a paucity of information available concerning sales prices. The Kyiv College of Real Estate has been established and has graduated its first class of appraisers. As the pool of qualified people expands, and as more and better sales data become available, the use of expert valuation should replace the normative approach.

There is another title problem related to lack of public funding. For many, the granting of title to land has not been accompanied by issuance of a certificate of title. The government states that it does not have the funds to survey the millions of plots in order to set boundaries and issue appropriate written documentation. On the collective farms, where people often hold half a dozen tiny plots, there is common understanding of which plot belongs to whom. This does not translate, however, into marketable title.

Mortgage and bankruptcy laws

Banks are unlikely to issue mortgages if the borrower's credit is difficult to ascertain. One component of evaluation of security of credit is the value of the property against which the mortgage is issued. If, as is the current situation in Ukraine, there is no open, accessible record of property transactions, the market for any given parcel of land is quite speculative. If the mortgage sought is for residential land, this poses even greater information difficulties, since projecting the future earning power of the prospective borrower is also speculative.

Banks are unlikely to lend to enterprises for another reason. Although there is a new bankruptcy law, commentators say it is very difficult to force an enterprise into bankruptcy and obtain title to the enterprise's assets, including land. While banks and other lenders prefer not to foreclose on land and other property because of their lack of liquidity, the power to foreclose is a necessary recourse.

Two persons interviewed stated a preference for fee title ownership over leasehold, in part based on their opinion that a leasehold interest cannot be mortgaged. Other people, two of whom represent foreign investors, stated that whether their clients held fee title or a leasehold was not a key factor in their investment decision. This difference in perspective points up the importance of context. Obviously, the mortgage law must permit mortgage of a leasehold or the issue does not arise. That said, it is then a matter of the context of the provisions of the lease and the financial stability of the prospective borrower/ lessee. Today in Ukraine, enterprise leases of land are likely to be for 49 years, renewable for another similar term. Rents are modest and leases are transferable. From a lender's perspective in calculating risk, this lease is tantamount to ownership in fee. The experience of the Belgian new town of Louvain la Neuve is instructive. The town was built on leasehold land, and the mortgage banks lent for construction on the basis that long-term leasehold was no riskier than fee simple.[13] Whether the tenure is leasehold or fee the probability that the would-be borrower can repay the loan is the critical factor to assess when determining whether to grant a mortgage.

The common practice in the U.S. for residential mortgages is for the bank issuing the mortgage to sell it at a discount to a consolidator of mortgages, which may or may not be a larger bank. The consolidator may then bundle a group of mortgages and offer them for sale, again at a discount, to a company that specializes in servicing and holding residential mortgages. As with enterprise mortgages, the creditor's rights include the right to foreclose if the debtor fails to make the payments that are due.

---

[13] Communication from President Pierre Laconte of the Foundation for the Urban Environment, February 7, 2000. The experience in Canberra and Hong Kong is similar to that of Louvain La Neuve in this respect.

Lack of a modern cadastral system

This is a serious impediment but one that appears near resolution. As with title registration, mortgages and bankruptcy, there has been serious study of the potential choices and extensive consulting advice from Western countries. The State Committee of Ukraine for Land Resources has prepared a draft law that would establish an automated cadastral system for the entire nation. The law will likely be enacted in 2000; upon approval, four pilot projects would be launched, three in regions and another in the city of Kyiv.

The Need for a More Active Judiciary

As the section of this article describing privatization of land demonstrates, there is no shortage of pertinent constitutional provisions, laws, and decrees. Even though some critical laws have yet to win acceptance by Parliament, much is already on the books. The impediment to privatization posed by this legislation is the confusion as to what is or is not authorized, either because of unclear language in a law or contrary provisions between two different pieces of legislation. Many laws enacted prior to the 1996 adoption of the Constitution have provisions that conflict with it.

Two illustrations of these conflicts are the uncertainty as to whether municipalities are authorized to transfer title to state property and the uncertainty as to whether enterprises may be sold public land in fee title. These matters go to the heart of the land privatization programs.

Concerning the first problem, Anton Tretyak predicts that revised legislation will be enacted that transfers around 90 percent of state land within cities to city ownership and 40–50 percent of state land outside cities to town and village ownership.

Without pointing to the litigious U.S. as a model, it is evident that a more active judiciary, with constitutional questions carried up to the constitutional court, can help resolve issues of conflict of laws. Further, court decisions must be readily accessible and widely disseminated for their impacts to be speedy and pervasive. A computer-based search system for laws and for the judicial opinions interpreting them could provide immediate access nationwide.

Corruption and Lack of Transparency

Two studies have sought to measure corruption in governments and to establish corruption indices. Transparency International has issued its Corruption Perceptions Index for five years and now has added a Bribe Payers Index; the latter is an index of bribery by corporate executives of those outside their native countries. In 1999, of 99 countries ranked on a scale of 1 to 10 in the Corruption Perceptions Index, with 10 being a perfect score, Denmark ranked highest with a perfect 10. Ukraine scored 2.6 and ranked 75th. Among other countries, the U.S. was in 17th place with a score of 7.5, Estonia ranked 27th with a score of 5.7, and Poland ranked 44th with a score of 4.2 (Crossette 1999).

The second study asked executives in 59 countries to rank their country for corruption, tax evasion and each of several other shortcomings on a score of 1 to 7, with 1 in this survey being worst (Sachs and Warner 1999). For tax evasion, Ukraine ranked 1.99, or 57th, while Russia ranked 59th; for favoritism by public officials to well-connected firms and individuals, Ukraine ranked 2.57, or 57th, while Russia ranked 58th; for irregular payments for permits, licenses, tax assessments or loan applications Ukraine ranked 2.46, or 58th, while Russia ranked 55th; and for personal bribes to senior politicians Ukraine ranked 57th.

The overall score on the corruption and tax evasion questions was compared to growth in 1998. Here Ukraine was 57th, with an average score of 3.04 and growth of –1.11. Russia was 59th, with an average score of 2.87 and growth of –4.53. The implication of these rankings for competitiveness is reflected in the report's ranking of Singapore as the most competitive of the 59 countries and Ukraine and Russia, respectively, as 58th and 59th, or the least competitive (Sachs and Warner 1999).

Neither study paints a pretty picture of Ukraine. People interviewed reported that in Kyiv a builder must add 15 percent to the cost of construction for bribes paid at various stages of construction permitting. Some suggested that a preference for negotiated sales of land rather than auctions sometimes reflects favoritism and bribes in the privatization process.

In a climate of suspected and actual corruption, lack of transparency is an even more serious problem than it would be in a country with a higher level of trust in public officials. Why, for instance, when city plans and development targets for specific sites are known to exist, are they not available for scrutiny by any interested person? Why should information about land title, building title and borrowing be registered in three separate locations? Many officials appear to hoard what stock of knowledge or power they have, perhaps only to reveal it in return for favors. This behavior, a holdover from socialist times, discourages investment, including that by prospective foreign enterprises.

This said, as of mid-2002 there is some reason for optimism. Since reelection, President Kuchma has recognized the importance of clarifying and revising land laws. His decree, On Measures about Development and Regulation of Market of Lands of Settlements, Other Lands of Non-Agricultural Destination,[14] is an important document that provides an overview of today's situation and a template for action. The Land Code of 2001 was passed over the strong opposition of the communist members of Parliament, who said, "To sell land is to sell the motherland." The code will begin to clarify what sales are allowed and will expedite the evolution, first, of an urban land market and, subsequently, of a rural land market. However, some 50 laws and decrees are required to specify what is to occur. Two provisions of the code relate to leasehold. One lists the types of rights in land that may exist. They are: fee ownership, perpetual or indefinite right of use, short-term leasehold of up to five years, long-term leasehold of up to fifty years and servitudes (easements). Another section of the code states that lessees may sublet with the approval of the lessor.

---

[14] #168/2000, February 4, 2000.

TENURE CHOICES: CONCLUSIONS AND RECOMMENDATIONS

At independence the only choices of land tenure, other than use or possession, were fee title for very small plots for gardens, garages or single family houses and leasehold for enterprises. In 1993 choice of land tenure became available for individuals as well as for enterprises with gas station sites and sites of unfinished structures, and in 1995 for other nonagricultural enterprises. Since then 10.7 million individuals have acquired fee title to small plots while 11.3 million others are holding plots through right of use. Entrepreneurs, on the other hand, have overwhelmingly chosen to privatize by right of use. Today, 93 percent of enterprises with privatized plots hold the land by gift of use, only 4 percent hold by purchase of fee simple, and 3 percent hold by purchase of leasehold.

To some extent the privatization choices reflect the reluctance of some municipalities to alienate land. Overwhelmingly, however, these choices reflect the fragile state of Ukraine's economy and the unsatisfactory structure of laws and practices governing privatization of land. Note that individuals privatizing plots that they formerly held under gift of use did not have to pay for these plots. Entrepreneurs, generally short of funds and without financing options, had a choice between gift of use or purchase of the fee title or leasehold. In the small percent of situations in which they chose either fee title or leasehold, payment of an average of 30 percent of the sales price has been deferred by the municipalities.

Lack of a clear, publicly accessible system for managing market transactions is another great disincentive to investment in land. Potential investors are more concerned with the existence of a reliable, stable and transparent structure than with the specific nature of property rights. The president's decree on February 4, 2000, addresses these problems directly and in considerable detail. If Parliament enacts the set of draft laws that has been submitted, there will be a new climate in which investment in land and advancement of credit for such investment will become sensible business activities. The government's hope that an active market in land will yield substantial tax revenues to support public services will become more realistic. The reform of land laws and practices alone cannot invigorate the economy, but it can play a significant role. Many draft laws have been submitted in recent years, only to perish in Parliament. Passage this year of a panoply of land laws is urgent.

The president's decree does not express a preference between sale of fee title and sale of leasehold, nor does it consider the appropriateness of the predominant present form of tenure, holding in use by gift. It is time now, while there is no great pressure from the private sector to acquire land, to review the arguments in favor of each type of tenure and reach some judgment as to which is preferable and under what circumstances.

Gift of use is a well-established practice for both land and structures. On one hand it produces revenue (in the form of land tax) and can provide flexibility to the public sector concerning future use of the property. On the other hand, it limits the users' options and does not place the property in the market.

Cities of Ukraine definitely face the need for redevelopment of older sectors. Much of the apartment construction after the Second World War does not meet today's standards and is in bad repair. Services and amenities are very limited. Many industrial structures are empty and abandoned. Giving land in temporary use where there is some demand for it, for whatever term of years is compatible with plans for redevelopment, would enable a city to reacquire the land, clear it to the extent desired and allocate it for new development. Short-term leasehold would achieve the same objectives but would likely prove less attractive to individuals and enterprises, since it imposes a greater commitment on them.

As in Kyiv, anticipation of future city expansion will lead to requirements for heavy public expenses for new infrastructure: roads, transit, water and sewer systems, and communication systems. If land intended for expansion has been sold in fee simple, its reacquisition for infrastructure systems will be difficult and expensive. Cities such as Rotterdam, Stockholm and Canberra have been able to realize their plans by holding expansion sites in public ownership, subject to short-term lease for agriculture, until they are needed for urbanization, then building the infrastructure and then placing the areas for development on long-term lease (Strong 1979; Bourassa, Neutze and Strong 1996). The cities of Ukraine have a considerable opportunity—if they retain fee ownership of urban fringe land and place it on short-term lease—to avoid expensive reacquisition costs and create efficient and attractive urban settlements.

Whether it is preferable to sell or lease land for new development or already developed urban land depends on many factors. Singapore, ranked first on the Competitive Index for 1998 and 1999, as the world's most competitive economy, uses long-term leasehold exclusively (Sachs and Warner 1999). It also is true that Singapore is perhaps the most highly regulated country in existence today. Yet, other governments, including several discussed in this book, have found that the legal right to resume title at the end of a lease term and the legal right to raise rents periodically are politically infeasible, making leasehold tantamount to fee simple.

Advocates of fee title insist that this form of tenure offers owners more freedom to determine what to do with land and is less subject to heavyhanded government intervention. Advocates of leasehold may agree with these perceptions, but see greater public control of land use as redounding to the general public interest. The ongoing, virulent battles in the U.S. today—between property rights forces who believe that a landowner is entitled to do whatever he or she wishes with that land, and growth management advocates who believe that there is a larger public interest that deserves protection—can be instructive to Ukrainians trying to decide where to set the balance. Whether UKRels, with its explicit advocacy of fee title and rejection of leasehold, is speaking for USAID and the U.S. government is questionable. Experience elsewhere shows overwhelmingly that public rights abandoned are difficult if not impossible to reclaim.

The degree of government intervention through regulation and taxation is not necessarily linked to the form of tenure. For instance, the highly specific, restrictive targeted uses for land in today's Ukraine equally affect holdings in fee or leasehold. In the U.S., there is tremendous variation from state to state in the restrictiveness of land use controls. In the arid west, where the majority of land in several states is in federal ownership with much of it leased to private ranchers for grazing, land use controls often are limited and loose. On the densely settled east and west coasts, where fee simple land ownership predominates, an intricate web of plans, zoning, building and sanitary codes, and public and private easements constrain use of land.

Selling the fee title may yield a larger initial sum to the municipality than sale of the leasehold. However, the terms of a lease may, by agreement, be revised to reflect subsequent market conditions and provide a higher yield over time. Also, at the end of the leasehold term the government will have the right to resume title to the land, if it is needed for a different use, without incurring the political and financial costs of expropriation. At present, the prices paid for either fee title or leasehold are certain to be substantially lower than they would be in a less risky institutional environment. This is a powerful argument for employing short-term leases until supportive financial and institutional structures are in place to provide a bulwark to investors.

Offering land at auction offers several advantages for Ukraine. Auctions are a relatively open process. In a country beset by corruption or the perception of corruption, transparency is a great asset. Auctions can attract many bidders and build firm evidence of the market value of land. As Ukraine seeks to build a cadre of qualified land appraisers, data from sales under competitive conditions will build an accurate market picture.

The government of Ukraine apparently intends to try to sell in fee title or lease for a long time all urban land not now needed for public purposes. This policy should be reconsidered. The allure of immediate income will be at the expense of lost greater future income. Sale of fee simple or long-term leases can hobble implementation of land use plans for future urbanization.

REFERENCES

Bancroft Group, PADCO Inc. 1997. *USAID urban land titling/registration, privatization and marketization project.* Contract #EPE-00114-I-00-5073.

Bourassa, Steven C., Max Neutze and Ann Louise Strong. 1996. Managing publicly owned land in Canberra: Rural to urban change of use. *Land Use Policy* 13(4):273–288.

Crossette, Barbara. 1999. A new index tracks bribe-paying countries. *New York Times,* October.

Committee for Land Resources. 1999. Information on fulfillment of presidential decrees on sale and lease of land plots of non-agricultural use.

Mace, James E. 1984. The famine: Stalin imposes a "final solution." *Ukrainian Weekly,* June 17, 24; July 1, 8.

Netzer, Dick. 1966. *Economics of the property tax.* Washington, DC: Brookings Institution.

Sachs, Jeffrey D. and Andrew M. Warner. 1999. *Year in review*. Cambridge, MA: Harvard University, Institute of International Development.

Strong, Ann Louise. 1979. *Land banking: European reality, American prospect*. Baltimore: Johns Hopkins Press.

Strong, Ann Louise, Thomas A. Reiner and Janusz Szyrmer. 1996. *Transitions in land and housing: Bulgaria, the Czech Republic, and Poland*. New York: St. Martin's Press.

State Committee of Ukraine on Urban Development and Architecture, State Committee of Ukraine for Land Resources, et al. 1995. *A guide to land auctions in Ukraine*. Kyiv.

Subtelny, Orest. 1988. *Ukraine: A history*. Toronto: University of Toronto Press.

U.S. Bureau of the Census. 1997. International database: *http://www.census.gov/cgi-bin/ipc/idb-sprd*. Ukraine data updated October 10.

Valletta, William. 1997. Black earth and bureaucracy: The land law of Ukraine. *Parker School Journal of East European Law* 4:53–105.

Vechirniy Kyiv. December 18, 1999.

Appendix

Pre-independence Laws Concerning Property Rights

The first pre-independence law affecting land rights was the 1989 USSR Fundamental Principles of Legislation on Lease.[15] This law authorized the state or its republics to lease property, including land; the primary emphasis was on leases to enterprises, although leases to individuals were included. The lease was to specify a term of years, the uses that might be made of the property and the payment due. Ownership of the lease could not be transferred, but if held by an individual could be inherited.

In 1990 the USSR Law on Fundamental Principles of Legislation on Land was adopted, authorizing the granting of some property rights to individual citizens and to enterprises:[16]

> First, individual citizens could be granted small parcels that were in the nature of "personal property" for gardening, recreation and residence. Use of these kinds of plots would not give rise to the need to hire other workers; thus, they were not "means of production" and could be allotted to individuals. Other lands...would be possessed by entities that would need to hire workers, thereby creating the potential for "landlords" whose monopolistic control of the land could be manipulated to exploit the workers. These lands would have to remain subject to a significant degree of state control (Valletta 1997, 59–60).

Individuals could possess land for life and pass it on to their heirs. Farm and forest enterprises could possess land in perpetuity. Urban enterprises could hold rights to use land, either temporarily or permanently. All categories of land rights: lease, possession and use, were to be subject to payments to the respective republic, with rents to be paid for leases and taxes to be paid for possession or use.

The USSR Land Code also was adopted in 1990.[17] It authorized individual land ownership for a residence, dacha, garage or garden up to a maximum of 0.4 hectare in cities and 0.6 hectare in villages. A moratorium of six years was set for private sales of such land.

---

[15] Issue #25, Item 481, enacted November 23, 1989, as amended Issue #12, Item 325, 1991.

[16] Enacted February 28, 1990, amended March 6, 1991.

[17] #562-12, December 18, 1990.

The USSR 1991 law, On Property,[18] stated that property ownership may be by individuals, the state or collectives, and that all forms of ownership are equal. This was a major departure from socialist doctrine.

POST-INDEPENDENCE, PRE-CONSTITUTION LAWS AFFECTING URBAN LAND

A substantial body of Ukrainian law was enacted between independence, in August 1991, and adoption of the Constitution, in June of 1996. Interpretation of pre-1996 laws, both those enacted by the USSR and by Ukraine, in light of the Constitution is ongoing in the courts.

On Forms of Land Ownership amended the 1991 law, On Property, by substituting the term *private* for *individual*, thus including enterprise land. It retained the statement that all forms of property are equal.[19]

The Land Code of 1992 substantially altered and augmented the Land Code of 1990.[20] As amended it is still in force; however, 96 of its 118 articles conflict with the 1996 Constitution, posing many quandaries. As of January 2002 revisions to the Land Code took effect. Summaries of a few of the important pre-2002 provisions follow.

Article 3. Local councils are responsible for public land management. They are authorized to transfer title or to lease land. Individuals holding title to land may lease it to others for up to three years.

Article 4. Nonagricultural land targeted for multifamily housing, commercial, or industrial use may not be sold, only transferred by the state for temporary or permanent use or for lease. The type of tenure is determined by current use, targeted use through plans and status of the prospective user.

Article 6. Individual citizens may own land for private farming, a residence and outbuildings, garden, dacha and garage.

Article 15. The State Committee of Ukraine for Land Resources is created and authorized to manage land use.[21]

Article 28. Land may be taken back by the state under circumstances that include: consistent failure to pay taxes or rents; use of the land for non-targeted purposes; and purchase, sale, gift or mortgage of the land by means other than those officially authorized.

Article 36. Use of land requires payment, either as land tax payable by owners or land rental payable by lessees.

Article 39. Owners and users of land may execute mortgages.

---

[18] Adopted February 7, 1991.

[19] Adopted January 30, 1992.

[20] March 13, 1992, as amended.

[21] The tasks of the committee were defined in the cabinet of ministers decree of June 22, 1992.

The Land Code incorporates several new departures. It strengthens the role of local government, by giving it power to transfer rights to state land and by allocating to it land tax revenues. What the Code does not change is that nonagricultural enterprises may not be granted fee title.

On Payment for Land amplifies Article 36 of the Land Code.[22] It reiterates that all landowners and users, except lessees, must pay a land tax. Lessees must pay rent. The law established a procedure for normative valuation of land by geographic area of a city, modified by coefficients for infrastructure, distance from the city center and distance from public transportation. The base for the land tax or land rent is 1 percent of the normative value. Parliament is responsible for setting tax rates. The rent may not be less than the land tax, and, for agricultural land, may not exceed it. Parliament is responsible for setting tax rates.

The law, On the Principles of Urban Development, for the most part retained pre-independence requirements.[23] All parcels of urban land are to have a target use. Planning approval proceeds by presentation of a use concept, issuance of a permit to plan, issuance of a permit to build and grant of a certificate of occupancy and grant of permanent tenure.

The decree of the cabinet of ministers, On Privatization of Land Plots, modified the prior authorization of 1990.[24] It reaffirmed that citizens who hold use rights to land for private farming, a house and outbuilding, garden, dacha or garage are entitled to free privatization of such land plot. Citizens may sell these plots, but for not less than the normative value. The agreement of sale must be notarized and registered in the cadastre, with the sale price recorded. This price, if higher than the normative value, becomes the value from which the land tax base is set.

The State Committee for Land Resources established regulations under this decree.[25] In cities, free land is not to exceed 0.1 hectare for a house or dacha, 0.12 hectare for a garden or 0.01 hectare for a garage. Citizens seeking plots must file an application and provide evidence of the parcel size. The local council is responsible for checking boundaries and issuing and registering titles.

The decree of the president, On Privatization of Objects of Incomplete Construction, sets forth procedures for privatizing unfinished, often abandoned enterprise structures and related land.[26]

The decree of the president, On Privatization and Lease of Non-Agricultural Land Plots for Business Activity, enabled individuals and enterprises, including those owning apartment buildings, to apply to buy or lease land.[27] Prior to this, land under privatized enterprises was given in either temporary or permanent use and was not considered a capital asset of the enterprise. For land that was to be sold by agreement, the sale price was to be the land's normative value.

---

[22] Adopted July 23, 1992, amended July 3, 1993.

[23] #52, Item #683, November 1992.

[24] Issued December 26, 1992.

[25] #10/93, February 15, 1993.

[26] Issued October 14, 1993.

[27] Issued July 12, 1995.

If the land was to be offered at auction, this value was to be the starting price. Land owned or leased under the provisions of this decree could be sold, given away, mortgaged or, in case of lease, sublet.

Parliament rejected amendment of the Land Code to incorporate the language of this decree. This action demonstrated continuing and substantial opposition to fee title sale of land to enterprises. It also, in the opinion of many, caused the decree to be inoperative. Whether this means that fee sales to enterprises are illegal remains a topic of considerable debate. In spite of this uncertainty, fee sales continue under the enterprise privatization programs.

THE CONSTITUTION AND POST-CONSTITUTION LEGISLATION

The Constitution of Ukraine was adopted on June 28, 1996. It establishes the structure of the government and includes a number of provisions relating to land.

» Article 13 provides: Property entails responsibility. Property shall not be used to the detriment of the person and society.... The land, its mineral resources, air space, water and other natural resources...are objects of the right of ownership of the Ukrainian people. On behalf of the Ukrainian people the rights as owner are exercised by the organs of state authority and local self-government in the order determined by this Constitution. Every citizen has the right to use natural objects of the right of ownership of the people, in accordance with law.... All subjects of ownership rights are equal before the law.

This last clause affirms the equality of forms of property as provided in the 1991 law, On Property. However, the statement that "the rights as owner are exercised by the organs of state authority and local self-government...." suggests that private fee ownership is not contemplated. This implication is refuted by the language of Article 14.

» Article 14 provides, "Land is the fundamental national wealth that is under special state protection. The right of property to land is guaranteed. This right is acquired and realized by citizens, legal persons and the state only in accordance with the law."

This language appears to overrule Article 4 of the Land Code that barred fee sale to nonagricultural enterprises.

» Article 41 provides that "every person has the right to possess, use and manage his/her property." The article also states that "No one shall be unlawfully deprived of property." Expropriation is allowed for social purposes with payment of fair compensation.

» Article 92 limits the authority of the president to issue decrees, stating that only Parliament may act concerning natural resources, including land. However, Chapter XV, Clause 4, authorized the issuance of Presidential

Decrees concerning economic matters not otherwise regulated by law for three years, or through June 28, 1999.

The 1996 law, On Land Payment,[28] governs taxation and rents for use of land and is a further development of the earlier law of 1992, as amended in 1993.

» Article 2 states that fee title owners and persons holding use rights of land will pay the land tax. Lessees of public land will pay rent as provided under contract. Parcel valuation is under the jurisdiction of the State Committee for Land Resources.

» Article 4 states that this law is the exclusive vehicle governing the land tax, including rates and payment.

» Article 7 reiterates the previous rule that the land's base value for taxation is to be one percent of normative value. It also prescribes factors to be applied in communities in which normative valuation of land has not yet occurred.

» Article 21 mandates that 30 percent of the payments be transferred to the State Committee for Land Resources and that 10 percent be transferred to the Republic of Crimea or the oblast in which the land is located.

» Article 22 limits municipal use of revenues to any targeted purpose. These include establishing and maintaining the cadastre, carrying out land reform, city planning, and building of infrastructure. There is a 100 percent penalty for use of funds for nontargeted purposes; penalty money goes to the state budget and is used for targeted purposes. State and oblast revenues are used for similar purposes.

The law, On Land Lease, specifies conditions under which land may be leased and sublet.[29] It reiterates that lease payments may not be lower than the land tax.

The following three decrees were among 60 decrees issued by the president in June 1999, to meet the deadline set by the Constitution. Of the 145 presidential decrees issued during the three-year window of opportunity from June 1996 through June 1999, as of the latter date 24 percent remained in force, 34 percent never came into effect because the draft law was rejected by Parliament, 10 percent did not come into effect because Parliament passed alternative legislation, and the remaining 32 percent did not become operative for other reasons.

The decree of the president, On the Delimitation of Land in Government and Communal Ownership,[30] was rejected by Parliament. However, the subject matter will be a chapter in the prospective Land Code.

---

[28] Adopted September 19, 1996.

[29] Adopted October 6, 1998.

[30] #722/99, issued June 27, 1999.

The decree of the president, On Amending the Decree of the President #1353/98, fixes land rent at a minimum of 1 percent of land value, increasing the minimum from the prior minimum of 0.5 percent.[31] This decree was confirmed December 3, 1999.[32]

The decree of the president, On the Measures Towards the Further Development of the Citizen's Individual House Plots, confirmed in December 1999, sets the size of the plot that may be privatized at no cost at a maximum of two hectares.[33]

Following the November 1999 presidential election, a new prime minister, Viktor Yushchenko, and other members of government were appointed. This government has withdrawn 161 draft laws that the former government had submitted to Parliament. The Committee for Land Resources has drafted a new Land Code, in part to eliminate the 96 areas of conflict between the 1992 Code and the 1996 Constitution. This draft includes sections on land lease, title registration and mortgages. It is this new code that passed first reading in Parliament in July 2000 and that will be presented for second and third readings in the fall.

---

[31] #749/99.

[32] #1529/99.

[33] #751/9 9, June 28, 1999.

LEARNING FROM LOUISIANA

LEASING MILITARY BASES

Christie I. Baxter

9

Like any large and dynamic organization, the United States military periodically finds itself with the wrong real estate for its current mission. At the start of armed conflicts—the Second World War, the Korean War and the war in Vietnam—the military acquired and built facilities to train and house troops. In the aftermath of these wars the military shed facilities (although shedding has always proved to be harder than acquiring). Most recently the changing nature of international conflict, including the end of the cold war and increased reliance on technology versus manpower in national defense, has again changed the military's need for land installations. Accordingly, four Base Realignment and Closure (BRAC) Commissions, acting between 1988 and 1995, ordered a 20 percent reduction in the number of major domestic installations by 2001. As a result, more than 200,000 acres of military property will become available for nonfederal users, such as state and local authorities and private parties (see Table 1).

Congress gave the U.S. Department of Defense (DOD) six years to implement the closures ordered in each BRAC round, and DOD intended to sell much of the surplus property to private buyers. Instead, a highly prescribed public land conveyance process, combined with the need for extensive and complex environmental cleanup, has significantly extended the timetable for property transfers. In addition, the need for significant investment to make the property saleable on the private market has limited the potential for "as is" sales, and made local redevelopment authorities (LRAs) key actors in the

I wish to thank the many people in central Louisiana who welcomed my questions about the redevelopment of England Air Force Base. Contributors of key information used in this chapter include: Travis Brann of the J. B. Hunt Driver Training School; Bruce Capps of Greiner Engineers, Inc.; Jon Grafton of the England Authority; Rod Knoles of Knoles-Frye Realty, Inc.; Keith LaBauve of Cleco Corporation; Garland Lawrence, formerly of Central Louisiana Electric Company; Mark L. Mavrinac of Cleco Services LLC; James L. Meyer of the England Authority; Elton Pody of the Central Louisiana Chamber of Commerce; and Edward (Ned) Randolph, Mayor of the City of Alexandria.

TABLE 1

SURPLUS LAND AT MILITARY BASES: BRAC 1988–1995 (LOCAL IMPACT
INSTALLATIONS)*

	Acres	%
Total surplus land	313,803	100
Federal-to-federal transfers	100,550	30
Available for nonfederal use	213,253	70

Source: Author's database compiled for the MIT Project on Base Redevelopment
* Local Impact Installations include 95 facilities whose closing or realignments were determined by the
U.S. DOD's Office of Economic Adjustment to affect a sufficient number of civilian jobs and/or release suf-
ficient land to the private market to warrant grant assistance to the local community.

redevelopment of the land.[1] Most LRAs wanted to take control of the property
quickly, to prevent building deterioration and permit the start of reuse.

Out of these circumstances has grown a "military leasing program" that
facilitates the transfer of property control from DOD to LRAs during the long
conveyance and cleanup processes. The specifics of this program have been
shaped by negotiations between LRAs, who will eventually own most of the
land slated for nonfederal use, and the individual military services—the Army,
Navy and Air Force—that controlled the land prior to closure. This chapter
illustrates how the military leasing program evolved, by exploring negotiations between the Air Force and officials in central Louisiana interested in
redeveloping the England Air Force Base. Participants in the case used leases
to (1) address problems with the traditional public land conveyance process;
(2) attract businesses that would create jobs to make up for those lost when
the Air Force left; and (3) manage development at the former base over time.
The England case is important because it set precedents for subsequent federal
policies. For example, Congress created a new kind of public benefit conveyance, known as the economic development conveyance or EDC, in part based
on the experience at England Air Force Base.

LEASING MILITARY BASES: AN OVERVIEW

The stringent terms of early leases reflected the expectation by the three military services that they would grant few leases. At the start of the post-cold war
closures, the military services generally refused to consider lease terms of longer
than one year. All leases permitted the relevant service to revoke the lease and
reclaim the property for military purposes at will with a 30-day notice to the
tenant. When lessees—mostly LRAs that ultimately stood to receive title to the
property—wanted to sublease property to other parties, the military services
insisted on reviewing and approving each sublease.

Today, things have changed. Although the military services do not compile
centralized data on leasing, available data suggest that most land at closed

---

[1] LRAs are public authorities or local governments designated as the entities responsible for the preparation of a redevelopment plan and directing its implementation for a closing military installation.

TABLE 2

DISPOSITION OF SURPLUS AIR FORCE LAND AS OF MARCH 2000, IN ACRES

	BRAC 1988 (%)	BRAC 1991 (%)	BRAC 1993 (%)	BRAC 1995 (%)	Total
Deeded	4,696 (24.6)	18,011 (43.4)	3,483 (17.2)	113 (1.3)	26,303 (29.3)
Long-term lease	14,280 (74.6)	17,568 (42.3)	818 (4.0)	1,027 (11.6)	33,693 (37.5)
Short-term lease	107 (0.6)	1,218 (2.9)	3,273 (16.2)	1,163 (13.1)	5,761 (6.4)
Not in reuse	42 (0.2)	4,737 (11.4)	12,678 (62.6)	6,577 (74.1)	24,034 (26.8)
Total	19,125 (100)	41,534 (100)	20,252 (100)	8,880 (100)	89,791 (100)

Source: Jenkins (2000)

bases is leased at some point in the redevelopment process, and substantial portions are leased for long periods of time. The Air Force, which does track its land-leasing activity, reported that 41,500 acres, or 46 percent of the total property it had declared surplus between 1988 and 1995, were under lease as of January 1999, most with terms longer than five years. It had deeded only 19,000 acres (21 percent of its surplus land) to various parties; and the remaining land was not in reuse at that time.[2] As Table 2 shows, by April 2000 the Air Force had deeded more than 26,000 acres (29 percent of the total surplus land) to designated recipients, and was leasing more than 39,000 acres (44 percent) of land.

Table 2 illustrates the importance of leasing. Twelve years after the first BRAC closures were announced, leasing remained the dominant form of land disposition for the Air Force in a context where conveyance by deed is the explicit objective.

Across the three services, the U.S. General Accounting Office (GAO) reported that by early 1998 the DOD had completed 85 percent of closures and realignments mandated by BRAC commissions between 1988 and 1995. Of the approximately 154,000 acres slated for nonfederal users, 31 percent (47,000 acres) had actually been transferred and another 25 percent (38,000 acres) was under some kind of lease arrangement (U.S. GAO 1998). The stringent provisions of early leases were no longer in evidence: lease terms varied widely according to the circumstances, and the military services no longer insisted on reviewing and approving the subleases issued by LRAs.

One reason for the increases in land leasing is because of the complexities of public land conveyances. Federal law dictates how federal land is conveyed, and over time Congress has imposed additional constraints that serve defined public interests but slow the process compared to private transactions. The most important governing statute, enacted in 1949, seeks a fair distribution of property within the family of federal agencies prior to private sale, a process known as *screening*.[3] Surplus federal real estate is first offered to other federal

---

[2] See the Air Force Base Conversion Agency website: *www.afbce.hq.af.mil/*

[3] The 1949 statute governs the actions of the General Services Administration (GSA), the federal agency responsible for most federal land transactions. Congress later delegated GSA's responsibilities to the DOD in the case of base closures.

agencies for their own use, and is then offered to other public entities under the sponsorship of federal agencies. For example, a local school district that wanted property would petition under the sponsorship of the Department of Education. Within the public claims queue, Congress has given priority to agencies providing for homeless people. Remaining property can then be sold to public entities at market price, with negotiated terms. Finally, any remaining property can be offered at auction to private buyers. Table 3 shows conveyances planned as of mid-1998 at 95 Local Impact Installations.

As Table 3 shows, the vast majority of conveyances planned as of 1998 have been for public benefit: under 4 percent involved auctions to private parties. Figure 1 describes where screening fits in the sequence of base redevelopment activities.

In addition to the screening process, all transfers of military land are subject to National Environmental Policy Act requirements. This generally means that the military service must prepare and file an Environmental Impact Statement (EIS) prior to transfer. However, because Congress did not want to allow private groups to derail base closure decisions through the EIS process, it defined the local reuse of the property, not DOD's closure decision, as the relevant action under the Act. This made the EIS process an integral part of the conveyance process. Figure 2 illustrates how the EIS relates to the conveyance process.

Since most military bases are in effect brownfield sites, the need for environmental cleanup further complicates the conveyance process. Almost all former military bases have some environmental contamination, and the military services are responsible for cleanup. Normally, no property conveyance can occur until the cleanup is complete. To illustrate how the military uses leasing to hasten these lengthy and complex procedures for base conveyance, a detailed case study is presented next.

TABLE 3

PLANNED CONVEYANCES AT LOCAL IMPACT INSTALLATIONS*

Category	Acres	% of Known Conveyances
Total identified conveyances	169,995	100.0
FAA conveyances	41,313	24.3
Education conveyances	2,856	1.7
Parks and recreation conveyances	20,842	12.3
Economic development conveyances	83,439	49.1
Other public benefit conveyances	8,840	5.2
Negotiated sales to public entities	5,746	3.4
Auctions to private buyers	6,400	3.8

Source: Author's database compiled for the MIT Project on Base Redevelopment

* Planned conveyances are as reported by the DOD as of August 1998; they account for 86 percent of all land available for nonfederal use.

FIGURE 1 ———————————————————————————————

ILLUSTRATIVE TIME LINE

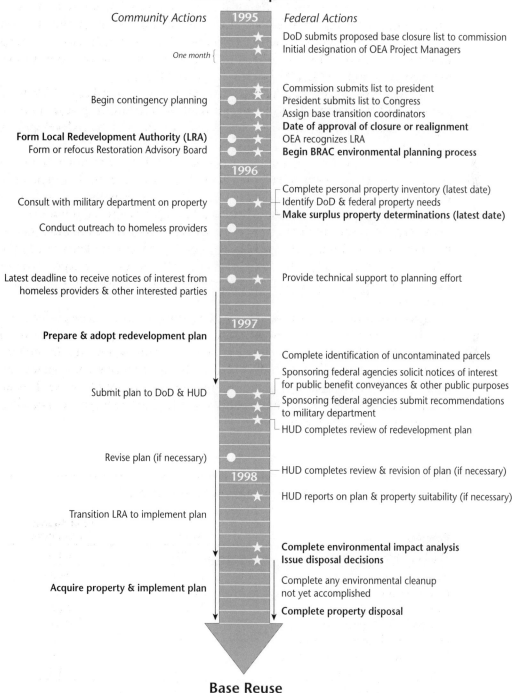

Closure Proposal

Community Actions 1995 *Federal Actions*

DoD submits proposed base closure list to commission
Initial designation of OEA Project Managers

One month {

Begin contingency planning

Commission submits list to president
President submits list to Congress
Assign base transition coordinators
Date of approval of closure or realignment

Form Local Redevelopment Authority (LRA)
Form or refocus Restoration Advisory Board

OEA recognizes LRA
Begin BRAC environmental planning process

1996

Consult with military department on property

Complete personal property inventory (latest date)
Identify DoD & federal property needs
Make surplus property determinations (latest date)

Conduct outreach to homeless providers

Latest deadline to receive notices of interest from
homeless providers & other interested parties

Provide technical support to planning effort

1997

Prepare & adopt redevelopment plan

Complete identification of uncontaminated parcels

Submit plan to DoD & HUD

Sponsoring federal agencies solicit notices of interest
for public benefit conveyances & other public purposes
Sponsoring federal agencies submit recommendations
to military department
HUD completes review of redevelopment plan

Revise plan (if necessary)

HUD completes review & revision of plan (if necessary)

1998

HUD reports on plan & property suitability (if necessary)

Transition LRA to implement plan

Complete environmental impact analysis
Issue disposal decisions

Complete any environmental cleanup
not yet accomplished

Acquire property & implement plan

Complete property disposal

Base Reuse

Source: U.S. DOD (1997)

FIGURE 2
BASE REUSE IMPLEMENTATION PROCESS FLOW CHART

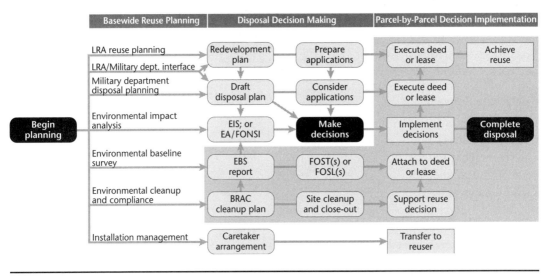

Source: U.S. DOD (1997)

ENGLAND AIR FORCE BASE

Over time, leases at England Air Force Base have covered a range of circumstances. The Army first made use of the site under a lease from the City of
Alexandria at the start of the Second World War. The Air Force took a fee
interest in the site during the Korean War. After the base was ordered closed in
1991 the Air Force used a lease to transfer interim site control to the England
Authority, a state-chartered public corporation, and in 1995 the Air Force
signed a long-term lease with the Authority. In turn, the England Authority
has leased individual parcels to a number of private and public tenants. The
Authority brought its first tenant, a private firm, onto the site before the Air
Force left, and soon thereafter the Authority leased part of the property to
the Army for war games training. Lease revenues help the England Authority
operate the facility and finance its redevelopment.

Background

Plantations once occupied the land that became England Air Force Base. In the
early 1940s the City of Alexandria assembled 1,339 acres of former agricultural fields to build a municipal airport. During World War II the Army leased
the property from the city for bomber crew training. After the war, the city
briefly operated the site as a civilian airfield, but the DOD reactivated the site
at the start of the Korean War. The Air Force acquired the original site plus
additional land in 1954.

Over the years the Air Force developed the land and buildings at the
base into a small city of almost 4,000 people. When the BRAC commission
ordered the base closed in 1991, it contained over 2.5 million square feet of

nonresidential buildings, 598 units of family housing (92 officers' units and 506 enlisted personnel units), and 13 dormitories (with a total capacity of 968) on 2,282 acres of land. There was a hospital, a school, a nine-hole golf course, a small nature preserve, an officers' club, plus all of the facilities and equipment necessary to operate the airfield and service military aircraft. Air Force inventories valued the base's real property at US$120 million and estimated its replacement cost to be US$602 million (U.S. DOD 1995).

The Single Conveyance

Local residents feared that the closure of England Air Force Base would devastate central Louisiana's economy. The 3,000 military and 700 civilian employees that would lose their jobs when the base closed represented 6 percent of employment in the Alexandria-Pineville metropolitan statistical area. Local leaders saw redevelopment of the base as the key to economic recovery. However, they worried that the piecemeal distribution of the base would damage their ability to create new economic activity at the site. Observers of the federal screening process at other bases suggested that the property looked like "Swiss cheese" by the time conveyance was complete, the choice parcels taken by various public entities and the homeless.

Leaders in central Louisiana wanted the DOD to return all of the land to its original donors, the City of Alexandria. As Mayor of Alexandria Ned Randolph put it, soon after the closure announcement, "Our aim will be to get title back to all of the property out there. We want title to and control of the whole shebang" (Caslin and Daye 1991, A-4).

To accept title to the site, the community created the England Airpark and Industrial District (the England Authority), a state-chartered public corporation. Legislation creating the Authority specified that it would be the sole agent to dispose of land locally, thus preempting claims that might come during a public screening process. The Louisiana legislature approved the creation of the England Authority just before the final closing announcement in June 1991.

A week or so later, Randolph met with Louisiana Senator John Breaux to discuss ways to ensure the England Authority gained control of the property. Louisiana Senators Breaux and Bennett Johnston decided to attach to the Defense Appropriations bill—then under consideration by the U.S. Senate—an amendment that reversed the order in which closed military bases would be turned over to other governmental entities nationwide, putting local communities first in line. The Senate passed the bill in a 93-1 vote, and a similar bill was introduced in the House of Representatives.

Concern that the passage of the Johnston-Breaux amendment might eliminate DOD's hopes for significant revenues from the sale of bases in strong real estate markets such as California, prompted DOD to begin negotiations with officials in central Louisiana. Meanwhile, local leaders were devising ways to make the federal screening process work in their favor. Federal sponsors could request and convey, as public benefit conveyances, properties that would be used for designated public purposes. Most interesting was the ability of the

Federal Aviation Administration (FAA) to transfer property to be used as airports. If the property at England were to be reused as an airport, which was likely, the Air Force could make a public benefit conveyance to the England Authority through the FAA. Conveyances under FAA sponsorship were made at no cost to the recipient.

Central Louisiana officials pursued negotiations with DOD to accomplish such a transfer at the same time the Louisiana delegation was pushing the Johnston-Breaux amendment in Congress. This dual strategy proved effective. Soon after the Senate's approval of the Defense Appropriations bill, as amended, giving property at military bases around the country back to communities at no cost, senior DOD officials agreed to negotiate with the Alexandria delegation to achieve a public benefit transfer through the FAA.

The Louisiana congressional delegation, local leaders, DOD lawyers and key Air Force decision makers agreed that if the Johnston-Breaux amendment were dropped, they would ensure that the England Authority received the base real estate. After the Air Force issued letters of intent to this effect, Breaux and Johnston withdrew their amendment. Defense Secretary Richard Cheney announced the agreement in November 1991. The conveyance would be subject to customary FAA rules requiring that the property remain public and that uses be aviation-related.

Leasing

Extensive reliance on leasing was central to the Authority's strategy to justify a conveyance of the entire site through FAA. While the Air Force had agreed to support such a conveyance, the England Authority still had to convince the FAA that the public benefit conveyance met its requirements. There were two issues to resolve. First, there had to be a commercial airport at England. Since central Louisiana already had a regional airport, the community had to commit to relocate its commercial operations to England. Second, typical FAA conveyances were restricted to airfields and the properties needed to support them. To achieve a single conveyance of the entire site, the England Authority had to show that lease revenues from the entire base were necessary to redevelop the airport and to support airport operations.[4] So, the England Authority commissioned a financial plan to support redevelopment and management of the entire site.

In the end, the England Authority decided to develop a civilian airport to serve commercial passengers, small private aircraft, defense installations remaining in the area (see the discussion below of the Army's Intermediate Staging Base) and air cargo carriers. The Authority would lease all nonairport property, mostly to business and industrial users. In addition, public entities that in other communities would have received property under the federal screening process—the county school department, which wanted the base school, Louisiana State University, which wanted classroom space, and the

---

[4] This broad interpretation of the public benefit conveyance was echoed in the 1994 Pryor Amendment, which defined economic development as a form of public benefit.

county, which wanted the hospital—would be paying tenants contributing to the self-sufficiency of the project.

J. B. Hunt Driver Training School

England Air Force Base was one of the first bases to close in the post-cold war BRAC rounds, and the first lease executed at England Airpark—with the J. B. Hunt Trucking Company—set several precedents. The lease negotiations tested the ability of the Air Force to enter into a lease with the England Authority and its ability to execute a simultaneous sublease with a tenant. Determining a lease price for Hunt set the framework for leasing the rest of the base. Getting a tenant to sign on before the Air Force actually closed the base generated critical momentum for the marketing effort and the reuse process in general. It also tested the willingness of the Air Force to accommodate such an action.

When lease negotiations began in 1991, J. B. Hunt was the largest publicly held truckload carrier in the country. The company owned a fleet of trucks and containers, hired and trained its own drivers and guaranteed customers door-to-door shipping services for a wide range of industrial freight. Hunt was outgrowing its driver training school. The company had been looking for space in the Lowell, Arkansas, area, and until conversations with the England marketing group began, Hunt had not considered locating outside of Arkansas.

England Air Force Base offered exactly the facilities Hunt needed: plenty of paved area for drivers to practice maneuvers, classrooms, housing for trainees and room for expansion. Despite these factors the director of the Lowell school doubted that local officials would be able to put the deal together, that it would drag on over time, and that the company would end up elsewhere.

The England marketing team calculated the rent it would charge Hunt based on estimates of its own costs to manage the real estate. It based its overall estimate on Air Force records for the management of nonairfield property at the base. The estimate was converted to square foot costs based on total available building area. Square foot rents necessary for the Authority to cover its costs if 70 percent of the base were leased, became the "break-even" rent it offered to Hunt. Subsequent negotiations focused on which facilities Hunt would lease and on potential federal and state financial assistance.

Soon after the marketing team made its proposal to Hunt, the Authority began negotiations with the Army, hoping it would locate a war games training facility at the former Air Force base. The Army needed a secure area adjacent to the existing hangers, which happened to be the area the Authority had designated for Hunt. The Authority wanted both tenants.

Providing another location for Hunt would require building a costly new concrete ramp for driver training. The Authority turned to the Economic Development Administration (EDA) and to the state for assistance. In May the EDA awarded the England Authority a $1.2 million grant to help finance construction of a new concrete apron to handle airfield cargo assembly and to support Hunt's driver training. The Louisiana legislature agreed to provide $800,000 in matching funds and agreed to help finance driver training through a new student loan program. With these agreements in place, Hunt announced its decision to lease a 13-acre site at the base. It would become England Airpark's first tenant.[5]

The England Authority set more challenges for itself when it decided to bring Hunt onto the base before it had title to the property and before the Air Force left. To accomplish this the Authority had to secure interim leases from the Air Force. However, despite the fact that by late 1991 the Air Force had agreed to convey the base to the England Authority through the FAA, restrictions on leasing at that time made subleasing extremely difficult. In addition, the Air Force claimed that as long as the DOD was owner of the property, it retained liability for any environmental contamination at the site, including any that Hunt might cause. To overcome this objection, the England Authority agreed to indemnify the federal government for any such responsibility related to the Hunt lease. These negotiations took time. The England Authority submitted its interim lease for the Hunt property to the Air Force in July 1992, and the lease had not been approved by October, when Hunt planned to move in. The Air Force briefly threatened to prevent access by Hunt until the lease approval was complete but finally backed down. Hunt occupied the site "by permission of the Air Force," without a lease, in October 1992. The Air Force approved the England Authority's interim lease two months later.

Ultimately the Air Force refused to consider a lease longer than one year to the England Authority, and Hunt wanted at least a five-year lease. Unable to convince the Air Force to consider longer lease terms, the England Authority decided to risk signing year-to-year interim leases with the Air Force and sublet space to Hunt for five years, with three five-year options to renew. As the Authority's executive director later characterized it, "The leasing process involved a lot of trust."

Leases for subsequent tenants took less time, but the process remained cumbersome. In 1993 the Authority requested that the Air Force enter into a 55-year master lease for all property at the base. The Authority would then take ownership of individual parcels as they were cleared for transfer. In March 1995 the Air Force and the Authority signed a lease in furtherance of conveyance with a 55-year term. At the time of the signing, the Authority had 12 year-to-year leases with the Air Force covering 470,000 square feet of building area. Most of the Authority's subleases were for longer terms.

Leasing an Intermediate Staging Base

In early 1992 word reached the England Authority that the Army was looking for a site to support war game training at nearby Fort Polk. The facility was known as an Intermediate Staging Base (ISB). The benefits of locating such a facility at the former England Air Force Base would be significant: under the contract that the England Authority eventually won, the initial lease payment of $1.25 million per year accounted for over 25 percent of the Authority's break-even budget. Having already rejected England as a potential site, the Army had set August 1993 as the deadline for making the ISB operational.

---

[5] Hunt has since closed all of its driver training schools, and left England Airpark in 1997.

Since England would not even close until late 1992, the Army assumed it would be impossible for England to meet the deadline. Through an acquaintance in the Air Combat Command in Langley, Virginia, the Authority's chairman convinced key Army decision makers that England could meet the deadline, and so remained a viable option.

The Authority had to mobilize significant resources to providing the facilities the Army needed, on time. The airport control tower had to be operational 24 hours a day, and the Authority secured a commitment from the Air National Guard to provide the necessary services. However, the Army would cover only the cost to operate the tower, beyond a normal 12-hour day. In addition the ISB would require more sophisticated and expensive air rescue and firefighting capability than those required for ordinary civilian use. Eventually, when the airport opened to commercial customers, the Authority expected to generate enough revenues to cover regular airfield operations, but it calculated that it would need $1.3 million a year for two years to operate the airport to Army standards.

England turned to the state for financial help and when the governor visited Alexandria in late spring 1992 local leaders secured a promise from him that if England got the ISB, he would provide funds for the Authority to operate the control tower for two years. The state legislature also earmarked $1.4 million in capital outlay funds for the ISB should the England Authority win the contract.[6] England won the contract later that year.

NONCOMMERCIAL LEASES

Leasing part of the air base to business and industrial tenants is important because replacing lost military jobs was a critical priority at the time the Authority was first negotiating with the Air Force. However, the Authority also leases the former base school to the county, which pays a rent that covers facility maintenance and common area maintenance costs only. It also leases former base housing to a nonprofit housing developer, California Lutheran Homes, which has created a 178-unit, moderate-income rental community for retired people, many former military personnel. Rents are targeted to households making between $25,000 and $35,000 per year. In another instance, however, the Authority chose not to lease base housing to low-income households, despite community pressure. Instead, the Authority leases the housing on a temporary basis to England Airpark tenants' new employees, while they find housing in the community.

Leasing to Manage Growth and Become Self-Sufficient

Accommodating the needs of various tenants at the Airpark over time will involve reorganizing land uses and shifting existing tenants, and the Authority

---

[6] This earmark was part of a $2.2 million authorization matching the EDA grant awarded that year.

has built the necessary flexibility into its leases. All leases give the Authority the absolute right to move tenants to equal or better space.

The Authority also tries to time lease expirations to coincide with planned redevelopment. For example, a passenger terminal completed in 1996 was designed as a short-term facility. The Authority planned to reconfigure the airport operation and built a new terminal in another location in 2002. All commercial leases in the interim terminal expired in August 2002, shortly before completion of the new facility. In another example the Authority undertook a major expansion of its existing nine-hole golf course; the new professional-level course has become the centerpiece of a new hotel and conference center complex. Since the existing golf course operator did not want to move, the Authority bought out the lease. The Authority also plans to use lease provisions to control the architectural design of the new complex.

Would the England Authority have been better off selling the land and using the capital raised to finance improvements? Not according to some. Before the England Air Force Base closed, the City of Alexandria sponsored development of an industrial park, where it sold sites to private buyers. According to a local bank president and member of the Port Authority board, early buyers (the first put an asphalt plant on the site) were not the most appropriate for the operations of the port. Had it sold the land, the Authority would have lost its flexibility.

England Airpark achieved its goal of self-sufficiency within five years of the base closure. As of September 1998 the England Authority had 64 commercial tenants renting more than one million square feet of space at the Airpark. The Authority also leased 140 units of housing. Annual lease income was $5.5 million out of total revenues of $6 million. (The Authority also received fuel flowage fees and interest on its reserves.) With expenditures of only $4.7 million, the Authority has been able to put funds aside for capital projects, and in fiscal year 1999 it allocated $5.3 million of its reserves for this use. Employment at the Airpark in 1998 totaled 1,569 people, more than twice the civilian employment at the base before it closed.

Opportunities and Dilemmas for Alexandria

Leasing has allowed the England Authority to take quick control of former military base property, provided a stream of revenues to finance the operation and facility redevelopment, and allowed the Authority to shift uses around as needed. However, leasing has been controversial in some communities, including central Louisiana. At England Airpark, competition between the former base—with its access to federal and state grants, advantageous leasing and conveyance terms from the Air Force, and exemption from property taxes—and private landlords has prompted some concern. Tenants who leased space at the Airpark, and local realtors who placed tenants in privately owned space both reported a rent disparity between the Airpark and comparable private properties. Another concern involves accountability. Because the airpark has no status as a political jurisdiction, it has no voters. Accountability and decision making rest with its board. The England Authority is independent of local government, although three legislative bodies appoint board members. Authority revenues are not available for general use in the community: according to provisions of the FAA conveyance, all revenues must go to the support of the Airpark itself.

LEASING SINCE ENGLAND AIR FORCE BASE

Based on the experience at England Air Force Base and other former bases around the country, Congress changed the legislative framework governing military base conveyances and leases. In 1994 Congress created a new kind of public benefit conveyance, known as the economic development conveyance (EDC), modeled on England's broadly defined FAA conveyance. Under an EDC, the military services can convey large sites to LRAs for comprehensive redevelopment. Since then, LRAs and real estate experts have lobbied hard to convince Congress that the investment in infrastructure and other improvements necessary to bring properties to civilian standards make many bases worth little "as-is" on the private market.[7] In 1999 Congress responded, authorizing EDCs to be made at no cost as long as the LRA invested net revenues in infrastructure improvements for at least seven years. EDCs have since become the conveyance of choice at former military bases.

With respect to military leases, Congress has authorized interim leases with terms of five years and longer. Termination-at-will clauses are no longer required. Congress has also turned to leasing to address the "Swiss cheese" problem, where federal agencies claim facilities within larger parcels. Using leaseback arrangements, DOD can now convey (through a deed or a lease in furtherance of conveyance) an installation to an LRA with the requirement that the LRA release a particular property to a federal agency at no cost. When and if the federal agency ceases to require the property, it reverts to the LRA without triggering a new screening process.

The attitude of the military services toward leasing has also changed dramatically. As evidence, the 1997 (and most recent) edition of the Defense Department's Base Reuse Implementation Manual summarizes the Department's philosophy and goal for leasing BRAC property as follows:

> Early leasing of property at a BRAC installation can spur rapid economic recovery and job creation and can reduce the Military Department's caretaker costs before the ultimate disposal of installation property. Therefore, leasing is one of the most important tools available to the Military Department and LRA for reaching common goals. (U.S. DOD 1997, 5-1)

To manage questions of responsibility for environmental contamination, DOD has fit leasing decisions into its normal environmental assessment process. One of the first steps in the environmental clearance process is the completion of an Environmental Baseline Survey that specifies current environmental

---

[7] The U.S. General Accounting Office (1998) noted that in early years the Defense Department anticipated receiving $4.7 billion in revenues from the sale of property from the four BRAC rounds.

conditions at the site. Based on this information, the service issues either a Finding of Suitability to Lease (FOSL) (or a Finding of Suitability to Transfer, in the case of a deed) for a particular parcel. FOSL specifies either that no hazardous substances are known to have been associated with the site, that cleanup of any known hazardous substances has been completed, or that the property contains some contamination but that it can be used safely with some restrictions.

To handle the variety of leasing situations, DOD has created three categories of model leases. Most recipients are LRAs. In those cases there are no lease payments. The benefit to the military service is that the lessee assumes responsibility for property management.

Interim leases are issued prior to a final decision about the conveyance of an installation. Uncertainties about the final conveyance decision do not concern whether the military service will convey the property to the LRA. Rather, they concern the details of the final reuse plan, for which the LRA is responsible. Interim leases allow LRAs to secure short-term tenants they may not want as long-term occupants. These leases have terms of up to five years and carry no commitment for the future use or conveyance of the property. However, they can be converted to long-term leases or conveyances if that is consistent with the final conveyance decision.

Leases in furtherance of conveyances are issued after the final conveyance decision and provide immediate possession of the property by the intended recipient of the deed. These leases can be long-term (55 years or more) and may be for all or part of the property conveyed to the recipient. (For instance, a recipient may choose not to take possession of a very contaminated parcel prior to cleanup.)

Master leases cover all or major portions of a facility and can be either interim leases or leases in furtherance of conveyances. Master leases include provisions for subleasing, freeing the lessee from getting clearances for each sublease from the military services.

Leasing prior to closure has also become an accepted practice. At a 1996 conference that brought together Air Force leaders and personnel with communities involved in base closures, the Air Force highlighted its execution of 17 interim leases prior to closure at Castle Air Force Base in Merced, California. DOD's Office of Economic Adjustment (OEA) shows similar preclosure activity. OEA tracks the performance of LRAs in the creation of new jobs, conveying land through deeds and lease transactions. Of seven due-to-be-closed bases that remained open in October 1999, LRAs at five sites had executed ten deeds and forty-one leases (U.S. DOD 2000).

Leasing has thrived because it has solved some immediate problems for the military services. With respect to the disposal of property, leasing has allowed the services to transfer operational control of facilities prior to the completion of cleanup and conveyance, and even prior to the final departure of all service operations on site. With respect to acquisition of property, leasing has allowed the services, for example, the Army, to obtain through leasing property needed for its training mission. A smooth conveyance process also has been essential to other federal agencies sponsoring public benefit conveyances. For example, leasing has allowed the FAA to transfer operational control of 20 military airfields, including the airfield at England Air Force Base, to communities around the country, allowing conversion to civilian use prior to the completion of the cleanup and conveyance processes.

SUBLEASING

Communities that receive former military bases often have few resources for the necessary redevelopment. Revenues from LRAs' tenants (or sublessees) have provided important revenues necessary for the operation and maintenance of base property and jobs to replace those lost when the military left. Even when an LRA plans major redevelopment necessitating the demolition of many existing buildings, it often leases them on a short-term basis until it completes planning and fundraising for more extensive work. According to OEA, as of October 1999 LRAs at 69 closed facilities had issued 147 deeds and 1,376 leases involving job-creating entities. These entities employed 57,429 people (U.S. DOD 2000). Tenant revenues can also finance capital improvements. The England Authority has been able to save net revenues to invest in capital. Other LRAs have elected to use future revenues to finance capital investment, floating revenue and tax increment bonds to raise the necessary capital.

CONCLUSION

The leasing experience at England Air Force Base reflects in several ways the international experiences in leasing public land. First, the public agencies involved turned to leasing as a way to transfer land control when impediments prevented an expeditious market sale. Second, leasing served as a developmental mechanism, allowing local organization to direct growth and to finance the infrastructure necessary to support it. Third, the lease revenues provided an important source of income for the local organization.

Internationally, leasing has allowed governments to manage uncertainty in land markets during periods of transition. This has been true, for example, in post-communist, Eastern European countries such as Poland and Ukraine, where private markets and the institutions necessary for their operation are poorly developed or where impediments to market operations exist. These countries have used leasing in the context of a transfer of land authority from central to local governments. In these cases leasing has enabled local governments to allow needed development and to avoid speculative land pricing while appropriate market institutions develop.

We might consider the transfer of federal land to local control associated with military base closures to occur during a similar period of transition. Frieden and Baxter (2000, 42) found that most former military land went through a process of normalization before it could be placed in the private market. Normalization involved "changing the status of a military base from a federal property unsuitable for private development in its present form and subject to uncertainties about future use and ownership to a property that can be integrated within the normal functioning of private real estate markets." During this transition period local governments and authorities often turned to leasing as a way to get the property into productive (and revenue producing) use until the normalization process was complete. The England case may have set precedents for leasing a former military base, but the federal government's subsequent creation of formal leasing arrangements reflects its recognition of the need for a transition period at most bases. The intent is that once the transition is complete, property can be transferred by fee ownership under normal private-market conditions.

Leasing is also a developmental (and redevelopmental) mechanism in many parts of the world, allowing communities to direct growth and finance the infrastructure necessary to support it. In the early days of Israel's existence, public land ownership and leasing served the national agenda of nation building and territorial stabilization. In Australia leasing facilitated the orderly development of urban Canberra from its rural origins. In Sweden leasing has allowed the City of Stockholm to stimulate the production of low-cost homes and apartments. Similarly, at England Air Force Base and other former bases around the U.S., leasing has allowed local authorities to direct the development and redevelopment for private use of former federal property. In Louisiana leasing allowed the England Authority to stage the growth of the airport, building an interim terminal in one location and a long-term terminal later in another location. The ability to move tenants around has also allowed the Authority to embark on the previously described major redevelopment project (hotel, conference facility and golf course). Such a project could not have been envisioned early in the base development process, when the market for such a project did not exist.

Finally, public entities around the world use leasing for financial reasons, to allow the public rather than private owners to benefit from land price appreciation and generate needed public revenues. Certainly, in Louisiana and at many former military bases around the country, lease revenues are important in financing the infrastructure necessary for the development of former military lands. In some cases, such revenues form part of the revenue stream necessary for bond financing. In addition, the England Authority has saved its excess revenues to invest in future improvements. The England Authority has also used leasing to create low-cost housing for retired people; the land lease allows the housing developer to price its housing based on a base land price plus the cost of building construction and maintenance, avoiding the effects of land-price inflation.

However, the England case bears closer and longer examination on the question of public revenues. The Authority, while government chartered, is not government, and its revenues by law can only be allocated for its own use. In the early years, when the Authority was struggling to finance expensive infrastructure, it needed all available resources. However, as the England Airpark prospers, it will generate ever-increasing revenues. Walsh (1978) argues that public authorities in general tend to maximize their own financial well-being and that this may not serve broad public goals.

There has been no systematic study of leasing at former military bases in the U.S. Yet, the evidence at England suggests that military leasing may provide fruitful models for other public leasing in the U.S. In addition, parallels to international leasing suggest opportunities for cross-country learning. At least two kinds of comparative studies come to mind. First, a study of the role of leasing during periods of market transition could help document ways different leasing arrangements can enable eventual private market transactions. Second, a study of leasing as a developmental mechanism could illuminate the role leasing can play in the implementation phases of land planning.

REFERENCES

Caslin, Susan and Raymond L. Daye. 1991. Mayor: It's worst nightmare. *Alexandria Daily Town Talk* (13 April):A-1; A-4.

Frieden, Bernard and Christie Baxter. 2000. From barracks to business: Report of the MIT Project on base redevelopment. Washington, DC: Economic Development Administration.

Jenkins, Richard. 2000. Air force base conversion agency report card. Fax to author. April.

U.S. Department of Defense (DOD). 1997. Base reuse implementation manual. Springfield, VA: U.S. Department of Commerce, National Technical Information Service. December.

U.S. Department of Defense, Office of Economic Adjustment. 1995. England Air Force base project narrative. Arlington, VA.

———. 2000. Base utilization status: Major base closures and realignments as of October 31, 1999. Arlington, VA. February.

U.S. General Accounting Office (GAO). 1998. Military bases: Status of prior base realignment and closure rounds. Report Number NSIAD-99-36. Washington, DC: Government Printing Office.

Walsh, Annmarie Huack. 1978. *The public's business: The politics and practices of government corporations.* Cambridge, MA: MIT Press.

POLITICAL ECONOMY OF PUBLIC LAND LEASING IN BEIJING, CHINA

10

F. Frederic Deng

This chapter investigates China's urban land reform, focusing on the adoption of public land leasing and in particular, the interrelations of land leasing, local public finance and local government behavior. Although China is not the only country where public land is leased to private land users, its ongoing economic reform makes its land leasing practice particularly interesting.

Compared to other economic reforms in China, land leasing started relatively late. Only in the late 1980s did China begin to experiment with public land leasing in addition to the traditional administrative allocation system. On September 9, 1987, the first lease was signed in Shenzhen, a booming city on the border with Hong Kong. That date was a landmark of China's urban land reform because at that time the Constitution of the People's Republic of China (PRC) explicitly forbade any land transactions, including leasing.[1] One year later the Constitution was amended to allow the possibility of land transaction. In 1990 China officially adopted land leasing as the basis for assigning land use rights to urban land users. Since then and especially after 1992, China's urban land reform has created a fast-growing real estate market that is now transforming its urban landscape.

Around the central issues related to the origin and functions of public leasehold in China, two questions are addressed here. First, what were the economic circumstances under which China adopted the land leasing system? Second, what are the special issues related to public land leasing under China's social and political environment, especially concerning local governments' behaviors as landowners? The second question relates to the economic role of political institutions. For example, most merits of public land leasing are based on the integration of landowner and other roles of the government. Are there any problems with local governments' multiple roles? How are local officials'

I thank Professor Peter Gordon for his guidance on my dissertation. The editors' helpful comments are gratefully acknowledged. This research is supported in part by a Lincoln Institute of Land Policy Dissertation Fellowship.

[1] This event shows the weak role of the law in China.

incentives aligned with the public interest? The answers to these questions are crucial to our understanding of public leasehold in China.

The history and common practice of public land leasing in China show that local government and the growth of the private sector are the two driving forces behind urban land reform. On one hand, severe problems with the administrative land allocation system indicate that the old system cannot be compatible with the growth of a market economy. The economy demands better delineation and protection of private property rights. On the other hand, under fiscal decentralization local governments are strongly motivated to maximize property-related revenues and to generate prosperity. As a result, public land leasing has become the basis for China's land allocation method. It may increase the efficiency of urban land use by creating an active real estate market.

In this chapter Beijing is used as an example to demonstrate that public land leasing has greatly vitalized local public finance that has traditionally relied heavily on local state-owned enterprises (SOEs). This success, as well as the successful implementation of urban land reform, indicates that a decentralized fiscal system is crucial for public land leasing in a large country like China. The emerging real estate market and its impacts on urban structure and housing clearly demonstrate the power of private markets. However, various problems in Beijing's land leasing system also point to the important role of political institutions in public land leasing. This case study indicates that the multiple roles of the local government, such as subsidizing local firms through administrative allocation, may cause role conflicts. One important finding from Beijing is that the political system is essential in aligning local officials' interests with the public wellbeing. There remains a tension between the growth of the private economy and the internal promotion system of the Chinese Communist Party (CCP). This helps explain why administrative allocation and private negotiation in leasing are so common in Chinese cities.

The following two sections provide a brief introduction to the history and common practice of China's urban land reform, respectively; they also provide some clues to the reasons for adopting public leasehold in China. Next, the urban land reform in Beijing will be analyzed. The last section summarizes the chapter and suggests future research topics.

CHINA'S URBAN LAND REFORM

As part of the economic reform in China that began in 1978, urban land reform is also a response to problems of traditional urban land use in socialist cities. The approach of the land reform is similar to reforms in other sectors, in that it is gradual, partial and dual track. As in other sectors, the successes and problems in urban land reform also stem largely from China's decentralized public financial system (Qian and Weingast 1996; Wang 1997).

Before the People's Republic of China was founded in 1949, private property was the foundation for land ownership. Property taxes were a major source of local public finance. This system was not immediately abolished until several years after the Communist Party came to power. In the mid-1950s all land transactions became illegal and a planned allocation system was established. Land as a private property or commodity disappeared for the next 30 years. Ironically, the nationalization of urban land was formally written into the 1982 Constitution after the economic reform had started and almost at the end of the traditional planned economy.[2] Item 10 of the 1982 Constitution states that all urban land belonged to the state, and farmland belonged to peasant collectives. It was emphasized that "any organization or individual cannot occupy, trade, lease or use other methods to transfer land." Under this planned system, land users (usually a work "unit" like a factory or school) had to apply to the government for land. Upon the approval of the application, land was then allocated to the land user, free and forever. This was the Three No system, which meant "no payment, no time limit and no transfer."

As the foundation of the planned economy, this administrative allocation system of urban land generated severe problems over time. First, although the state was and still is nominally the owner of land, the land user or unit has the real control over land. Since all units were part of the larger hierarchy of the state in a communist economy, it was never clear who represented the state. When land was allocated out, it was extremely difficult for the government to reallocate it to other units. In this sense, any theoretical argument for a planned system of land allocation lost its ground.

Second, land users' demand for land became unlimited because land was free. The more powerful unit within the administrative hierarchy was able to obtain more land without regard to its real economic need. It was common in China that many large, state-owned enterprises occupied a lot of land—which remained vacant for a long period—while many smaller units operated within very crowded space.

Third, the administrative allocation system also created a peculiar urban structure that reflected its inflexibility. Most Chinese cities had a high percentage of industrial land, about 25–30 percent (Deng, Li and Zhang 1994). It was also very difficult to renovate downtown or old areas (Lin 1998). Bertaud and Renaud (1994) noted that one consequence was a flat, or even rising, urban density function.

Fourth, the planned land use system affected local public finance and distorted government behavior. Due to the government's heavy subsidies on industrial production, there was no stable revenue source for urban construction before economic reform. Only in 1978 did the government begin collecting urban maintenance fees and allocating 5 percent of enterprise profits as a special fund for urban infrastructure construction and maintenance. The result was that, on one hand, urban infrastructure lagged far behind urban residents' basic needs, and on the other, local governments were motivated to invest in high value–added industries such as tobacco and petrochemical industries. Many city governments commonly operated their own small tobacco or petrochemical

---

[2] This also shows the new awareness of the importance of the law. Obviously, people did not foresee the coming urban land reform at that time.

firms, which was a misallocation of public resources. This in turn impeded the basic government function of providing public services, especially for the development of the market economy after economic reform.

As the private economy and foreign investment expand, increases in the demand for public infrastructure have prompted local governments to explore alternative methods of public finance. The need was especially urgent for newly developed cities. In 1982 Shenzhen—a special economic zone that had the discretion to experiment with all kinds of reforms—started to collect a land use fee ranging from 1 to 21 yuan (US$0.12–$2.53) per square meter annually.[3] Most cities gradually followed suit. In 1988 the State Council formalized and standardized this practice and began to levy a land use tax all over the country.[4] The tax rate was 0.2–10 yuan (US$0.02–$1.20) per square meter. Although this tax provided local governments a source of income from land, its magnitude was very limited. More important, it did not assist the development of a land market.

On September 9, 1987, the city government of Shenzhen leased a 5,322 square meter parcel of land to a local company. The price was 200 yuan (US$24.10) per square meter and the term was 50 years. This event could have been considered "illegal" according to the Constitution at that time, thus an amendment was deemed necessary. In 1988 the Constitution was amended so that "land use right can be transacted according to the law." The formal framework of public land leasing was established in 1990, as specified by State Council Decrees #55 and #56, Provisional Regulations on Urban Public Land Leasing and Transfer and Provisional Regulations on Foreign Investment in Large-Scale Land Development, respectively. Yet, due to political events in 1989, land leasing was largely limited to several coastal cities and almost came to a halt in the early 1990s. Only after an important 1992 speech by Deng Xiaoping did economic reforms in all sectors start to come back on track again.[5] Urban land leasing reached a peak around 1994, with the huge flow of foreign investment into real estate.

Since the beginning of the urban land reform, the old administrative allocation system and public land leasing have been coexisting. Although local authorities claim to use administrative allocation only to assign land to government agencies and nonprofit public organizations, many SOEs have also received land through this method. For foreign and private firms, land leasing may be the only option. In recent years the central government has tried to reduce the scope of administrative allocation, but the effectiveness of this policy remains unclear.

Another feature of the dual-track approach is that land leasing is applied to vacant urban land, newly acquired farmland and redeveloped urban land only.

---

[3] The official exchange rate is about 8.3 yuan for US$1.

[4] Before 1988 there was a lot of discussion and confusion about whether this should be called *fee* or *tax*. Although it is now formally called tax, people usually understand it as a kind of land rent due to government ownership of land.

[5] During his tour of South China in 1992, Deng Xiaoping made a speech that reversed the antireform trend emerging after the suppression of the 1989 student democracy movement.

Leasing is also applied to companies that issue stocks to the public. To some extent it is equivalent to the company redistributing previously allocated land rights to the public by allowing acquisition of equity in the firm. Land obtained by users before the reform, through the traditional administrative allocation system, will not be affected. The distinction helps local governments capture land value without disturbing existing land users. In practice, however, it is still very common that local officials may assign land to private users through administrative allocation.[6]

In the past two decades, local governments and the emerging private economy are the driving forces behind the Chinese urban land reform. According to an official document (State Council Decree #55), the goal of urban land reform is to "improve urban land use system, develop and manage land rationally, strengthen land management and promote urban construction and economic development." In other words, two major goals of public land leasing are to improve local public finance and to optimize urban land use through the reestablishment of private property rights. The first goal is obviously the motivation for local governments; the second is what private and foreign firms need.

The key to the successful introduction of public land leasing is fiscal decentralization in China. As pointed out by Oi (1992) and Montinola, Qian and Weingast (1997), the fiscal relations among different levels of government represent a style of fiscal federalism. Some Chinese scholars even worry about excess fiscal decentralization (Wang 1997). Before the 1994 tax reform, governments at various levels were subject to a bottom-up revenue-sharing system within which the formula of revenue sharing sometimes depends on the negotiation between the central and local governments. Local governments are allowed to maintain "off-budget" accounts, about which the central government has limited knowledge. Other factors—including widespread cash transactions and the possibility of private bank accounts under false names—also restrict the central government's ability to tap local revenues. Compared to centralized reforms in some other countries, China's decentralized fiscal structure encourages local governments to create prosperity and revenues (Zhuravskaya 1998). Because some local governments can avoid sharing lease revenues with the central government, fiscal decentralization might have created the opportunity for the wide adoption of public leasehold.

Driven by this fiscal structure, why do local governments not just sell land and collect property tax? Both in theory and reality, there are problems with land taxation. In 1991 several prominent U.S. economists wrote an open letter to then-USSR President Mikhail Gorbachev, urging him to retain public land ownership (Tideman et al. 1991).[7] The motivation of their proposal was derived from frustration with property taxation for local public finance, and other land use problems associated with private land ownership. The underdevelopment

---

[6] This is always a problem for this kind of dual-track approach. See Byrd (1987) and Murphy, Shleifer and Vishny (1992) for discussions on this topic.

[7] These economists include three Nobel Prize winners: Modigliani, Tobin and Solow. In their letter, the authors urged Gorbachev to retain public ownership of land and raise government revenue by charging market rent for the use of land.

of market institutions, the lack of respect for the law and widespread corruption in China may also make problematic the levy of any land taxes. Many Chinese still are not used to the concept of paying tax. Tax had disappeared from Chinese society for 30 years before the economic reform.

In 1990 there was a debate over public land leasing, triggered by a Japanese company leasing a large amount of land in Hailan Province. Many old cadres angrily denounced the experiment of land leasing as selling the national sovereignty. Although this event was largely ideological and did not hinder the urban land reform, it showed the strong legacy of socialist ideology. Given the fact that even leasing land could generate such strong emotions, the potential political resistance toward selling land is then obvious.

Unlike selling land, leasing has many attractive features. First, it is politically more feasible than selling land because it allows the government to retain the land title. A politically powerful but economically weak government must give up some control over property rights to allow the growth of a private sector in a planned economy. Second, land leasing fits into China's general track of economic reform, which is gradual and partial (Lin 1995; Naughton 1995). Third, China is in a period of rapid urbanization, and large-scale urban infrastructure construction is needed. Retaining public land ownership, at least in theory, may help to implement land use controls and urban construction projects. Fourth, the land leasing experience in Hong Kong may also have some influence on China's adoption of public leasehold (Yeh 1994). This may explain why land leasing first started in cities close to Hong Kong.

COMMON PRACTICE OF GROUND LEASE IN CHINA

According to the Land Law, the government owns all urban land in China. Yet, the law does not stipulate which level of the government is the owner. Private parties can lease urban land from the government, then sell or mortgage the land use rights. Unlike urban land, all farmland belongs to peasant collectives (formerly called communes) and cannot be transacted. Although in recent years there seem to have been experiments that allowed farmland to be alienated, farmland transaction is generally prohibited by law. The government controls the conversion of farmland into urban land; no one can acquire farmland. Local governments use their power of eminent domain to acquire land from farmers with limited compensation only. Then, urban land users have to lease the land from local authorities.

The maximum lease terms are 70 years for residential land, 50 years for industrial and 40 years for commercial. There are three ways to obtain a land lease: private negotiation, private tender and public auction. Private negotiation is the most common. It is a direct negotiation between the land user and the government over land price and land use conditions. In private tender, multiple land users bid for a parcel of land with an offer price and a land use plan. It can involve either open or closed bids, and the winner may not necessarily be the highest bidder. In contrast, the winner at a public auction must offer the highest price. There are usually restrictions on who can participate in the latter two methods of leasing. Participants must be real estate developers with licenses issued by the government.

Payment for leasing land usually consists of three major components: lump-sum premium, urban infrastructure fee and community infrastructure fee. The difference between the last two items is that the former is for infrastructure for the whole city, while the latter is only for the neighborhood. All three components must be paid up front to the government at the beginning of the lease. Nominally, each city has a standard guideline that stipulates land prices for different parts of the city. These standard land prices are supposed to serve as minimum leasing prices. However, since they are produced by questionable techniques and only updated every five years or longer, most cities also rely on some market-based land valuation methods to adjust leasing prices to account for changing market conditions. It is also true that most leasing prices depend on negotiations between local governments and developers.

After obtaining the land lease, the lessee must pay a land use tax every year. The tax rate varies according to location and is adjusted periodically. The land use tax is very small compared to the up-front premium. For example, in 1993 the land use tax in Beijing was only 0.5–7 yuan (US$0.06–$0.84) per square meter, while the standard leasing premium ranged from 15 to 5,400 yuan (US$1.81–$650.60) per square meter. The urban infrastructure fee ranged from 460 to 800 yuan (US$55.42–$96.39), and the community infrastructure fee from 150 to 400 yuan (US$18.07–$48.19), all in per square meter charge.

There are also many kinds of fees that vary across cities. For example, Beijing charges a land acquisition fee (75–150 yuan or US$9.04–$18.07 per square meter), building demolition and residents' relocation fee (5,900–7,800 yuan or US$710.84–$939.76 per square meter), and other fees. Among these major payments, only the land use tax is fixed. The others may deviate from the standard guideline.

Land use conditions—such as land use types, floor area ratio and building restrictions—are usually attached to the lease. These are usually planning requirements from the urban planning agency. However, writing the planning requirements into the lease contract does not mean lessees no longer have to care about other planning regulations. Urban planning in China is regarded as separate from land leasing. After obtaining the lease, the lessee still must apply for a planning permit before developing the land. In Land Administration Law almost nothing is mentioned about urban planning, and in Urban Planning Law there is little mention of land leasing. Urban planning is regarded as state power and superior to lease contracts. To this point, China's urban planning has not encountered problems such as compensation for regulatory taking, because respect for private property rights, contracts and even the law is far from established. Hence, it is not surprising that the government generally does not use lease contracts to implement urban planning. Urban planning agencies and land administration agencies are usually separate, and the power struggle between them is a serious problem both in the central and local governments.

The lease usually requires the lessee to complete a certain portion of land development within two years. Its original purpose is to prevent land speculation, but the extent to which this clause is enforced is questionable. Some local governments may charge a vacant land fee after the first two years, but many parcels still remain vacant after the time limit. This was most obvious after the real estate bubble burst in the late 1990s. From 1992 to 1994 there was a huge inflow of speculative capital into Beihai City, Guangxi Province. The city leased a lot of land to real estate investors. After the speculation bubble burst in the mid-1990s, many parcels remain undeveloped. Obviously the two-year limit does not work in practice.

A lessee can negotiate with the local government for a lease renewal when the lease expires. In the absence of a renewal, the land and improvements revert to the government. China's land leasing started only about 10 years ago, so the many potential contractual problems—such as lease renewal, lease modification, and regulatory takings and remedies—have not yet arisen. Further, there is no well-defined legislation that governs these operations; instead, whenever they emerge, the government deals with these leasing issues through negotiation. Obviously, the government does not like to bind itself to the rule of law, but the growth of the market economy will suffer from lack of explicit legislation (Weingast 1995). ·

There is sharing of land management between different levels of government. The county or district government can usually approve leasing a parcel of land less than 10 mu (one mu is about 667 square meters). The city government also has an upper limit in land leasing, which depends on the administrative level of the city. For example, Beijing's upper limit in land leasing is 1,000 mu for farmland and 2,000 mu for other land. Other cities' limits may be lower than Beijing's. Leasing a parcel of land over the size limit must be approved by the central government. According to this categorization, most urban land leasing is under the management of city government. Yet, lower levels of government may sometimes circumvent the size limit by subdividing land. Revenues from land leasing are also shared between different levels of government. Back in the early 1990s the central government tried to retain 30 percent of the lease revenues. Although a law was enacted, the central government found it difficult to enforce because local governments hid their lease revenues. As a result, an amendment was made to the Land Law in 1998, that the central government would no longer ask local governments to surrender a portion of their lease revenues. The central government will receive only 30 percent of the revenues generated from leasing the newly acquired farmland. In sum, city governments are in charge of land leasing and retaining the lion's share of the revenues.

PUBLIC LAND LEASING IN BEIJING

This section concentrates on the case of Beijing, to study the extent to which public leasehold has helped policy makers achieve their goals. Problems of the current public land leasing are also analyzed. After a brief introduction to Beijing's history, the focus turns to three groups of questions and how the case of Beijing may help us answer them.

Historical Background of Beijing

Located on the northern end of the North China Plain, Beijing became the national capital as early as the thirteenth century, largely due to its importance in controlling North China rather than its importance as regional economic center. In recent centuries Beijing was a capital city with little modern industry or prospering agriculture. The economic center of China had moved to the Yangtze River Delta even before the Ming Dynasty. In 1949 more than 80 percent of Beijing's industries were small handicraft workshops. Only several dozen had more than 100 employees.[8] After 1949 Beijing's investment focus was on industrial production. Before the economic reform, more than 70 percent of investment had gone to industrial production, of which about 55 percent went to heavy industry. Many large industrial companies, such as the Capital Steel Mill and Yanshan Petrochemical Co., were built in Beijing in this period. The city was quickly transformed from a consumer city to a large industrial city. In order to be the purest socialist city in China at that time, Beijing completely eliminated private and foreign firms.

After the economic reform began in 1978, Beijing also experienced significant changes to its social and economic structures. The ratio between production-oriented and consumer-oriented investments changed from 71:29 to 53:47. The investment share of the tertiary (service) sector rose from 46 percent in 1978 to more than 70 percent in 1998. The tertiary sector has now become the largest, compared to the secondary and primary sectors, employing over 52 percent of the labor force. Due to its past concentration of intellectuals under the socialist economy, Beijing's high-tech industry has been developing rapidly, and its Zhongguanchun area has become China's Silicon Valley.

Beijing's industrial development does not have a strong regional base, and its agriculture and township enterprises lag behind those of many coastal cities. Compared to the Pearl River and the Yangtze River deltas, the North China Plain does not have a strong regional economy that can provide any reasonable justification for Beijing's growth. The only reason is its status as the national capital and the associated benefits from China's highly centralized social and economic structures. That is why many Chinese say that Beijing has been built not by Beijing's citizens but by all Chinese people.

More accurately, the Chinese government built Beijing with resources from all over China. Urban infrastructure in Beijing is the best among all the Chinese cities. In spite of various measures to restrict migration, the city has been expanding in a strangely uniform monocentric way, thanks largely to old socialist planning principles. Despite strict controls on urban development, the city promoted a spatial pattern that emphasized several possible satellite cities

---

[8] All data in this section comes from Beijing Statistical Bureau (1999), except noted otherwise.

in the suburbs (Beijing Urban Planning and Design Institute 1993). However, the feasibility and effect of this dispersed development pattern has been debated because of Beijing's transportation condition. The new master plan, made in 1993, adhered to the principle of the old pattern but introduced more flexibility in urban development. Beijing imposes strict control on land supply while facing tremendous immigration pressure.

Although Beijing's built-up area urban increased from about 62.5 square kilometers in 1949 to 391 square kilometers in 1988 and 488 square kilometers in 1996, its inner-city area had remained largely intact. Most of Beijing's new construction was located outside the inner city, and large housing complexes rose in what was then suburbs. This phenomenon, which may be peculiar to socialist cities, was noted and studied by Bertaud and Renaud (1994). Housing in the inner city is largely in the traditional Si He Yuan style that does not use land very intensively. This construction pattern is neither compatible with Beijing's huge, socialist-style, monocentric city planning nor the new land use dynamics under market economy.[9] Urban renewal has been an important social and economic issue for Beijing, even though this city may have been the best in providing housing in China in the past. According to the latest 1990 survey there are still 202 old or dilapidated housing areas, with about 952,000 residents, 258,000 households and 10 million square meters of housing in Beijing, even after excluding the outlying suburbs (Lin 1998). With rising housing standards and the inevitable population growth in a fast urbanization process, pressure for urban renewal will not decrease in the near future.

Due to the presence of the central government in the city, Beijing also faces some unique problems. If any policy is inconsistent with the interests of central government agencies, implementation becomes politically difficult. The central government agencies had been allocated a large quantity of land in Beijing under the administrative allocation system in the past decades. Thus, it is quite difficult for the city government to implement any planning or land use policies without affecting the interests of central government agencies. This may be the reason for a special Capital Planning and Construction Committee inside the central government, responsible for all important decisions about Beijing's urban planning and land use. In 1995 the State Council stipulated that the approval of the National Planning Committee must be obtained for all high-end real estate projects with total construction areas of more than 100,000 square meters, a total investment of more than 200 million yuan or foreign investments of more than US$30 million (Lin 1998). In this sense, Beijing's city government should be more constrained by the local-central relationship and should not be as autonomous as other cities. Like other cities, however, Beijing is capable of playing games with the central government.

---

[9] Although the traditional inner city has long been cherished by some scholars and planners in Beijing, a close look at these areas shows they are used in a very intensive or crowded way, which is obviously not the original design of Si He Yuan. Even if these inner city areas need to be preserved, the size of the preservation area and the tradeoff between their historic value and economic development should be carefully studied.

Success of Urban Land Reform

Two goals of urban land reform are to expand sources of local public finance and to transform the Three No system. How successful is urban land reform in Beijing, in terms of not only achieving the two goals but also of promoting housing development and urban renewal?

The first case of ground lease in Beijing occurred in 1992 after Deng Xiaoping's speech during his trip to South China. On March 26, 1992 the city leased eight parcels of land in Shangdi Information Industry Base, a development zone in Haidian District. In the same year the city enacted several local laws to implement the ground lease system.

It is difficult to obtain accurate land leasing data from Chinese cities because they all have strong incentives to hide lease revenue from the public. Figure 1, showing Beijing's "commodity building" prices, clearly indicates the rise of real estate prices in the 1990s. The Beijing city government now has an estimated average income of about 3 billion yuan (US$361 million) from land leasing each year. The numbers for 1995 and 1996 are 3.7 and 3.2 billion yuan (US$445.8 and $385.5 million), respectively. This is a significant amount, given the city's total budgetary revenue of about 15 billion yuan (US$1.8 billion) in 1996 and 20 billion yuan (US$2.4 billion) in 1997.

The demand for land comes from real estate development. In the 1990s Beijing's real estate market grew rapidly (see Figure 2), especially in the 1995 boom that was characterized by large amounts of foreign investment in real estate. There were two peaks of land development around 1992 and 1995,

FIGURE 1

BEIJING: COMMODITY BUILDING SALES AND PRICE

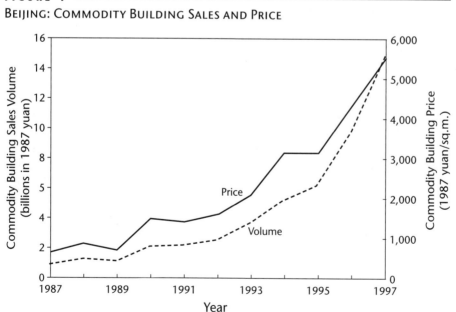

Source: Beijing Statistical Bureau (1999)

FIGURE 2 ───

BEIJING: REAL ESTATE INVESTMENT AND LAND DEVELOPMENT

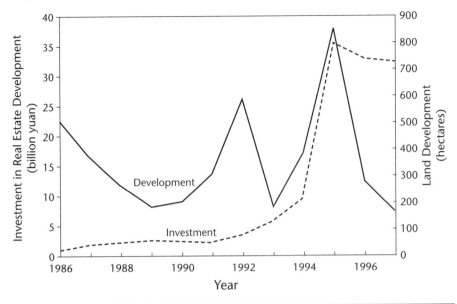

Source: Beijing Statistical Bureau (1999)

respectively. The first peak in 1992 was a response to Deng Xiaoping's speech and the widespread practice of setting up development zones on urban fringes. The second peak corresponds to the large flow of foreign money into China's real estate market (see Figure 3). At that time almost all Chinese cities experienced varying degrees of real estate boom.

Given the current social political system in China and the importance attached to the national capital, it is not surprising that urban land reform has had a strong impact on Beijing's urban development. In the absence of strong regional competitors, Beijing's land leasing has created an important real estate market for private investors. The revenue from land leasing becomes an important source for urban infrastructure construction. In recent years Beijing has finished many important public infrastructure projects, such as new freeways, gas plants and pipelines, and upgrading the Second, Third and Fourth Circle Roads to expressways. In addition to investment from the central government, the city government has financed many projects by lease revenues. For example, in 1998 local investment in fixed assets was about 20 billion yuan (US$2.4 billion) excluding foreign loans. Since infrastructure investment accounted for about 30 percent of investment in fixed assets,[10] local investment in urban infrastructure was roughly 6 billion yuan (US$722.9 million). Comparing this estimated investment figure with the 3 billion yuan (US$361.4 million) of lease revenues indicates that public land leasing played an important role in financing urban infrastructure construction in 1998.

─────────────────────────

[10] This is only a rough estimate because total investment in fixed assets includes those from the central government.

FIGURE 3

BEIJING: FOREIGN DIRECT INVESTMENT

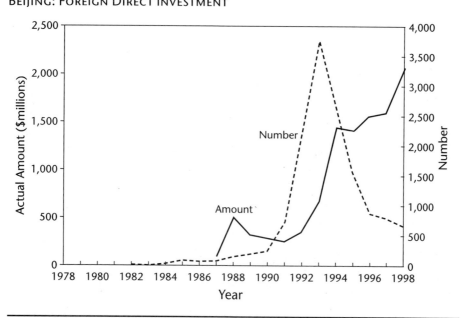

Source: Beijing Statistical Bureau (1999)

Housing is also greatly affected by urban land reform. Before economic reform, work units provided workers with housing as a kind of employment benefit. When work units were restructured, this housing benefit had to be reformed as well. But before the introduction of land leasing, housing reform was stagnant because it was still largely inside the planning system instead of the market system. After the start of public land leasing a real estate market emerged. Many foreign and domestic developers entered the residential housing market. Housing supply increased dramatically, and it became easier to sever the relationship between housing and work units. From 1980 to 1990 Beijing's new housing supply per year increased from about 3,969,000 square meters to about 5,730,000 square meters, about a 40 percent increase. But from 1990 to 1998 new housing supply almost doubled. The impact of public land leasing on housing reform was very prominent.

Urban land reform has also had an impact on urban renewal. Before the economic reform, Beijing had tried to reconstruct some old inner city areas, but these attempts largely failed (Lin and Li 1992; Lin 1998). Most urban reconstruction projects relied on limited rents from public housing and government investment. Many pilot studies were terminated because of the lack of funds (Yang 1989; Zhu 1990; Cai 1994). Although some experiments had been attempted in an effort to improve urban renewal, the lack of economic resources led them to failure (Wu 1993).

These problems were resolved after 1992. Land leasing had opened the door of real estate development to the private sector, which resulted in an urban renewal boom. From 1990 to 1996 the city government of Beijing reconstructed 114 areas of the inner city, moving 113,000 households and reconstructing a total area of 10.2 million square meters (Lin 1998). Attracted by high real estate prices and current low densities in the inner city, real estate developers showed strong interest in urban renewal.

Problems of Multiple Government Roles

Under the Chinese public leasehold system the government is simultaneously the landowner, provider of collective goods and owner and manager of SOEs. Is there a possible conflict of interest for a single entity to play these multiple roles? If so, what is the impact of this potential problem on the development of a land market?

In China the multiple roles of the government may pose problems unique to public land leasing. Unlike private firms that are always trying to maximize profit, there is no single objective that can synchronize the multiple roles of the government. Under the traditional planned economy, the identities of land user, landowner, firm owner and collective goods provider all disappeared behind the single cloak of an omnipresent government. In this sense, public land leasing actually is a step toward separating land user and landowner. It also makes clear the different identities of landowner and collective goods provider, even though these are part of the same government.

Another role probably unique to Chinese local governments is their place in the vertical political hierarchy. They are not as autonomous as their Western counterparts, let alone as private firms, and they must compete with each other under the constraints of the political hierarchy. Beijing is a typical example that demonstrates this delicate relationship with the central government.

At the start of urban land reform, Beijing was relatively more conservative than many coastal cities. The first ground lease in Beijing was issued in 1992, several years later than in Shenzhen and Guangzhou. This might be attributed in part to the impact of the 1989 student democratic movement, but the basic reason is the presence of the central government. Under the direct surveillance of the central government, the city has not dared to indulge in many of the experiments other cities have explored.

This close relationship with the central government poses a paradox to Beijing. On one hand, the strong role of the central government in China's socialist economy has greatly increased the attraction of the capital city to private or foreign investors. This factor is further strengthened by good urban infrastructure and accumulated human capital, as a result of the prolonged preferential policies to Beijing under the traditional planned economy. The fast growth of the high technology industry in Beijing is a good example. High demand for real estate is obviously based on the comparative advantages of Beijing as the national capital.

The presence of the central government, on the other hand, imposes more constraints on Beijing's urban land reform. Beijing usually follows the central government's policies very closely and few institutional innovations have started there. Complicated political relations produce complex underground deals in the land market. The city government appears unable or unwilling to create a more efficient and transparent market for land leasing, since many parties involved are more powerful than the city itself. The dilemma faced by Beijing can be improved only when China becomes more like a real market economy, which is not going to happen in the near future.

Although land leasing has been adopted, other aspects of urban land use still are largely the same as under the planned economy. The strict control on land supply is a typical example of the legacy from the past. High demand coupled with supply constraint on land has propelled Beijing's real estate prices to very high levels. Many people complain about poor housing conditions and environmental problems, but few question the rationality for strict control on land supply and the rigid planning concept of a monocentric spatial pattern. For instance, in the latest master plan of Beijing, the State Council (1993) asked Beijing to "prevent the inner city area from being connected to the outside towns." Transportation planning still emphasized the monocentric, radial style spatial pattern (Beijing Urban Planning and Design Institute 1993). Without the decrease of government intervention in the private sector, the pressure for Beijing's expansion will not subside. Without the change of planning concepts and land supply policy, problems associated with a highly concentrated, monocentric city cannot be reduced.

The relationship between planning and leasing raises another problem of the government's multiple roles. Again, the local government plays the roles of the landowner, collective good provider and owner of SOEs. Even if we do not consider government officials' personal interests, these three roles of government may create problems that undermine the efficiency of public land leasing. For example, leasing is regarded as a possible mechanism for implementing planning requirements. But when the planning bureau follows the legacy of socialism and the land leasing office allocates land though an emerging market mechanism, the two agencies act differently. For example, the planning bureau may prefer development in certain areas or directions according to urban planning, but the land leasing office wants to lease as much land as possible and tries to accommodate developer's location choice. The solution to this problem usually is determined by the more powerful agency, or by the local government that presides over both agencies. Local governments sometimes try to attract foreign investment by offering investors inexpensive land. The effectiveness of this policy remains doubtful because the location choice of most foreign firms does not depend on land only. Besides, land prices across China are already much cheaper than those in developed countries. In the case of Beijing, the use of land for this purpose is uncommon because being the national capital is already very attractive.

Another more probable role conflict is local governments' interests in SOEs or local firms, as well as other public organizations (like the army). Local governments tend to subsidize SOEs in the form of free or cheaper land, so that they can survive competition. But in the long run this is inefficient, given the objective of market-oriented reform. Local governments also like to allocate free land to local firms so that this asset can be kept in local hands. This way, the central government will have no knowledge of the actual amount of revenue generated locally. This is the main feature of China's fiscal federalism, but it may reduce the efficiency of land allocation.

Beijing's land supply system is a typical example. Land suppliers in Beijing vary according to location, although the final paperwork must be done at the Beijing Housing and Land Administration Bureau (BHLAB) (Meng, Mo and Zhang 1998). Land within the inner city is available from the Urban Renewal Offices (UROs) of the districts or counties, or from development companies owned by the UROs. Land must be obtained from the management commit- tees in 30 development zones set up by the city. Most suburban land in edge towns is already owned by five large local state-owned real estate companies. Developers or land users pay a high price for these companies to transfer land. Interestingly, the real estate companies pay nothing for land; they pay only the leasing price when they develop the land themselves or transfer the land to others. The relationship between BHLAB and those intermediaries is very complex. This land supply system shows the complexity of the so-called public ownership of land in China. The real question—who really represents the public—has never been solved. Theoretically, this relatively decentralized land supply system might increase competition between suppliers. But, given Beijing's land supply constraint imposed by its strict planning, the land market may largely be a seller's market with land brokers benefiting from their special relationship with the city. This may also be an indirect way for the city to retain leasing revenues under central government surveillance, but it masks the transparency and makes transactions dependent on personal relations.

Incentive Alignment: The Role of Political Institutions

An evaluation of public leasehold must deal with government behavior. Given the capitalization of collective goods into land rent, land leasing is usually regarded as being good at aligning the interests of collective good provider and landowner. But, with public land ownership and no democracy in China, can land leasing still be a device of incentive alignment? What is the relationship between public land leasing, fiscal decentralization and the promotion system inside the CCP?

Conventional theories about local public finance suggest that intergovern- mental competition can bring about efficiency. The Tiebout model regards jurisdictional competition as a device for sorting and matching between con- sumer preference and public service (Tiebout 1956). However, it takes for granted a democratic political system that can effectively align government official's interests with those of the citizens' (more exactly, the voters'). Profit maximization—which synchronizes the interests of landowner and collective goods provider—is also the basic assumption underlying the arguments for intercommunity competition in the ground lease–based land use system (Deng 2002). It is not clear in the existing literature how all these apply to a one- party political system. Qian and Weingast's (1997) theory on market-preserving federalism is partly derived from China's experience.[11] They focus on the role of intergovernmental competition as a disciplinary force to align the interests of government officials and citizens. But to what extent is this true? Prybyla's

TABLE 1

STATISTICS FOR ADMINISTRATIVE ALLOCATION OF LAND IN BEIJING (1992–1995), IN HECTARES

Year	Renewal	Commercial	Office	Residential	Industrial	Mixed Use	Others	Total
1992	151.5	5.4	11.5	22.6	12.0	6.3	10.0	219.5
1993	204.2	31.4	9.0	28.7	1.0	19.1	9.6	302.9
1994	365.1	19.5	6.8	11.1	0.0	2.8	9.6	414.8
1995	183.1	1.1	4.7	18.1	0.2	4.1	17.6	229.0
Total	903.8	57.4	32.0	80.5	13.3	32.3	46.9	1,166.2

Source: Qinghua University Real Estate Research Institute (1997)

TABLE 2

BEIJING LAND LEASING AND LAND USES (1992–1995), IN HECTARES

Land Use	Land Area	Planned Construction Area
Commercial	73.07	34.26
Commercial mixed w/ office, apartment, etc.	1,485.14	1,580.70
Residential	511.57	658.43
Industrial	616.61	585.33
Others	56.55	12.44
Total	2,742.94	2,871.16

Source: Qinghua University Real Estate Research Institute (1997)

(1994) critique of China's economic reform raises questions about the effectiveness of market-preserving federalism. In fact, as Qian and Stiglitz (1996) pointed out, the internal promotion system of the CCP plays an important role in local government behavior. This is definitely an important factor in any study on Chinese local governments.

Many problems with Beijing's public land leasing are related to China's relatively decentralized fiscal system and the one-party political structure. The first phenomenon is that, behind the spotlight of land leasing, a large amount of land has been allocated administratively (in other words, free of charge) to some special land users. Tables 1 and 2 list the statistics of administrative allocation and land leasing. We can see that the area of land assigned by administrative allocation is about half of that by leasing. Within land leasing, 54 percent is for commercial use, 19 percent for residential and 27 percent for industrial. Most administratively allocated land is for urban renewal. Although these figures initially show the tilted policies toward urban renewal, a second look reveals the problems. First, Urban Renewal Offices or districts obtain most land for urban renewal. They can then transfer land to state-owned real

---

[11] The theory of market-preserving federalism emphasizes the effect of federalism in aligning the incentives of political officials and citizen welfare. "Specifically, providing the central government less information and power in particular areas increases the credibility of commitment. This combines with the induced competition among local jurisdictions to provide local political officials with the incentives to pursue citizen interests" (Qian and Weingast 1997, 85).

estate companies. Real benefits obviously go to these intermediary government agencies. Second, as Bertaud and Renaud (1994) point out, there seems to be an inverse urban density function in Chinese cities. If this is true, there are large profit opportunities in urban renewal. Therefore, urban renewal should need little subsidy, even though it may incur higher costs than does the development of new land.

A direct problem brought about by administrative allocation is corruption. Although no statistics at the city level are available on this issue, widespread news reports confirm the severity of the problem. According to the local law, land uses eligible for administrative allocation are: facilities for government agencies, party organs and other nonprofit public institutions; urban infrastructure, public facilities and public welfare; important energy, transportation, defense and water irrigation projects approved by the state; and other land uses approved by the city government (BHLAB 1996). The last eligibility requirement has given local officials a lot of discretion in allocating land rights administratively. The biggest recent scandal concerning Beijing was a bribery case involving the former mayor and other officials in a large real estate project financed by a Hong Kong real estate tycoon. The vice mayor in charge of the city's finance committed suicide. The former mayor, once a member of the powerful politburo of the CCP, was sentenced to jail. By bribing local officials, many people can obtain land free through administrative allocation and then lease the land to actual land users.

Another practice in ground lease—namely, private negotiation—also facilitates corruption. Most land in Beijing was leased through private negotiation instead of through public auction or tender (few auctions or tenders were conducted in Beijing). One explanation is that the city's past attempts to auction land leases had failed to attract adequate investment. But, as admitted by some insiders, the reason investors were not interested in auction was that they could buy land at much lower prices through private negotiation. Although in recent years the Ministry of Urban Construction began to require all cities to hasten the adoption of auction and tender in land leasing, progress remains doubtful, given the status quo of the political institutions.

According to China's political system, the only link between officials' personal interests and citizen welfare is the internal promotion system of the CCP. In the past the internal personnel system strongly emphasized ideology. Although it now places more weight on economic performance, it is in essence still an ideological system. Its compatibility with market economy remains questionable. Widespread corruption in Chinese cities shows tension between the CCP's personnel system and the growth of a market economy. As the market economy expands, officials' interests become less motivated or constrained by the CCP's personnel system. Instead, they are more interested in exploiting opportunities available in the private sector. Therefore, the effect of public land leasing on incentive alignment depends critically on the reform of political institutions.

CONCLUSION

Public land leasing is the core of the urban land reform in China that began in the late 1980s. Generating local public fund and correcting problems associated with the old land use system are two driving forces behind the reform. To understand why China chose the particular form of land leasing that it did, other factors are also important. They include: a government that is politically powerful but economically weak; government roles in large-scale urban infrastructure construction; the socialist legacy; and the influence of the Hong Kong public leasehold system.

The case of Beijing shows the success of urban land reform and its impacts. In addition to generating local revenues and freeing land from the rigid planned system, public land leasing assists urban renewal and housing reform. Nevertheless, there are problems related to public land ownership. Because local governments are owners of SOEs, they have strong incentives (or face pressure) to subsidize these enterprises by granting land to them at no cost. Beijing's land allocation system is a clear example: five local real estate companies obtained large volumes of land from the city, through administrative allocation, then leased these holdings to actual users at lucrative prices. This conflict of interest can be traced back to the nature of Chinese political institutions.

The effects of public land leasing on local public finance and the land market depend critically on the behavior of local officials. In this sense political institutions are important in the evaluation of public leasehold. Many scholars argue that fiscal decentralization in China leads to an efficient intergovernmental competition (Qian and Weingast 1996). But it should not be taken for granted that competition has a strong enough effect that government officials always behave in the public interest or always try to maximize fiscal revenues. In a democratic society the link is the flow of votes; in China, the only link is the internal promotion and disciplinary system within the CCP. But both theoretical reasoning and empirical evidence indicate the tension between the development of the market economy and the CCP's internal promotion system. On one hand, this promotion system is necessary for any efficiency gains from intergovernmental competition, and on the other, the growth of the market economy eventually erodes this kind of ideological system. Corruption in China's public land leasing shows the severity of this problem. If local officials' interest is not aligned with public interest, many properties of public land leasing will be lost. In this sense, the interaction between economic and political systems is crucial to our understanding of public land leasing.

What can other countries learn from China's experience? The experience of public land leasing in China suggests that it may be an appropriate transitory land tenure arrangement for transitional economy. Strong intergovernmental competition could be an important factor that contributes to the efficiency of public land leasing. This point leads to a caution that China's success is built on a decentralized fiscal system.

China's experience also suggests potential problems associated with the multiple roles played by local governments in leasing and managing land. Some careful institutional design of local government may help officials mitigate these problems.[12] For example, it may be desirable to sever the relationship between government and enterprise.

Another lesson from leasing practices in China is that political institutions are important to the functioning of public leasehold. The traditional bureaucratic system within the CCP is obviously unable to fulfill this task, at least in the long run. Officials should take into account the costs of leasing public land. The Chinese government currently does not pay much attention to the potential contracting problems, such as complications involved in lease renewal and contract modification, but it must face these issues sooner or later.

There are some research topics that deserve our attention. First, the influence of public land leasing on intracity land uses, such as spatial structure, is important for future research. Second, there are many contract forms and related contracting costs in public land leasing. What are the costs and benefits of choosing a particular form of contract? Hong's (1998) analysis of the transaction costs in Hong Kong's public land leasing is a good source for research. More general study is needed, especially with regard to contract theory and the role of political institutions. Third, the government's decision on land supply and its impact on the real estate market should be studied. Usually, planning for land supply is needed in a public land leasing system. How should land supply be planned for in the context of intergovernmental competition? What are the tradeoffs involved in this kind of regulated land supply? Fourth, in the context of transitional economy, if public land leasing is regarded as a transitory form only, what should the next step be? Last, it will be interesting to study which institutional structure can mitigate the problems associated with the multiple roles of government in public land leasing.

---

[12] In Chapter 2, Max Neutze suggests setting up a quasi-independent body to manage public land leasing. This is a good example of the use of institutional arrangements to solve the problem of role conflicts.

REFERENCES

Beijing Housing and Land Administration Bureau (BHLAB). 1996. *Guide to ground lease and transfer in Beijing*. Beijing. In Chinese.

———. 1997. *Real estate industry statistics (1996)*. Beijing. In Chinese.

Beijing Statistical Bureau. 1999. *Beijing 50 years*. Beijing: China Statistics Press. In Chinese.

Beijing Urban Planning and Design Institute. 1993. Introduction to Beijing's master plan (1991–2010). *Beijing City Planning and Construction Review Supplement* 31:6–34. In Chinese.

Bertaud, Alain and Bertrand Renaud. 1994. *Cities without land markets: Lessons of the failed socialist experiment*. Washington, DC: World Bank.

Byrd, William A. 1987. The impact of the two-tier plan/market system in Chinese industry. *Journal of Comparative Economics* 11:295–308.

Cai, Jinshui. 1994. New perspectives are needed for urban renewal. Mimeo. In Chinese.

Deng, Feng, Biao Li and Zhiqiang Zhang. 1994. Urban land use and land price in Xiamen City after economic reform. *Urban Problems* 4:19–23. In Chinese.

Deng, F. Frederic. 2002. Ground lease-based land use system versus common interest development. *Land Economics* 78(2):190–206.

Hong, Yu-Hung. 1998. Transaction costs of allocating increased land value under public leasehold systems: Hong Kong. *Urban Studies* 35(9):1577–1195.

Li, David D. 1996. A theory of ambiguous property rights in transition economies: The case of the Chinese non-state sector. *Journal of Comparative Economics* 23:1–19.

Lin, Cyril Z. 1995. The assessment: Chinese economic reform in retrospect and prospect. *Oxford Review of Economic Policy* 11(4):1–24.

Lin, Jian. 1998. Urban renewal: A comparative study between Hong Kong and Beijing. Unpublished working paper. Beijing: Peking University. In Chinese.

Lin, Jian and Feng Li. 1992. Current problems and solutions for Beijing's inner city renewal. *Beijing Real Estate* 4:22–24. In Chinese.

Meng, Xiaoshu, Tianquan Mo and Jin Zhang. 1998. *Beijing real estate yearbook (1998–1999)*. Beijing: China Planning Press. In Chinese.

Montinola, Gabrialla, Yingyi Qian and Barry R. Weingast. 1997. Federalism Chinese style: The political basis for economic success in China. *World Politics* 11(4):83–92.

Murphy, Kevin, Andrei Shleifer and Robert W. Vishny. 1992. The transition to a market economy: Pitfalls of partial reform. *Quarterly Journal of Economics* 107:889–906.

Naughton, Barry. 1995. *Growing out of the plan: Chinese economic reform, 1978–1993*. New York: Cambridge University Press.

Oi, Jean. 1992. Fiscal reform and the economic foundations of local state corporatism in China. *World Politics* 45:99–126.

Prybyla, Jan S. 1994. The political economy of development in communist China: China and the market. In *The collapse of development planning*, Peter J. Boettke, ed., 61–89. New York: New York University Press.

Qian, Yingyi and Joseph Stiglitz. 1996. Institutional innovations and the role of local government in transition economies: The case of Guangdong Province of China. In *Reforming Asian socialism: The growth of market institutions*, John McMillan and Barry Naughton, eds., 175–220. Ann Arbor, MI: University of Michigan Press.

Qian, Yingyi and Barry R. Weingast. 1996. China's transition to markets: Market-preserving federalism, Chinese style. *Journal of Policy Reform* 1(2):149–86.

———. 1997. Federalism as a commitment to preserving market incentives. *Journal of Economic Perspectives* 11(4):83–92.

Qinghua University Real Estate Research Institute. 1997. Research report on planning and management of ground lease in Beijing. Manuscript. In Chinese.

State Council, PRC. 1993. The state council's reply to Beijing's master plan. *Beijing City Planning and Construction Review Supplement* 31:2–5. In Chinese.

Tideman, Nicolaus, et al. 1991. Open letter to Mikhail Gorbachev. In *Now the synthesis: Capitalism, socialism and the new social contract*, Richard Noyes, ed., 225–230. London: Center for Incentive Taxation.

Tiebout, Charles M. 1956. A pure theory of local expenditure. *Journal of Political Economy* 64:416–424.

Wang, Shaoguang. 1997. *The bottom line of decentralization*. Beijing: China Planning Press. In Chinese.

Weingast, Barry R. 1995. The economic role of political institutions: Market-preserving federalism and economic growth. *Journal of Law, Economics and Organization* 11:1–31.

Wu, Liangyong. 1993. *Beijing inner city and Ju'Er alley*. Beijing: China Architecture Press. In Chinese.

Yang, Jirui. 1994. *Institutional innovation in China urban land use.* Chengdu, PRC: Sichuan University Press. In Chinese.

Yang, Yanmin. 1989. Current situation and a historical review of Beijing urban renewal. In *A collection of studies on urban renewal*, Xing Li, Yanmin Yang and Yicheng Zhu, eds., 29–38. In Chinese.

Yeh, Anthony G.-O. 1994. Land leasing and urban planning: lessons from Hong Kong. *Regional Development Dialogue* 15(2):3–21.

Zhu, Yicheng. 1990. A brief introduction to the history of Beijing's urban renewal. In *A collection of studies on urban renewal*, Xing Li, Yanmin Yang and Yicheng Zhu, eds., 12–15. Beijing, PRC. In Chinese.

Zhuravskaya, Ekaterina V. 1998. Incentives to provide local public goods: Fiscal federalism, Russian style. Cambridge, MA: National Bureau of Economic Research. Working paper.

LONG-TERM PUBLIC LEASEHOLDS IN POLAND

IMPLICATIONS OF CONTRACTUAL INCENTIVES

David Dale-Johnson and W. Jan Brzeski

11

The long-term ground lease, or land leasehold, is a type of interest in real property that in one form or another is used in many countries around the world. In Poland almost all nonurbanized land is freehold and some portion of the urban land is public leasehold.[1] The form of long-term ground lease used in Poland, known as *perpetual usufruct*, is a variation somewhat unique and peculiar to Poland. Land is leased for a period of between 40 and 99 years, and the lessee owns the improvements built on the leased land. Consequently, existing improvements (if any) must be purchased by the lessee upon the granting of the lease. In Poland today, this form of leasehold can be created by the state or a local government only, typically a municipality. Similar contracts within the private sector have been proposed and debated, but are not legally possible at this time. Another type of partial land interest is private or public land leasehold, but this is for shorter periods of up to 20 years, and lessees may not have an ownership interest in the improvements. Also, the interest itself is not a real property right registered on the title record of property, as is the case with perpetual usufruct.

During the transition of the 1990s in Poland, perpetual usufruct has been debated in both political and legislative realms. Some have argued for their elimination—as "relics of the socialist system" that have no place in a modern market economy—apparently in ignorance of the Hong Kong experience.[2] Others have wanted to preserve these types of leases because they are "in the

---

[1] The proportions vary substantially; in the City of Krakow (the third largest city in Poland) the breakdown is as follows: public freehold (21 percent), public leasehold (15 percent), public enterprises (13 percent), private freehold (46 percent) and other (5 percent). The capital city of Warsaw and cities in western and northeastern Poland have much higher proportions of leaseholds, since most of the land was nationalized after the Second World War.

[2] In Hong Kong, "through its ownership of Crown land and the sale of land leases, the government plays a very active role in urban planning, infrastructure provision and social housing," and yet "the real estate economy of Hong Kong is one of the most dynamic and sophisticated in the world" (see Renaud, Pretorius and Pasadilla 1997).

public interest." There have been no attempts to provide economic justification for the long-term ground lease or to determine if it makes sense to consider alternative structures of this instrument in the interest of economic development. It seems appropriate that the economic rationale for such contracts be examined before this type of property right is eliminated as a result of uninformed debate.

Some attempts have already been made to reduce the use of perpetual usufruct in the private sector by individual residential lessees. In the late 1990s the Parliament, under pressure from individual lessees, adopted a law allowing the lessees to buy out "their" land for low compensation, provided the land had been developed in compliance with zoning regulations. As a result, local governments lost valuable residential land assets that were producing a sizable portion of their autonomous revenues, that could not be subsequently replaced by the area-based property taxation system.[3] Given the state of the nascent zoning regulatory structure, local governments simultaneously lost an effective planning instrument. Nonindividual (institutional or corporate) owners of residential land did not benefit from this legislation. In 2000 this leasehold conversion law was declared unconstitutional because it infringed on local government land ownership rights by providing them with unjustifiably low compensation. A lengthy political process to reconcile the situation ensued.

Nevertheless, municipalities have retained the right to grant new leaseholds, which cannot subsequently be bought out by the lessees. The Ministry of Housing and Urban Development began to emphasize the role of land leaseholds in land use policy, urban development and development financing. In 1998 the government of Poland adopted a broad-ranging Medium Term Strategy for the Sectors of Town and Country Planning, Real Estate Market and Housing Construction. The document, developed by the State Office of Housing and Urban Development, states that there is a frequent *misconception* about perpetual usufruct in the policy debate in Poland, where it is claimed that the institution of long-term land leasehold is not practiced in democratic market-based countries (Section II 1.11). The document notes that land leasehold is known and practiced in various European and American countries, and that

---

[3] Potential current revenue from all public leaseholds (if they were bought out) would be as follows. Of 1,245,000 leaseholds, 797,000 are residential and 199,000 are nonresidential. About 20 percent of leaseholds were already prepaid, so no running ground rents apply. Government estimates of annual ground rent for residential leaseholds (1 percent of land value) is US$150; for nonresidential leaseholds (3 percent of land value) is US$450. Thus, for residential leaseholds the public sector owner (state and municipalities) receives US$119 million per annum, and for nonresidential leaseholds US$90 million for the total annual revenue of US$209 million. These ground rents are deemed to lag changes in market values by about 10 percent, so the government estimates that after adjustment the total revenue figure should stand at US$230 million. To this figure could be added newly granted leaseholds, which charge an upfront amount of 15–25 percent of land value, but these statistics are not available. Revenues from this source are not large. The annual revenues of US$230 million from ground rents should be compared to other local government revenue sources (excluding central government transfers) of US$1,780 million. Full compensation for conversion to freehold would bring a lump sum of US$2,090 million (US$1,195 million for residential and US$895 million for nonresidential).

it is a convenient instrument for investors lacking equity for land acquisition. It is further stated that long-term land leaseholds are granted in Poland on public land only, but this right should be extended to cover all or some cases of privately owned land. This should provide private landowners with more alternatives for disposal of their land. Further, the extension of this right to private property should lead to increased availability of building lots, secure regular income for landowners and additional transactions in the real estate market. Such a change would require amendments to the Civil Code and the Land Management Act, but no further action has been undertaken on this issue since 1998. There has, however, been a renewed government impetus to improve rather than eliminate long-term land leaseholds.

This chapter seeks to provide a perspective on the debate regarding long-term public leaseholds in transitional economies. We focus on contractual and economic aspects of land leasing, as well as on improving land leasehold instruments in terms of their effect on redevelopment timing and intensity. These issues are critical for the land use component of urban redevelopment strategies that are part of broader economic transition strategies. While we provide a broad perspective on public leasehold in Poland, we choose to focus much of our analysis on the differences between some of the contractual elements of public leasehold in Poland and a generic public leasehold contract employed in North America. The specific contractual elements we focus on are the right to renew or extend leaseholds and the ownership of the improvements to the land. With the right to renew or extend, and with ownership of improvements, a public leasehold interest begins to emulate a freehold interest in terms of some of the critical property rights. The reason we choose to focus on these contractual provisions is that they have a significant impact on the incentives to redevelop the property when economic growth provides the impetus for land use change.

Here, we provide a brief summary of this chapter:

1. A historical evolution of perpetual usufruct in Poland;

2. The legal and contractual elements of perpetual usufruct;

3. An alternative structure;

4. Long-term land leaseholds in transitional economies, and incentive problems in the redevelopment decision;

5. Relevant theoretical literature;

6. Long-term leaseholds, redevelopment and our approach to evaluate alternative contracts (the model developed in this section is presented in the appendix);

7. Analysis and results; and

8. Conclusions and implications for urban form.

THE HISTORY OF PERPETUAL USUFRUCT IN POLAND

Although perpetual usufruct was introduced in Poland in 1952, similar forms of long-term use rights can be traced to the Roman legal system, which provides the basis for much of Poland's legal tradition. The Roman legal system had developed two institutions similar in character to perpetual usufruct: perpetual right to use agricultural land *(emfiteuze)* and perpetual right to a building lot *(superficies)*. The perpetual user had the rights to profit from, sell, encumber and bequeath the land. This involved full ownership by the user of any improvements. Later, after the fall of the Roman Empire, a divided ownership right was developed permitting two owners a separate claim: a direct land ownership right *(dominum directum)* and the right to use of the land *(dominum utile)*.

By the end of the eighteenth century various derivatives of these rights evolved in Europe. Poland, partitioned among three foreign powers (Russia, Prussia and Austria), developed different institutions, depending on the region and the occupying power. In the former Kingdom of Poland, which was part of the Russian occupied territories, a tradition of "perpetual leases" developed for both rural and urban land, with the land lessee (user) retaining significant control relative to the lessor (landowner). In the Austrian occupied territories an institution of divided ownership was used but was replaced in 1912 by building right *(baurecht)*. The baurecht was developed in response to the need to build affordable housing for those who could not afford to buy the land. The baurecht was patterned on the German *erbbaurecht*, which treated a building right as a sort of easement. The institution of erbbaurecht inspired several countries, including Russia and Switzerland. In the rest of the Russian occupied territories, which were integrated with Russia, an institution of building right *(zastroika)* was used.

Upon regaining independence during the world wars, Poland leaned heavily on the tradition of Erbbaurecht and the Austrian baurecht, but treated the building right not as a claim or easement but as a full ownership right to the building, distinct from ownership of the land, and registered as a distinct property right.

Immediately after the Second World War, in 1945, a decree was issued "municipalizing" land in the capital city of Warsaw (which was virtually destroyed during the war) and choosing the perpetual lease over the building right as the dominant solution.[4] The perpetual lease remained controversial and in 1947 a concept of *temporary ownership* was introduced. This concept had its roots in the old Roman notion of divided ownership. Temporary ownership assumed that the temporary owner is a full owner and the reversionary owner held a right in the form of a claim against the temporary condition. Temporary ownership, while operational and focused on facilitating housing

---

[4] The building right, even though quite popular in many European countries, was deemed by contemporary decision makers to be too rigid and focused on building up the land rather than taking a broader land management perspective.

supply, did not survive criticism from the left that it was a form of reprivatization of nationalized land.

Consequently, the decree, issued in 1952, introduced a perpetual right to residential building lots, but without abrogating temporary ownership. During the next few years the housing crisis was not alleviated, so, in 1957 the 1952 decree was abrogated and the temporary ownership concept revived through a law on sale by the state of residential buildings and lots. In the meantime, work was proceeding with development of a new Civil Code, which sought a new, more permanent solution. The process was concluded in 1961 with a new Law of Land Management in Cities and Communities, which introduced the institution of perpetual usufruct and abrogated other rights regarding public land. The sources of law on perpetual usufruct were split between the new law and the Civil Code. This duality of sources created problems that were worsened by placing the institution of perpetual usufruct between freehold ownership and lesser interests in land. On one hand it is a limited material claim right, but on the other it is deemed as a separate category between freehold and lesser interests in real property in the Civil Code. The right is fully alienable and inheritable and confers ownership of a building. It is recorded on the title of the property and can be mortgaged.

Upon the inception of the transition process in 1990, perpetual usufruct was confirmed as one of the basic property rights. In fact, the law restituting local governments in Poland provided that they take over most of the state land used for residential and municipal purposes, and the various legal entities using this land were granted perpetual usufruct to that land, subject to municipal land ownership. The state land that was not transferred to municipal ownership, and was used by state enterprises, institutes and cooperatives, was granted to these users in the form of perpetual usufruct, subject to restitution claims. This way, much of the most valuable urban land—the portion covered by land use plans—became vested with perpetual usufruct.[5] During the late 1990s Parliament introduced a law allowing individuals to buy out their leaseholds by paying a formula-driven amount. The formula was appealed by cities and changed to one more favorable to local government interests. The main reason for introducing this option was to let the people in Western Poland, which was regained from Germany after the Second World War, possess freehold interests in land and thereby be in a stronger position against possible claims from the prewar owners from Germany.

Legal scholars continue to debate whether perpetual usufruct should be replaced by something less connected to the communist period in Poland. Some claim that the country should revert back to temporary ownership, which would confer stronger rights on the lessee. The perception is that temporary ownership is very close to freehold, with the state owning only a residual claim (apparently not likely to be exercised), while perpetual usufruct divides the

---

[5] The share of urbanized public land held in the form of perpetual usufruct is just under 30 percent. Just under 20 percent of the total land supply in Poland is urbanized.

ownership right, with the state retaining ownership of the land. The real issue is practical, having to do with policies regarding lease extension in each scenario. The debate, however, is usually thin on economic and financial arguments and driven by historical perceptions.

The Structure of Perpetual Usufruct in Poland: Residual Claim Shared by Lessor and Lessee

We begin by describing the contractual terms of perpetual usufruct as defined by law in Poland.[6] In the case of improved land, the granting of a perpetual land leasehold must be linked with the sale of improvements to the leaseholder (lessee). It follows that no one but the leaseholder can be the owner of improvements. If the lessee wants to sell the improvements, the lessee also must sell the perpetual usufruct rights. In case of the sale of land (by the state or a municipality) for the development of condominium apartments, what is subsequently sold is the condominium unit, with a concurrent granting of a land leasehold right to a fraction of the land parcel under the condominium building.[7]

The granting of the leasehold takes place in one step through a civil law contract executed by a notary public. Perpetual usufruct right must be registered at the land title registry in order to be enforceable.

The granting of a perpetual leasehold interest requires that the state agency or local government impose competitive tender procedures requiring a 21-day public notice. There is open public bidding with strict rules described in the law on real estate. The government can constrain the land use and thereby pre-select bidders. Anyone without a criminal record can bid after lodging a security deposit (which can be quite high). The public tendering procedures may be waived in cases where:

» persons have statutory priority to obtain leasehold of particular land;[8]

» there is a transfer between two government agencies;

---

[6] The two main sources of law are the Civil Code and the Real Estate Act. The theoretical notion of the leasehold is embodied in the Civil Code, which codifies this property right, allowing it to be registered in the land title registry in the same way as the freehold right. Consequently, it is an alienable, transferable, inheritable and mortgageable right, and thus even subject to possible subordination. This right can be established on state and municipal land only. The Real Estate Act regulates how this right is to be exercised by the state and local governments.

[7] When a newly completed project on leased land is sold, the developer includes provisions that the new owners will agree to respect a majority vote with respect to a later sale. In respect to old buildings on leased land (usually, apartments sold by a municipality or cooperative), little can be done since no restrictions can be imposed on individual owners. Thus, there are cases where some owners hold out, but lawsuits can be lodged against them on the grounds of "obstructing communal life." Such lawsuits are not often successful. Properties with multiple leaseholders can be difficult to redevelop because individual leaseholders can hold up redevelopment. Due to high negotiation costs, developers have little incentive to initiate redevelopment projects. This problem, however, also exists for developers when condominium owners have a freehold interest. One subtle difference is that the developer in a leasehold environment is likely a master lessee who, in turn, leases to the individual lessees.

[8] These usually are former owners who are unable to achieve restitution in kind (Poland has not adopted a universal law of reprivatization and restitution).

» the lessee is engaged in charitable, custodial, cultural, healthcare, educational, scientific, or sports and recreational activities;

» there is an exchange or gift;[9]

» the subject property improves the use of the adjacent property;

» the land is an in-kind contribution to the formation of a company or foundation;[10]

» the lessee is acquiring the land after having developed it; and

» the land is to be used for housing purposes (buildings or infrastructure) by nonprofit organizations pursuing the goals of housing provision.

The highest bid for the land is then used as a basis for establishing the initial payment ranging from 15 percent to 25 percent of the land price, which may be paid in installments. In addition, beginning the year after the granting of the lease, the new lessee pays an annual ground rent that is a fixed percentage (usually between 1 and 3 percent) of the land price or value. Later we will discuss subsequent adjustments triggered by revaluations.

The ground rent percentage rate depends on the land use stipulated in the lease. For land uses connected with national defense, state security, fire protection, religious uses, charities and cultural, medical, educational, scientific and research and development activities, the rate is not less than 0.3 percent of the land price. For residential land uses, technical infrastructure and sports and recreation, the rate is not less than 1 percent. Finally, for other land use purposes (mostly business) the rate is not less than 3 percent. In case of an approved land use change, the percentage rate and the value change accordingly. There are further possibilities for granting special discounts as motivated by, for example, income (affordability) or heritage building criteria.

The ground rent percentage rate does not change over the term of the leasehold (40–99 years). In the first year the lessee (tenant) pays ground rent based on the land value at the start of the lease. Later, the value of the land can be adjusted by the landowner if warranted by market value changes or inflation. These changes can take place as frequently as every year, although practice shows that municipalities have not used this right annually, due to the high cost of reappraisal and manpower shortages. The changes may be requested by the lessee or made by the landowner. In both cases, an official

---

[9] Some people were paying toward their future apartments during the communist period, and had not received these apartments when the economic system changed. The government devised a scheme in which municipalities can grant land in lieu of the once-promised apartment, but only when the claimant relinquishes the claim to a future apartment from the state. In other cases, municipalities can grant land to some special public and semipublic initiatives as in the case of charitable foundations or nonprofit rental housing projects.

[10] Local governments are free to form public-private partnerships that are then subject to other regulations. City councils must approve or select the private partner. Once the partner is chosen the land cannot be subject to competitive bidding, but is to be valued by independent appraisal. Obviously, this creates some possibilities for corruption, although city councils are very careful since they act under public scrutiny.

appraisal by a state-licensed appraiser is required. The lessee may appeal the new ground rent through a tribunal, and ultimately in court. So far, few appeals have taken place.

The leasehold agreement specifies what kind of land use is permitted. If the goal is to develop the land with permanent improvements, the agreement has to specify:

» the date of commencement and completion of building activity;

» the type of buildings and other improvements;

» the duty to keep them in proper condition;

» terms and conditions for rebuilding in case of damage to and demolition of buildings and improvements; and

» compensation (based on an appraisal) to the lessee for buildings and improvements upon termination or expiration of the leasehold.

The agreement stipulates the type of land use the tenant is to implement. If the land use implies new construction, the agreement must specify the date of commencement and completion of the building activity. These terms may be extended if events beyond the lessee's control take place. Upon violation of stipulated dates, the landowner may impose an additional penalty equivalent to 10 percent of the initial land price (upon granting the leasehold) for each calendar year of delay. In practice, the ability to impose a penalty successfully is case-specific.

These contractual provisions are revealed in title registration records, which means that these covenants are binding not only on the initial lessee, but they run with the land, thus obligating every successive lessee.

The initial leasehold term of 40–99 years can be extended for another term of 40–99 years. A valid public purpose is the only reason the state or municipality may not grant an extension. The Civil Code is silent on the issue of further extensions. Termination of the perpetual usufruct right may be sought by the state or municipality prior to the contractual termination date through a judicial procedure if there is a violation of contractual provisions. Upon termination of the leasehold, either due to expiration or as a result of legal action, the landowner must compensate the lessee for the value of land improvements, as of the termination date. Early termination of the leasehold rights may take place if the lessee does not comply with stipulated land use or does not complete the stipulated land improvements in time. In this case, the landowner returns the initial payment and the amount of ground rents prepaid for the period beyond the date of termination. The prepaid ground rents are to accrue interest but the total amount of money returned to the lessee cannot exceed the value of the leasehold rights at the date of termination.

In 1998 a new law was passed, allowing individuals who are leaseholders to request conversion of their leasehold rights into freehold rights prior to the end of the year 2000. Conversion requires payments by the lessee. If the lease has been in place less than five years, the first payment must be made within

14 days followed by the equivalent of 15 annual payments. If the lease has been in place more than five years and less than 20, there is an equivalent of 10 annual payments. For leases in place more than 20 years, there is an equivalent of five annual payments. The payment structures were consistent with the differential pricing attached to properties that had been leased for a longer time period. There are various exceptions to these payment arrangements. Although the contemporary perpetual usufruct rights were created for sitting tenants in 1990 the first property rights construed as perpetual leaseholds were granted as early as 1961, thus explaining the existence of leases that have been in place longer than 10 years. This law has recently been challenged in the Constitutional Court as alienating the rights of the state and local governments.

AN ALTERNATIVE STRUCTURE: FULL OWNERSHIP OF THE RESIDUAL CLAIM VESTED WITH LANDLORD

In the following section we describe a generic lease based on the typical North American long-term ground lease. Particularly in the U.S., both public and private leasehold arrangements are often similar and many public and private long-term land leases have the following structure. Land is leased by the landowner to a tenant, usually for a period of at least 50 years. That 50-year term is often comprised of an initial 10- or 20-year term with options for two or three 10-year renewals. The lease, including options to renew, may be as long as 99 years. Longer leases (more than 99 years including renewals) are viewed as sales from a tax perspective in the U.S. and are seldom used.[11]

The length of the lease allows sufficient time for return of capital invested and amortization of debt in the case that leasehold improvements are financed with debt. Lenders are reluctant to finance improvements on ground-leased property unless the term of the lease, including extension options, exceeds the amortization period associated with the debt.

The landowner typically will agree on (and may even dictate) the nature of development before finalizing the lease, and in many cases will seek proposals from competing developers. In the end, the landowner is usually a silent partner, but at the time the development program is decided the landowner will be heavily involved, as it is here that the parameters that determine the revenue stream from the lease are set. Usually the ground lease will assess penalties if the development does not occur as planned or when planned. Often, there will be a date at which the lease can be terminated if the ground tenant or developer has not performed. The typical forms of rent include:

» Holding rent: usually a fixed dollar amount, paid until commencement or completion of construction;

» Base rent: a fixed dollar amount adjustable at specified intervals (usually every 5 or 10 years) using an agreed upon approach or formula;

---

[11] Sale treatment normally would cause the lessor to pay capital gains tax on the imputed sales price, even though the lessor retained the fee interest, thus incurring an unnecessary tax obligation.

» Percentage rent: determined as a fraction of the rents received from and/or gross sales by the occupying tenants payable annually in the amount, if any, by which percentage rent exceeds the minimum rent.

The key attribute of the participation in the performance of the property is that the effective ground rent fluctuates with the revenues generated by the property or the sales of occupants of the property. This is a way for the lessor to ensure the rental stream matches the performance of the property. If the base rent adjusts only every 10 years, a participation clause allows rents to increase periodically, provided the gross income from the property or sales of tenants in the property are increasing.

In North America this type of lease commonly has been used by public agencies including ports, airports and local governments (especially redevelopment agencies). Although they entail some risks, such contracts provide a steady stream of revenues for public agencies. Also, the lease permits a degree of long-term control during operations. This may allow a public agency to recoup subsidies, including the write-down of land, over time, without unduly burdening the project during the development and startup periods, when cash flow may be critical to the project. It also permits an agency to exert closer control over the development. If a public purpose for the land is envisioned, retaining public control through ground lease rather than sale seems justified. Thus, ground leases are viewed as an effective tool in public-private partnerships (see Frieden and Sagalyn 1989).[12]

Similar leases are used by private landowners who want long-term revenue from land but lack the interest or expertise to develop and manage the improvements to the land.[13] These and other owners may use the ground lease to defer paying a capital gains tax on land with a low depreciable basis. Non-developer-owners may choose ground leasing relative to selling because that approach allows them to generate an ongoing income stream without personal responsibility for development, while deferring the tax on any capital gain far into the future. A tax-free exchange would accomplish the tax deferral goal, but would leave development of the new site in the hands of the taxpayer and, if income is the goal, the new parcel still must be developed. So, for investors in developable parcels, tax deferral seems to provide a rationale for the existence of long-term ground leases. On the other side of the transaction, ground leases provide an alternative to financing the land component of a development transaction, so, for some developers a ground lease may present, at some price, a preferable mechanism for financing a development. In general, it is more

---

[12] The difficulty of effective contracting is an ongoing debate. Some observers argue that the difficulties of contracting are so profound that joint ventures between landowners and developers are preferred, where feasible.

[13] Many heirs to the families granted lands by the king of Spain during the late 1700s or early 1800s in what is now California, currently receive ground lease revenue from urban land developed in the twentieth century.

difficult to justify long-term ground leases as a tool for private investors, as tax-deferral seems to be the only argument.

The holding rent is designed to facilitate development and reduce out-of-pocket costs of the ground lessee during the predevelopment, development and construction periods. The base rent is the least risky ongoing revenue source for the ground lessor. This component of the rental stream should yield the equivalent of a relatively low-risk return for the term of the lease. The actual payment often is computed on a notional amount equivalent to the land value in highest and best use (presumably the existing use) at the time the lease begins. Since the market value is unobservable, an appraisal is required periodically to determine the expected market value. In practice, such appraisals to determine lease rates are costly and used at long intervals only. Thus, the base rent may adjust periodically (usually every five or ten years) when triggered by a change in the value of the land. Such changes in value are normally determined by an appraisal, although some creative draftsmen have tried to finesse the need for valuation to trigger changes in the base rent.[14] Other indexing mechanisms or participation clauses may serve to index the lease revenue to the inflation rate or property performance.[15] However, there is no reason to expect changes in such revenue streams to be proportional to changes in highest and best use land values.[16]

Landlords cannot unreasonably withhold transfer of the ground lease by the developer to successors. However, the contract may permit the landlord to renegotiate the terms of the lease. At a minimum the landlord will require that the transferee have an acceptable credit rating. These contingencies may be part of a contract with either a public or private lessor.

If the highest and best use changes, many North American leases (where lessors are either public or private) are silent about what should happen. It may be presumed that the lease will be renegotiated, but without a clause addressing this issue in a lease there is no mechanism to bring about renegotiation, let alone optimal redevelopment. The ground lease represents an unusual allocation of property rights. Hart (1995) develops a simple property rights model that

---

[14] The interest rate (yield) should be determined by adding a spread to an equivalent maturity risk-free rate. The value of the land is the notional amount against which the rate is applied to determine the actual lease payment. That value should be a value of the land in highest and best use, not the existing use. Some leases, particularly those having participation rents, have used the average of the last few years' gross ground rental income to determine the new base rent. This process, of course, may bear no relationship to the ground rent that might be determined through a valuation process. However, it has the advantage of being easy and cost effective to implement.

[15] Using such an index mechanism for commercial real estate is straightforward because the asset periodically generates measurable income that can be audited. Unfortunately, for residential real estate, obtaining meaningful rents is not as easy. Thus, the indexing mechanism can be troublesome and a political nightmare for the landlord (Orange County Register 2000). If the index is based on market value, substantial volatility is possible.

[16] Indexing land lease payments to the consumer price index can squeeze lessees as payment obligations may continue to rise, even though the property is performing poorly.

allows him to conclude that a party is more likely to own rather than rent an asset, if that party is expected to have an important investment decision with respect to the productivity of the asset. The redevelopment decision is such a decision. As well, Hart argues, highly complementary assets should be under common ownership. Land and buildings are complementary assets. Hart's focus is on determining the boundaries of the firm. So, Hart would argue that the ground lease separates complementary assets allowing management by separate firms. Thus, it is a contract that creates an unnatural boundary between activities associated with complementary assets (land management and real estate management) that should be undertaken by one firm. It would seem, then, that the ground lease must provide contractually for activities that in a perfect world would be undertaken by the same entity. That is, the contract should provide incentives that provide the landlord and tenant jointly the same potential benefits as the landlord alone would have as the fee owner.

LONG-TERM LAND LEASEHOLDS: THEIR ROLE IN THE TRANSITION PROCESS AND POTENTIAL PROBLEMS

In Poland real estate markets are increasingly being integrated into broader capital markets, as well as becoming a useful tool in the management of urban growth and redevelopment. The long-term ground lease can be viewed as an additional financial instrument allowing market participants another contractual mechanism to meet their particular requirements. The leasehold instrument, however designed, should not only supplement the basic freehold property rights granted by the state, but also should be extended into the private market, allowing private entities to grant long-term leaseholds if there is a market.

The extension of the right to grant a leasehold interest on privately held land is consistent with the goals of market-oriented governments that aim to remove legal and bureaucratic barriers to market innovation. In financial markets, there has been spectacular growth in the number of instruments allowing significant choice in the market. Similar evolution should be encouraged in real estate markets facilitating sale as well as development, financing and leasing. Below, we describe the attributes of long-term land leaseholds that are particularly relevant in a transitional economy. Our presumption is that more contractual alternatives are better than less, and that debate should be focused on contract design. We are particularly interested in the issue of redevelopment decisions by lessees faced with the prospect of lease termination and the forfeiture of building capital.

In an economy in transition, where the economic and political processes are critically interrelated, the ground lease may be an important tool for facilitating higher urban productivity, land redevelopment, stronger urban governance and autonomous local government finance. Here, the long-term public leasehold may be a pragmatic resolution to the problem of institution building:

1. Where local land use planning systems may not be in place, the long-term ground lease provides a mechanism for local governments to influence the land use of key parcels owned by the state (while still placing the parcels under the effective control of the private sector).[17]

2. Where local governments are responsible for building local infrastructure but lack sources of revenue due to limited local taxation systems (such as an area-based property tax versus a value-based property tax), public leasehold systems provide local governments a critical revenue source.

3. Public leasehold systems also allow local governments to benefit from the growth in land values that the government, in part, facilitates through the creation of infrastructure. This ultimately is dependent on the interplay among growth, validity of the infrastructure investment and the effectiveness of the lease contract.

4. If the availability of equity capital is limited and mortgage markets are in their early stages, public leasehold systems permit local governments to finance the use of land for private purposes (creating a capital market where one does not exist).

5. Where land is transferred to local governments to provide a source of wealth as a basis for building urban infrastructure, a public leasehold system provides a means of benefiting from that wealth, given that capital markets are just beginning their evolution and property tax systems are likely not in place.

6. Public leasehold systems allow local governments a significant role in determining future patterns of land use and to be proactive regarding changes in the pattern of land use that is the legacy of the prior economic system.

7. Public leasehold systems may provide more flexible land disposition instruments, allowing a local government to postpone sale until more stable market conditions evolve. This assumes that planners can anticipate market movements, although there is no consensus that this is feasible.

8. Public leasehold systems may provide a more politically palatable mechanism for making land available to nonresident investors for needed urban development.

9. Public leasehold systems can use contracts similar to those used in mature market economies, allowing the contracts to be readily understood by international investors while enhancing the choice of instruments.

---

[17] The relationship between public land leasing and urban planning has to be treated with extreme care. As some cases indicate, the development of planning and leasing should coincide. If the lease term is long, conditions specified in land contracts will be effective for many years. If the government has no land use plan to guide land contracting now, some current lease conditions may conflict with future planning regulations when the government tries to implement urban planning later. Hong Kong is an example. We are indebted to the editors for this point.

10. While public leasehold systems may be viewed by some as unnecessary relics of centralized or planned economies, long-term ground leases have a long history in many market-based economies.

While there seem to be numerous practical reasons for public leasehold systems in transitional economies, research has suggested that long-term ground leases are contracts that, unless carefully drafted, create the potential for significant divergence of incentives between lessor and lessee during the life of the lease. If the benchmark is a system of freehold, in a public leasehold system, over time, the lessee begins to act less like a landlord, to the detriment of the lessor (see Dale-Johnson 2001). If lease extension or renewal is automatic, this divergence goes away. Thus, one must question whether the potential benefits of public leasehold systems in transitional economies are offset by negative externalities resulting from the divergence of incentives problems. It is important to distinguish exactly what is meant by divergence of incentives. If a lessee does not have long-term control or rights to the value of improvements, lessees will undermaintain as the termination date of the lease approaches. If redevelopment is feasible, it may not be undertaken. If undertaken, it will occur at a lower density than if the lessee were the fee owner. These are economic responses having nothing to do with the zoning decisions of the public sector. We will illustrate this in the analysis that follows.

First, it would be helpful to fully understand the divergence of incentives problems. Ground leases are long-term contracts where there is significant uncertainty as to the future outcomes that may influence the value of the contract to the parties involved. While perpetual usufruct requires the ground tenant to own the improvements, in many other systems, at the end of the lease, the improvements revert to the landowner (ground lessor) who has the residual claim.[18] Who owns the residual interest in the improvements turns out to have a critical impact on the behavior of the lessee during the life of the lease. In order to appreciate fully the impact of perpetual usufruct on the behavior of the lessee, we will compare it with a generic ground lease similar to that used by public and private entities in the U.S. In the latter, at the termination date of the lease, both land and improvements revert to the landowner. In the former, the lessee owns the improvements. Where improvements are in place at the inception of the lease, the lessee must buy them.

Without the right of extension, the property rights associated with ground leases yield the leaseholder less value than fee simple ownership. The lessee has no rights to the land at the termination of the lease, thus, the terminal value of the land to the lessee is zero. As of the same date, the value of the land to the owner of the fee simple interest is the present value of the future cash flow associated with the land. Regarding the improvements, a public or private North American ground lease yields the leaseholder no terminal value for the existing structure or any redevelopment. Perpetual usufruct, on the other hand, gives the leaseholder the right of ownership to the improvements

---

[18] In most public leasehold systems, once the lease expires the land and improvements revert to the government with no compensation paid to the lessee. This is the case in China.

(or any subsequent redevelopment undertaken during the term of the lease) at the termination of the lease. Moreover, any subsequent lessee must purchase the improvements.

The option to redevelop provides value to whoever controls the improvements and the right to redevelop and the consequent cash flow stream. The redevelopment option has more value the longer the timeframe over which the option can be exercised and the longer the timeframe that the owner of the option can benefit from the redevelopment cash flows. In the case of both public and private North American leases, the redevelopment option is less valuable to the lessee because any capital expenditure has zero terminal value (see Capozza and Sick 1991). The redevelopment option is worth more if the lessee has a residual claim equal to the value of the improvements and any associated capital expenditure, as is the case with perpetual usufruct.

Usually, when a ground lease is initially negotiated, it is in the interests of both landlord and ground tenant that the property be developed to the highest and best use, that is, the use that yields the highest land residual or the most profitable use. The landlord has the leverage to have the site developed at highest and best use because the landlord can withhold from contracting with any party that will not commit to the development the landlord believes is the highest and best use. However, once the site has been developed, time has passed and market conditions have changed. Depending on the terms of the contract, redevelopment may not be optimal for the ground tenant, even if there is a higher and better use for the site. Sometimes redevelopment may be optimal but not at the scale most optimal for the fee owner. The motivations of the ground tenant will be driven by the terms of the ground lease. Most public and private ground leases are silent about the issue of redevelopment, even though during the 30-or-more-year term of a typical contract the likelihood that a higher and better use will arise is very real.

LITERATURE

We now turn to the literature that provides the background for analysis of alternative types of leasehold systems. This line of research provides a framework to evaluate the ability to extend a lease along with the property right associated with the improvements. Williams (1991) uses the option pricing approach, with both analytic and numerical techniques, to determine the optimal timing and density of development and timing of abandonment of a property. Conceptually, the model considers multiple rental growth outcomes and a "development" production function. The value of the development option is the expected value of the most profitable development scenarios that arise from rental growth paths randomly selected from a prespecified distribution of such paths. Capozza and Sick (1991) examine the value of long-term ground leases relative to fee ownership. They find, using option pricing theory, that the discount in the value of a ground lease relative to the fee is not simply the result of the termination value of the lease to the ground tenant; it is also the result of the reduced redevelopment opportunity afforded the lessee as a consequence of the foreseeable termination of the lease. Thus, as noted earlier, a ground lessee will redevelop sooner and at a lesser intensity than a fee owner would in the same economic circumstances. The redevelopment is at lower density because the ground tenant does not benefit from the revenues after the termination of the lease, and it occurs sooner, so the ground tenant can benefit from the enhanced revenues for a longer period. This behavior is nonoptimal from the lessor's point of view, as the present value of the ground lease revenues will be lower than they would have been had the lessee built at the same time and to the same scale as would have the landlord. Capozza and Sick consider the possibility of one redevelopment opportunity for either the fee owner or the ground lessee.

It is clear from the literature that the prospect of redevelopment, along with the loss of the residual value at the termination of the lease, causes the value of ground leased land to be less than the value of the fee simple. However, Capozza and Sick did not focus on the nature of the contractual arrangement between lessor and lessee. Dale-Johnson (2001) extends the work of Capozza and Sick to examine alternative ground lease contracts in which there is an option to extend if redevelopment occurs. As well, the author considers a lease contract where the residual claim to the improvements may be owned by the lessee, as in the case of Poland's perpetual usufruct. In both cases (lease extension and residual sharing), the value of the leasehold is enhanced as a consequence of the enhanced value of the redevelopment option. Thus, in the remainder of this chapter we examine perpetual usufruct as one of a number of contractual options, and discuss some of the implications of the results for transforming economies.

REDEVELOPMENT, GROUND LEASES, SECOND BEST AND OUR APPROACH

In a perfect world, a landowner (either public or private) would like to negotiate a ground lease that yielded a rental stream consistent with the value of the underlying asset (the land) in highest and best use, given an acceptable city plan. This would be the first-best outcome. As we have discussed, there are a number of reasons the lessee's incentives might diverge from those of the lessor over time. Exploring alternative contractual arrangements may allow us to come closer to the second best alternative.

In a real estate development environment, the value of a property is a function of the expected path of rents, the development technology, the expected interest or discount rate and the expected cost of construction plus any option value related to future redevelopment. The optimal development decision involves choosing the optimal time and intensity of development. Here, we build on the approach used by Capozza and Sick (1991), with some exceptions. First, our model includes a value or rent for both the land and the improvements (building). This permits the building to be treated as an asset separate from the land. Thus, at termination of the lease, the value of the building can flow to the lessee (as is the case with perpetual usufruct) or to the lessor (as is the case with a typical North American ground lease).

Thus, the rental stream generated by a property is comprised of building rent and land rent: both are stochastic but land rent adjusts to its theoretical market value at the time of redevelopment.[19] We employ Monte Carlo sampling and a genetic search algorithm to determine the optimal values of the fee simple and the lease contracts and the related timing and intensity of redevelopment for both landlord and ground tenant. Starting rents, interest rates, lease terms, construction costs, conversion technology (efficiency) and building and land growth rates, and volatility are fixed parameters. We do not consider multiple or sequential redevelopment alternatives at this point, but we do consider the possibility of lease extension.

The model for each lease contract is created to simulate the redevelopment decisions faced by a ground tenant. The ground tenant leases the land from the landlord and then leases the building to the space users. When the current land use is no longer at its highest and best use, the ground tenant has to decide if and when it is optimal to redevelop (convert) the land to its best use. Even though the property may not be at highest and best use, the lease contract may not provide the same incentives for the ground tenant to redevelop the property as in the case of the fee owner.

We seek to identify contractual alternatives that would be preferred by both the lessor and lessee. Rational redevelopment by a fee owner would create value. The present value of the future incremental revenue would exceed the costs of redevelopment. In the case of land leasehold, the incremental benefit would be shared between lessee and lessor.[20]

Monte Carlo techniques, combined with simulation, can be used to estimate the current value of a development option by simulating many sample paths of development, finding the maximum value in each sample path and averaging the present discounted value of the maxima over all sample paths to yield an expected value. In the case of possible redevelopment, that expected value, less the value in the current use is an estimate of the value of the development option.

Boyle (1977) was the first to use numerical techniques to value financial options and subsequently numerous others have used these approaches particularly for model specifications where partial differential equations are difficult to solve analytically (see Capozza and Sick 1991; Childs, Riddiough and

---

[19] This means the rent attributable to the land takes on a value consistent with the most profitable use at the time of redevelopment. In the model, land prices are driven by the existing use. This is consistent with many ground lease contracts in which periodic payments are a function of the land value for the existing use. When the existing use changes to a new higher and better use, the land rent adjusts accordingly.

[20] How the benefits are shared at the time of redevelopment is important. In this analysis we assume no lump-sum payments when the lease is renewed, extended or when redevelopment occurs. In our model the periodic rents (land lease payments) adjust to reflect the new use. Periodically, the rent also adjusts to the current market value for the land for the existing use. We believe there is the potential for holdup by the lessee if redevelopment is optimal. This is a topic for future research.

Triantis 1996). Childs, Riddiough and Triantis solve the problem by finding numerical solutions using a backward dynamic programming approach. A three-dimensional lattice is constructed involving the two stochastic variables and time. At each point in the lattice, the present value of baseline development in each of several possible mixes is compared to all alternative values net of redevelopment costs. If redevelopment is optimal the new present value replaces the old. This process starts at year 50 (the terminal year) and is repeated backwards to the present. The final present value computed is the value of the baseline development plus the redevelopment option.

We use an alternative approach: a combination of Monte Carlo sampling and a genetic search algorithm, to simulate alternative outcomes to choose the optimal behavior of the lessee or the fee owner in the case of each contract or fee ownership, respectively. Genetic algorithms optimize the results of a procedure (such as determining the value of a contract), by repeatedly trying alternatives through changing predetermined choice variables and reproducing and mixing the components of the better solutions, to maximize or minimize a target variable (the value of the contract). If properly specified, the process converges to an outcome where subsequent changes in the choice variables do not lead to improvement in the outcome (the statistic describing the target variable). Goldberg (1989) and Holland (1992) summarize the evolution of genetic algorithms and provide a number of illustrations of their use in economic, search and mathematical optimization problems.[21] This approach has been used to price financial options (see Chidambaran, Lee and Trigueros 1999; Keber 1999).

The choice variables in our model are development timing and intensity, and the target variable is the present value of the contract with the goal being to choose combinations of development timing (choice of time τ) and density (the quantity of rentable space $q(k)$ or capital K) that maximize $NPV(R_L, B, \tau, K; T, \Omega)$ where T is the terminal date of the contract, Ω defines the terms of the ground lease contract and R_L and B are the market rent flows. The growth rate in building rents (R_L) and the growth rate in land rents (B) are stochastic. We assume that the two growth rates (g_1 and g_2) are perfectly correlated.

The key variables are: the target variable (the present value of the contract); the choice variables (the time and intensity of development); and the uncertain variables (the periodic rents). A number of other parameters are fixed. The optimization process can be described by referring to two stages. In the first stage, a time of development and intensity of development are chosen by the analyst and provided as inputs to the model. The model randomly assigns rents to each year of the analysis where the choices are governed by prespecified distributions. The growth rates g_1 and g_2 each have log-normal distributions with standard deviations σ_1 and σ_2. The model iterates using a search algorithm to identify new combinations of τ and K and the resultant

---

[21] We implement the approach using RISKOptimizer, an Excel-based software package designed by Palisade Corporation for solving optimization problems involving uncertainty.

contract value. This process continues until there is convergence. A number of search algorithms can be chosen based on assumptions about how τ and K might vary. We use a process where τ and K can vary independently. In other words, we do not presume that higher τs would automatically require higher expenditure of K. The choice of the new combination of τ and K is also governed by the crossover and mutation rate. These exogenously determined parameters of the algorithm influence the scope of search in choosing the new set of choice variables. Convergence determines the present value for the subject contract and a combination of τ and K for that simulation. A new simulation then begins with the choice of a new combination of τ and K as a starting point along with a new set of randomly assigned rents drawn from the prespecified distribution. Each simulation determines a combination of PV, τ and K that is saved. Multiple simulations are undertaken and the procedure repeats itself until the statistics of interest converge (in this case, the mean present value of the contract reaches a maximum). The combination of τ and K consistent with the mean of the individually maximized simulations is the optimal τ and K for the contract.

Use of genetic algorithms to solve difficult optimization problems is common. We chose this approach to allow flexibility to adjust the nature and particularly the complexity of the contract. For example, we were not sure we could devise an approach to solve the lease extension problem using the backward dynamic programming approach used by Childs, Riddiough and Triantis (1996). Our model appears in greater detail in this chapter's appendix.

ANALYSIS AND RESULTS

We explore the contractual structure of two types of long-term land leaseholds: the typical North American ground lease and the public leasehold contract used in Poland, perpetual usufruct. Since one objective is to simulate how lessees would behave with respect to redevelopment opportunities, we also consider a leasehold extension that would coincide with any redevelopment undertaken by the lessee. Behind this exercise is the idea of determining an optimal structure for a long-term land lease where the lessee would be motivated to act as would a fee owner (in the absence of a ground lease). A first-best or optimal outcome for the landowner would be redevelopment at a time and intensity identical to one the fee owner would undertake, were the fee not subject to a ground lease. We assume the party that has the use rights to the land will behave optimally when those rights are complete, subject only to planning constraints or police power provisions. This would imply long-term use rights with no uncertainty as to their termination, and also imply ownership of the improvements as well as the land. Public leasehold systems have the potential to reduce the rights provided in a freehold system if, for example, the state need not renew the lease or compensate the lessee for property improvements at lease termination.

Our model is used to determine values for the redevelopment scale and year for each of the contractual alternatives below. The following are specific alternatives we consider:

1. Baseline case: Standard North American ground lease with a 50-year term and no residual claim for the lessee.

2. Perpetual usufruct: Polish public leasehold (50 years): Modeled after perpetual public land leasehold in Poland. A 50-year term is assumed for comparison purposes. In this analysis we begin with the assumption that renewal is not automatic. The model permits the relaxation of this assumption to capture the "expectation" in the Polish market.

3. Lease extension (step-up rents, no residual claim): the lessee may redevelop at any point in the first 50 years (the initial lease term), but may extend the lease by the number of years expired in the initial lease. For example, if the lessee chooses to redevelop in year 40, the lease is extended 40 years, becoming a 90-year lease.

4. Fee ownership: Landowner is presumed to own the property in perpetuity.

The baseline case assumes a land rent of $16 and an equivalent building rent. The growth rate for values and rents of land and buildings is assumed to be 1 percent. Buildings are depreciable, so we assume the 1 percent building growth rate is the net result of a 2 percent market growth rate and a 1 percent depreciation rate. Depreciation is assumed to influence rents as well, so rents grow at the rate of 1 percent rather than 2 percent. The variance of the land growth rate is 0.3 and the variance of the building growth rate is 0.2. The interest rate is assumed to be 5 percent and the cost of capital $100. With an interest rate of 5 percent and a growth rate of 1 percent, the appropriate capitalization rate is 4 percent, resulting in an initial value of $800 for each square foot of leasable space. Given our assumptions about production efficiency (see this chapter's appendix), an additional square foot of leasable space can be generated with one unit of capital. However, two square feet of additional space would require four units of capital. In other words, a marginal expenditure of $100 would be required to create an additional square foot of leasable space on a square foot of land. A marginal expenditure of $400 would be required to create two additional square feet of leasable space.

To provide perspective for the analysis of the ground lease contracts, we compare ground lease contractual outcomes with fee simple outcomes using similar market assumptions. That is, if the building rent growth rate is assumed to be 2 percent with a depreciation rate of 1 percent, we determine the optimal redevelopment timing and intensity for both the ground lessee and the fee owner (the lessor) under the same circumstances. Table 1, Case 4, reports the results and parameters for a fee simple (fee owner) scenario. Specifically, Case 4 involves a fee owner with a 100-year horizon who may redevelop only once during the 100-year period. Depreciation of the building is assumed. Redevelopment occurs in year 46 at a scale of 26.98 with a resulting rent

TABLE 1

COMPARISON OF ALTERNATIVE LEASE CONTRACTS

Case	Scale (Rent Multiple)	Period 0 Value (NPV at τ) Mean NPV	Year of Redevelopment	Lease Escalation (Years to Step Up, 0 = Mark-to-Market)	% Land Growth Rate	Land Growth Rate Variance	% Market Building Value Growth Rate	Building Value Growth Rate Variance	Option to Extend	% Depreciation Rate	Residual Claim	PV to Lessor (Value of the Leased Fee)
(1) North American lease	2.93 (1.71)	346 (515) 331	29	0	1	.30	2	.20	No	1	No	500
(2) Perpetual usufruct (Poland)	21.07 (4.59)	346 (1,532) 858	22	0	1	.30	2	.20	No	0	Yes	780
(3) Automatic lease extension	27.5 (5.25)	383 (2,522) 897	38	0	1	.30	2	.20	Yes*	0	No	852
(4) Fee owner	26.98 (5.19)	400 (3,357) 731	46	N/A	1	.30	2	.20	N/A	1	Yes (fee owner)	N/A

Source: Compiled by the authors

* Lessee has option to extend the lease by the number of periods that have passed if redevelopment occurs.

Interest rate = 5 percent

Capitalization rate = 4 percent

Production efficiency γ = 0.50

PV = present value

NPV = net present value

multiple of 5.19. Scale refers to the units of capital expended. The redeveloped property has a new floor-area-ratio (FAR), or the ratio of floor area to land area) of 5.19, equivalent to the rent multiple. Thus, the new rent generated is 5.19 times the old rent. The scale and rent multiple appear in the second column of Table 1. The third column reports that the initial value of the land is $400 and the present value of the eventual redevelopment is $731. Thus, the redevelopment option is worth $331. The present value of the project in year 46, at the time of redevelopment, is $3,357. This outcome is also plotted in Figure 1 and appears as the darkest line that slopes upward to the right with one step-up in the 46th year.

Table 1 illustrates all of the input assumptions and key parameter values as well as the outcomes associated with each case. The outcomes describe the timing and intensity of redevelopment. Specifically in Table 1, column 2, in reports, for each case, the intensity of redevelopment and the rent multiple. The rent multiple is equal to the capital applied per unit of land raised to the power γ, where γ is the capital elasticity of substitution or the production efficiency. We assume that $\gamma = 0.50$ in most of our runs. Column 3, reports respectively, for each case: (1) period zero value of the asset assuming no redevelopment; (2) period τ value of the asset (when redeveloped); and (3) period zero value of the asset assuming redevelopment occurs at the optimal time and with the optimal intensity. Column 4, reports the timing of redevelopment. Column 13 reports the period zero value of the leased fee when optimal redevelopment has occurred. The remainder of the table reports input parameters or attributes of the contract.

Now we can proceed to evaluating the outcomes for the alternative ground lease contracts. Our results show a dramatic difference between the intensity of redevelopment that would be undertaken by the fee owner and that which would be undertaken by the ground lessee in the baseline case. In Case 1 (the typical North American ground lease) of Table 1, we see, as was demonstrated by Capozza and Sick (1991), that the lessee redevelops at less intensity than would the fee owner. Redevelopment by the lessee occurs in year 29, before redevelopment in the fee owner scenario. As well, the value of the leasehold declines to zero at the date of the termination of the lease. The scale of development by the fee owner is much greater than in the case of the lessee. The ground lessee would only apply 2.93 units of capital per square foot of land, resulting in a rent multiple of 1.71, compared to the fee owner's 26.98 units of capital and 5.19 rent multiple. Capozza and Sick suggest that, since the ground lessee has no residual claim, it makes sense to redevelop at a lower intensity than would the fee owner. The finding that the lessee redevelops sooner than the fee owner is also consistent and reflects the lessee's desire to earn the enhanced income over as long a period as possible. A dashed-and-dotted line is used to plot this outcome in Figure 1.

Case 2 is meant to illustrate perpetual usufruct (the Polish public leasehold structure). Since one of the challenges facing the ground lessee is the recovery of capital investment when the passage of time foreshortens the recovery period,

FIGURE 1

GRAPHICAL COMPARISON OF ALTERNATIVE LEASE CONTRACTS (VALUE OF
PROPERTY RIGHT TO FEE HOLDER OR LESSEE)

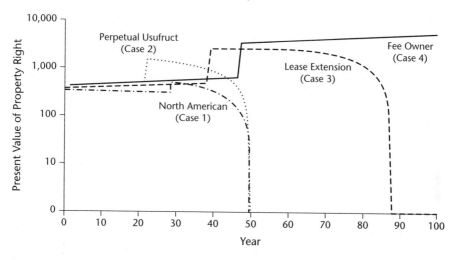

Source: Compiled by the authors

giving the ground lessee a residual claim to the value of the improvements
should reduce, if not eliminate, this problem. At the same time the lessor retains
the residual interest in the land. In the analysis we assume no depreciation of
the improvements. At lease termination the lessee receives a payment from
the lessor or the new lessee equal to the value of the redeveloped building.
The lessee redevelops sooner (in year 22) and at less intensity (21.07 units of
capital) than would the fee owner. It is clear from this result that giving the
ground lessee a residual claim (ownership of the improvements) has a significant
effect on the lessee's behavior. In particular, redevelopment occurs at a higher
intensity more in line with that which the lessor would undertake. However,
redevelopment occurs sooner in the perpetual usufruct case than in the fee case.
This result is plotted in Figure 1 (dotted line).

Case 3 demonstrates the impact of providing the ground lessee the option
to extend the lease at the time redevelopment occurs. We assume that the
extension permitted equals the period of time already passed in the existing
50-year lease. For example, if the ground lessee wished to redevelop in year 10,
the lease could be extended another 10 years, so the original lease would then
have a life of 60 years. As previously noted, the fee owner would redevelop in
year 46 using 26.98 units of capital to generate a rent multiple of 5.19 in the
case of a 100-year horizon. Remember, the fee owner owns the residual rights
to the property forever. On the other hand, we have parameterized our model
so that the ground lessee is normally subject to a 50-year limitation on right of
use. We found in Case 1 that the ground lessee would only apply 2.93 units of
capital in year 29. With the ability to extend the lease as described above, the

ground lessee chooses to apply 27.5 units of capital in year 38 to generate a rent multiple of 5.25. The result in Case 3 is plotted in Figure 1 (dashed line).

Note that in column 13 we report the value of the leased fee (the freehold interest subject to a lease) in the case of redevelopment at the intensity and time determined by the simulation of the ground lessee's alternative contract. In the baseline case (Case 1), the value of the leased fee, assuming redevelopment occurs in year 29 at an intensity (scale) of 2.93, is $500. In all other cases (Cases 2 and 3), the value of the leased fee exceeds the baseline value of $500. Thus, it appears that in all of the alternative contractual arrangements, the owner of the leased fee is better off than in the baseline case. [22]

URBAN FORM AND REDEVELOPMENT DECISIONS: IMPLICATIONS AND CONCLUSIONS

These results have some interesting implications with respect to land use in communities where long-term land leaseholds are ubiquitous. If there is uncertainty about the ability to extend the lease, and if the lessee has no residual claim to the value of the improvements, redevelopment will occur sooner and at less density than if there was fee ownership of the land. This means that, if everything remains the same, land use densities will be lower in cities where public leasehold is common and the contractual arrangements are as described above.[23] In the case of Poland and perpetual usufruct, the clear definition of the ownership rights of the lessee, with respect to the improvements, significantly changes the outcome. While redevelopment will still occur sooner and at lower density than with of fee ownership of the land, density is much greater than would be the case without ownership of the improvements. Moreover, in Poland the likelihood of the extension of the leasehold is also high (since a valid public purpose is the only reason to refuse such an extension). Our results suggest that if the extension is tied to the decision to redevelop, the outcome is even closer to the fee outcome. Certainly, the combination of a residual claim and the extension option would create a second best outcome.[24]

Earlier, we noted that there are clear pragmatic economic benefits to long-term land leasehold systems in transforming economies. Many of the benefits fade away as capital markets evolve, alternative sources of local public revenue are developed and land planning and regulatory systems are put in place. Given the expediency of public leasehold systems we focus on the nature of

---

[22] Another alternative would be to maximize the aggregate value of the leased fee and the leasehold and permit the two parties to bargain regarding the split of the cash flows and the costs. We leave consideration of this alternative for later research.

[23] We are indebted to Bertrand Renaud for this insight.

[24] Combining the right to extend and the residual claim on the improvements would clearly bring the ground lessee closer to the fee owner with regard to property rights. Redevelopment would occur later but still before the fee owner outcome. Development would also be at higher density but still not as high density as in the fee owner case.

the contract itself with the goal of enhancing what seems to be a necessary institution. At the same time we view the property rights inherent in a freehold system necessary to encourage ongoing private investment.

Thus, in this chapter we consider alternative contractual arrangements for long-term land leaseholds. The key alternatives we consider are the sharing of the residual claim at the termination of the lease and the option to extend the lease. An example of the former is if the lessee owns the improvements, as is the case in the public leasehold system in Poland. In the former case, we consider entitling the ground lessee to a payoff equal to the market value of the improvements to the land (the building). Thus, when the improvements are redeveloped, the lessee owns the redeveloped asset. In the latter case, we propose a contract that is automatically extended by the number of years elapsed if redevelopment occurs. We find that both these alternatives enhance the value of the redevelopment option to the ground lessee, and result in redevelopment that is more consistent with that which the fee owner would have undertaken. Note that in the U.S. most leases are silent about the issue of redevelopment.

The results of this research are promising in that they suggest that the contractual terms of a long-term land lease have significant implications with respect to the behavior of the lessee during the life of the lease. In private lease transactions, this has implications for the value of the asset delivered to the lessor at lease termination and the size of the lease payments during the life of the lease. We presume in this analysis that more intensive uses by the lessee generate higher revenues to the lessor if and when they occur. In public leasehold environments, particularly where leaseholds dominate the scene, the contractual terms potentially have significant implications for urban form and for revenues to local governments. If lessees redevelop at lower density, cities will evolve at lower density if the leaseholds are North American style. While the local government can capture public leasehold revenue from a "flatter" city by simply expanding the city boundary, there may be significant incremental cost to providing the infrastructure for that flatter city.

The nature of the long-term land leasehold is such that the landowner cedes control of the asset to the lessee for a significant period of time usually in excess of 40 years. In a growing city, the probability that the highest and best use of a particular site will change is relatively high over that long time frame. Thus, ground lease contracts should provide incentives that encourage lessees to behave more like fee owners. Perpetual usufruct, as it has been implemented in Poland, has attributes that allow it to approach the first-best outcome with respect to the redevelopment decision. In this chapter we have shown that this type of contract is superior to the generic North American contract because of the high probability of extension and the lessee's residual claim to the improvements. Thus, if long-term public leasehold systems are critical to facilitate transfer of land use to private entrepreneurs, generate local government revenue and facilitate land planning, perpetual usufruct is an expedient measure as these institutions evolve.

REFERENCES

Boyle, P. 1977. Options: A Monte Carlo approach. *Journal of Financial Economics* 4:323–338.

Capozza, D. R. and G. Sick. 1991. Valuing long term leases: The option to redevelop. *Journal of Real Estate Finance and Economics* 4:209–223.

Chidambaran, N. K., C. H. Jevons Lee and J. R. Trigueros. 1999. Option pricing via genetic programming. In *Computational finance*, Y. S. Abu-Mostafa et al., eds. Cambridge, MA: MIT Press.

Childs, P., Riddiough, T. and A. Triantis. 1996. Mixed uses and the redevelopment option. *Real Estate Economics* 24:317–339.

Dale-Johnson, D. 2001. Long term ground leases, the redevelopment option and contract incentives. *Real Estate Economics* 29:(3)Fall.

Frieden, B. J. and L. B. Sagalyn. 1989. *Downtown inc.: How America rebuilds cities*. Cambridge, MA: MIT Press.

Goldberg, D. 1989. *Genetic algorithms in search, optimization and machine learning*. Reading, MA: Addison-Wesley.

Hart, O. 1995. *Firms, contracts and financial structure*. Oxford: Oxford University Press.

Holland, J. H. 1992. *Adaptation in natural and artificial systems*. Cambridge, MA: MIT Press. First edition [1975], Ann Arbor, MI: University of Michigan.

Keber, C. 1999. Option valuation with the genetic programming approach. In *Computational finance*, Y. S. Abu-Mostafa et al., eds. Cambridge, MA: MIT Press.

Orange County Register. 2000. Condo owners feel hammered: Land leases up 389%. March 27.

Renaud, B., F. Pretorius and B. Pasadilla. 1997. *Markets at work: Dynamics of the residential real estate market in Hong Kong*. Hong Kong: Hong Kong University Press.

Williams, J. 1991. Real estate development as an option. *Journal of Real Estate Finance and Economics* 4:191–208.

APPENDIX
THE MODEL

In describing our model, a number of variables and parameters have been identified. A formal statement of the model follows. The growth rates (g_1 and g_2) for market land rent (R_L) and market building rent (B) each follow log-normal distributions (Wiener processes). Both of the growth rates are positive. Thus

$$dR_L / R_L = g_1 dt + \sigma_1 dz \tag{1}$$

and

$$dB / B = g_2 dt + \sigma_2 dz \tag{2}$$

where dz is a standard Wiener process. We expect a strong relationship between g_1 and g_2. In fact, we would expect that in a competitive environment the two drifts would move in tandem. This would be the case with respect to new properties. However, in our simulations we include depreciation so that g_1 may not equal g_2 (the effective growth rate after depreciation may be $g_2 - \varepsilon$, where ε is the depreciation rate).

The ground tenant pays contractual ground rent to the landlord, which may or may not equal the market land rent, depending on the lease structure Ω. The rest of the rent flows are the income to the ground tenant. We assume for the purposes of this chapter that building rents "mark to market." That is, lease rental rates adjust instantaneously to market rent levels.[25]

Assuming the ground rent specified by the lease defined by Ω is R_S, then the rent flow or income to the ground tenant is equal to:

$$R(t) = R_L(t) + B(t) - R_S(t). \tag{3}$$

It is assumed that, after redevelopment (conversion), where new construction is homogenous,[26] both land rent and building rent increase by the same multiple. If the redevelopment occurs at time τ, the rent flow after the redevelopment becomes:

$$R'_L(\tau) = q(k)R_L(\tau) \tag{4}$$

$$B'(\tau) = q(k)B(\tau) \tag{5}$$

---

[25] This is a strong assumption. However, relaxation of this assumption would unnecessarily complicate the model without providing further insight into the structure of the ground lease.

[26] The expenditure of capital increases density, not quality.

The rent multiple is determined by a Cobb-Douglas–type production function such as:

$$q(k) = K^{\gamma} \tag{6}$$

where γ is the capital elasticity of substitution, K is the amount of capital per unit of land, and $q(k)$ is the resulting rentable space per unit of land. The cost of applying a unit of capital is c so:

$$\{[K^{\gamma}B(\tau)] / (i - g_1)\} + \{[K^{\gamma}R_L(\tau)] /(i - g_2)\} - Kc \tag{7}$$

is the value of conversion at any period τ. Note that the land rent (land residual rent) increases with the ability of the property to generate income that results from increases in the FAR (the rentable space per unit of land).

In both models of certainty and uncertainty, the ground tenant tries to maximize the net present value (NPV) of the project at time 0 given the opportunity to redevelop at some point τ in the future, where $0 < \tau < T$. The NPV consists of four elements: rent flow before and after the redevelopment, the cost of redevelopment (c per unit of space), and the compensation value or the residual value (m), if any, when the lease expires.

Assuming the property is redeveloped at time τ to a density q, then the present value of the leasehold at time 0 is:

$$\begin{aligned} NPV(R_L, B, \tau, K; T, \Omega) = {}& PV(R_L, B, \tau) + q(k)PV(R_L', B', T - \tau) \\ & - PV(kc) + PV(m) - PV(R_S) \end{aligned} \tag{8}$$

where T is the term of the lease. Here, the formula to calculate the present value (PV) is the standard discrete one.

$$PV(R) = \sum_{t=1}^{N} \frac{R_t}{(1+r)^t} \tag{9}$$

Therefore, in a single certainty scenario, the optimal timing and optimal scale (density) of the redevelopment is the solution to the following problem:

$$\max_{\tau,k} NPV(R, \tau, K; T) \text{ for each contract of form } \Omega. \tag{10}$$

This problem can be solved using numeric optimization techniques. To find the optimal solution under uncertainty, we use Monte Carlo sampling and a genetic algorithm to simulate each contract as discussed in the prior section.

The following table summarizes the exogenous variables, derived parameters and endogenous variables in the model. The exogenous parameters include:

1. interest rate, cost of capital;

2. starting land rent, its growth rate and "sigma";

3. starting building rent, its growth rate and "sigma";

4. the building depreciation rate;

5. production efficiency; and

6. the correlation coefficient between the land rent and the building rent.

The derived parameters include:

1. land value;
2. real building rent growth rate;
3. building value;
4. rent multiple; and
5. capitalization rate.

The results of the analysis include:

1. conversion year (redevelopment timing) and
2. conversion scale (redevelopment intensity).

We can also further describe each outcome with the following information:

1. rent multiple;
2. period zero value of the asset assuming no redevelopment;
3. period value of the asset (when redeveloped);
4. period zero value of asset assuming redevelopment occurs at the optimal time and with the optimal intensity; and
5. period zero value of the leased fee when optimal redevelopment has occurred.

To implement the model, we apply the depreciation rate to the building rent only. Thus, the real growth rate used in the Wiener process for the building is the market growth rate less the depreciation rate. To determine asset value, a capitalization rate is derived from the land rent growth rate and the interest rate.

Thus, the capitalization rate[27] is constant throughout the lease term. The building value and the land value are calculated by dividing the current rent by the capitalization rate. The same method is used to determine the residual value of the building at the termination of the lease.

The landowner's position must also be considered as the contractual arrangements are changed. For the landowner to consider negotiating an alternative contact, the landlord must be better off than with the original contract. In other words, there must be a joint optimization process. In this analysis we simply compute the value of the leased fee and demonstrate that under some of the alternative contracts the landlord or the owner of the leased fee is better off than in the case of the baseline contract.

---

[27] This is based on the Gordon growth model or growing perpetuity model where asset value is equal to $CF/(r-g)$. The denominator is equal to the overall capitalization rate.

PART IV

CONCLUSIONS

Rethinking the Future Roles of Public Leasehold

12

Yu-Hung Hong and Steven C. Bourassa

This chapter summarizes the land leasing experiences presented in this book, focusing on the importance of the design and development of institutions and organizations for public leasehold systems. Because our discussion concentrates on the three questions stated in Chapter 1, it would be useful to recapitulate them here:

» To what extent can governments accomplish their desired policy goals by leasing public land?

» How do institutions and organizations affect governments' ability to achieve their policy objectives?

» If there is a common set of enabling institutions and organizations for public leasehold systems, what are the critical issues involved in building and maintaining them?

Answers to these questions form the basic structure of this chapter, with each section devoted to a detailed examination of one question.

We would like to emphasize that our statements are not intended to be conclusive, for they pertain only to the case studies examined in this volume. As mentioned in Chapter 1, there are other public leasehold systems, such as those in Singapore, Vietnam and Russia, which we did not analyze. Our aim is to show how the accomplishment of land leasing goals (or the lack of it) is connected to the unique institutional environment in each case study. A clear understanding of these relationships, we believe, would help policy makers design land leasing policy that matches the special institutional settings of their countries, thereby enhancing their chance of obtaining the benefits and avoiding the pitfalls of public leasehold systems.

ACHIEVING LAND LEASING GOALS

In assessing the extent to which governments could accomplish their policy goals by leasing public land, we limit our analysis to the six established public leasehold systems: Canberra, the Netherlands, Sweden, Finland, Israel and Hong Kong. We exclude the case studies in Part 3 of this book because those leasing experiences have not existed long enough to generate sufficient information for making an assessment. Nevertheless, they are helpful in indicating, for countries in transition, if public leasehold can facilitate timely transfers of state-owned land to private entities for development.

Raising Public Funds

Among all the case studies, the Hong Kong public leasehold system appears especially instrumental in assisting the government to raise public funds for financing public infrastructure and social services. From 1970 to 2000 the government generated US$71.1 billion (in 2000 values) by leasing public land, largely from lump-sum premiums paid at the beginning of the lease. This income accounted for 16 percent and 18 percent of total government annual revenues and expenditures, respectively. More important, for the same period, these proceeds were more than enough to cover the costs of public works and land development, indicating that land leasing has been a profitable undertaking for the government in Hong Kong.

Public leasehold systems in the Netherlands, Sweden and Finland also help municipalities generate public funds, although the lease revenues of these countries play a far less important role in financing public expenditures than in Hong Kong. While all three systems rely mainly on annual land rents to collect leasehold charges, lessees in the Netherlands also have the right to convert all annual rental payments into a premium (discounted to present value) and pay the entire amount in a single payment at the beginning of the lease. According to Needham, although net income from land leasing in Amsterdam (US$43.8 million) was equivalent to as much as 43 percent of total property tax revenues in 1999 (US$101.5 million), it could cover only 1.3 percent of municipal expenditures. Mattsson found that lease revenues in Sweden account for only a small percentage of total municipal incomes (5 percent in 1999). As for Finland, although the municipal governments have attempted to recoup land value by adjusting land rents regularly, the key objective of land leasing is not to maximize lease revenues. Instead, the municipalities have employed land leasing primarily to facilitate urban and housing development. In making this comparison, one thing has to be borne in mind: fiscal structures in most Western European countries are centralized, whereas Hong Kong was financially independent of Britain prior to 1997 and has remained so since it reunited with the People's Republic of China (PRC). Owing to the lack of intergovernmental subsidies, Hong Kong must rely on lease revenues, as corporate and income taxes are low, to defray its government expenditures, thus explaining in part why lease revenues play such an important role in public finance.

The Canberra leasehold system, as Neutze argues, has not helped the government generate much public funds. The fiscal objectives of land leasing are set within the consideration of broad public objectives, especially with regard to maintaining low land costs for the construction of public facilities and housing. In addition, the government was unable to increase revenues from leasing public land because of the infrequent adjustments of land rents prior to 1970, and then the abolition of land rents for all residential leases in 1971. It has also failed to request lessees to pay either additional premiums or land rents at full market value when they change the use of their land. Because of these problems, the potential of public leasehold for capturing increases in land values has never been realized in Canberra.

Freeholders and leaseholders in Israel face the same real estate tax obligations, including a local betterment levy and the national Added Increment Tax on real property. The only difference is that lessees must pay an extra permit fee for any change in land use, which is calculated at 50 percent of the increase in lease value caused by redevelopment. Although the public leasehold system does provide the government with an additional mechanism for recouping increases in land values, a large portion of these increments is normally captured by other property taxes. In turn, the well-designed property taxation system renders the role of public leasehold in capturing land value unnecessary in Israel.

Among all case studies examined here, the Hong Kong leasehold system clearly represents the most aggressive approach to collecting leasehold charges (see Chapter 7). Under this system the value of the land lease is determined by competitive bids at public auction. The highest bidder will win the contract with the entire initial premium, which is equal to 100 percent of the final offer, payable in lump sum within 30 days. By using this method, the Hong Kong government is essentially requesting lessees to buy development or use rights at full market value.

Unlike Hong Kong, other land leasing systems require lessees to pay land rents or premiums based on the assessed, not market, value of leasehold rights (or simply based on the estimated land value when the duration of the lease is long and the land rent is either nil or set at a minimal level). For instance, negotiation between the municipality and the lessee generally determines the level of land rent in the Netherlands, Sweden and Finland. The base for calculating ground rent is the assessed land value, which is normally below the market value. In Israel the government requires lessees to pay a leasehold charge equivalent to 91 percent of the assessed value of the property, a value that had been grossly underestimated by the government up through the 1970s. Although the government assessors have appraised properties at a more realistic level in recent decades, the interest rates used to calculate the annual leasehold charges and the up-front, discounted payment (both 5 percent) have stayed the same for many years, despite the great vicissitudes of the Israeli real estate and financial markets. Because public officials in all of these cases have in one way or another made certain concessions (or downward adjustments to assessed land or property values) in collecting leasehold payments, it is not surprising that the Hong Kong system generates more revenues than do the others.

One matter must be clarified here: we are not advocating the premium system in which lessees will purchase the leasehold rights with a capital sum rather than lease them on payment of annual rent. Indeed, there is no reason to believe that a government would collect more revenues from a premium system than a land rent system if the base for setting either premiums or land rents is the same. Although the premium system will allow the government to collect the entire lease value up front, there will be no opportunity for it to recoup any land value increments by requesting additional payments from the lessee, except when there is a land use change or the lease expires. Those options, as will be discussed later, are not always viable as well.

In contrast to the premium system, a system based on rents may allow the government to amend the rent level periodically through the term of the lease to recapture unanticipated increases in value—a potential advantage over the premium system, at least in theory. Of course, rents may also have to be adjusted downwards in a declining market. Just as additional premiums can be charged in a premium system, the government can establish new land rents when lessees request additional land rights for redevelopment or seek to renew their leases. Again, the frequency of rental adjustments and the level of resistance to rent increases from leaseholders will determine whether the government can actually raise substantial public funds by collecting land rents. As a whole, whether the government is better off adopting a premium system or a land rent system will depend on the possibility of collecting extra payments from lessees at three occasions: lease modification, contract renewal and rent adjustment. Thus, it is worthwhile to discuss them in detail.

As Neutze, Alterman and Hong suggest, asking lessees to pay the entire lease value at the beginning of the lease and no (or little) land rent could affect the negotiation between the government and lessees for payments at the time of lease renewal. Allowing lessees to purchase leasehold rights in entirety may give them the impression that they have acquired a significant portion of equity in land, especially when the term of the lease is long and renewable. The reason to distinguish the possession of leasehold rights vis-à-vis equity in land is that the former should, in principle, cease when the lease expires. With the exception of perpetual leases, what the lessee acquires from the lessor by paying a premium are specific leasehold rights for a limited time. Certainly, when the lease is automatically renewable, which allows the land rights to continue for a long time (as in the case of all established leasehold systems examined in this volume), the expiration date of the lease becomes meaningless. In this situation, the value of the long-term lease should be close to the freehold value of the land, if charges for changes in land use will be the same whether land is leasehold or freehold. Thus, paying the entire lease value in a single payment is tantamount to buying the fee title of land. If lessees believe that they are the de facto landowners, the government will encounter great difficulties in requesting leaseholders to pay an additional premium for renewing their land contracts. As shown by the Hong Kong experience, when the government tried to ask holders of renewable leases to pay a new land rent calculated at the fair market value of land for extending land leases, lessees argued that they had already purchased the right to extend their leases when they first established the contracts with the government. As the dispute intensified, lessees organized public protests against the policy, which eventually compelled the government to concede. The experience of the Israeli system in this respect was similar during the 1970s.

Does this mean that not issuing renewable leases would avert the problem? Unfortunately, we believe that the answer is negative, for there is a common perception that the government should be responsible for ensuring security of land tenure. Because of this belief, government lessors in our case studies seldom repossess land when leases expire. Concerns about the negative impacts of land repossession on private incentives to invest could deter public officials from asking lessees to pay the full market value of the lease when reissuing land contracts. This is particularly true when the lessor is a government that is accountable to and elected by lessees. If a large number of leases are expiring at the same time, it is highly possible that the government will yield to public pressure and extend all contractual agreements with leaseholders automatically. This may explain why most leases in our case studies are renewable for a nominal or zero fee.

In sum, granting automatically renewable or perpetual leases would prevent problems associated with renegotiating contract renewal and may enhance security of tenure, but it removes the government's ability to reclaim the right to benefit from land. Insistance on recapturing land value during lease renewal does not seem desirable either, for, based on the experiences of our case studies, it is unclear if the idea can ever be put into practice. Governments should bear these issues in mind if they expect to collect from lessees full market premiums or land rents for renewing leases.

Collecting additional premiums from lessees when they modify the use of their land is not trouble-free, either. In principle, under a premium system, lessees purchase at the beginning of the lease the right to use land for a specific purpose. If lessees change the land use, they are exercising different land rights that may not be allowable according to the original contractual agreements. Therefore, the government is entitled to an additional premium (similar to betterment charges under freehold systems) if the new land use will lead to increases in lease value.

Collection of extra payments for modifying land leases shows mixed results in our case studies. While lessees in the Netherlands, Finland and Israel do not seem to oppose the adjustment of land rent for a change in land use, renegotiation for a similar kind of payment in Canberra, Sweden and Hong Kong has been problematic. There is no evidence to show that public leasehold can ease the problems of collecting betterment charges. For example, the levy of the change of use charge in Canberra for lease modification has been controversial. The current rate is set at 75 percent of the increase in land value, and was only 50 percent between 1971 and 1990. So far, it has not been politically feasible for the government to maintain a betterment charge designed to capture the full increase in land value. In Hong Kong lease modification premiums do not account for a significant share of total lease revenues because the negotiation costs involved in assembling leasehold rights are high. High negotiation costs, coupled with a 100 percent betterment charge on land use changes, Hong argues, might have discouraged some developers from undertaking land redevelopment projects, thereby eliminating the chance for the government to recoup the land value increments at the time of lease modification. These experiences seem to show that governments may be unable to collect a substantial amount of revenue from lessees for amending lease conditions.

Governments that depend on the collection of land rents to capture land value also seem to face difficulties in readjusting rent levels. In Sweden not only does the calculation of land rents vary from one municipality to another, but the determination of their base and rate frequently leads to lawsuits as well. Prolonged litigation, in turn, increases the administrative costs of collecting and renegotiating land rents. In addition, some local governments do not want to tie up capital in land and thus have begun to convert public leaseholds into freeholds. In 1986, in the Netherlands, the government of The Hague decided to implement a series of legislative changes that allowed lessees to convert their leases into perpetual leaseholds to avoid any potential conflict involved in renegotiating new land rents at lease expiration. Only certain municipalities in Finland, which normally adjust land rents every 30 years to real increases in land value, as well as annually according to the cost of living, appear to face very little resistance from lessees. In sum, both the premium systems and land rent systems have major hurdles that governments need to overcome. In terms of using land leasing to raise public funds, one thing is clear: there appears no easy way to collect leasehold charges. No matter which system governments use to collect lease payments, they must be vigilant about potential problems and creative in devising ways to minimize them.

As found in our case studies, another reason for the different experiences in generating lease revenues is related to the priorities individual governments set for achieving their land leasing goals. Indeed, we must evaluate the financial outcomes of land leasing in conjunction with government attempts to accomplish other policy objectives, because, for example, the aim to reserve land for developing public housing or government facilities may be in conflict with the objective of maximizing lease revenues. The opportunity cost of allocating a land site to a public agency at a concessionary price would be the forgone revenue the government could have collected were the land leased at its full market value. Put differently, if a government wants to maximize lease revenues and encourage the development of affordable housing, it may not be able to achieve both objectives through the leasehold system. The experience of Hong Kong is a good example. The government's reliance on lease revenues to finance public expenditures had inflated property prices in the private housing market for many years. When the post-1997 government took over the administration of Hong Kong and wanted to increase home ownership by setting production targets for both public and private developers, expected increases in housing supply triggered a series of sharp declines in property values. Powerful developers and the propertied class immediately opposed the policy, which eventually forced the government to abandon its initiative.

The Hague's government faced a similar dilemma in the 1980s. The government attempted to use land leasing to capture land value, and at the same time tried to employ lease conditions to regulate land use. Leaseholders began to feel that the government had exerted too much control over their property and started to pressure local politicians to change the leasing policy. Some even proposed that the government should abolish public leasehold altogether. To save the public leasehold system, public officials had to give up their aim of recouping land value. Had the municipality been unwilling to compromise, the public would have demanded the eradication of the land leasing system—an outcome that could have caused the government to lose not only the lease revenues but also the ability to control land use through lease conditions.

Judging from these experiences, inherent tradeoffs appear to exist among the public policy goals some analysts believe to be achievable by leasing public land. For instance, accomplishing financial goals may have to be at the expense of other objectives. In Hong Kong, as stated earlier, the government has only a few alternative revenue sources and thus must choose to achieve its financial goals above the other purposes. For other cases, different aims—such as building the national capital in Canberra or extending Jewish settlements to the peripheries in Israel—seem to prevail over the importance of raising public funds. The different priorities for land leasing may explain why Hong Kong employs a more forceful approach to levying leasehold charges than is used in the other countries.

Because policy goals may sometimes be mutually exclusive, none of the governments in our case studies was able to attain all of its targets. Governments must pay special attention to the potential benefits, as well as costs, of achieving particular public purposes, and find ways to balance tradeoffs. Similar to all other tenure arrangements, public leasehold systems will never solve all land management problems. It would be unduly optimistic for policy makers or analysts to believe that governments can avoid difficult policy dilemmas by adopting public leasehold systems. Setting unrealistic expectations for the performance of public leasehold systems could only lead to disappointment.

Building Affordable Housing and Government Facilities

Among all purposes of land leasing, reserving land for the construction of public housing and facilities appears to be most achievable. The prime example is Canberra, where public leasehold was established primarily for building the nation's capital. Land was reserved according to the Griffin plan for the construction of government buildings, foreign embassies and other public infrastructure to allow the city to function as the political center of Australia. Even Neutze, who is quite critical of the performance of the Canberra leasehold system, admitted that public leasehold allowed the government to implement the ambitious Griffin plan and avoid land price inflation and speculation. Although critics complained about the extravagance of creating Canberra, the building of the city would have been even more expensive if the government was not the landowner and had to acquire land from private individuals.

In the Netherlands, Sweden and Finland, municipalities have employed land leasing to negotiate with developers for either monetary or in-kind contributions toward the provision of public infrastructure in land development. They also grant concessionary land contracts to private agencies for building affordable housing. Some Swedish municipalities have discounted land rents as much as 33 percent for leasehold sites used for single-family dwellings. Similarly, one key purpose of preserving the public leasehold system in Israel, despite the gradual privatization of land ownership, is to maintain the government's ability to use land to encourage the presence of Jewish settlements in peripheral areas, which has important geopolitical implications for stabilizing the country's territory and demographic distribution. Even in Hong Kong, where the primary goal of leasing land has been to raise public funds, the government has from time to time granted land sites to industrialists at below market value to promote the development of key industries. More important, the government has also allocated land sites at either no cost or for a concessionary premium for public housing development to mediate the negative impacts of high land and housing costs on the poor.

Both the Canberra and Hong Kong governments have also tried to influence housing costs by inserting provisions into land contracts that oblige lessees to complete their housing developments within a specified time. Unfortunately, enforcement of these lease conditions has not been effective in both cases. Since market forces determine the supply and demand of housing, it is difficult for the government to distinguish whether delays in development by the lessees are to meet unexpected dips in demand or to make speculative profits. Because of this uncertainty, both governments have failed to set heavy enough fines to deter developers from delaying land development, thus rendering their control over housing supply through lease conditions ineffective.

To what extent should governments be involved in housing and industrial development? If government can actively influence the economy by leasing public land, what will happen when government programs, albeit well intentioned, fail? Our case studies clearly show that public leasehold has provided governments with useful tools to balance both public and private interests in land. Public leasehold has enabled governments to influence urban development without severely impeding private incentives to invest in land and improvements—the flexibility that state land ownership under some former socialist regimes did not provide. All our cases, and especially the Israeli experience, exemplify the remarkable flexibility of public leasehold in accommodating changing public and private involvements in land development according to varying circumstances. Free market advocates may still argue that the real estate markets in, say, Israel and Hong Kong could have been even more vibrant if all land were freehold. Similarly, believers of state intervention may insist that the governments of Canberra and The Hague could have been more "successful" in controlling land use had they fully exercised the power of being sole landlord in each city.

Although these are legitimate challenges against public leasehold, they are not the right assessments given the specific historical contexts and missions of the public leasehold systems in our case studies. For instance, Canberra's major mandate has been to become the world-class capital of Australia—an objective that cannot be achieved by state control or private investment alone. Similarly, if all land in Israel were privately owned, that government would have been unable to utilize public land to mobilize the mass migration of the population from urban centers to rural areas. The public leasehold system has helped the Israeli government balance the two seemingly conflicting objectives: to retain public control over land to serve the nation's geopolitical purposes and to satisfy the growing demand for private property. In the eyes of the Israelis, public leaseholds are tantamount to freehold rights. Leasehold rights are so secure that homebuyers and investors rarely ask if they own or lease land when they decide to invest in real estate. Freehold in Hong Kong has never been a viable option because of Hong Kong's status as a British colony in the past, and as part of the PRC at present. In this situation public leasehold represents the best possible arrangement.

Urban development requires both public and private investment in land. State involvement is needed to facilitate certain types of economic and social development, such as public housing and infrastructure, for which there may not be incentives for private investment. And in areas where private investors can do a better job of utilizing scarce resources, the role of the government should be maintained at a minimal level. Public leasehold systems should have the paramount aim of bridging the gap between the needs of public control over land and private interest in property investment. Certainly, government involvement does not always bring forth positive outcomes. The same is true for investment decisions guided solely by unregulated private markets. There is no simple answer to what constitutes an appropriate level of government intervention in private markets, because such a determination can be made only on a case-by-case basis in view of the unique institutional environment of a country (or a city). Moreover, whether a government should employ land leasing to play an active role in land development is a political issue. Only affected citizens (or residents) have the right to decide, for they are the ones who must live with their collective decisions. In making their decision, involved parties may consider the flexibility to accommodate both public and private interests in land demonstrated by most of the leasehold systems analyzed in this book.

Regulating Land Use

Public leasehold systems examined here do not appear to play a significant role in controlling land use. In Sweden municipalities that adopted public leasehold used lease conditions to control land use until 1953. Since then, local governments have relied on their statutory power to impose restrictions on land development. They also employ public land banking and special allocations to influence land use. Finnish and Israeli governments do not rely on land leases to control land development at all; instead, they depend on separate planning legislation and agencies to implement land use regulations. The functions of planning and leasing are independent in these countries. In cases involving change in land use, the planning department decides whether to approve or reject an application. The lessee would only need to apply to the land administrative agency for a lease modification and pay the necessary premium or new land rent.

Although land use controls are specified explicitly as part of the leasing agreements in Canberra, the Netherlands and Hong Kong, enforcement of these lease conditions has been lax. In order to guarantee security of public leaseholds, the Canberra government has been reluctant to exercise its right to repossess land even if lease conditions are violated. Besides, lease conditions established before the Second World War are not well formulated, thus making their enforcement difficult. In the Netherlands there is no active government monitoring of lessees' compliance with lease conditions related to land use. The government takes action to deal with violation only when a third party reports the incident to relevant public agencies. In Hong Kong not only were lease conditions not strictly enforced, but they also created confusion as to which set of rules—the statutory zoning plans or lease conditions—developers should follow. To make matters worse, using lease conditions to control land use before the establishment of statutory plans has complicated the planning process. Old land leases that do not have well-specified land use conditions (or have conditions that are in conflict with the existing land use regulations) have made it difficult for the government to require holders of these leases to convert their land uses in order to conform with recent statutory plans. Lessees claim to have preexisting contractual agreements with the government, thus, any new restrictions on their property rights would constitute a violation of those agreements. The government may have to compensate these lessees for any loss in their lease values if updated land use regulations reduce the amount of development rights. The Hong Kong case, though unique, showed that public leasehold could become an impediment to, rather than an instrument of, planning. Most of our authors have suggested that controlling land use through public land leasing is unnecessary if well-established, separate institutions and organizations are in charge of planning. The relationships between public leasehold and planning as two separate institutions for governing land allocation and development are important issues to which we will return in the last section of this chapter.

Facilitating Urban Redevelopment

While public leasehold systems seem to be instrumental in assisting governments to influence initial land development, there is no evidence to show that they are equally helpful in facilitating urban redevelopment. In principle, because the government is the landowner, it should be able to take back land from the lessee for redevelopment when the lease expires—a major advantage over freehold systems in which land assembly for public purposes is normally conflict-ridden and expensive. After updating the land use and infrastructure of the repossessed land, the government could lease the site to a private entity at a higher premium or land rent, thereby capturing the full betterment generated by redevelopment. Yet, experiences found in our case studies do not support this proposition.

In Canberra, despite being the landowner, the government has taken a passive role in redeveloping land. As pointed out earlier, leases are renewable in Canberra, and the government hardly ever repossesses land. Between 1971 and 1990, the government decided to encourage land redevelopment by imposing a change of use charge equal to only 50 percent of the estimated increase in lease value caused by redevelopment. However, as Neutze indicates, the policy produced the opposite result: land redevelopment was delayed due to higher selling prices demanded by property owners who were keen to maximize their share of the 50 percent windfall gains. Although the government has raised the charge to 75 percent since 1991, there is no assessment of how the new policy has affected redevelopment.

Even though the Hong Kong government has taken a more active role than the Canberra government in land redevelopment, its unique tenure structure complicates the negotiation process of assembling leasehold rights for renovating obsolete properties. Most construction in Hong Kong is in the form of multistory apartment buildings, and a single lease for a site could have hundreds of lessees. Negotiating the transfer of land rights for redevelopment with numerous lessees increases the costs of the undertaking tremendously. Besides, as described before, if developers need to change lease conditions before they can redevelop land, they must pay the government a modification premium. All these costs could become quite taxing on the financial as well as human resources of developers. As a result, land redevelopment in Hong Kong has been sluggish, despite the fact that land and property prices are extremely high. In sum public leasehold in both Canberra and Hong Kong does not seem to ease the problems of land assembly for urban redevelopment.

Promoting Industrial Development

In principle, governments in public leasehold systems can attract investment capital to their jurisdictions by granting land contracts to industrialists and investors with premiums or land rents set below market value. As discussed in previous chapters, governments have used this approach for promoting development of key industries. Yet, giving concessionary land deals to investors to induce investment is a practice that does not pertain to public leasehold systems only. Many local governments in the U.S., where urban land is generally freehold, have also tried to achieve the same objective by giving land to investors at very low cost, if not for free, or by granting them generous tax abatements.

In some of our case studies, small local governments that do not sell land freehold may be in a disadvantageous position to compete with municipalities where the opportunity for obtaining fee simple is available. This is especially true when investors prefer freehold and the municipalities are not situated at strategic locations. As shown by the experiences in the Netherlands and Finland, public leasehold is not popular in small municipalities because they do not have the locational advantages to compete with major cities. Besides, small municipalities may not have the resources to hire staff qualified to administer public land leasing.

At first glance, some of our case studies seem to imply that public leasehold may not survive the competition if the system is operated within an environment where the option of buying land freehold is available elsewhere. Contrary to this perception, potential investors in Ukraine, Strong argues, are indifferent to either leasehold or freehold. As long as land transactions are transparent and well supported by legal institutions, whether investors own or lease land is secondary. Lessees in Finland who have the right to convert their leasehold rights into freeholds are not keen to exercise that option because public leaseholds are secure. Besides, leasing land can help homebuyers and investors avoid the financial burden of raising the initial capital or arranging financing for acquiring land for housing or commercial purposes. It is also noteworthy that the Finnish land leasing experience seems to defy the common trend found in other case studies, where public leaseholds are either being sold or transformed into freehold-like tenure arrangements. Virtanen has suggested that the reasons for the resilience of the Finnish public leasehold systems include the long tradition of public land leasing; the belief in socially bounded land ownership; and the government's ability to create institutions and organizations to protect leasehold rights and inform citizens of the social and financial benefits of public land leasing. We examine these factors in detail later. Hence, regarding the question of whether public leasehold may enhance or weaken the ability of local governments to attract investment, the answer seems to depend more on the institutions that affect the investment climate and security of property than on the land tenure choice.

Conveying Public Land into Private Use

One important lesson we learned from land reforms occurring in Eastern Europe and the PRC is that governments cannot restructure land tenure overnight. The process takes time because the changeover of institutions and organizations from the previous socialist arrangements to market-oriented systems has encountered political resistance and technical problems. When everything is in flux and the future is highly uncertain, governments need a transitional mechanism for reallocating land from the state to private entities for development. More important, this mechanism must be flexible enough to allow governments to experiment with different property rights arrangements without committing to one system prematurely. Our authors, who studied experimentation with public leasehold in transitional economies and the U.S., have reached a similar conclusion: land leasing could be a flexible instrument for allocating land resources when institutions necessary for the functioning of markets are still underdeveloped. Assigning public land to private investors by interim leases may prevent the situation in which a government that is eager to use private incentives to develop land sells fee title at excessively low prices. Revenues from land leasing may also help the government raise much-needed public funds for infrastructure development when a property tax system is not yet in place.

Some analysts may claim that short-term leases cannot provide investors with enough long-term security. Yet, as argued by Baxter, when the ownership, future uses and environmental cleanup of the England Air Base were unclear, the private sector remained uninterested in investing in the property for the long term. By using a master lease, the Department of Defense transferred the Air Base to a local agency, which in turn kept the property in use by granting short-term leases for individual parcels to interim users. This method reduced the waiting time caused by the complex and long conveyance process mandated by several federal agencies. Not only did this leasing system expedite the transfer of property from the federal government to a local agency and prevent the property from being idle, it also raised the required revenues to leverage government funding for a major redevelopment project. Because of these leasing arrangements, the local government minimized the negative impacts of military base closure on local employment. This experience is particularly telling for Eastern European countries, where public officials are facing similar problems—poorly developed markets, vaguely delineated land ownership and ill-defined land development plans. Both Strong and Deng, who studied the public leasehold systems in Ukraine and Beijing, respectively, have also proposed the use of short-term leases to assign land to private entities in transitional economies. With additional case studies and further experimentation, we will be able to ascertain if public land leasing can indeed facilitate the transfer of public land into private uses during periods of transition.

INSTITUTIONS AND PUBLIC LAND LEASING

One fundamental function of any land tenure system is to direct resources to their best possible uses by facilitating exchanges. Through the delineation of property rights supported by formal and informal rules, parties interested in a transaction will know with whom they must bargain, what price they must pay for the property and how agreements are enforced. Because of the infinite ways in which formal and informal rules are intertwined to form unique institutional environments to support land tenure systems, there is no universal model that can work in all contexts.

For the same reason, the public leasehold systems examined in this book are diverse. The basic ideas of land leasing have undergone numerous transformations in these countries (or cities) according to the changing conditions of their institutional environments. In most cases, transformations are driven by disputes over the delineation and assignment of property rights as well as obligations. As discussed earlier, the Dutch and Hong Kong governments wanted to collect additional payments from lessees for renewal of land leases. Their intentions were challenged by lessees, thereby bringing public officials and lessees back to the bargaining table to renegotiate lease conditions and related legislation. Similar conflicts over payment for changes in leasehold rights occurred in most of our case studies. These processes of renegotiating land leasing rules are dictated by (and may later lead to changes in) the design of enabling institutions and organizations. Thus, it is useful to analyze further how public leasehold is interconnected with other formal and informal institutions and organizations.

Constitutions and Legislation

The constitution of a country normally contains the most important doctrine for defining land ownership. It also specifies explicitly, based on the philosophy (or ideology) of the nation, the roles of the state and private entities in possessing and controlling land resources. Apart from delimiting property relations, constitutional rules provide guidelines for making legislation, specifying the major principles used to formulate law, the selection of lawmakers, and procedures for proposing, passing and amending legal rules. Because of their importance in shaping all aspects of lawmaking, constitutional rules are designed, at least in most democratic countries, to be particularly difficult to amend. The intention is to instill a sense of stability and consistency in the minds of citizens, that the making and remaking of law are not arbitrary. The certainty is critical for lowering the risks involved in real estate investment.

In each of the established public leasehold systems examined here, constitutions or special legislation provided the necessary legal framework for governments to lease public land and for lessees to transfer their leasehold rights to other parties. Had there been no law to define and enforce the legal status of leasehold rights, it would have been difficult for governments to convince their constituents to accept public leasehold as a viable tenure arrangement. Using leasehold rights as collateral to apply for a mortgage loan to finance purchase of property would also be unattainable. Thus, without special constitutional and/or legislative rules, neither public land leasing nor the achievement of related policy goals would have been possible in these countries.

In addition to setting the legal framework for involved parties to practice land leasing, constitutional rules and special legislation may set the priority for land leasing. For instance, as discussed in the Hong Kong case, guidelines issued in 1841 for public land leasing had already focused on how the government should raise the maximum amount of revenue at public auction. These guiding principles, which later became part of the quasi-Constitution until 1997, explain in part why the Hong Kong government has remained firm in upholding its approach of auctioning land rights publicly. Although there are similar legal mandates under the Canberra, Swedish and Finnish systems for governments to capture land value, there are other principles, such as providing low cost land for the development of housing and public facilities, that policy makers must consider. These different mandates, enabled as well as constrained by constitutional and legislative rules, can also elucidate the dissimilar results of achieving land leasing goals among the public leasehold systems.

One important observation related to constitutions and legislation is that public leasehold and freehold are not necessarily mutually exclusive, at least under the law. Constitutions in several of our case studies provide equal legal protection to both leasehold and freehold rights. Indeed, if property in land is treated as a bundle of rights, and each element of the bundle can be assigned to and possessed by various private entities, leasehold rights can be protected as private property. The coexistence of the two tenure options in a country, or within a city, can bring an important benefit: government will have the flexibility to accommodate varied property rights preferences. If certain homebuyers or developers are willing and able to raise the required up-front capital for acquiring full equity in land, the option of buying land freehold will be available. If others do not want to tie up capital in land or simply do not have the funds to buy land, leasing land on payment of annual land rent is also feasible. Governments can even combine the two options, as practiced by some Finnish municipalities, by allowing developers to lease land initially for a specified term and then have the option to buy out leasehold rights when the leases expire.

These flexible arrangements, we believe, are especially useful for transitional countries where domestic and foreign investors are reluctant to commit to any long-term investment until they see political and economic reforms in these countries progress to more mature stages. Thus, leases with a buyout option may provide some degree of assurance for the duration of land tenure and at the same time allow investors to adjust their investment strategies as the future development of these countries continues to unfold. A practical land tenure system should be flexible enough to accommodate changing and sometimes incompatible interests in society. Only through the ability to adjust flexibly to the majority's preference could a land tenure system win the acceptance and confidence of public and private investors. In this respect the Israeli and Finnish public leasehold systems are good examples.

However, there is one cautionary note on the argument for flexibility of public leasehold: special interests must not dominate the process of renegotiating land leasing rules or the system could lose its credibility. Neutze has alluded to this danger by arguing that commercial leaseholders in Canberra are better organized than are residential lessees. Therefore, they have supported persistent lobbying efforts to undermine the planning and fiscal functions of the public leasehold system. Similarly, the conversion of leasehold rights into fee simple in Sweden might have been influenced by neoliberal sentiment and the desire of local governments to raise funds to cover their immediate fiscal shortfalls. It was unclear, Mattsson argues, whether municipalities had considered the long-term welfare of their communities before selling off public leaseholds.

Indeed, when a government lessor must rely on political support from lessees to stay in power, there is always a chance that politicians, political parties and lobbyists may exploit the political process of reformulating leasehold policy. Corruption may occur when public officials have the power to bend rules in the name of trying to be flexible to accommodate special circumstances. Favoritism may emerge that will subsequently undermine the confidence of investors and developers. Without a system of checks and balances to ensure both flexibility and consistency in implementing leasehold policy, land leasing may become unpredictable, thus rendering long-term investment impossible.

The public leasehold systems in Ukraine and Beijing, as described by Strong and Deng, seem to suffer from these problems. Designing flexible yet consistent leasehold policy is the topic of the final section.

Informal Rules

Outcomes of leasing public land in a country are governed not only by the constitution and legislation but are also shaped by informal rules, such as ideology, conventions and social norms. As mentioned earlier, the emergence of neoliberalism during the 1980s, which advocated the downsizing of public programs, led governments to retreat from using public land leasing to influence urban development in our case studies. The changeover of public leasehold in Canberra from a land rent system to premium system was, Neutze found, an early harbinger of the trend. The initiation of perpetual leases in The Hague, and the divestitures of public leaseholds by Swedish municipalities might have resulted from this shifting ideological belief as well. The declining support for public leasehold and the diminishing use of land leasing as a policy instrument during the 1980s and 1990s in these cases contributed to their increasingly unimportant roles in raising public funds and controlling land use.

On the opposite side of the ideological spectrum, the communist legacy of opposition to private property in some former socialist countries has blocked proposals to institute a public leasehold or freehold system. For example, when President Kuchma of Ukraine issued a decree in 1995 to empower local governments to sell or lease enterprise land, the Parliament rejected his order and refused to amend the Land Code. Some members of the Parliament insisted that the state could retain greater control over land under the old system than it probably could under a freehold or leasehold system. In Russia, when the Parliament considered permitting Russian and foreign investors to buy urban land in fee simple, the Communist Party and its allies fiercely opposed the bill and staged demonstrations inside and outside the lower house of the Parliament. Nevertheless, the bill was finally passed in 2001.

This is the most troubling aspect of ideology—no matter whether it is neoliberalism, communism or other beliefs. An ideological conviction will become an obstacle to change when the holders of the belief are blind to other possible alternatives. As argued before, a system that works in a specific place and time may not work when adopted in other situations. Hence, any belief in a single, universal model of land tenure will only increase the chance of making erroneous policy decisions. In view of the ideological barrier, many governments in Eastern Europe have begun to realize that the process of transition will take longer than originally expected because institutional change requires more than just the introduction of a set of formal rules and enforcement procedures. Instead, it demands a deep understanding of how ideology shapes people's preferences and what tools are available to modify informal institutions. Ideological changes occur slowly; thus, governments and analysts should not expect to accomplish land reform in a short time.

Supporting Organizations

Under the framework set by both formal and informal rules, parties involved in land leasing will negotiate a set of lease conditions for guiding land investment and the distribution of land benefits. To perform these functions, lease conditions require continued maintenance and rigorous enforcement carried out by supporting organizations, such as:

» a land registry to record and secure public leasehold rights;

» mortgage banks to finance purchases of leasehold property;

» a well-designed judicial system to interpret laws and mediate disputes between the lessor and lessee; and

» professional groups to appraise lease values and facilitate transactions.

The effectiveness of these organizations will determine the extent to which a government can accomplish its policy objectives by leasing public land.

In Sweden some municipalities sell public leaseholds because the enforcement of their contractual right to increase land rents has too often led to time-consuming, expensive litigation. These disputes relate mainly to the assessment of land value upon which rent is calculated. Despite the accumulation of legal precedents that have gradually helped professional groups standardize the methods of land rent adjustment, the process remains technically complex and controversial. Because land rents are set at low levels with the possibility of any future increases limited by the threat of potential lawsuits from lessees, some local governments have decided to sell public leaseholds at a large discount. Similar problems associated with the determination of land rents or premiums for lease modification and renewal in Canberra, the Netherlands and Hong Kong have also hindered governments from capturing increases in leasehold values. Differences in government ability to enforce lease conditions, which is affected by supporting organizations, could partly explain why the Hong Kong government has collected more lease revenues from public auction than from lease modification, contract renewal and the collection of land rent.

Notwithstanding the legal problems in assessing lease values and setting land rents found in our case studies, no public leasehold system could have persisted without a judicial system or professional appraisers to ease land leasing conflicts. Indeed, as property relations are in constant flux, differentiating the portion of land value belonging to the lessee from the portion that should be retained by the public lessor has been a daunting task. A public leasehold system (or, for that matter, any form of land tenure) must provide proper channels and flexibility to enable parties involved in a dispute to articulate their arguments, debate key issues and arrive at a compromise. The presence of an impartial juridical system and a group of well-trained professionals will provide the proper forum and technical assistance, so that disputing parties can reconcile. The lack of an established profession of real estate management in Australia during much of the twentieth century might have caused the gradual erosion (using Neutze's term) of the Canberra public leasehold system.

At the same time, competent administrations, staffed by highly trained real estate surveyors, may explain why public leasehold has been so well received in Finland. Policy makers in both established and emerging public leasehold systems must pay special attention to these supporting organizations to make land leasing functional.

INSTITUTIONAL AND ORGANIZATIONAL DESIGN

In the concluding sections of their chapters, several authors raised issues about the institutional and organizational design for public leasehold systems, questioning the extent to which the state should directly administer public land leasing. In view of the unsatisfactory performance of the Canberra government in managing public leasehold, Neutze proposed the creation of a quasi-public agency to be in charge of land leasing. Although this independent entity would have an arm's length relationship with the state apparatus, it would be subject to government regulation, like any other private developer. Both Needham and Deng also warned of potential conflicts of interest when the state is both the regulator of land use and the landowner. Hong questions whether the Hong Kong government, whose primary aim of leasing land is to generate public revenue, can balance its fiscal objective with other social needs of the population, such as affordable housing. To continue with these discussions, we explore the idea of having a quasi-public or private agency administer public leasehold. There are at least three reasons such a proposal may be able to deal with the concerns raised by our authors.

First, as Deng pointed out, the multiple roles of local governments as regulators, controllers of state-owned enterprises and custodians of public land have created conflicts of interest and tensions between public agencies within the local government of Beijing. While the Planning Bureau wants to restrict development to certain urban areas, the leasing office prefers to lease as much land as possible in any location to satisfy developers' needs. With the two agencies operating within the same government, tensions have emerged. Inconsistency and favoritism become a problem when disagreements are resolved, not according to the rule of law, but based on the power structure within the bureaucracy or personal connections. By separating the operations of public leasehold from the government apparatus, the land leasing agency will be unable to influence the decisions made by the planning department and vice versa. Although a similar result can be obtained by creating a system of checks and balances within the government, this will never be as transparent and credible as having an independent entity perform the function. It is especially relevant for some former socialist countries where governments might have lost the confidence of the public, due to the misdeeds of the past regime, and would need a long time to rebuild trust relations with citizens.

There are, of course, issues involved in creating an independent land leasing agency in transitional countries. Questions that need to be examined carefully prior to implementing the proposal include:

» How can policy makers create incentives for local governments to relinquish control over land?

» What are the constitutional or legislative requirements for facilitating the transfer of public land to a quasi-public or private agency?

» What is the proper governing structure for the agency?

» By whom should officers in charge of the agency be appointed or elected?

» How can an election, if it appears necessary, be conducted in countries where democratization is still in its infancy?

All these matters are related to political and government reforms. Policy makers must examine these issues thoroughly before considering the idea of using an independent agency to manage public land leasing.

Some readers may worry that allowing a separate, private agency to manage land leasing would undermine government's ability to use lease conditions to regulate land use and reserve land for the construction of affordable housing and public facilities. Regarding the possibility of using land leasing as a means to regulate land development, our authors seem to agree that the approach would be unnecessary when there is well-established planning legislation enforced by other public agencies. Again, there is no evidence to show that public leasehold can provide such overwhelming benefits for planning that public land leasing must reside within government domain. As for reserving land for public development, the agency can continue to allocate land to public bodies at either below market value or no cost. To help make the allocation of land for public purposes efficient, the agency must record the fair market value of land assigned to government units. This way, the community's land assets will no longer be treated as free when they are used for public purposes. The agency should record the potential lease revenues forgone for public allocation in its annual report to ensure the accountability of reporting the real costs of subsidizing public development.

Second, creating a non- or quasi-government entity to manage public land leasing may also eliminate the confusion between leasehold charges and taxes. While the former are forms of compensation to the public landowner for leasing development or use rights to lessees, the latter are fees that citizens pay to the government for public goods and services, such as roads, parks, education, fire protection and crime prevention. In Canberra, as indicated by Neutze, most residents confused land rents with rates, which are similar to property taxes in other countries. This confusion influenced the decision to abolish land rents, because policy makers and analysts believed that shortfalls in rental incomes could easily be offset by increases in rates—an idea that never materialized due to the inability of the government to raise rates. In principle, a public landowner, if it acts like a private investor, should expect to earn a required return on investment by collecting from the lessee an annual rent through the term of the lease. In addition, the required return should include any potential capital gains of selling (or releasing) the land to the same or another party at full market value when the lease expires. With the abolition of land rents and the automatic renewal of all leases, the hope for the Canberra government to obtain a reasonable return on its land holdings waned. If a quasi-public agency were in charge of land leasing in Canberra, the distinction between land rents and rates would have been more apparent, for two different entities would have collected these payments separately. As the collections of land rents and rates went into the same coffer, voters might have mistaken the elimination of land rents as another tax cut without realizing that it was indeed an actual loss of the community's property.

In addition, as stated before, maintaining a different account for land leasing could show voters how much is earned on their public land assets. Not all governments in our case studies have informed their citizens about their land leasing operations. It is critical for public review of the performance of public leasehold systems to have an independent agency responsible for land leasing, and mandated to publish a yearly report summarizing the community's land holdings, lease revenues generated and the manner in which funds are used. Only when citizens have a good understanding of the pros and cons of public leasehold can they determine if the tenure system serves their own wellbeing and that of their community.

Third and finally, separating land leasing from the machinery of government may prevent public officials from forfeiting the community's land assets to achieve short-term political or other personal gain. Governments normally face multifaceted demands from their constituencies that are not always compatible with each other. By establishing an independent entity with a single mandate to protect public property in land, the agency's performance will be judged largely on a commonly agreed upon return on land investment. This performance indicator may be able to align the managers' incentives of maintaining their jobs with the financial wellbeing of the community, thereby minimizing corruption and political pressure from special interests.

This book began with the argument for a pluralistic approach to examining public leasehold systems. It ends with the suggestion that a private or quasi-public entity may manage public leasehold. Although the proposed idea is presumptive, the exercise has clarified our pluralistic view: there are innumerable ways for policy makers to structure public leasehold systems. We have learned from this project not to be overly optimistic about the usefulness of public leasehold. Indeed, the implementations of public leasehold systems in our case studies have not been trouble-free. Public land leasing is unlikely to solve all our land management problems. Yet, to put this statement in proper perspective, neither could other land tenure options. For example, in the U.S., where most land is freehold, there are ongoing and virulent struggles between private property rights protectors and growth management advocates in determining the limits to what individual private landowners can do with their land. Heavy-handed government intervention through absolute public land ownership is certainly not the way to go in the future either. The damage that this land tenure system has done to housing and infrastructure development in some former socialist countries should certainly deter governments from following a similar path. The delineation of public and private property in land, we believe, will remain contentious regardless of land tenure choice. In dealing with property rights controversies, a land tenure system has to be amendable in response to changing circumstances and preferences. Perhaps the flexibility of public leasehold systems, which we have emphasized here, may allow these land tenure arrangements not only to endure in industrialized countries but also to remain as a viable option for economies in transition.

About the Lincoln Institute

The Lincoln Institute of Land Policy is a nonprofit and tax-exempt educational institution established in 1974. Its mission as a school is to study and teach land policy, including land economics and land taxation. The Institute is supported primarily by the Lincoln Foundation, established in 1947 by John C. Lincoln, a Cleveland industrialist who drew inspiration from the ideas of Henry George, the nineteenth-century American political economist and social philosopher.

The Institute's goals are to integrate the theory and practice of land policy and to understand the multidisciplinary forces that influence it. Through its curriculum development, courses, conferences and publications, the Lincoln Institute seeks to improve the quality of debate and disseminate knowledge about critical issues in its departments of planning and development and valuation and taxation, and in the program on Latin America and the Caribbean.

The Institute does not take a particular point of view, but rather brings together scholars, policy makers, practitioners and citizens with a variety of backgrounds and experience to study, reflect and exchange insights on land and tax policies. The Institute's objective is to have an impact—to make a difference today and to help policy makers plan for tomorrow. The Institute is an equal opportunity institution in employment and admissions.

Lincoln Institute of Land Policy
113 Brattle Street
Cambridge, MA, USA 02138-3400

Phone: 617/661-3016 x127 or 800/LAND-USE (526-3873)
Fax: 617/661-7235 or 800/LAND-944 (526-3944)
Email: help@lincolninst.edu
Web: *www.lincolninst.edu*